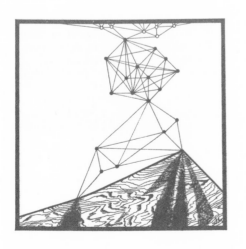

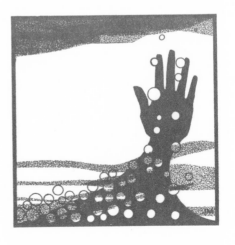

Economics for Urban Social Planning

Economics for Urban Social Planning

By

William S. Hendon

University of Utah Press
Salt Lake City, Utah

Endsheet illustrations: Jerry McKinney

To my parents, who made it all possible, and to Mary Ann, Anna, Willie, Claude, and Earl the Wonder Dog.

Contents

Figures

Tables

Preface

In setting out to write this book I had in mind the many things which economics has to say to people but the many times the formal rigors of the discipline prevent anyone from drinking at the well without almost drowning in prerequisites and formal course work. This book hopes to bring some current economics to a variety of people in a way in which they may read and understand it. The basis of the book is microeconomics; the subject matter is human resources in the city and the politics and evaluation of policies which local governments currently pursue but only in fragmentary ways.

The book is designed for undergraduate economics students, although many students outside of economics at most levels might profit from its reading. One chapter has been used in principles of economics; the entire book has been used in senior-level economics courses and in graduate-level interdisciplinary courses in urban affairs. In this latter instance, the book serves to provide planners with some of the economics they need to know. For the economics student, this book represents a second book for the urban economics course. Coverage attempts to round out the things about cities which other books do not include. Urban economics, to me at least, is too narrowly perceived, as represented in current texts. Hopefully, this work will be of assistance to others of like mind.

Many persons have left their mark on this book, both figuratively and literally. My debt to other economists is considerable and my debt to colleagues in other disciplines is great. I would like to acknowledge my colleagues in the Department of Urban Studies for their careful readings, their useful comments and suggestions: Edward Hanten, Gerald Pyle, David Cox, Frank Costa, James Richardson, Ashok Dutt, Frank Kendrick, Yong Cho, and James Huber. To my colleagues in economics here at Akron and at other institutions I owe similar debts: Ali Fatemi, James Robinson, Arthur Ford, Jack W. Nickson, and Milton Russell.

I would like to acknowledge the help of my students, John Pierson, Allen Pearson, Dick Boyce, Kelvin Carlisle, Dick Boyd, Suzanne Page, Michelle Marx, Peter Leahy, Tom Koegel, Al Papa, Doug Nodine, Jack Litzenberg, June Bland, and Bill Schwab.

In particular I would like to acknowledge Mrs. Barbara Wade of the Center for Urban Studies for her considerable aid in editing the manuscript and making numerous suggestions.

I would also like to acknowledge James Shanahan, my colleague in economics at the Department of Urban Studies, for his careful reading of the manuscript, his encouragement, and his suggestions.

Part of this book was made possible by a research grant from the University of Akron.

I wish also to thank Mrs. Arlene Lane and the members of her secretarial staff who typed the manuscript.

The final debt is a significant one, and goes to scholars Wilbur Thompson, Jack Knetsch, Burton A. Weisbrod, Herbert Klarman, Eli Ginzberg, T. W. Schultz, Nelson Peach, and others whose works have influenced my thinking.

Any errors or omissions, of course, are my own.

William S. Hendon
Akron, Ohio
January 1973

Economics for Urban Social Planning

Introduction

This is a volume concerned with human resource development in the city and describes the economics of manpower, education, health care, and recreation in the city within the context of local public and private institutional policy. Included within these discussions are elements of cost-benefit analysis, useful in the evaluation of policies. Throughout the volume there is a consideration of policy evaluation and implication with the objective of making the city a more effective instrument of man's purposes.

It has been said that cities were built by man for man. As necessity arose people congregated together for protection, for economic intercourse, and for social interaction. They grouped together in villages, in forts, in towns, and, eventually, in cities. We speak of the development of American cities as a result primarily of the development of agricultural technology and secondarily as a result of the development of industrial technology. But a city is also a process of extending the interdependence of people and fills their need to participate in groups and communicate with others. In this sense, cities are a result of an increasing complexity of economic and social organizations and of the interdependence which arises among men in well-developed economies of advanced societies.

Yet, in recent years, the city has come under increasing criticism for failing to support man and his activities. The city impedes man's development. Nothing is more conforming than the modern American city; nothing is more lonely than the modern American city; and nothing is more insecure than life in the modern city. The individual's attempts to develop his own potential, to generate a higher technology, and to create for himself a sense of well-being have been thwarted by events in cities. Man must lock up his possessions, his family, and himself behind barred doors. We cope with our neighbors in the city rather than live with them. We increasingly confine ourselves to easy chairs in front of television sets to escape the immense complexities of everyday urban existence.

1

It appears that cities in North America were developed by a population of single individuals with single-minded purposes for specific and particular kinds of activity. Man did not come to the city to seek the fulfillment of all of his desires and to generate a life for himself which was better in all respects than he had had in the village or on the farm. Rather, he came to the city in hopeful pursuit of a specific goal, such as a particular job or business venture, the accomplishment of which he hoped would bring the other perquisites of the good life. These perquisites, however, were only dimly perceived in the shadows of his mind. Also, not all men came to cities voluntarily; migrations to cities in America need not be seen as patterns of hopeful and ambitious Americans seeking to improve their lot. It is possible that many were dragged to cities out of desperation, out of hopelessness, and because life in towns, villages, and rural areas was simply no longer possible for them.

But pessimism is reasonably inexpensive. It does not require much imagination to become pessimistic about what cities do to or for people. The fact of the matter is that cities exist now and will continue to exist, and anyone who imagines that a great decline in American cities is about to take place is naïve. Any community of a reasonably large size in the United States today will likely exist in the future. There is little question that for certain types of man's economic activities the city still fits very well. For example, the activities of large banks, newspapers, and other services are more efficiently pursued where there is considerable density of population. Likewise, much large-scale manufacturing is not possible in isolated locations.

Cities are essentially commercial undertakings. Cities are no longer necessary to protect one from invaders; they are not even necessary for the educational development of man except insofar as large educational institutions are considered more effective. People do not need cities for outdoor recreation, religion, or medical care. Today we need not live in the city to have electricity, water, indoor plumbing, varieties of consumer goods, or personal transportation such as the automobile; nor is the city essential for the better care and rearing of children. Fundamentally, the city is necessary as an economic undertaking, and while it may make many of the needs, desires, and wants of people more readily available, the city is essential mainly because private capitalistic development still requires large-scale organizations and large numbers of people.

Human Development: The Major Purpose

If the city is primarily organized as an economic unit, then one may wonder if it meets man's noneconomic needs. The success of cities is measured not merely by economic efficiency, but more broadly by the quality of the life of the individual man living in the city. Unless the individual citizen and his neighbors are profiting from a full life in the city, the entity as a social experiment may be deemed a failure.

This book supports the idea that cities should be for the purpose of a full life for individuals. A successful city is a framework of economic and social institutions which respond to the needs of the citizens of that community. A further premise is that in addition to the individual's responsibilities, the local government is responsible for the protection, maintenance, and development of the citizen whether or not the citizen is a productive member of, or a surplus to, the local economy.

In employment matters the local government must become an employer of last resort. Further, local government has the duty of providing educational, recreational, and health care opportunities for all of the citizens in the community. To accomplish these aims, local government's role must be vastly enlarged.

Though an important part of urban policy, general welfare and income guarantee policies are not treated in this volume. The extent of the income policy discussed encompasses manpower policy only: policy designed to provide employment for those in the city who are psychologically willing and physically able to be placed in jobs. The vast majority of persons on welfare would not be directly assisted by local manpower policy, because welfare recipients are individuals with multiple problems for which even an expanded manpower policy is apt to be deficient. Although welfare is increasingly the province of the federal government, it is still primarily a matter of state responsibility. Annual income guarantees also do not appear to be within the jurisdiction of local government; rather, these policies are national government functions.

Improvements to the urban condition which are based upon a gestalt concept concerning the quality of life for individuals in the city might lead one to discount the importance of narrow policy in the urban area. However, such is not the case since local government policy, carefully conceived, is probably central to all urban development. Concern is not simply with the development of urban economic institutions but with all urban institutions and the impact of these institutions upon individuals. Urban development is a term to be perceived more broadly than urban economic development.

Urban Development

Urban development is concerned with comprehensive knowledge and a comprehensive perspective of the development of cities. The term comprehensive is used with special purpose; in order to understand urban development, one is forced to make use of all the social sciences and humanities if one is to include the many variables relevant to urban development. No matter what traditional discipline utilized, development is concerned with the interrelationships of social, political, economic, and cultural variables. Analysis of a city's total development adds dimension even to other disciplines. Cumulative causation, backwash effects, and spread effects are no longer the sole property of a single discipline;

rather, they are reflections of processes and sequences of change and interaction which demand tools from many disciplines in broad application. While we draw from many disciplines, we must begin to think in new categories.

The nature of urban development lends itself to certain forms of questions, the answers to which could lead to broad urban theories. For example:

1. Are there typical sequences of socioeconomic change, or are there regularities in these transformations?

2. Which features of modern urban economies, societies, and cultures generate resistance or receptivity to innovations?

3. Given the fact of the economic modernization of cities, how and why do traditional social organization and culture change?

4. What defines "successful" urban development?

5. What similarities and dissimilarities can we find in developmental patterns between cities in countries at various stages of development?

6. To what extent are processes of social and economic change at the urban level small-scale counterparts to national development?[1]

The foregoing questions tend to suggest that urban development must be comprehensive as a field of study in order to prevent the fragmentation of effort. This does not disallow specialization, but merely puts it in a context of debt to a larger whole. In urban development it is necessary to relate these fragments to a larger theory, and, therefore, the following tentative assumptions might be made:

1. Development of cities does not simply mean economic development, or development in any other traditional context.

2. Because it is a complex set of interrelationships, no single social science or humanities study provides sufficient methodology or data for understanding, urban development.

3. Not all tools developed within the traditional disciplines upon which urban development draws are likely to be relevant, and, indeed, most of the tools drawn from other disciplines must be redesigned to form an urban theory and method.

4. Urban development is a complicated process which takes place over a long period of time, and if sufficient improvement in certain spheres of the city are successfully undertaken, they will be mutually reinforcing.

5. Urban development implies the need for continuous and significant formal planning.[2]

---

[1] Adapted from George Dalton, comp., *Economic Development and Social Change: The Modernization of Village Communities* (Garden City, N.Y.: The Natural History Press, 1971), pp. 20–21.

[2] Adapted from Dalton, comp., *Economic Development and Social Change*, pp. 20–21.

Institutions and Urban Development

When we speak of urban development we refer specifically to four dimensions of urban institutions. An urban institution is an *organization involved in collective action.* Local government, churches, social clubs, schools, labor unions, political parties, and other organizations are involved. Closely related to these organizations are the major ideas or mythologies which permeate a city and arise from its ways of doing things. In this sense collective action moves from *popular myths or ideologies* which become the urban value system — that is, social forces capable of directing human behavior and which may arise from either irrational or rational origins. This conventional wisdom may be the result of clear knowledge or it may be purely ignorant and superstitious.

Aside from organizations involved in collective action and the value systems which rise to the fore as strong social motivators, the institutions of the city must also be thought of in terms of *power.* To accomplish particular aims, urban institutions exert energy and contain relative degrees of power. The urban landscape is a field of competition and cooperation, a contest which some groups win and others lose. But power does not reside merely in the large bureaucratic organizations of the city; power structures arise informally as well as formally, and powerful individuals and groups may collude to gain particular ends. Thus, while the city is a field of competition and cooperation, it is also a field for collusion. In all instances, the exertion of power may be legal or illegal and it may be either antisocial or social.

In addition to expressions of power, urban institutions (organizations, ideas, and informal power structures), once they arise, have among their particular ends the *desire to survive.* The local organization (commercial, governmental, etc.) wishes to survive and does so by monopolizing urban space or activity. The popularized social myths (we got rhythm, etc.) arise by dint of the citizen's unwillingness to face complexity, and major myths become popular slogans used by formal and informal urban institutions as a means of social control, and, thereby, preservation of their power and their very existence. The power structure survives by control of the market for its activities (where is public housing located, etc.).

The Individual in the City

The major means of accomplishing individual aims in the city is through collective action and participation in urban institutions. If good wages and job security are desired, labor unions are formed. If better health care is desired, we buy health insurance or health cooperatives are formed. If better recreation is desired, groups are formed to pressure for actions from local government. If more responsive governments are desired, individuals join political parties. In short, no matter what the activities desired or the goals sought, the individual who does best in the city does so by the extent to which he belongs to strong urban institutions. People who do least well are those who suffer directly from local ideologies and myths and who do not belong to strong urban institutions. Collective action places the city dweller in prospect of gaining his own personal ends and desires.

A person's accessibility to effective urban institutions is the principal determining factor in the quality of his life in the city. Accessibility for the urbanite is characterized by the ready availability of political, social, and economic institutions. Accessibility is determined by (a function of) distance (where one is located in the city), income (whether one may pay the price if he chooses), social class, education (a prerequisite to wide political, economic, and social choice), health (whether one has mental and physical well-being), and recreation (whether one has both leisure time and recreational skills). If the urbanite has sufficient income, education, health, and recreation then he or she may overcome to some extent the problem of lack of access (exclusion). To prosper in the city is to have access to the advantages of the city and the means to overcome some of the disadvantages of urban living.

An individual who fails to have access to any one of these urban institutions may fail significantly in attaining a high quality urban life. Determinants of accessibility are not equally important for all individuals. Tastes and preferences may vary; conditions may differ. Yet the fact remains that relative failure exists when a person does not possess access to institutions in sufficient quantity. And, as noted earlier, access for the individual depends upon effective collective action.

If the purpose of collective action is to satisfy individual aims, then the institution (organization exerting power within a value structure) must be democratically derived. Aside from powerlessness, urban institutions fail because they become bureaucratized, which, by definition, thwarts the original purpose of serving individuals. If an institution begins to serve a mere survival function and fails to respond to its constituency, it becomes a force for urban degeneration rather than development. The only means we have of testing the quality of an institution in this manner is to investigate the practical effect of its actions upon its members and the rest of the urban citizenry. This test of practical effect is basically a test of responsiveness and is discovered by the extent of democratic participation by the members in its activities.

Urban Economic Development

As a part of a yet underdeveloped urban theory, urban economic development is concerned with the progressive or positive economic change which occurs in cities. Schumpeter's theory of development (transposed to urban areas) states that development is spontaneous and discontinuous change in the channels of economic flow — disturbances of equilibrium which alter and displace the previous equilibrium position.[3] This definition is dependent upon perceiving an eco-

---

[3] Joseph A. Schumpeter, *The Theory of Economic Development* (Cambridge, Mass.: Harvard University Press, 1934), p. 64.

nomic system as a circular flow tending toward an equilibrium position and into which an internal change is introduced. This internal change alters the flow and causes the economy to move forward to a different position.

New Combinations

If one imagines an urban economy as one in circular flow, economic development moves that flow from one level to another. The internal change which is labeled "development" can be called such only when the process of change results in net economic gains. In discussing national economies, Schumpeter notes that the internal change is to be found in the process of carrying out new combinations.[4] New combinations are innovations in the economy which generate growth and which Schumpeter classifies into five major cases:

> (1) The introduction of a new good — that is one with which consumers are not yet familiar — or of a new quality of a good. (2) the introduction of a new method of production, that is one not yet tested by experience in the branch of manufacture concerned, which need by no means be founded upon a discovery scientifically new, and can also exist in a new way of handling a commodity commercially. (3) The opening of a new market, that is a market into which the particular branch of manufacture of the country in question has not previously entered, whether or not this market has existed before. (4) The conquest of a new source of supply of raw materials or half-manufactured goods, again irrespective of whether this source already exists or whether it has first to be created. (5) The carrying out of the new organization of any industry, like the creation of a monopoly position (for example through trustification) or the breaking up of a monopoly position.[5]

Role of the Entrepreneur

The carrying out of new combinations is the work of the entrepreneur. Finding relevant opportunities among alternatives, the entrepreneur generates economic activity in one of the five mentioned forms. Who are these individuals in the community? Traditionally they tend not to be found among the largest corporate enterprises but among those new or existing small to middle-sized businesses in the community for which there is growth potential and for which the entrepreneurs seek venture capital for expansion. While the large, well-established concern may generate the current stability in a city and the major amount of employment, it is likely that future development will come from some small, new, or existing business firms. In addition, local government may generate development of the local economy through its revenue and expenditure patterns and in the future by direct action.

The dynamics of urban economic development appear to move in spurts as cities take economic jumps from prior economic structure. This form of discontinuous movement suggests the relevance of viewing urban economic development as a set of stages.

[4] Schumpeter, *The Theory of Economic Development*, p. 66.
[5] Schumpeter, *The Theory of Economic Development*, p. 66.

Stages of Urban Economic Development

The dynamics of economic development are more clearly understood when one combines the stages suggested by Wilbur Thompson and the stages of economic development posited by Walt W. Rostow.[6]

The *traditional society*, according to Rostow, has some features which suggest small towns of particular types in the United States. The traditional city has very limited production functions; a high proportion of its activities are supported by agriculture; there exists in the community a kind of long-run fatalism (relatively) and little hope for alteration of the particular local economic condition. Incomes are low, and income distribution is characterized by most incomes at lower than the national average combined with a few incomes which are quite high. Like William Faulkner's Jefferson, many small towns in the West, Southwest, and South appear to have these characteristics. Politically, control falls to the wealthy. The local economies are not completely static but they tend to be limited by a kind of ceiling of development possibilities.

If economic change occurs either from internal or external intrusion, innovation can move this traditional city to a *stage of export specialization*. In this stage the city depends very heavily upon a single export activity. While many factors determine growth, there is little doubt that most cities in this particular historical development stage may well be in the position similar to preconditions to a "takeoff period." City development, like historical development of nation states, demands the right place at the right time for development to occur. The variables of growth must be such that the developing smaller community can begin to rapidly grow or "takeoff" if some form of innovation occurs. Examples of innovation are numerous: the location of a defense plant during wartime, the sudden rise in demand for a particular new or existing product, the location of a military base, the location of a state college, and the attraction of some industry expanding out of its old domains. For the city to move from the traditional stage to the single export stage, the introduction of a new industry producing either goods or services is required. Transition out of the export specialization stage appears to call for some significant economic innovation in the community; this is usually not a purely external intrusion, but a mix of local development efforts culminating in innovation. A city economy can broaden or deepen either backward or forward to attain momentum for further development.

If the export specialization stage is a preconditioning period, then it might be argued that innovation leads to a *takeoff period* in which the community, if it becomes an *export complex*, grows rapidly for a period of several decades. This urban takeoff reflects a rise in population and a corresponding rise in

---

[6] Wilbur Thompson, *A Preface to Urban Economics* (Baltimore: Published for Resources for the Future by Johns Hopkins Press, 1965), pp. 15–16; Walt W. Rostow, *The Stages of Economic Growth: A Non-Communist Manifesto* (Cambridge: Cambridge University Press, 1960), pp. 4–12.

per capita income over a sufficient period of time to achieve the beginnings of the *economic maturation stage,* or what might be called the drive to maturity. As a mature city, the economic activities are characterized by a diverse export base and an increasing tendency to replace imports with locally produced goods. In addition, the local service sector has reached a state of diversity of development which does two things: (1) it reinforces basic (manufacturing) exports, and (2) it may become part of local exports. Stabilized economic development and growth of per capita incomes are achieved as a city grows to large size and diversifies its outputs. Diversity demands a wide variety of manufacturing and services.

The next stage of development might be called a *stage of regional metropolis,* assuming the city develops to that point. Most cities do not since the competition from other similarly situated communities is intense. A community that becomes a regional metropolis, Thompson notes, is characterized by its nodal location as a point of control for a region and hinterland of some size around it.[7] The regional metropolis as a mature city is diverse in its exports and local service sector. Its social overhead capital is highly developed, and such communities are apt to be capable of regeneration in the economic development sense. Economies of this diversification and level of development are characterized by their ability to move from one export base to another as innovative activity maintains the flow of development.

The final stage, as noted by Thompson, is the *stage of technical professional virtuosity* in which a city has advanced through all of the previous stages and has reached a level of development making it a national center for a particular skill or technical ability. Houston and its heart specialists, Detroit and its autos, Los Angeles and its aircraft industry, Pittsburgh and its steel, all represent instances of high national recognition in particular activities. In addition, we should note the cultural center achievements among cities. New York, a financial capital, is also the center of the performing arts in the United States. Universities, museums, orchestras, and park systems can all bring recognition.

It is convenient to think about the development of urban economies in terms of a set of stages. With the appropriate data, it is possible to use the stages approach to compare the relative development of a group of cities in a well-developed nation such as the United States.

As one considers cities moving in circular flow from one stage to another, the concept of size is implicit. Cities of large size in the United States all represent maturity even if they are not regional metropolises. Size appears necessary for urban development to persist because of the fact that size implies diversification. Also, as Thompson points out, the large city represents a social investment which no country can afford to discard. Large cities are more nearly self-sufficient be-

[7] Thompson, *A Preface to Urban Economics,* p. 16.

cause they are producing for their own consumers. While there may not be a higher rate of innovation in large cities relative to small cities, in large cities innovation is regular and consistent; thus, growth or at least maintenance is insured and stability of growth is enhanced. To be effective, power politics, which aids the growth stability, also demands large city size.[8]

Local Income Analysis

The foregoing discussions have dealt with matters of economic growth and development in a broad context. To narrow the discussion further, we need to turn to how we might measure economic development in a city. The most widely used measure of economic performance in cities is per capita income. We use per capita income as a quantity measure of economic development. Though a loose average, we can adjust per capita income to be a more sensitive test of local economic performance. The first adjustment necessary is to relate the per capita income figures for cities to the consumer price index in order to turn from money to real income. By inflating or deflating per capita incomes with the consumer price index, we achieve an improvement in sensitivity. However, we need further to separate property income from labor income if we are to get to the "nut" of urban income. An understanding of labor income is the essence of analyzing income differences among cities and consequently noting developmental differences among cities.

Income differences and income distributions among cities appear to be accounted for by differences in education, manufacturing employment, regional income, and city size. As education, manufacturing employment, regional income, and city size are greater, per capita income will be higher, but will income be more equitably distributed? Our second test of economic performance is the relative equity of income distribution. It is a performance measure of the quality of economic development.

In the use of income as the measure of performance, the reader should recognize that many cities in the United States are well developed, thus the rate of development, i.e., the rate of change in per capita income, may be slight among American cities.

Human Development: The Economic Purpose

A city is a set of labor skills and the development of these skills should serve to better the individual who acquires them and the city in which he works. Our interest in the economics of human development lies in the long-run aim of high quality urban life accomplished by effective manpower, educational, health, and recreational policies, leading to long-run economic growth.

Local government can aspire to a positive role in local economic development by having a significant impact upon the local labor force, particularly the poten-

[8] Thompson, *A Preface to Urban Economics*, pp. 22, 23.

tial labor force, or that segment of structurally or chronically unemployed labor that is lost to the local economy. By employing these wasted human resources, local government can provide some stability of growth and be an innovator in the field of urban public services. We may not have central economic planning, but we can at least create a useful manpower development role for local government.

Technology

The impact of technological change upon the local labor force is largely beyond the control of local government. Government may put constraints on technology and does so in the form of zoning, pollution controls, billboard ordinances, building codes, public health ordinances, and licensing of labor. But such constraints are nearly always a negative or preventive form rather than a positive manipulation of local technology. Without central economic planning, it is unlikely that cities will ever be able to do more than nudge technology slightly to attempt to curb the most negative aspects of technological change. Even city authorities who attempt to safeguard public employment may find that scarce budgets do not permit the local government to overlook a technological efficiency through automation which might reduce government employment.

On the other hand one may argue that while we may not be able to locally control technology in a positive way, we can effect improvements to urban life by attempting to eliminate some technological problems such as pollution.

Evaluation of Local Policy

As we move from chapter to chapter the reader should recognize the increasing possibilities of local public institutions for allocating resources for urban economic development and urban development generally. Usually in combination with private institutions, the policies in manpower, education, recreation, and health care can be consciously generated to turn toward a nucleus of expanded local planning — something we will see more and more of in the future.

An additional feature of this book is its heavy reliance upon cost-benefit analysis and planning, programming, budgeting systems (PPBS) as a means of evaluating local policy. To achieve effective and efficient local policy, local programs will have to begin to be evaluated on a regular and consistent basis. Cost-benefit analysis, which weighs the gains of a program against the costs of the program, can be a powerful tool of local policy. If cost-benefit analysis is used to select one goal over another or to generate a strictly economic evaluation of a local program, then the analysis has been misused. The role of cost-benefit is to provide a systematic and as complete a picture as possible of the program and its alternatives to ascertain whether or not resources are being allocated in an efficient manner. In so doing, it serves as a policy making aid, not a substitute for decisions by local policy makers.

The New Entrepreneurs

What gets done in cities is the result of both institutional collective action and the action of strong individuals. The idea of the entrepreneur as theorized by Schumpeter fails to consider the innovative role of these institutions. The new entrepreneurs consist of public and private agencies and corporations. While such institutions can be characterized as essentially bureaucratic, they may also, in some instances, do more than merely protect their interests by resisting change. The protection of interests sometimes generates actions which serve to develop the city and may represent new combinations on the urban landscape.

Yet private corporations in cities or other commercially involved power groups tend to aim more for short-run profit than for long-term urban gain. In the future we must look to the development of stronger quasi-public agencies and departments of local government which will undertake the planning and development of the city. These local government and quasi-public agencies we call (somewhat optimistically) the new entrepreneurs, and the goods and services which they produce will likely alter the current short-run profit pursuits of local economic units. Aside from strong departments of local government, we will see increasing numbers of consumer groups, conservation groups, and others who will offer both positive programs and checks against current power groups.

Other new entrepreneurs in the city include special programs agencies of local government such as the recently cut Model Cities (HUD) and community action (OEO) programs, special park districts, university connected action groups, housing cooperatives and other cooperatives, fair housing contact groups, legal aid societies, tenants' rights organizations, welfare rights groups, action oriented museums (educationally oriented), assorted private social clubs, historical societies, and many others. Their numbers are large and increasing as their budgets increase. Their role is local improvement in some cases and only group interest in other cases, yet most have some power, and even in their protection of their members interests, they become in some sense advocates.

What is lacking among these new advocates is coordination and long-run planning. It is the need for this ingredient, in which local government is increasingly competent, that may in the future shift more of these activities into local government. As the actions of the new entrepreneurs become more widely recognized and accepted, there will be increasing pressure for local government to provide such services for all. Thus it is that local government is the key institution to promote high quality urban development in the future.

The scope of such local government planning activity is not at this time known, but chances are the major city in the region will be the focal point, likely contracting services for smaller towns in the region as well as rural communities. Funding for such planning and programs as may arise will probably come from local, state, and federal sources.

Having discussed briefly the major features of urban development with local government being the primary agent for local development in the future, we turn to chapters which highlight some of the major facets of the urban political economics of human development. The next two chapters deal with unemployment and the local government role in alleviating unemployment. The chapter on education discusses the economics of education, its relation to human development, and its possible relation to urban economic development. The chapter on recreation is concerned with the use of leisure time and the local government role in providing efficient parks and recreational services. The chapter on health care discusses some of the economics of health and some additional urban requirements. The chapter on technology treats technology as a social cost. Though this may be a narrow concept, the point is that technology arising in the city generates significant social costs and a balance should be found between privately produced goods and other aspects of high quality urban life. Finally, a few concluding comments are made which reemphasize the need for strong local institutions to provide checks and balances on existing power in cities, but no proposal is made for a superagency simply because the ideal development agency in the community is not yet perceived.

1

Urban Planning:
The Human Context

City planning is of increasing importance in the creation of a viable city, but what do we mean by planning? What do we hope to accomplish by it? To the economist, planning is "the systematic management of assets," [1] i.e., planning is the management of the resources available to the community to attain desired goals. Of primary importance is the identification of the family of objectives toward which the management of resources is directed. The assets upon which any economic unit — in this case the community — can draw are definitely limited. For individuals, companies, cities, nations, all resources are scarce.

For effective use, scarce local resources must be directed toward those ends which are most desired. When alternate ends are discussed, the notion of opportunity costs arises; the opportunity cost of utilizing assets in one way in one objective is the next best gain to which those assets might have been directed. Second, management of assets involves the integration of several strategic strains of decision making which are necessary if the assets or resources are to be successful in accomplishing the proposed objective. A third aspect of asset management involves time. Since both the objective and the strategic decisions made are not one-time affairs but are indefinitely continuous throughout the life span of the community, one must be aware of changes over time due to a variety of influences. Further, the community also must make decisions to preserve existing assets for the production of future income. Conservation in this sense is the accumulation of further resources in some kind of meaningful group pattern which involves net new investment out of current income.

Probably the most difficult process in the entire concept of planning is also the key function of management planning: coordination. Basically two forms of coordination are necessary. One activity involves the coordination of things, especially technology, machines, equipment, materials, schedules, etc. The sec-

[1] Neil W. Chamberlain, *Private and Public Planning* (New York: McGraw-Hill, 1965), p. 4.

ond form involves coordinating people. Efficiency and internal consistency are necessary for the successful operation of any planning system. Following Chamberlain, an overall concept of planning has to include at least three principal aspects:

1. *The ideological* — the framing of objectives or goals both present and future;
2. *Technical and economic* — the most efficient hypothetical means of achieving the system's objectives; and,
3. *Organizational and political* — a management which can coordinate coherence and activity of the participants in the system.[2]

Aside from major war planning, public planning has been almost exclusively urban planning, and even in this instance only in a limited context. Planning by governments in the United States has historically been limited due to a national bias which favored the market mechanisms of capitalism as the sole allocators of resources. Until recent years planning in the economic sphere was almost a dirty word. In many circles this bias against planning is still prevalent. Thus, American urban planning has rather a curious history, namely a responsibility for the planning of physical assets in the city space yet no responsibility for planning for economic resources. Urban planning is somewhat like the parking lot attendant who parks other peoples' cars but cannot afford one of his own. He can move the cars and manipulate them furiously in the lot when the owners are not in view, but when an owner returns, the attendant loses all control. Unless economic planning is available to urban planners, their role may continue to be like the parking lot attendants', manipulating within a system in minor and possibly inconsequential ways. The private economy dominates; the planner follows.

We appear, however, to be in an era of change. Future local governments may have a larger role in the total development, including economic development, of the community. This larger role will include a number of tasks which local governments have not historically performed. Many of these tasks will be in very sensitive areas, such as juvenile delinquency, birth control, personal and family services, and numerous others for which there is no particular well-developed ethic in local government or in the community. City authorities are still not used to thinking in terms of social and economic programs such as those undertaken in Model Cities planning that offer health services centers, special educational ventures, day care centers, and others. Local government and local planners will in the future be more effective in the sense of total welfare of the citizens rather than the largely physical dimensions of current city planning activities.

The purpose of this chapter is to discuss some philosophical implications of urban planning in the larger human context. The main point is that city

---

[2] Chamberlain, *Private and Public Planning*, p. 9.

authority should become primarily involved with programs designed to generate increases in the general welfare of individual citizens.

I. Urban Planning

The ability of the planning profession to pursue the widened horizons of urban policy is questioned by planners as exemplified in a recent copy of the *Journal of the American Institute of Planners*: ". . . we remain divided over which of our fundamental societal problems other than space allocation are 'planning' problems, frustrated with our record to date, and uncertain how to proceed." [3] It is widely believed that urban planning has not developed workable concepts for the future, and there is disagreement among planners as to just what, if anything, can be done.[4] These disagreements among planners appear to be widespread and may be in part due to the somewhat dissimilar views of the two most prominent "schools" of planning.

The two "schools" of planning are referred to as the comprehensive future-oriented group (the larger, traditional school) and the special-interest advocate group.

Comprehensive planners seek to determine the general public good and to base the future physical configuration of the community upon their perception of the present and future public good and interest. The problem here is that in a pluralistic society it is often impossible to determine the general public good. Consequently, comprehensive planning has succeeded only in those societies which possess a high degree of cultural homogeneity.

The special-interest advocate seeks to advance the interest of his own particular client group. His goal is to obtain an equitable share of present and future public facilities and benefits for his clients.

Comprehensive City Planning

Rapid changes in the thinking of city planners are occurring. While there is increased interest in social as opposed to physical planning, it would still be accurate to state that comprehensive city planning emphasizes physical planning. The work of city planners has concentrated on the physical aspects of city building for a number of reasons. First, funds for planning in cities have always been limited; second, funds for community development have generally been scarce. A third possible reason is that city planning has until recently been dominated by planners with particular skills and interests who pursued the spatial aspects of physical design since they were eliminated from economic decisions and were largely ignorant of the social aspects of cities.

---

[3] John L. Hancock, "History of the American Planning Profession: Introduction to a New Biographical Series," *Journal of the American Institute of Planners* 38 (September 1972): 274.

[4] Hancock, "History of the American Planning Profession," p. 274.

Traditionally, cities have been planned from three particular viewpoints as noted by Melville Branch. First is the *initial city*, where no city exists; second is the city planned from the standpoint of a *superimposition*, or radical change, in its present design. Major design surgery is required in this case to remedy existing problems, and often urban renewal is thought of as a partial attempt at this superimposition. A third view, which can be called *emergent*, seeks to guide urban growth in a continuous and gradual way. In this last case, city planning undertakes a long-term guidance of the development of the physical form of the city by following a flexible master plan. These three views of planning can also be seen as a series of overlapping stages to the extent that all are apparent in any city's current planning activities.[5]

What is the current state of the art among physical planners? The planner operating on the urban space has developed a current "agreeable" thinking on physical planning; again we turn to Branch for an informative listing. Branch's summary is probably accurate as far as it goes, but it does mainly present only spatial concerns and so shows the major interests of planners, but not their complete interests.

I. Transportation[a]

  1. Organization of community-wide networks of primary roads and railway lines according to radial-concentric systems. In larger cities radial limited-access highways extend outward from a loop about the central business-commercial area. These are crossed at intervals by circumferential routes of increasing radius which provide connection between outer sectors of the city without traversing the center city. A portion of the outermost circumferential route usually functions as a bypass around the city for interregional traffic. Railroad lines are also planned as a radial-concentric system but the pattern is usually less complete.

[a] Urban Traffic and Transportation Board, City of Philadelphia, *Plan and Program, 1955*, Philadelphia, 1955, 123 pp.

Parsons, Brinckerhoff, Hall, and Macdonald, *Regional Rapid Transit* — A Report to the San Francisco Bay Area Rapid Transit Commission, San Francisco, 1956, 105 pp.

Department of City Planning, *Basic Policies for the Comprehensive Plan of CHICAGO*, Chapter 10: Transportation, Chicago, August 1963, pp. 70–81.

Advance Planning Department-LARTS, California Division of Highways, *Los Angeles Regional Transportation Study*, Volume 1: *Base Year Report*, Los Angeles 54 (P.O. Box 2304, Terminal Annex), December 1963, 61 pp.

Paul Ritter, *Planning for Man and Motor*, Oxford (Pergamon Press), 1963, 384 pp.

Report of the Steering Group, *Traffic in Towns — A Study of the Long-Term Problems of Traffic in Urban Areas*, London (Her Majesty's Stationery Office), 1963, 224 pp.

Robert Herman and Keith Gardels, "Vehicular Traffic Flow," *Scientific American*, Vol. 209, No. 6, December, 1963, pp. 35–43.

[5] Melville C. Branch, *Planning: Aspects and Applications* (New York: John Wiley & Sons, 1966), pp. 132–34.

2. Interrelation of proposed types and densities of land use with the transportation system, traffic projection, and network design.

3. Street and highway design according to function and best contemporary practices, utilizing automated signaling and central electronic computer control.

4. Discouragement or prevention of abutting and nearby land uses which impair the efficient functioning of the primary transportation systems; prevention and elimination of commercial and high-density residential "ribbon development" along present and proposed major thoroughfares unless it is separated by a service road or otherwise designed to reduce traffic conflict.

5. Adequate off-street parking throughout the community where and as needed.

6. Elimination of on-street and roadside parking in areas of heavy traffic.

7. Designation of primary truck routes into and through the city.

8. Elimination of unnecessary or duplicative railroad tracks and facilities. Provision of separated grade crossings.

9. Consolidation of terminal facilities.

10. In larger cities, design and development of a mass transit system of rail transportation to and from the central city, related to existing and proposed areas of higher density within the municipality and metropolitan region. Provision of feeder bus service or automobile parking at rail transit stations.

11. For cities with water transportation, continued improvement of waterfront facilities and interconnecting rail and highway systems.

12. Location and extension of airport sites for much-expanded air traffic, as close to the city as feasible. Provision of express transportation between airports and terminal points in the city.[6]

It would appear that the planner perceives transportation as an orderly process of circulation which forms, molds, and guides development of the urban space. The principal idea appears to be a smooth flow of transportation of goods and people through and around the space. While orderliness is of high priority, there seems to be no connotation of optimum except as a maximum. That is, planners think in terms of the smoothest or rapidest rather than the most efficient in economic terms. That is not to suggest that the planner would propose using all urban space for transportation, but, from the above points, there is no sense of what might be subservient to an urban transportation system. Transportation in the eyes of the physical planner seems to take precedence over most other urban activities and land uses.

Turning again to Branch, planners appear to reach some agreement about the spatial aspects of industry in the city.

[6] From *Planning Aspects and Applications* by Melville C. Branch, pp. 134–38. Copyright © 1966, John Wiley & Sons, Inc. Reprinted by permission.

II. Industry[b]

13. Location of new industry and gradual consolidation of existing scattered industry in particular zones of districts of considerable size.
14. Special location, isolation, or physical separation of "noxious" industrial activities.
15. Industrial "parks" designed to provide the quality sites, utilities, services, environmental amenity, and other features desired or needed by many modern productive operations.
16. Under special control, the occasional location of industrial activities with few environmentally disruptive characteristics — such as research and development and manufacturing medical laboratories — in or close to residential areas or small commercial centers.[7]

[b] Theodore K. Pasma, *Organized Industrial Districts — A Tool for Community Development*, Area Development Division, Office of Technical Services, United States Department of Commerce, Washington, June, 1954, 111 pp.
  Thompson Ramo-Wooldridge, Inc., *Ramo-Wooldridge Laboratories*, Bunker Ramo Corporation, Canoga Park, California (Form 248–59), 1959, 6 pp., enclosure.

There are numerous constraints which the planner places on industrial location. The above gives the impression that industry should be clustered, isolated if it is "obnoxious," and generally controlled to avoid having it located so as to harm the environment. While controls are present, no sense of the amount of urban space allocated to industry is observed.

Business location is also important. Planners suggest a number of principles.

III. Business-Commercial[c]

17. Regional, district, and neighborhood shopping centers in decreasing order of size: planned to serve a designated population and trade area, immediately accessible to but not along arterial streets, providing adequate off-street parking for customers and employees, with separate service access, and integrated design features.
18. Replanning and urban renewal of downtown or city center to provide: improved circulation and reduced congestion, central mass transit facilities and interchange, consolidation of related activities and services, adequate vehicular parking within structures, off-street loading

[c] Ministry of Town and Country Planning, Advisory Handbook on *The Redevelopment of Central Areas*, London (His Majesty's Stationery Office), 1947, 99 pp.
  National Research Bureau, Inc., *1964 Directory of Shopping Centers in the United States and Canada*, Chicago, 1963, 900 pp.
  Victor Gruen and Larry Smith, *Shopping Towns U.S.A., — The Planning of Shopping Centers*, New York (Simon and Schuster), 1960, 288 pp.
  J. Marshall Miller (Editor), *New Life for Cities Around the World — International Handbook on Urban Renewal*, New York (Books International), 1963, 233 pp.

[7] From *Planning Aspects and Applications* by Melville C. Branch, pp. 134–38. Copyright © 1966, John Wiley & Sons, Inc. Reprinted by permission.

and unloading, often a pedestrian shopping mall, and areal design, landscaping, and other physical features upgrading the aesthetic quality of the central city environment.

19. Provision in new construction and the redevelopment of established strip commercial zones of sufficient off-street parking for customers, visitors, and employees on the property or close-by.

20. Elimination of incompatible, nonconforming, commercial and industrial land uses from residential neighborhoods.[8]

The location of business and commercial activities hinges on a number of ideas. A control factor is implied by regional shopping centers serving particular populations in the urban space. This suggests a limitation on the number of shopping centers. Further, "strips" of commercial activity appear to be undesirable as are "nonconforming uses." With regard to strips, the implication is that one is primarily concerned with off-street parking and circulation. As to nonconforming uses, there seems to be no particular basis for such ideas except in extreme examples. Cities with mixed use may well be as attractive as cities with strict zoning; living and working may be more efficient when mixed commercial and residential patterns are possible. Economic efficiency does not appear to be significant among these ideas. On the other hand, a kind of aesthetic conventional wisdom does obtain. One gains the impression that urban ugliness is in part due to commercial "strips" and "nonconforming uses."

Residential patterns in the urban space are an additional area of agreement.

IV. Residential[d]

21. Organization of land and structures into neighborhood units of varying type and size. The resident population in the unit and its area are related to the efficient radius of one or more service functions; to date, the elementary school has been the main determinant of size. Neighborhoods are delineated by some physical boundary or separator: arterial street, other right of way, park, or appropriate feature on the ground. In newly developing areas, street design, lot layout, and an arrangement of open spaces are encouraged or required which will create natural neighborhood units.

22. Use of larger "superblocks."

[d] James Dahir (Compiler), *The Neighborhood Unit Plan — Its Spread and Acceptance* (A Selected Bibliography with Interpretative Comments), New York (Russell Sage Foundation), 1947, 91 pp.

Committee on the Hygiene of Housing, American Public Health Association, *Planning the Neighborhood*, Chicago (Public Administration Service), 1960, 94 pp.

Federal Housing Administration, *Planned-Unit Development* with a Homes Association (Land Planning Bulletin No. 6), Washington (United States Government Printing Office), 1963, 64 pp.

William H. Whyte, *Cluster Development*, New York (American Conservation Association), April 1964, 130 pp.

[8] From *Planning Aspects and Applications* by Melville C. Branch, pp. 134–38. Copyright © 1966, John Wiley & Sons, Inc. Reprinted by permission.

23. Avoidance of highly regular, gridiron layout of streets.
24. Increased percentages of multistory, rental, or condominium apartment buildings and subsidized housing for low-income families.
25. Taller apartment buildings covering a smaller proportion of the land, with correspondingly larger surrounding open space.
26. As an alternative to single-family houses with yard spaces on all sides: clustered arrangements of dwellings or "town houses" joined together by one common wall with the yard space thus saved added to surrounding open space for private and common use.
27. Reduction in the heterogeneity of land uses within small areas, grouping together of similar types of uses.
28. Greater variety of design in land layout and buildings.
29. Reduction in single-family lot sizes and corresponding increase in residential densities.
30. Large-scale project or planned unit developments incorporating different land uses and residential building types.[9]

For planning residential areas one perceives that aesthetics play a part in the planners' thinking about housing. The elimination of grids, the interest in "neighborhoods," and the interest in variety all suggest a sense of environment in which the planner may most nearly approximate a "social planner." This aspect of physical planning appears to be the only one we have discussed thus far which is not primarily subservient to circulation. On the other hand, residential "slurbs" would appear to reinforce the planners' interest in transportation. Thus, while one may not choose to be able to control densities, one may be able to build expressways out to residential suburbs.

Another significant area of urban planning has to do with recreation. Planners have reached some agreement concerning the spatial aspects of parks.

V. Recreation[e]

31. Public neighborhood parks and playgrounds located with respect to population, access, and frequency of use.
32. Properly distributed regional and district parks for a population with increasing leisure time.
33. Location, design, and preservation of parks, recreational areas, open spaces, agricultural and other land of low-intensity use so that it comprises an interrelated system which assists in delineating neighborhood units, appropriately divides land uses or districts, and otherwise acts to improve the physical form and amenity of the community.

[e] Wayne R. Williams, *Recreation Places* (New York: 1958), 302 pp. National Recreation Association, *Recreation and Park Yearbook* (New York: 1963 and earlier).

[9] From *Planning Aspects and Applications* by Melville C. Branch, pp. 134–38 . Copyright © 1966, John Wiley & Sons, Inc. Reprinted by permission.

34. Incorporation of recreational areas as an integral part of privately developed subdivisions and planned projects.

35. Preservation of natural recreational resources within the urban area: water- and beachfront, wooded areas, scenic outlooks, and other places with unique potential for public recreation and enjoyment.[10]

Recreation is one area in which the planner proves himself distinctly physical in approach except in the aspect of preservation of unique resources. Recreation to the planner is largely the planning of parks and facilities where recreation presumably takes place. Just as a house is not a home, a park may not be a recreation area. Concerned planners today however appear to concentrate on parks and open space to a larger degree as an attempt to become involved with social aspects of planning. Unfortunately, while one may plan for a motorcar without knowing its occupants, one may not truly plan a park without considering its direct users. Many confusions thus arise when the park is considered an end rather than a means.

Under a miscellaneous category, Branch notes:

VI. General and Miscellaneous[f]

36. A town or civic center, branch administrative centers in larger cities.

37. Location of operating elements of the municipality — such as schools, libraries, police and fire stations, and public utility facilities — to function efficiently with respect to service area, expansion, accessibility, and related urban-wide systems. Superior technical and aesthetic design which can serve as an example for private development.

38. Tax policies favoring the retention of existing open spaces in the city such as private golf courses and designated agricultural land.

39. Recommended use of "greenbelts" as a method of structuring the city into neighborhoods or separate sections, interrupting continuous urban development at the periphery, favoring the organization of new suburbs as distinct communities of limited size, and providing open recreational space threading through built-up areas.

40. Recognition that the impact of limited-access automobile expressways on urban form, neighborhoods, and abutting land use is an essential consideration in their location and engineering design.

41. Preservation of the air resource over cities by controlling its pollution.

42. Preservation of historical sites.

[f] Such a variety of objectives are included under this heading that specific references are not listed. See one of the number of bibliographies available on city planning or the "Planners Library" in each February, May, August, and November issue of *ASPO Newsletter*, American Society of Planning Officials, Chicago (1313 East 60th St.).

[10] From *Planning Aspects and Applications* by Melville C. Branch, pp. 134–38. Copyright © 1966, John Wiley & Sons, Inc. Reprinted by permission.

43. In ascending order within large buildings: separate layers of restricted commercial, parking, office, and apartment-residential uses. Regulated by "horizontal" zoning.

44. A comprehensive zoning plan and supporting ordinances which include: (a) reduction of excessive commercial zones and "ribbon development" abutting arterial streets, (b) provision for planned unit developments or projects, (c) provision for cluster and other inventive dwelling design and layout which observe established standards for safety, health, and amenity, (d) limitation of the number of less restrictive uses permitted in single-purpose zones without special approval, (e) elimination of incompatible nonconforming land uses after a reasonable period for amortization and removal.

45. Minimum standards for various areal, spatial, and physical elements and provisions within the municipal police power, ranging from minimum side yards and floor-area ratios to standard street sections and grading or soil retention requirements.

46. Subdivision and comparable controls which include: (a) approval, by the public planning body and municipal departments directly concerned, of the intended street layout, lot size and shape, utility installations, and other physical features and provisions of private land development involving more than one parcel, (b) prohibition of lot sizes, shapes, and arrangements which depreciate the environment or create undue difficulties for related city services and activities, (c) modification of normal requirements in hillside and other special terrain, (d) provisions encouraging desirable design treatment and environmental features.

47. A building code supporting city planning requirements and objectives.

48. Participation by the public planning body in the municipal long-range capital improvement program with respect to projects included and their priority.

49. Formal involvement of all major municipal departments and agencies in the planning process.

50. Use of electronic computers for data processing, storage, and analysis.

51. Application of systems engineering, operations research, and other advanced quantitative techniques of analysis to comprehensive city planning.[11]

The last category, general and miscellaneous, suggests a rounding out of the planners' interests in the urban space. Included are concepts of environmental quality, institutional clustering, and a variety of controls and standards for spatial planning.

These are the ideas of the comprehensive planners and are the major ideas which obtain in existing city planning agencies. Perhaps this discussion of "current thinking" has been unduly critical given the constraints under which city planners have worked in cities. The overriding impression that one gets, how-

---

[11] From *Planning Aspects and Applications* by Melville C. Branch, pp. 134–38. Copyright © 1966, John Wiley & Sons., Inc. Reprinted by permission.

ever, is that city planners have not been attuned directly to many social needs of people living in cities in their physical planning.

Perhaps the most interesting planning ideas relate to the radical kinds of change which are taking place today in advocacy and other forms of social planning. By way of illustration, let us note a typical Model Cities program set.

Model Cities: A Form of Advocacy Planning

Model Cities programs are the result of the passage in Congress of the Demonstration Cities and Metropolitan Development Act of 1966. The goal was to coordinate all other urban programs, focus them on a particular area of the city, and, with local government, develop means for reducing what we call urban poverty problems. There were six basic objectives:

1. To develop rational solutions to specific urban problems.
2. To develop rational solutions on a "balanced" attack basis.
3. To generate involvement of affected peoples in the total process of problem solving.
4. To coordinate existing programs affecting people in the selected area in order to minimize duplication of services.
5. To implement additional programs and/or expand existing programs according to the developed rational solutions and administrative strategy.
6. To monitor program accomplishments and to evaluate the effects on the "quality of urban life" of the residents of the area as a result of implemented programs and the "balanced attack."

Thus, the City Demonstration Agency becomes a focal point of planning, coordinating, and implementing programs to attack the human problems of a segment of the population of the city.

The vicious circle of poverty is very much in evidence in American cities; figure 1 presents a typical scheme of urban poverty problems. The interrelatedness of factors in the figure argues strongly for the necessity of a "balanced attack" against urban poverty problems. A balanced attack involves a set of comprehensive and interrelated programs which attempt to eliminate urban problems. Much of today's policy moves in a single-purpose way (housing programs build only housing) and results are mixed. Most programs that fail do so in part because of their small impact on what is not a single urban problem but a complex of problems.

The enormous conceptual differences between comprehensive planning and the social-physical planning of a Model Cities program can best be seen in the projects proposed for the Akron, Ohio, Model Cities Commission and City Demonstration Agency. While not all of the programs were funded, the Model Cities programs which were implemented were to some great degree free of traditional planning limitations.

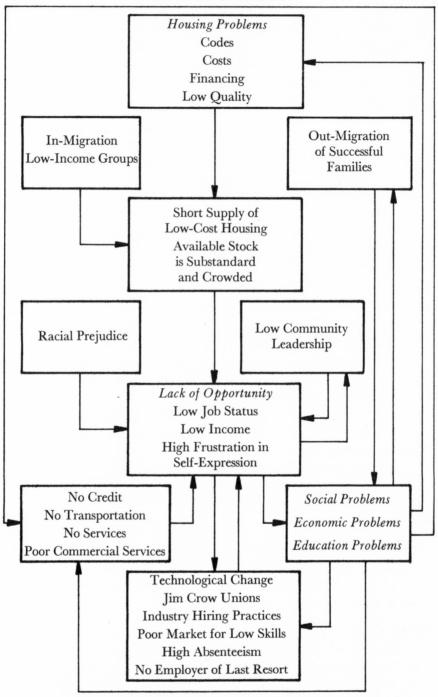

FIGURE 1
THE CIRCLE OF POVERTY

Housing Problems
Codes
Costs
Financing
Low Quality

In-Migration
Low-Income Groups

Out-Migration
of Successful
Families

Short Supply of
Low-Cost Housing
Available Stock
is Substandard
and Crowded

Racial Prejudice

Low Community
Leadership

Lack of Opportunity
Low Job Status
Low Income
High Frustration in
Self-Expression

No Credit
No Transportation
No Services
Poor Commercial Services

Social Problems
Economic Problems
Education Problems

Technological Change
Jim Crow Unions
Industry Hiring Practices
Poor Market for Low Skills
High Absenteeism
No Employer of Last Resort

Source: Used by permission of Management Information Services.

Projects Proposed for Akron, Ohio,
Model Cities Program 1969–70

Economic Projects

1. Consumer Protection and Education Agency
    a) Debt counseling
    b) Consumer advice
2. Job Placement Center
    a) Testing counseling
    b) Research and data bank
    c) Training
3. New Careers Program
4. Cooperatives
    a) Investment
    b) Business and buying
    c) Credit union
5. Neighborhood Development Corporation
6. Income Supplement — Income Guarantee Experiment
7. Trade School Program
8. Housing Assistance Center
    a) Fair housing
    b) Have maintenance and improvement education
    c) Relocation of workers
    d) Loans for housing improvement and home purchase
9. Market Feasibility Studies

Social Planning Projects

1. Montessori School
2. Neighborhood Health Center
3. Multipurpose Social Service Center
4. Youth Services Bureau
5. Adult Rehabilitation Organization (Seven-Step Foundation)
6. Project Follow Through, a Dropout Program
7. Nongraded Primary School
8. Neighborhood Recreation Council

Physical Planning Projects

1. Improvement of Bus Schedule and Routing Service
2. Transportation for Hard-Core Unemployed
3. Rehabilitation Specialist
4. Neighborhood Arts Program

5. Neighborhood City Hall for Environment Services
6. Metropolitan Housing
   a) High rise for elderly
   b) Scattered site
   c) Improve recreation facilities
7. Summit Lake Survey
8. Ohio Canal Improvement
9. Perkins Woods Redevelopment
10. Lane Field Redevelopment
11. Perkins Square Redevelopment
12. (2) Tot Lots
13. Expand Demonstration Trash and Collection for Whole Area

Three categories of programs were discussed; economic, social, and physical. Most of the proposals are self-explanatory but a few may need description. For example, by isolating physical planning it is obvious that the Model Cities people thought first in terms of social and economic services; thus physical programs were designed to support the social or economic programs. Note the physical planning programs under various categories. A structure for housing the development corporation, a site for a housing assistance center, a structure for housing the organization of neighborhood recreation councils are all physical structures to serve a social or economic purpose. Perhaps this is the example which best reveals the subtle conceptual difference between traditional physical planning and social planning, as evidenced in Model Cities. Model Cities programs cast the physical in a subservient role to the broader human context. Planning in the future will probably be much more like this Model Cities listing than traditional planning. Planning will be more extensive and less limited in scope.

II. Perspectives on Social Planning

Problems of Social Planning

If planning is a formal attempt to develop means for managing community resources to accomplish social ends, it is important to understand that decisions we make through an enlarged planning concept may bind future human beings as no other decisions have. We stand in prospect of being able to deal with individual human problems in a context we could not perceive before. What things will we leave behind? What things will be overlooked? What essential ingredients will be lost? As Margaret Mead suggested, the islanders of the South Seas forgot how to build canoes and so were forever prisoners on a group of islands to which they had come as competent mariners. Is it possible for modern man to forget an essential human relationship? Probably it is, and planning puts us in direct prospect of so doing, for planning, no matter how well conceived, is an oversimplification of human experience.

Another danger of planning efforts lies in dealing only with the "needs" of human beings rather than needs and aspirations or human potentialities. By our considerable ability to equalize the performance of persons (eyeglasses, education, work, training, minimum health protection, etc.), the risk is run of stressing the compromises that are necessary to accomplish the "social goal" to the disadvantage of the individual and his or her potential. While we need to know our limitations, we need to know our potentialities as well.

Still a further possible area of problems exists in planning. On a somewhat negative note, any planning for residents has as an essential part a desire to control that population. For example, in recreation it may well be that a central desire of planning for children is to control them. If society is interested in planning as a control mechanism, then it is easy to develop a recreational program which leads to this goal. One simply devises means for using up the child's time and stimulates him to participate in these means. Similarly, if society decides to deal with the problem of juvenile delinquency, it does so largely because delinquency is a felt "social problem." Unless we consider juvenile delinquency as primarily an individual problem (that is, we hope to support, aid, and assist the individual with the problem) there exists an improper context — that of mere social control. Juvenile delinquency is a "social pain" as generally conceived; thus the elimination of the pain requires that the person so "diseased" must be "cured" or "isolated." In fact, there are great satisfactions and pleasures for the juvenile delinquent in terms of status and belonging to the subculture. Thus the alternative for the "cured" juvenile delinquent may simply be to become a member of the alienated blue-collar work force and, in so doing, settle down and give up the immediate (although transitory) pleasures of the juvenile delinquent subculture.

To amplify this kind of thinking consider that the primary historical motivation for organizing social change has been fear; to wit, our recent interest in programs for the ghetto. Unfortunately, since fear is probably still our greatest motivator, when we plan social programs or think about such programs we have to be certain of the integrity of them in order to avoid social manipulation of individual human beings. If we are to avoid manipulation, our planning must be in a different context than the organizational planning that we have pursued historically. Planning must be fully democratic.

Until recent years, the major planning in our cities has been in the form of private planning, principally undertaken by business firms to accomplish specific profit motives. Public planning on what some might call a human scale is a recent idea that is not widely understood. The human joy of living in the city is not a primary motive in city development. Cities have grown on expediency and personal profit, and the primary guiding force of this growth has been effective economic centralization for the benefit of effective machinery and an efficient economy. Probably one of the most articulate and vocal critics of city planning on this basis (which is substantially no planning at all) has been Frank Lloyd Wright. What Wright suggested is that planning processes have not supported a consistent human philosophical position.[12] There has been no value system which has been purposely introduced. Successful planning for the future is going to have to be developed on a human scale, i.e., developed around the idea of the individual's wishes.

The Role of Free Choice

To be effective, social programs must be heavily ingrained with freedom of choice. It is one essential requisite of democratic planning. As R. H. Tawney argues, there is no freedom in the abstract.

> Whatever else it may or may not employ, freedom involves the power of choice between alternatives; a choice which is real, not merely nominal, between alternatives which exist in fact. It means the ability to do or refrain from doing definite things at a definite moment in definite circumstances or it means nothing at all; because a human being is most a human being when he thinks, wills, and acts.
>
>   . . . Every individual possesses certain requirements ranging from material necessities of existence to the need to express himself in speech and writing, to share in the conduct of affairs of common interests, and to worship God in his own way or refrain from worshiping him; the satisfaction of which is necessary to his welfare. Reduced to its barest essentials, his freedom exists in the opportunity secured him within the limits set by nature and in the enjoyment of similar opportunities by his fellows to take the action needed in order to insure that these requirements are satisfied.[13]

Tawney goes on to describe what is necessary for an effective guarantee of freedom for the individual. First, it must be measurable that the human being has not been prevented from making a choice.

> The right to vote and to combine is valueless when the use of the former means eviction and the latter, unemployment. The right to the free choice of an occupation is eliminated when the expenses of entering a profession are prohibitive; the right to earn a living is absurd if unemployment is rampant; the right to justice is nonexistent if few men of small means can afford the cost of protecting their rights to life, liberty and the pursuit of happiness. . . .[14]

12 Frank Lloyd Wright, *The Living City* (New York: New American Library, 1963), pp. 19–29.

13 R. H. Tawney, *The Attack and Other Papers* (London: Allen & Unwin, Ltd., 1953), p. 83.

14 Tawney, *The Attack and Other Papers*, p. 84.

In the second place, Tawney argues that the rights essential to freedom must be available to all, not just a minority.

> Marriage would not be regarded as a national institution if, while five percent of the population were polygamous, the majority passed their lives unsolaced and unencumbered by husbands or wives. The same is true of freedom. A society in which some groups can do much what they please, while others can do little of what they ought may have virtues of its own; but freedom is not one of them. It is free only insofar as all the elements composing it are able in fact, not merely in theory, to make the most of their powers, to grow to their full stature, to do what they conceive to be their duty, and — since liberty should not be too austere — to have their fling when they feel like it. Insofar as the opportunity to lead a life worthy of human beings is restricted to a minority, what is commonly described as freedom would be more properly called privilege.[15]

In continuing his argument, Tawney notes that while the meaning of freedom is not complex, its application through policy is quite difficult. Values are translated into power by the degree of interest which people take in them.[16] Past values though held through power are still values, but the policies which purport to represent them may no longer do so. Simply stated, power resides in the hands of a few and only those few have freedoms in great number. To create general freedom is to constantly strive toward the prevention of power in the hands of the few.

> Classes already at the top of the ladder may fall, but they cannot rise. The constrictions which they put upon liberty are the result of that position. Whether consciously or not, it is, in large measure, a defense mechanism. Put in a nutshell, it is a doctrine of liberty which purports not action to extend opportunities and raise individual faculties to the highest possible levels, but the continued enjoyment by individuals and groups of such powers, advantages and opportunities as past history and present social arrangements may happen to have conferred upon them.[17]

In urban communities someone must make rules and see that they are kept or life becomes impossible and the wheels do not turn.

> If public power does not make these rules, the effect is that they are made by private power — by landlords interested in increasing rents or by capitalists interested in increasing profits. The result in either case is not freedom, but a dictatorship, which is even more oppressive because it is largely unconscious and because those whom it profits regard it, quite sincerely, as identical with liberty.[18]

[15] Tawney, *The Attack and Other Papers*, p. 84.
[16] Tawney, *The Attack and Other Papers*, p. 85.
[17] Tawney, *The Attack and Other Papers*, p. 85.
[18] Tawney, *The Attack and Other Papers*, p. 34.

When beginning to plan for the personal lives of others, there is always the risk of manipulating their lives and constricting their freedom; yet, when nothing is done, many persons are sentenced to personal imprisonment. The social programs created must recognize the latter and attempt to deal judiciously with the former. While planners may argue that "opportunity" is freedom, there is little credence to the idea that planning in cities has truly provided more opportunities than restraints.[19]

The Bureaucratic City

The problem of freedom is of course simpler in a democratic society of little complexity, but in a large bureaucratic society, freedom is less readily identifiable. Freedom demands easy comprehension, and the resident of a less complex and agrarian world may see his freedom as being interdependent upon the freedom and welfare of his fellows. The city removes from man the direct responsibility to protect his freedom by protecting that of others. Civil order is not personally identified with self and assisting others as much as it is with large social and political institutions in the city. When man forms the city he is more capable of individually creating and pursuing his own goals but less capable of being "civil" or "civilized." That is, the city may support the individual's freedom to choose and take action, but it renders him more isolated and less aware of his own responsibilities toward the group.

Isolation of the urbanite is both technological and economic. Labor specialization is required for the local economy and yet serves to isolate one worker from another and places the majority of citizens in work which decivilizes them. Job specialization thus creates a limited man. At the same time, increasing complexity of organization which characterizes the modern city takes issues and decisions out of the hands of the common citizen and beyond his understanding.

In the wake of the limited man and complex organizations, decision making moves higher and higher into the hands of a few. Yet, as Harvey Wheeler notes, the human being is still the best and cheapest computer available.[20] Thus one might argue that the most efficient mode of decision making in cities is the one in which maximum autonomy is given to individuals to make their own decisions. Democracy evidences this efficiency in spite of the fact that the city is increasingly a bureaucratic organization.

The Planning Unit of One

What then is the decision mode or planning unit most acceptable for planning? It is not the control functions that the city has exercised over land use;

[19] Alan A. Altshuler, *The City Planning Process: A Political Analysis* (Ithica, N.Y.: Cornell University Press, 1965), p. 312.

[20] John Harvey Wheeler, *Democracy in a Revolutionary Era: The Political Order Today,* A Center Occasional Paper (Santa Barbara, Cal.: Center for the Study of Democratic Institutions, 1970), p. 75.

nor is it merely the circulation patterns to ease movement. Albeit important, these two major forms of planning activity are distinctly inferior to the development of institutions in a democratic society which are more essentially supportive of individuals. Educational institutions, while ostensibly for this purpose, fail in this regard; recreation services fail; health services are exclusive; job programs are limited; and guaranteed employment is nonexistent. Bureaucratic institutions function in an atmosphere of conformity and control, and, like traditional planning activities, fail to the extent that they do not place the smallest planning unit, the individual, as the focal point of their consideration.

If the individual is so important, how is he to become a recognized, functioning part of planning? The planner must learn to approach the people in smaller and smaller numbers, making distinctions about what is in fact welfare to the smaller and smaller units of population he serves. It is not likely that these small units can be used in all urban decisions, but in traditional areas of planning, the planner can become more aware of protecting the minority in his attempts to please the majority.

Most importantly, the planner can begin to function in his more relevant areas — the social programs which have been discussed and exemplified in our look at the Model Cities programs. Even the most massive programs of medical care, or recreation, or manpower, or education can be planned around units of population as small as one person.

Finally, specific programs developed for individuals are easier to evaluate than aggregate programs. A chest x-ray program is simpler to assess than a highway program. A recreation program for a particular group of teen-agers is easier to evaluate than a park system. Thus specific programs which have an immediate impact upon the lives of the beneficiaries are usually more defensible than complex, long-run programs such as urban renewal. It is not merely simplicity nor is it long-run and short-run differences that make human programs more desirable than large-scale physical capital programs. It is simply the ability to know whether or not the program was worth doing and the fact that a known group of human beings is being directly aided.

Grass-roots: A Counterpoint to the Planning Unit of One

While the individual should be the basic planning unit wherever possible, the student of the city recognizes that power is an essential part of urban policy. Power tends to flow to the top, and business and other leaders also become civic leaders forming a power structure which represents leading economic (private and public) interests of the city.

As a counter to this form of power concentration, there appears to be strong need for active participation by citizens to create effective decisions. "Citizens' participation," as exhibited in Model Cities programs, has been explicit policy but has had a mixed record of success. The "official" granting of political decision-making power from the "rich" to the "poor" is apt to be fundamentally self-serving on the part of the rich and not efficacious for the poor.

While a lengthy discussion of recent experience in officially sanctioned citizen's participation is not the intent of this section, some mention should be made of one form of "unsanctioned" participation which does appear effective, namely the radicalism practiced by Saul Alinsky.

Alinsky, in his efforts at organizing the powerless into power groups, was not in favor of violent revolution. "We start with the system because there is no other place to start from except political lunacy," said Alinsky. Instead of destroying the system, Alinsky believed that the system was sufficiently dedicated to freedom to enable individuals to achieve their potential. Working within the system but in opposition to existing power structures to gain political power appears to be the central point of the approach. ". . . We are concerned with how to create mass organizations to seize power and give it to the people." [21]

The basic requirement for an effective political method is the recognition of the world as it is, ". . . an arena of power politics moved primarily by perceived, immediate self-interests, where morality is rhetorical rationale for expedient action and self-interest. . . . A world not of angels but of angles." Alinsky, for purposes of political activity, divides the world into the Haves, the Have-Nots, and the Have-a-Littles, Want Mores. These class distinctions are merely emphatic descriptions of the socially, economically, and politically rich, poor, and middle class. The mode of change toward improved conditions resides in the extent to which men recognize that their welfare depends upon the welfare of others.[22]

The reader should seek out Alinsky's *Rules for Radicals* since it is not possible in this brief section to do more than allude to some of his major ideas about strategy. He actively seeks to have established authority attack the radical leader or his organization. By so doing, the "establishment" provides a cohesive force which brings support to the organization and aids in its creating a viable political group. By committing "antisocial" (antisocial in the minds of the power structure) but legal acts, "The enemy properly goaded and guided in his reaction will be your major strength." The resources of the Have-Nots are people and not money. "Aside from voting, use the power of the law by making the establishment obey its own rules." Alinsky suggests that organized groups seeking power "go outside the experience of your enemy," emphasize tactics that your people enjoy, and recognize that the threat is usually more terrifying than the tactic itself.[23]

[21] Saul D. Alinsky, *Rules for Radicals: A Practical Primer for Realistic Radicals* (New York: Random House, 1971), pp. xxi, xxiv, 3.

[22] Alinsky, *Rules for Radicals*, pp. 12–13, 18.

[23] Alinsky, *Rules for Radicals*, pp. 136, 138, 139.

In one city the threat of an "antisocial act" generated gains. Alinsky proposed that the Have-Nots buy one hundred tickets for one of Rochester, New York's, symphony performances. The one hundred blacks would have an enormous preperformance dinner of baked beans. The result at the concert would render ridiculous the establishment, symphony goers, and the symphony.[24] The threat of such an act carries as much weight as the act itself and places the organized Have-Nots in a position of bargaining for gains for their group.

While outrageous to some, such tactics can be characterized as legal, nonviolent, and potentially effective. Alinsky's form of politicizing the Have-Nots is essentially competitive and within the system. Such activities represent a significant form of generating responsive government and form a potentially useful counterpoint to planning from the top with the grass-roots essentially coming up. The major point is that individual freedoms and opportunities are protected only by participation in collective action.

The Costs of Social Interaction

While we may recognize the planning unit of one as an ideal of democracy, its implementation in a complex society is difficult and not without costs. Not every urban policy decision can seek the approval of every citizen; the costs would be enormous. The costs of citizens cooperating for their mutual benefit have been referred to as a form of *social interaction cost*. People with differing views are forced to make cooperative decisions or compromises in which all may have to incur certain kinds of costs.[25]

Among the major urban power groups are politicians, local bureaucrats, local citizens groups, business interests, and, occasionally, individuals who are most affected by a coming decision. In a way this interaction is a kind of bargaining process in which individuals or groups act to gain their own points of interest. As Buchanan and Tullock have pointed out, one aspect of costs associated with this bargaining can be called decision costs.[26]

Decision costs, or the costs of bargaining, can arise from the values placed on effort and time as well as the direct costs of bargaining.[27] Logically, if two people can be seen as the smallest bargaining unit, decision-making costs arise as soon as a bargaining unit is formed. Further, such costs will rise as the group becomes larger. Those who have worked on committees well understand the problem of the optimum workable size of a committee; a committee too large demands increased bureaucratization, repetition, considerable time, and sometimes pa-

[24] Alinsky, *Rules for Radicals*, p. 140.

[25] Robert L. Bish, *The Public Economy of Metropolitan Areas* (Chicago: Markham Publishing Co., 1971), p. 35, and James M. Buchanan and Gordon Tullock, *The Calculus of Consent: Logical Foundations of Constitutional Democracy* (Ann Arbor: University of Michigan Press, 1962), pp. 97–116.

[26] Buchanan and Tullock, *Calculus of Consent*, pp. 68–69.

[27] Buchanan and Tullock, *Calculus of Consent*, pp. 68–69.

tience as compared to a small committee. A committee too small cannot generate sufficiently reliable inputs to arrive at an appropriate decision. Further, costs can rise since there are possibilities for strategic bargaining, a situation in which a person in the bargaining can, by holding back his support, gain a larger share from the decision. If a graph were drawn showing decision-making costs, the curve (costs) would rise as the number of individuals in the bargaining increases (see figures 2 and 3).

In addition to the decision costs, another form of social interaction cost is that of political externalities. *External costs* arise when the action by the group generates costs for other individuals. This cost is in the form of a by-product; thus in an economic transaction when A and B are engaged in bargaining and this creates costs for C, an external effect of the transaction has been created. Likewise, when a local government imposes a tax, those who disagree with the tax bear an additional cost over and above the dollar amount of the tax which is disagreeable to them. If everyone agrees with the tax, then there are logically no political externalities for all are willing to bear the agreed upon tax. Therefore, we would expect that a curve showing political externalities and their costs would decline as an increasing number of persons agreed with the political action.[28] Note that terms have shifted from bargaining unit to political entity, since the political jurisdiction is, in making decisions, a bargaining unit.

As would be expected, and as noted in figures 2 and 3, the more persons agreeing on a particular decision the lower the political externalities costs. For example, there are little or no political externality costs to a decision such as a proclamation on the wondrousness of mother's apple pie. Here total agreement is reached (assuming that mother can in fact bake a decent apple pie), and no person bears significant costs. If, on the other hand, the decision has to do with slum removal, the external costs can be quite high, thus agreement is difficult to reach if bargaining includes all affected parties.

Combining decision costs and political externality costs one gains social interaction costs. The most efficient decision in this case would be where the lowest combined costs were achieved. While it is not possible to attain perfect harmony in political decision making, it is possible to work toward a compromise which is in theory reached at that point where the two curves combine to generate the lowest point of costs.

With these two forms of social interaction cost in mind, it should be recognized that decisions in the urban community are far from costless. Further, various forms of government might lead to different social interaction costs. For example, in a dictatorship it would be possible to eliminate most costs of decision making, but political externalities might be high indeed. Likewise, on the other end of the political spectrum and under conditions of full citizens' participation

[28] Buchanan and Tullock, *Calculus of Consent*, pp. 64 and 115.

FIGURE 2
SOCIAL INTERACTION COSTS

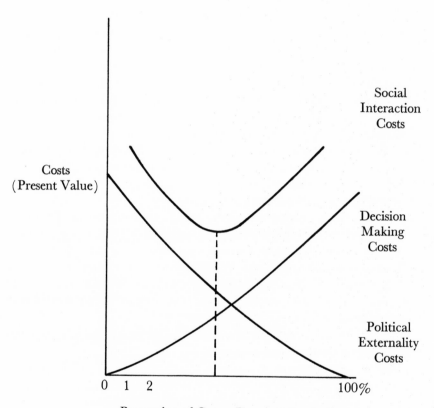

Proportion of Group Required for Action

Source: Robert L. Bish, *The Public Economy of Metropolitan Areas* (Chicago: Markham Publishing Co., 1971), p. 40. Reprinted by permission of Markham Publishing Co.

FIGURE 3

SOCIAL INTERACTION COSTS

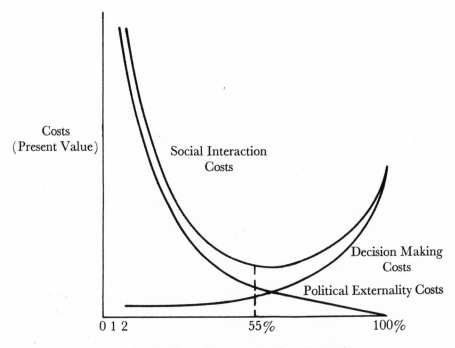

Source: Robert L. Bish, *The Public Economy of Metropolitan Areas* (Chicago: Markham Publishing Co., 1971), p. 40. Reprinted by permission of Markham Publishing Co.

in all decisions, political externalities might be reduced or even eliminated, but decision costs would be relatively higher.

An additional feature of social interaction costs is that they may shift as a result of new information during the period of consideration of the decision. As Leibenstein suggests, it is easy enough to establish agreement on rules in a game prior to the beginning of the game, but quite difficult to do so after the game is under way.[29]

In reality, planning in the city demands some delegation; by that we mean that the people entrust political decision makers with power to select from among the various choices which are open to citizens in cities. It is not our task to go into great detail on the organization of local government. Suffice it to say that particular organizational forms bear particular costs, and any city government which is responsive to citizens is likely to be less costly in the long run than one which is not.

Returning briefly to a comparison of the traditional city planning of most cities and the social planning of the Model Cities Agencies, decision costs would likely be higher in Model Cities where there is more citizens' participation than in traditional city planning. On the other hand, in traditional city planning political externality costs are likely to far exceed those of the participatory planning of Model Cities.

III. Urban Goals

Planning in cities without well-recognized goals is not effective. Cities must have goals in order to bring their designs to fruition and to evaluate the results. A city without stated goals is a city without a predictable future; the invisible hand and the Protestant ethic are not sufficient. Let us explore some community goals and relate them to urban planning.

Taylor illustrates the goals around which programs are budgeted in a particular government. These goals represent a philosophy of policy to some degree and are a first-level consideration of the progression of goals to programs. In addition to goals of government management the following obtain:

1. Improve the standard of living for all people*
   a) Remove social and economic barriers
   b) Develop economic environment
2. Improve health of all people*
   a) Physical
   b) Mental
   c) Environmental

* Most important human development areas.

[29] Harvey Leibenstein, "Long-Run Welfare Criteria," in *The Public Economy of Urban Communities*, ed. Julius Margolis (Washington, D.C.: Resources for the Future, 1965; distr. by Johns Hopkins Press, Baltimore), pp. 43–46.

3. Provide formal education*
   a) Pre-school
   b) Elementary and secondary
   c) Higher education
   d) Continuing education
4. Provide adequate transportation
   a) Water
   b) Air
   c) Urban mass transit
   d) Motor vehicle transport
5. Provide satisfactory physical environment
   a) Water supply
   b) Land development
   c) Waste disposal
   d) Conservation and beautification
   e) Drainage and flood control
6. Provide cultural and recreational opportunity*
   a) Build and operate facilities
   b) Conduct recreational and cultural programs
7. Safeguard the individual, his rights and his property
   a) Crime prevention and control
   b) Traffic law enforcement
   c) Civil dispute adjudication
   d) Fire prevention and control
   e) Disaster prevention and control
   f) Standards of service control[30]

* Most important human development areas.

While the above suggestions for goals are relevant, they do not represent plans of attack, they do not imply specific programs, nor do they contain much which will guide a process of program development and its evaluation. How do we make this translation?

While the items under numbers 1 through 7 are really broad, general goals, the items under a, b, etc., do begin to imply a notion of programs. Thus, the process of arriving at program goals does occur even within this simple listing. For example, while "improving the standard of living" is too general to use as an implied program, topic a, "remove social and economic barriers," moves away from generalization toward areas of potential programs. Development stems from generalized statements to the more specific and thence to potential programs.

One may ask at this point where economics fits into this goal building. It does, but in a rather narrow context. Economics is largely a discipline of capi-

[30] Graeme M. Taylor, "Designing the Program Structure," in *Program Budgeting and Benefit-Cost Analysis: Cases, Text, and Readings,* comp. Harley H. Hinrichs and Graeme M. Taylor (Pacific Palisades, Cal.: Goodyear Publishing Co., 1969), pp. 38–39. Copyright © 1969, Goodyear Publishing Co. Reprinted by permission.

talistic and individualistic activities. Even microeconomic theory avoids the issue of groups by assuming the motivations of individuals are additive. Urban economics has no central philosophical position; it has no all-encompassing notion of the welfare of citizens. It depends upon materialism and acquisitiveness as the manner of behavior of people and it tends to deal in strict material modes. It does not provide a substitute for philosophy. As discussed in the next chapter, economics does not contain a useful social welfare concept. The point is simply that while economics can have a distinguished role in individual, social, and public urban activities, the discipline cannot truly be called political economy; that is, we cannot assert that through economic reasoning an urban philosophy can come to the fore suggesting a new direction for urban development.

If economics is merely a single perspective of the urban scene, how does it relate? Principally in this fashion: After choices for goals and priorities have been established for public expenditures, then economics can be of considerable aid. The efficient allocation of resources among various uses is the center of economics, and this the discipline can do well. However, this is only after the wishes of citizens have been made known and are understood by political leadership. Once political entities begin to introduce specific programs to attack urban problems (work toward achieving goals), then the rigors of economics can have much to say about the logic and form of the expenditure and its efficiency.

The Relevant Context of Goals: Good Information

Starting from broad, general goals is an accepted rational approach to urban planning; however, it fails to include the necessary participation of all affected residents. Citizens' views of goals and programs may not coincide with the planner's views. Since participation of both elements is required, how is the input of the citizenry to be developed?

First, we must regularly ascertain the beliefs and feelings of the population about current and proposed issues that will directly affect them. This can be accomplished in participatory neighborhood meetings where problems are elucidated and priorities of problems (urgencies) are indicated. A regular opinion survey and publication of pro's and con's on public issues can aid in this participation. Some basic economic and demographic data for given neighborhoods is essential in order to put some substance into this mechanical listing and to determine the urgency of problems.

Secondly, from a questionnaire and/or from published sources a current and regular picture should be drawn of conditions in the city — for example, numbers of persons who live on what incomes and in what classes. The accumulation of sufficient data is necessary to evaluate the basic statistical condition of persons in the area as they relate to the felt needs, the planning philosophy (Taylor), and the priorities as cited by the residents.

The massive amounts of information now available and necessary to make improved decisions in cities call for an urban institute, a new information system. Such an institute would serve a number of functions:

1. A twenty-four hour information service
2. A permanent exhibition center
3. A seminar center
4. A publications center
5. A city archive[31]

The complexity of interrelationships is immediately apparent when dealing with urban problems in a social or an individual context. This complexity and interdependence of variables makes any evaluation process difficult. We cannot arbitrarily move into problem solving without an understanding of how one fact interacts with another. It must be recognized that the kinds and forms of data used will affect the analysis of ultimate impacts. (See Chapter 1 Appendix.)

If we have an initial picture indicating the disadvantages in all the areas of income, health, education, etc., in the community, what is to be done with this initial composite picture? The next step is to decide which goal or goals the public seeks to strive for. Is it truly ideal? Is the city seeking the best of all possible worlds? Perhaps so, but it would be banal to suggest that the goal is to provide all residents in the city with the standard of life maintained by Ari and Jackie. What represents a "good life" as an approximation for some unattainable ideal? What is a first substitute?

One substitute for the ideal might be the allocation of resources to achieve the quality of life in the city that will bring residents up to the "statistical" national urban average. This would be a first step and likely a desirable one. First the disparity which exists between area residents (in all the major goal categories) and the "average urban American," must be determined from figures for the national average of metropolitan areas and from data collected in the city. Thus if mean income in one neighborhood is $4,000 and mean income nationally for families is $9,000 in metropolitan areas, then the degree of disparity is .44 or 44%. Such coefficients of disparity could be generated for each category of concern. For descriptive purposes, a table would show disparity coefficients for each of the questions of substance in the questionnaire. This table might reflect what could be called the implied "First Level Goals" in a sequence of goals. Explicitly, the "average" in the United States cities is a goal. While this is not ideal, it is a stage in a sequence of achievement of goals.

By sequence it is meant that there is a concern for doing more than just passing on the national metropolitan average as a device for the "ideal." At the same time we move toward the average in medical care, income, education, etc., it is

[31] Arnold Rockman, "The City as an Information-Processing Machine," *Habitat* 10 (Jan./Feb. 1967) : 47.

necessary to be aware that middle-class life in the city has its grubby aspects and is generally unfit as an ideal. It is at this recognition level that "new," "experimental," and unusual devices must be sought to imagine an ideal. In short, the ideal is not a set of programs which are being undertaken with great success in "Burbank"; to some degree the ideal is a set of programs which have not yet been attempted. The only hope is that some have been "imagined" by artists, planners, philosophers, and others whose task it is to generate the ideal for us and that citizens express interest in such directions of change.

The ideal is not an absolute; it is not a final point of perfection; it is essentially this and nothing more: a measured improvement over the way in which the city now does things. That is to say, the ideal is a direction implying an ongoing process. It is essentially experimental, and, as Don Juan in Shaw's *Man and Superman* says, "As long as I can imagine something better, I cannot be satisfied with what is." We must think in terms of improvement as a kind of operational ideal, a working toward rather than a stationary state. The challenge then becomes one of ascertaining with some validity whether or not any improvement is measurable. The appendix at the end of this chapter suggests a means of implementing the development of a set of general urban goals and the data currently available which relates to those goals.

As a note of caution, it should be recognized that when the urban analyst and the policy maker begin to think about citizens, they think in terms of averages or average people. Since the data available to cities is aggregated, it is still necessary to analyze individual cases concerning human welfare in the city. While federal data collections are aggregates, there is no reason why a recurring sample of individuals cannot be taken at the local level in which life in the community is seen through individual statements of concern, interest, and satisfaction. If well done, the detailed statements through regular opinion polls go far toward a description of the "quality" of urban life to be compared with the average statements of federal and much local data.

A National Urban Policy

While local planners may aid the community in formulating goals, and, through improved communication with citizens, develop more relevant programs for cities, the success of such ventures depends in large part on the existence and form of national urban policy. Local resources and institutions cannot be expected to be completely sufficient for the achievement of community goals. As well, local goals can be offset or made ineffective by various national policies.

There are a number of arguments in favor of a comprehensive national urban policy. First, federal programs already have a significant effect upon the location of the population, the economic growth of cities, and the character of urban development. Federal programs such as the Federal Housing Administration (FHA), programs of the Economic Development Administration, Model Cities,

Office of Economic Opportunity (OEO), and others have significant impact upon urban development. Second, federal programs are single purposed, and a coordination is necessary to make any one of them effective. Their relative success is based on their interdependency — in some cases individual programs may work at cross-purposes with each other. A third argument suggests that the consequences of uncontrolled growth, many of which are undesirable, demand some controlled policy applications.[32]

A fourth argument for a national urban policy is that it could be used to eliminate some of the trends of growth which aggravate discrimination and thus could create favorable opportunities for minorities. Central-city decay creates particular problems for inner-city minorities, and some of these problems are the result of the form of economic growth in cities. A fifth view is that current growth trends in states mean some will become increasingly weak economically in comparison to others, resulting in a general weakening of the ability of states to respond to their own problems.[33]

A sixth argument for a national urban policy is that there must be adequate planning to insure that once goals are established resources can be generated to affect the goals. A final and very persuasive argument lies in the need for immediate solutions to many current problems of urban residents.[34] Some problems are of such serious urgency that immediate steps should be taken to eliminate them.

On the obverse side, arguments can be made against a coordinated national urban policy. Even if a good case can be made for the problems of cities, for example, lack of information or suitable techniques mean urban policy would be ineffective. A second argument is that since urbanization is inexorable, the expenditure of funds to stem the form and content of urbanization is merely squandering the funds. A third argument would suggest that a good policy would only be as good as its implementation, and the record of past urban programs implementation is poor. Many failures have dotted previous efforts. Another argument against a national urban policy is that a competent policy might require a selective process with some cities being left to die; such policy, it is argued, would be politically infeasible. A rational policy might come to the conclusion that, for one or more reasons, it is undesirable to continue to support a city, say for example, Newark, New Jersey, and the citizens of Newark might be opposed to such an idea.[35]

A fifth idea which argues against a national policy is that essential market forces of economics do sufficiently well to distribute people geographically and

[32] U.S. Advisory Commission on Intergovernmental Relations, *Urban and Rural America: Policies for Future Growth: A Commission Report*, publication A-32 (Washington, D.C.: Government Printing Office, 1968), pp. 125–26.

[33] U.S. Advisory Commission, *Urban and Rural America*, pp. 125–26.

[34] U.S. Advisory Commission, *Urban and Rural America*, pp. 125–26.

[35] U.S. Advisory Commission, *Urban and Rural America*, pp. 127 and 128.

to eliminate poverty, and policy would merely interfere with the market.   Some economic institutions should die if they are significantly inefficient, and policy aimed at saving such enterprises would be undesirable.   Sixth, a national urban policy can be used as a pretext to develop massive spending programs for essentially useless purposes.   Arguments against a national urban policy could be considered numerous.[36]

A national urban policy may be desirable, but the extent to which effective national urban policy can be generated is still unsettled; the question of competence is relevant and logrolling is highly likely.   Yet, cooperation is necessary, and effective planning and implementation of policy can aid the desired growth processes and at least mitigate some of the undesirable growth consequences for urban areas.   A national urban policy is thus deemed necessary.

Summary: Urban Planning

Cities have engaged in limited planning for many years.   Planning as a process consists of framing objectives, determining the most efficient means of gaining the objectives under conditions of scarce resources, and managing these means to gain the desired goals.

Urban planning has had three particular viewpoints: planning the initial city where no city existed previously, superimposing on or making radical changes in an existing city, and planning from the emergent view in which a flexible master plan is drawn and serves as a long-run guide to the growth of the city.

Urban planning has been largely concerned with providing and developing transportation systems (streets and rails), industrial locations and land use, business and commercial land, residential land, and recreational land.   In addition, development of town centers, public facilities, and green belts or buffers have attracted the attention of city planners.

Zoning, building codes, land use, space controls, pollution controls, public health ordinances, tax policies, and police power have been the tools of the city planner in his attempt to impose a sense of order on the areal, spatial, and physical elements of a city.   City planning has not traditionally dealt directly with most local human or individual concerns.

Model Cities programs are an expansion of city planning into the human or social problems of a city.   Programs are devised that emphasize social and then physical planning through the planning unit of one, the individual city resident.

When a city initiates social program planning, certain problems arise.   Any attempt to comprehend human problems is an oversimplification.   It is not possible to account for all the varieties of man, and, in intervening in his life, society runs the risk of causing a loss of skills and knowledge.

Another concern lies in dealing with mere needs instead of needs and aspira-

[36] U.S. Advisory Commission, *Urban and Rural America*, pp. 127 and 128.

tions. Urban policy may accentuate the common or similar "needs" of men and discount individual aspirations and potentials.

Planning human activity may become mere control. Controlling people through planning cannot be viewed as necessarily positive. Manipulation of human lives is a high-risk venture, and a consistent, articulated philosophical position is required to maintain a human scale of planning.

Effective social planning requires considerable free choice by the individuals directly affected. If free choice is to be real, the individual must not be prohibited or prevented from exercising choices. As well, rights essential to freedom must be guaranteed for all. The only sound test of a political doctrine or a social policy is its practical effect upon the lives of human beings affected by the doctrine or policy. To not pursue policy can be as dangerous as manipulations through policy, because to fail to intervene may be to support a set of undesirable customs or practices.

Democratic planning is costly. Costs of decision making can be analyzed by the inclusion of political externality costs. An analysis of social interaction costs, which includes decision-making costs and externalities, reveals that as people are excluded from decision making, decision costs decline but political externality costs increase. If decision costs are expanded by the inclusion of more people participating, political externality costs will decline. As one might expect, decision costs are higher in Model Cities programs than in other local public decisions. Conversely, political externality costs are apt to be lower in Model Cities decisions than decisions arrived at by other local public agencies.

Cities, it was argued, must have stated goals toward which they move. Standard of living, health, education, transportation, physical environment, cultural and recreational opportunities, and protection through fire department and police activities are all areas of responsibility toward which local government should direct its attentions.

Planning toward goals requires an intimate knowledge of the citizens of the community. Complex data systems are required to develop indicators for the human condition in a city. Chapter 1 Appendix includes some necessary indicators.

Arguments for and against national urban planning policy were presented. Arguments centered on the inability of government to generate effective policy as opposed to arguments favoring such policy on the basis of urgency of urban problems.

Chapter I Appendix

The following indices measures are drawn from *Criteria for Evaluation in Planning State and Local Programs*, a study done by Harry P. Hatry of the George Washington University State-Local Finances Project and presented to the Subcommittee on Intergovernmental Relations to the Committee on Government Operations of the United States Senate, published by the United States Government Printing Office in July of 1967 as a Committee Print.

Included in the criteria are data suggestions for evaluating the progress of communities toward their stated goals. In each case the general objective is stated and suggestions are provided for the data to serve as a continuous means of evaluation. Progress toward goals as a result of specific programs may be noted by a systematic collection of information.

I. Personal Safety

Objective: To reduce the amount and effects of external harm to individuals and in general to maintain an atmosphere of personal security from external events.

A. Law Enforcement

Objective: To reduce the amount and effects of crime and in general to maintain an atmosphere of personal security from criminal behavior. (To some persons the punishment of criminals may be an important objective in itself as well as a means to deter further crimes.)

1. Annual number of offenses for each major class of crime (or reduction from the base in the number of crimes).

2. Crime rates, for example, the number per 1,000 inhabitants per year, for each major class of crime.

3. Crime rate index that includes all offenses of a particular type (e.g., "crimes of violence" or "crimes against property"), perhaps weighted as to seriousness of each class of offense.

4. Number and percent of populace committing "criminal" acts during the year. (This is a less common way to express the magnitude of the crime problem; it is criminal oriented rather than "crime oriented.")

5. Annual value of property lost (adjusted for price-level changes). This value might also be expressed as a percent of the total property value in the community.

6. An index of overall community "feeling of security" from crime, perhaps based on public opinion polls and/or opinions of experts.

7. Percent of reported crimes cleared by arrest and "assignment of guilt" by a court.

8. Average time between occurrence of a crime and the apprehension of the criminal.[a]

9. Number of apparently justified complaints of police excesses by private citizens, perhaps as adjudged by the police review board.

10. Number of persons subsequently found to be innocent who were punished and/or simply arrested.

Notes

a) Criteria 1 through 6 are criteria for the evaluation of crime-prevention programs. Criteria 7 and 8 are aimed at evaluating crime control after crimes have occurred (i.e., when crime prevention has failed). Criteria 9 and 10, and to some extent 6, aim at the avoidance of law-enforcement practices that themselves have an adverse effect upon personal safety.

[a] A major purpose of criterion 8, as used in this list, is to reflect the psychological reduction in anxiety due to the length of this time period. Note that it is not the purpose of this or any of these criteria to evaluate the efficiency of the police organization.

Criterion 6, and to some extent 8, aim at indicating the presence of a fearful, insecure atmosphere in the locality.

b) Some argue that the primary function of criminal apprehension and punishment is to prevent future crimes and, therefore, that criteria 7 and 8 would not be sufficiently "end oriented," but rather "means" oriented and would not be included in the list.

c) For many analyses it would probably be appropriate to distinguish crime activity by the type of criminal, including such characteristics as age, sex, family income, etc. (Juvenile delinquency is an obvious subcategory.)

B. Fire Prevention and Firefighting

Objective: To reduce the number of fires and loss due to fires.

1. Annual number of fires of various magnitudes (to be defined).

2. Fire rates, for example, number per 10,000 inhabitants per year.

3. Annual dollar value of property loss due to fire (adjusted for price-level changes).

4. Annual dollar value of property lost due to fire per $1 million of total property value in the locality.

5. Annual number of persons killed or injured to various degrees of seriousness due to fires.

6. Reduction in number of fires, in injuries, in lives lost, and in dollars of property loss from the base. (These are primarily different forms of criteria 1, 3, and 5 and can be substituted for them.) This reduction might in part be obtained by, for example, drawing inferences from the number of fire code violations (by type) found.[b]

7. Average time required to put out fires from the time they were first observed, for various classes of fires.

Notes

a) Criteria 1 through 6 are intended for evaluation of fire prevention programs. Criteria 7 and to some extent 3, 4, and 5 can reflect the results of programs which aim at the control of fires after they have started. Criterion 7 also is a proxy for the anxiety related to duration of fires.

b) It may be appropriate to distinguish among geographical areas within the jurisdiction.

II. Health Care

Objective: To provide for the physical and mental health of the citizenry, including reduction of the number, length, and severity of illnesses and disabilities.

1. Incidence of illness and prevalence (number and rates).[c] (Armed Forces rates of rejection for health reasons of persons from the jurisdiction could be used as a partial criterion.)

[b] From current data on the violations found, estimates could be prepared of the number of additional violations that would be found and corrected if more fire-code inspectors were added. However, the more important (that is, the higher level) criterion is not the number of violations found and corrected but the reduction in the number of fires and in the loss of lives and property. To get to this higher level criterion, estimates would have to be made of the consequences of not finding and correcting such violations. This footnote is included to indicate the kinds of inferences that are likely to be needed in program analyses. Similar situations can be identified for many of the other criteria presented in this list.

[c] Here and in the following material the term "illness" is also intended to cover disability and impairments.

2. Annual mortality rates by major cause and for total population.[d]

3. Life expectancy by age groups.

4. Average number of days of restricted activity, bed confinement, and medically attended days per person per year. (Such terms as "restricted activity" need to be clearly and thoroughly defined. Also, probably more than one level of severity of illness should be identified.)

5. Average number of workdays per person lost due to illness per year.

6. Total and per capita number of school days lost owing to illness per year.

7. Number of illnesses prevented, deaths averted, and restricted-activity days averted per year as compared with the base. This is primarily a different form of such criteria as 1 through 6.

8. Average number of days of restricted activity, of bed confinement, and of medically attended days per illness per year.

9. Number and percent of patients "cured" (of specific types of illnesses and various degrees of cure).

10. Some measure of the average degree of pain and suffering per illness. (Though there seems to be no such measure currently in use, some rough index of pain and suffering could probably be developed.)

11. Some measure, perhaps from a sampling of experts and of patients, as to the average amount of unpleasantness (including consideration of the environment in the care area) associated with the care and cure of illnesses.

12. Number of percent of persons with after effects, of different degrees, after "cure."

13. Number of percent of persons needing but unable to afford "appropriate health care" — both before receiving public assistance and after including any public assistance received.

14. Number of percent of persons needing but unable to receive "appropriate health care" — because of insufficient facilities or services.

15. Some measure of the overall "vigor," the positive health of the populace, rather than simply the absence of illness — such as "the average per capita energy capacity." Meaningful measures are needed.

Notes

a) A number of subobjectives can be identified for this major program area. Those subobjectives and the criteria that attempt to measure each are as follows:

(1) Prevention of illness — criteria 1 through 7.

(2) "Cure" of patient when illness occurs including reduction of its duration — criteria 1 through 7.

(3) Reduction of unpleasantness, suffering, anxiety, etc., associated with illness — criteria 10 and 11.

(4) Reduction of aftereffects — criterion 12.

(5) Making necessary health care available to the "needy" — criteria 13 and 14.

Note, however, that during consideration of the overall problem of health, these subobjectives will often compete with each other. For example, with limited funds, they might

[d] Suicide rates should be included; these are likely to provide some indication of the overall mental health of the community. Note that reducing mortality from certain causes would presumably increase mortality from other causes. Life expectancy, criterion 3, is thus a more important overall criterion.

be applied to programs aimed primarily at preventing an illness or at reducing its severity (or at some mix of these programs). Also note that criteria 1 through 7 are affected by programs that are directed at curing illnesses as well as those directed at preventing them.

b) The criteria can be defined to distinguish among specific types of illnesses as well as to consider the aggregate effect on individuals of all possible illnesses. For certain problems the incidence of a specific disease may be of concern, whereas for other problems the incidence of illness per person per year, regardless of specific disease, might be the appropriate criterion. One such breakdown which is very likely to be desirable distinguishes mental health from physical health, though even here there will be interactions.

c) Note that such common measures as "hospital-bed capacity" or "utilization rates of available medical facilities" are fundamental indicators of the effectiveness of health programs.

d) As with most of the major program areas, program analyses will need to consider the contributions of other sectors, including private institutions and activities undertaken by other jurisdictions.

e) The role of governmental jurisdictions may emphasize health services for certain specific target groups such as the needy and the very young. Therefore, it will frequently be appropriate to distinguish target groups by such characteristics as family income, race, family size, and age group.

f) To further focus on the positive side of health, in addition to the use of criterion 15, such criteria as 4 might be replaced by such criteria as "average number of healthy days (appropriately defined) per person per year."

III. Intellectual Development

Objective: To provide satisfactory opportunities for intellectual development to the citizenry. See also Notes (b) and (c) below.

1. Annual number and percent of persons satisfactorily completing various numbers of years of schooling.

2. Annual number and percent of dropouts at various educational levels.

3. Annual number and percent of each age group enrolled in educational institutions.

4. "Intellectual development attainment" measures, such as performance on various standardized achievement tests at different ages and educational levels.[e] Major educational areas; for example, reading skills, reasoning skills, and general knowledge, might be measured.

5. Performance on the achievement tests indicated in criterion 4 as related to intelligence tests (to indicate attainment relative to capacity).

6. Annual number and percent of students continuing their education at post-high school educational institutions.

7. Participation in selected cultural and civic activities (and perhaps the number of persons who read newspapers, or at least certain parts of them).

Notes

a) Criteria 1, 2, and 3 emphasize quantity of formal education received. Criteria 4, 5, 6, and 7 attempt to indicate the quality of education received. Since formal education is not the only means to intellectual development, criteria such as 4, 5, and 7, when various age groups are considered, should be applied to persons regardless of whether they are in school

[e] Armed Forces rejection rates — for intelligence reasoning — of persons from the jurisdiction could be used to provide a partial measure.

or not, or how much formal education they have had. Criterion 6 also provides some information as to the success of education to stimulate intellectual curiosity. None of the criteria provides much help in measuring the development of individual creativity, if it can indeed be developed.

b) Education not only affects intellectual development but also social development. The above criteria (with the minor exception of 7) fail to measure such things as "social adjustment," "responsible citizenship," and increased "personal pleasure." Such criteria as crime rates, juvenile delinquency rates, including school vandalism, etc., such as are used for major program area I, "personal safety," might be used to draw inferences to certain aspects of social adjustment.

c) "Education" clearly may be a means to other ends (for example, to lower crime rates) as well as an end in itself. In fact some persons may consider education to be primarily a means to increase future dollar earnings and therefore would consider the above criteria solely as proxy measures for getting at earnings. If so, education programs would better be considered under major program area V. Economic Satisfaction and Satisfactory Work Opportunity for the Individual. The perspective here is that education and, more broadly, intellectual development, have more than economic value to individuals and society, and is, therefore, an important end in itself. The objectives: to increase earnings, to increase job opportunities and job satisfaction, and to supply needed scarce skills are, in the categorization used in this paper, considered under major program area V. Education programs are some of the means to these ends and in this role would need to be considered in performing such program analyses.

d) To estimate quality of formal education, frequently such "proxy" indicators are used as "annual expenditures per student," "professional-student ratios," "number of professionals with advanced degrees," "teacher salary levels," etc. These are less direct, lower-level criteria than those given above, but nevertheless may be of some use if qualified sufficiently.

e) The role of government in intellectual development varies considerably among jurisdictions.

f) It will frequently be appropriate to distinguish target groups by such characteristics as: race, family income level, family size, and sex.

IV. Satisfactory Home and Community Environment[f]

Objective: To provide opportunity for satisfactory living conditions.

A. Satisfactory Homes

Objective: To provide opportunities for satisfactory homes for the citizenry, including provision of a choice of decent, safe, and sanitary dwellings in pleasant surroundings at prices they can afford.

1. Number and percent of "substandard" dwelling units. More information would be provided by identifying more levels than just two. In any case, "substandard" should be fully defined; the definition should include consideration of crowding, physical deterioration, unsatisfactory sanitation, etc.

2. Number and percent of substandard units eliminated or prevented from becoming substandard. (This is essentially another form of 1.)

---

[f] Two subcategories have been singled out for illustration: "satisfactory homes" and "satisfactory water supply." Others such as "maintenance of satisfactory air environment," "noise abatement," and "sanitation," can also be identified as subcategories and require selection of appropriate criteria that also help to evaluate home and living conditions.

3. Acres of blighted areas eliminated and other areas prevented from becoming blighted areas.

4. Total number and percent of persons and families living in substandard dwelling units.

5. Number and percent of persons and families upgraded from one level of housing (for example, "substandard") to a higher level (for example, "standard") or prevented from degrading to a lower level. This is essentially another form of 4.

6. Measure of neighborhood physical attractiveness. Perhaps (a) as indicated by the number of negative conditions estimated by neighborhood inspectors, including adverse physical appearance, excessive noise, lack of cleanliness, offensive odors, excessive traffic, etc.; or (b) an index based upon a public-opinion poll of persons passing through the neighborhood and/or experts.

7. Measure of neighborhood psychological attractiveness. Perhaps an index based upon a public-opinion survey of persons living in the neighborhood and/or experts.

8. Average and distribution of property values adjusted for price level changes. Expected changes, from year to year, in property values might also be used as a criterion.

9. Number of fires, other accidents, deaths, and injuries resulting from housing deficiencies.

Notes

a) Important secondary effects (such as changes in crime and juvenile delinquency rates, in health conditions, in fire problems, and in job opportunities) are likely to result from changes in housing conditions and urban redevelopment. Criteria relating to these effects are included under the other major program areas.

b) It will frequently be appropriate to distinguish target groups by such characteristics as family income, race, family size, and location.

c) Criteria 1 through 5 aim at provision of housing, with 4 and 5 probably the most important, since they directly evaluate effects on people rather than things. Criteria 3 and 6 and probably 7 evaluate the physical attractiveness of the neighborhood. Criteria 7 and 8 are attempts at evaluating the overall quality of the housing and living conditions. Criterion 8 is included here rather than under major program area V as a measure of the overall quality of the neighborhood; that is, property values are used as a proxy for the many features contributing to the attractiveness of the property. Criterion 9 measures the safeness of housing.

B. Maintenance of a Satisfactory Water Supply

Objective: To provide sufficient water in adequate quality where and when needed.

1. Water-supply capability relative to average and to peak demand.

2. Number of days per year during which water shortages of various degrees occur. (Downtime for repairs should be included.)

3. Measure of "quality of water" (e.g. biological oxygen demand and percent of solid waste removed) supplied to homes or businesses. (If waste water is not recycled, the quality of the effluent fed back into streambeds, etc., could be used as a criterion.)

4. Measures of taste, appearance, and odor of water — perhaps based upon such factors as amount of chlorination or upon opinion samplings of water users.

5. Measures of hardness and temperature of water.

6. Annual number of illnesses and other incidents due to low quality water.

7. Annual number of complaints of water odors due to low quality water.

Notes

a) Criteria 1 and 2 are measures of the sufficiency of the quantity of water supplied. Criteria 3 and through 7 are measures of the quality.

b) Each of the quantity measures is also dependent upon the minimum quality level established. That is, more water can generally be supplied if the quality requirements are reduced. Program analysis will need to consider such tradeoffs.

c) The seasonal and diurnal effects of water supply and demand has to be considered in the analysis.

d) It may be appropriate to distinguish individual user needs such as water for home consumption, for industrial use, for recreational needs, for irrigation, etc., each of which will have its own quantity and quality characteristics.

V. Economic Satisfaction and Satisfactory Work Opportunity for the Individual

Objective: To permit each family and each person to meet basic economic-physical needs, while maintaining dignity and self-respect. To permit any employable person desiring employment to obtain satisfactory employment without loss of dignity and self-respect.

1. Annual number and percent of persons of families whose incomes before receiving public assistance placed them in the "poverty" class. More evaluation information would be provided by identifying more levels than just "poverty" and "not poverty." In any case, "poverty" should be fully defined, the definition should probably take into consideration such factors as family size, ages of persons in the family, location, cost of living, etc. (Note that programs which reduce the cost of living are alternatives to programs which increase income.)

2. Average and distribution of per capita or per family income. (This criterion essentially supplements 1.)

3. Annual number and percent of persons or families whose incomes, considering any public assistance received, still place them in the "poverty" class.

4. Annual number and percent of persons or families whose economic condition is improved through public assistance (preferably further grouped by the amount of total public assistance per person or per family).

5. Some measure of the "standard of living" levels of all residents.

6. Number and percent of persons or families formerly in the "poverty" group that achieve self-sufficiency during the year.

7. Number and percent of persons in job market who are unemployed or underemployed (in terms of number of hours worked).

8. Number of persons previously "unemployed," or who would become unemployed, who are placed in jobs during the year. (This is essentially another form of criterion 6.)

9. Index of individual job satisfaction, perhaps based upon a sampling of the employed and/or upon expert opinion. Another measure would be the number of persons whose jobs did not appear to match the workers "capacities." Both current capacity as well as "potential" probably should be considered.

Notes

a) This major program area can be considered to include two major subcategories: "welfare" and "employment" programs. These subcategories are both complementary to and competitive with each other in meeting the objective to achieve overall "economic satisfaction." However, the human need for worthwhile activity is probably not met by welfare but can be by employment. In addition other types of programs, e.g., general education, can contribute to the objectives. (Vocational-oriented education and training are here considered as being one type of "employment" program.)

b) Criteria 1 through 5 emphasize the evaluation of economic satisfaction (regardless of employment condition) whereas 6 through 9 are work opportunity oriented.

c) Criterion 9 is needed to measure the extent to which individuals are matched to satisfying, rather than just any, jobs.

d) It will frequently be appropriate to distinguish target groups by such characteristics as family size, race, and age.

VI. Satisfactory Leisure-Time Opportunities

Objective: To provide year-around, leisure-time opportunities for citizenry which are accessible, permit variety, are safe, physically attractive, avoid uncomfortable crowdedness, and are in general enjoyable.

1. Number of acres of recreation and of various types per 1,000 population (perhaps as compared to standards that may be available). Or for indoor activities, some such measure as the number of square feet, or number of seats, per 1,000 population for each type of activity.

2. Number of percent of "potential users" within, say one-half mile and/or a 10 minute walk of neighborhood recreational area (note that for some facilities such as large state parks, people who live farther away may account for more use of the facilities than persons living close by).

3. Number of man-days usage per year for each public leisure-time activity (perhaps related to some usage standards).

4. Ratio of attendance to capacity, during specified critical periods for certain activities (both as a measure of attractiveness and "crowdedness" of the facilities).

5. Number of different leisure-time activities available.

6. Average waiting times, during specified key periods, for use of certain public facilities (such as golf, tennis, and boating) or average requests for attendance turned away such as at concerts, theater shows, etc.

7. Number of accidents in recreational areas related to usage, e.g., per 1,000 man-days usage per year.

8. Number of persons unable or unwilling to take advantage of available leisure-time opportunities who would if they could (categorized by the reason for their disuse of available opportunities).

9. Number of persons who would use currently unavailable leisure-time opportunities if made available.

10. Some measure of overall pleasurableness and sufficiency of leisure-time opportunities, perhaps based upon a public opinion poll sample.

Notes

a) For many analyses, such criteria as 1, 2, and 5 will need to consider private leisure-time facilities as well as public facilities.

b) Criteria 1 through 6 and 9 are indicators of whether leisure-time opportunities are provided in sufficient quantity. Criteria 3, 4, and 8 are indicators (unfortunately, indirect ones) of the quality of the opportunities. Criterion 5 aims at measuring the amount of variety available. Criterion 7 measures the safeness of the activities. Criteria 3, 8, and 9 are also indicators of the "pleasurableness" of the opportunities (such things as overcrowdedness are not included in the concept of the term "quality" as used above and therefore "pleasurableness" is also used). Criterion 10 is an overall measure that probably encompasses all of the attributes. Note that except for criterion 10 the criteria do not attempt to measure what is achieved from the leisure-time activities; the degree of pleasure that is derived from each type and quality of activity is not addressed in 1 through 9.

c) Criteria 8, 9, and 10 will be particularly difficult to measure. Well constructed surveys and polls will probably be needed to provide meaningful information.

d) Leisure-time opportunities in addition to being considered ends are also means to meet other major program area problems such as physical and mental health (major program area II) and crime and delinquency (major program area I). Effects on the criteria in these other program areas, therefore, have to be considered when evaluating leisure-time program alternatives.

e) It may be appropriate to distinguish target groups by such characteristics as age and family income level. (For example, recreational opportunities for the aged, for the poor, and for youth are likely to be of particular concern).

VII. Transportation-Communication-Location (See Notes (a), below, for clarification)

Objective: To transport needed amounts and types of "traffic" quickly, safely, and pleasurably.

1. Average time for performing specific tasks. The criterion "average trip time between selected locations" would be an appropriate form of this criteria if only physical transportation systems are being evaluated.

2. Average delay times at selected locations during selected parts of the day, week, and year.

3. Number of passenger-miles transported per day and the passenger mile capacity of the system (probably categorized by the different types of transportation systems).

4. Number of transportation accidents, injuries, and deaths per year.

5. Transportation accident, injury, and death rates, e.g., per so many passenger-miles or per trip.

6. Some measure, or measures, of the overall pleasantness of the travel or of such individual characteristics as physical attractiveness, noise, crowdedness, convenience, and comfort, perhaps indexes based upon a public opinion poll of travelers or opinions of "experts." (A proxy measure such as the average number of trees per mile of road, or the percentage of roadway that is landscaped might be helpful but could be quite misleading if not carefully qualified.)

Notes

a) This major program area is intended to include all types of systems including communications and locational programs as well as automobile, rail, water, mass transit, and pedestrian physical movement. The former affect the amount of physical transportation required. The term "traffic" is meant to convey the concept of the transmission of "messages" as well as physical objects and people. Physical transportation systems may be specific means to transmit messages of certain types but are not the only solution. For example, the function of shopping might be supported by a lengthy transportation system, by originally locating the shops near the users, or by audio-visual telephone selection of goods with mass delivery provided by the shops. Thus, programs to avoid the need for physical movement of people or goods may be effective in reducing the overall problem.

b) This major program area is not really an end in itself. Rather it is a means to satisfy other human needs, such as employment (commuter service), economic progress, accessibility to recreational areas, etc. However, because of its importance in most communities and the need to consider these "transport" systems in an integrated manner, identification as a separate major program area, with its own criteria, seems reasonable. In the evaluation of transport alternatives, however, these basic purposes of transport must be considered. For the same reason, such potential negative effects as air pollution and noise generation must also be considered.

c) Criteria 1, 2, and 3 attempt to measure the adequacy of the transportation system to move needed traffic and to move it quickly enough. Criteria 4 and 5 measure the safety of system. Criterion 6 attempts to indicate the pleasurableness content in the system.

d) It may be appropriate to distinguish user target groups by such characteristics as geographical location, income level, whether the users are commuters, shoppers, leisure-time activity seekers, commercial users, etc.; and whether they are acting as pedestrians, drivers, or in other roles.

Selected Bibliography

Planning

AGENA, KATHLEEN. "Tahoe." *ASPO* (American Society of Planning Officials) *Newsletter, Planning* 38 (1972): 3–16.

ALTSHULER, ALAN A. *Community Control: The Black Demand for Participation in Large American Cities.* Pegasus Series on Decentralization and the Urban Crisis, vol. 1. New York: Western Publishing Company, Pegasus Books, 1970.

BAUMOL, WILLIAM J. "Urban Services: Interactions of Public and Private Decisions." In *Public Expenditure Decisions in the Urban Community,* ed. Howard G. Schaller, pp. 1–18. Washington, D.C.: Resources for the Future, 1963; distr. by Johns Hopkins Press, Baltimore.

BISH, ROBERT L. *The Public Economy of Metropolitan Areas.* Chicago: Markham Publishing Co., 1971.

BLUMENFELD, HANS. "The Modern Metropolis." *Scientific American,* Sept. 1965, pp. 64–74.

BOLAN, RICHARD S. "Emerging Views of Planning." *Journal of the American Institute of Planners* 33 (1967): 233–45.

BRANCH, MELVILLE C. *Planning: Aspects and Applications.* New York: John Wiley & Sons, 1966.

BRANDT, RICHARD B., ED. *Social Justice.* Englewood Cliffs, N.J.: Prentice-Hall, Spectrum Books, 1962.

BUCHANAN, JAMES M., AND TULLOCK, GORDON. "Public and Private Interaction Under Reciprocal Externality." In *The Public Economy of Urban Communities,* ed. Julius Margolis, pp. 52–73. Washington, D.C.: Resources for the Future, 1965; distr. by Johns Hopkins Press, Baltimore.

———. *The Calculus of Consent: Logical Foundations of Constitutional Democracy.* Ann Arbor: University of Michigan Press, 1962.

CHAMBERLAIN, NEIL W. *Private and Public Planning.* New York: McGraw-Hill, 1965.

CHAPIN, F. STUART, JR. *Urban Land Use Planning.* 2d ed. Urbana: University of Illinois Press, 1965.

DAKIN, JOHN. "An Evaluation of the 'Choice' Theory of Planning." *Journal of the American Institute of Planners* 29 (1963): 19–27.

DANFORTH, RICHARD S. "The Central City and the Forgotten American." *Journal of the American Institute of Planners* 36 (1970): 426–28.

DAVIDOFF, PAUL, AND REINER, THOMAS A. "A Choice Theory of Planning." *Journal of the American Institute of Planners* 28 (1962): 103–15.

———. "A Reply to Dakin." *Journal of the American Institute of Planners* 29 (1963): 27–28.

DOWNS, ANTHONY. "Alternative Forms of Future Urban Growth in the United States." *Journal of the American Institute of Planners* 36 (1970): 3–11.

DOXIADES, C. A. "Man's Movement and His City — Cities are Systems Created by Man's Need and Ability to Move." *Science*, Oct. 1968, pp. 326–34.

———, ET AL. "The Great Lakes Megalopolis." *Ekistics* 33 (1972): 462–69.

DUTT, ASHOK K. "A Comparative Study of Regional Planning in Britain and the Netherlands." *Ohio Journal of Science* 70 (1970): 321–35.

———. "Levels of Planning in the Netherlands, with Particular Reference to Regional Planning." *Annals of the Association of American Geographers* 58 (1968): 670–85.

DYCKMAN, JOHN W. "Social Planning, Social Planners, and Planned Societies." *Journal of the American Institute of Planners* 32 (1966): 66–76.

———. "Transportation in Cities." *Scientific American*, Sept. 1965, pp. 162–74.

FEISS, CARL. "Planning Absorbs Zoning." *Journal of the American Institute of Planners* 27 (1961): 121–26.

FINKLER, EARL L. "New Orleans is a City Looking Ahead Over Its Shoulder." *ASPO* (American Society of Planning Officials) *Newsletter* 37 (1971): 15–23.

FRIEDEN, BERNARD J. "The Changing Prospects for Social Planning," *Journal of the American Institute of Planners* 33 (1967): 311–23.

FRIEDMANN, JOHN, AND ALONSO, WILLIAM, EDS. *Regional Development and Planning: A Reader*. Cambridge, Mass.: M.I.T. Press, 1964.

HALLMAN, HOWARD W. *Neighborhood Control of Public Programs: Case Studies of Community Corporations and Neighborhood Boards*. Foreword by Royce Hanson. Praeger Special Studies in U.S. Economic and Social Development. New York: Praeger in cooperation with the Washington Center for Metropolitan Studies, 1971.

HANDLER, A. BENJAMIN. "What is Planning Theory?" *Journal of the American Institute of Planners* 23 (1957): 144–50.

HANSEN, NILES M. *French Regional Planning*. Bloomington: Indiana University Press, 1968.

HARRIS, BRITTON, ED. "Urban Development Models: New Tools for Planning." Special Issue of the *Journal of the American Institute of Planners* 31 (1965): 90–184.

HEILBRONER, ROBERT L., AND FORD, ARTHUR M., COMPS. *Is Economics Relevant? A Reader in Political Economics*. Pacific Palisades, Cal.: Goodyear Publishing Co., 1971.

HINRICHS, HARLEY H., AND TAYLOR, GRAEME M., COMPS. *Program Budgeting and Benefit-Cost Analysis: Cases, Text, and Readings*. Pacific Palisades, Cal.: Goodyear Publishing Co., 1969.

INTERNATIONAL CITY MANAGERS' ASSOCIATION. *Principles and Practice of Urban Planning*, ed. William I. Goodman and Eric C. Freund. Washington, D.C.: International City Managers' Association, 1968.

KAUFMAN, JEROME L. "Trends in Planning." *ASPO* (American Society of Planning Officials) *Newsletter* 35 (1969): 49–52.

LEIBENSTEIN, HARVEY. "Long-Run Welfare Criteria." In *The Public Economy of Urban Communities*, ed. Julius Margolis, pp. 39–51. Washington, D.C.: Resources for the Future, 1965; distr. by Johns Hopkins Press, Baltimore.

LEWIS, HAROLD M. *The Planning of the Modern City*. Vol. 1. New York: John Wiley & Sons, 1961.

MASON, EDWARD S. "The Planning of Development." *Scientific American*, Sept. 1963, pp. 235–44.

MAYER, MILTON S. *On Liberty: Man v. the State.* A Center Occasional Paper, vol. 3, no. 1. Santa Barbara, Cal.: Center for the Study of Democratic Institutions, 1969.

McCAHILL, ED. "Detroit — Motown at the Crossroads." *ASPO* (American Society of Planning Officials) *Newsletter* 38 (1972): 29–39.

McNEESE, MOSE. "Neighborhood Planning Agencies: An Evaluation." *ASPO* (American Society of Planning Officials) *Magazine* 38 (1972): 232–38.

MOCINE, CORWIN R. "Interpretation: Urban Physical Planning and the 'New Planning.'" *Journal of the American Institute of Planners* 32 (1966): 234–41.

REICHEK, JESSE. "On the Design of Cities." *Journal of the American Institute of Planners* 27 (1961): 141–43.

ROTHENBERG, JEROME. "A Model of Economic and Political Decision Making." In *The Public Economy of Urban Communities*, ed. Julius Margolis, pp. 1–38. Washington, D.C.: Resources for the Future, 1965; distr. by Johns Hopkins Press, Baltimore.

RUSSELL, BERTRAND. *Human Society in Ethics and Politics.* New York: New American Library, 1962.

SCHNORE, LEO F. "The Timing of Metropolitan Decentralization: A Contribution to the Debate." *Journal of the American Institute of Planners* 25 (1959): 200–6.

SCOTT, MEL. *American City Planning Since 1890.* Berkeley: University of California Press, 1969.

SEELEY, JOHN R. "What is Planning? Definition and Strategy." *Journal of the American Institute of Planners* 28 (1962): 91–97.

SHAW, BERNARD. *Man and Superman.* Act III, pp. 110–80. Harmondsworth, Engl.: Penguin Books, Ltd., 1952.

SPENCER, MILTON H. "Uncertainty, Expectations, and Foundations of the Theory of Planning." *Journal of the Academy of Management* 5 (1965): 197–206.

TAWNEY, R. H. *The Attack and Other Papers.* London: Allen & Unwin, Ltd., 1953.

WEBBER, MELVIN W. "Comprehensive Planning and Social Responsibility." *Journal of the American Institute of Planners* 29 (1963): 232–41.

WHEELER, JOHN HARVEY. *Democracy in a Revolutionary Era: The Political Order Today.* A Center Occasional Paper. Santa Barbara, Cal.: Center for the Study of Democratic Institutions, 1970.

WRIGHT, FRANK LLOYD. *The Living City.* New York: New American Library, 1963.

YLVISAKER, PAUL N. "Diversity and the Public Interest: Two Cases in Metropolitan Decision-Making." *Journal of the American Institute of Planners* 27 (1961): 107–17.

ZIMMERMAN, JOSEPH F. "Are Neighborhood Governments a Desirable Institutional Change?" *ASPO* (American Society of Planning Officials) *Magazine* 38 (1972): 224–31.

2

The Evaluation
of Local Government Policy

The local government produces a variety of goods and services. While seldom perceived in this light, there is little doubt that government production is an important allocator of local resources. In traditional economic development theory we speak of social overhead capital as the supportive outputs of government, but in the future we will likely discuss the role of local government as an economic planner and developer of the city. In order to begin to understand the role that local government might take in urban development, it is necessary to evolve a set of analytical tools for evaluating the efficiency of government production. The purpose of this chapter is to elaborate upon the essential tools. Following a brief discussion of welfare economics and planning, programming, and budgeting systems (PPBS), the major segment of this chapter will describe cost-benefit analysis as the basic tool in the PPBS activity.

Economics and the Idea of Social Welfare

Not only is liberty perceived as fundamental to the democratic ideal as was discussed in the previous chapter, but individual freedom is the foundation of modern economic thinking as conceived in welfare economics. That individuals are the best arbiters of their welfare is demonstrable in terms of competitive economic theory. From the analysis of the economics of competition, economists have long been aware of the fact that interpersonal comparisons of utility are not possible. Historically, this argument has been behind much discussion of what constituted the "best" income distribution but also alludes to the difficulty of a social or political body making decisions for individuals.

Most relevant today is the idea of the inability to measure interpersonal utilities among persons when we consider public policy. If it is not possible to determine that one person's satisfaction from a particular good is greater or lesser than another person's satisfaction from the same good, then the basis for government production of goods and services is considerably weakened. In the private sector, the market mechanism is thought to reflect individuals' choices, thus some knowledge of the demand curve is at least partially sufficient for private production. In the production of public goods, however, the market mechanism does not function in the same way; the prices that people are willing to pay are not generally known to the public producer. If price is not known, then the basis for how much of a good to produce and at what price is not explicit.

The failure to know a market price results in the need to develop shadow prices. *Shadow prices* are essentially nothing more than proxies for market prices. If what people are willing to pay is evidenced by price in the private sector, then what people are willing to pay can be estimated by a shadow price in the public sector. Knowing that shadow prices are estimates leaves the public producer with very weak signals from the marketplace.

Some economists have argued that in a planned economy public authority can establish a schedule of prices which will allow decentralized decision making to effect an approximation of the competitive market mechanism. Thus the plant manager in a socialist economy can "maximize his profit," and the artificial creation of competition appears to work. But can such a translation be made to the producer of goods that are not replicated in the private sector? Can a bureau chief in charge of parks where no charges are levied and no fees are paid be expected to "maximize his profits"? While the socialist government can set prices which it considers "best" and have the plant managers respond to that price schedule to create economic efficiency, such is not the case with many goods produced by local government.

This lack of price setting either by the central authority or the local public producer leads many to argue that fees should be charged to consumers of public goods. Such fees would be based on the marginal cost of producing that particular additional level of output. Marginal cost pricing appears relevant where average costs are increasing; but where average costs are decreasing, marginal costs are below average costs, with the end result that producers do not cover costs. Such might be the case in a sewer system where declining costs appear common as the sewer system size increases. Marginal cost pricing appears to be useful in developing expressway systems where extra costs are required to create a sufficiently large system of highways to accommodate peak load uses. Where applicable, marginal cost pricing is thought to be more efficient than many other charges or revenue producing payments.

The basis of marginal cost pricing depends on the individual consumer's willingness to pay. If there are difficult areas in pricing and producing public goods, the economist would generally suggest that the public authority develop as much knowledge as possible about individual preferences for goods and attempt to produce directly for individuals. After all, economic welfare in the city is the extent to which individuals in the city are "best off."

How does the local government know when it is an efficient producer? In welfare economics efficiency is achieved and welfare improved when any change in economic activity in the community benefits some and harms none. This criterion for optimal efficiency, developed by Vilfredo Pareto, is not applicable under most conditions. What, for example, happens when we see a public decision which benefits some and causes losses for others? In further response to this situation, Pareto's optimality is not sufficient because it does not deal with questions of income distribution. Pareto optimality assumes the existing distribution of income.

Kaldor proposed another criterion which attempts to deal explicitly with income distributions. Using money as the common denominator, Kaldor suggested that when we have a situation where some win and some lose, the proper criterion is to compare the dollar values which both groups place upon their respective wins and losses. Scitovsky recognized that the Kaldor criterion could lead to undesirable results in those cases where a change in policy (which is beneficial to some and costly to others) is made but for which a return to the original state (eliminate the new policy) is also beneficial. Scitovsky suggested that a proposed change is beneficial only when a change is beneficial and when a return to the old point is not beneficial.[1]

Another approach to social welfare lies in the explicit welfare function as devised by Abram Bergson. He argued that optimality can only be achieved when goals are derived from value judgments and made explicit. The idea of the explicit welfare function has much to recommend it, yet has come under criticism by Kenneth Arrow when he investigated the relationship between social and individual choices. Arrow's work led him to the Impossibility Theorum which suggests that making a choice among all alternatives violates some of the conditions that social choices must meet if they are to represent individual choices. The four conditions for individual choices are: (1) social choices must be transitive; (2) social choices must not be dictated by anyone either in or outside the society; (3) social choices must not respond in an opposite direction from changes in individual choices; and (4) the social preference between two alternate choices must depend only upon those two alternatives rather than on opinions about other alternatives. As a result of Arrow's work it is possible to suggest that at this point in time economic theory has not created a useful guide for decision makers in the area of maximizing welfare for the citizenry. If the conditions for making social welfare decisions are not met, then there is little basis for knowing whether the local government is making good social decisions for the individual.[2]

[1] Nicholas Kaldor, "Welfare Propositions of Economics and Interpersonal Comparisons of Utility," *Economic Journal* 49 (1939): 549–52; Tibor Scitovsky, "A Note on Welfare Propositions in Economics," *Review of Economic Studies* 9 (1941): 86.

[2] Abram Burk [Bergson], "A Reformulation of Certain Aspects of Welfare Economics," *Quarterly Journal of Economics* 52 (1938): 310–34; Kenneth J. Arrow, *Social Choice and Individual Values*, Cowles Commission for Research in Economics, monograph no. 12 (New York: John Wiley & Sons, 1951), pp. 46–60, 89.

As a moderating notion on the rather hopeless result, the theory of the "second best" in economics implies that there is little point in requiring a Pareto optimal decision in one sector of the economy when the conditions for efficiency are not met in other segments of the economy. Thus, in a highly monopolistic economy, welfare at the local level may not be optimal even if we could generate an "optimal" local decision.[3]

In conclusion, welfare economics to the policy maker may look like a dog chasing its own tail, but its contribution lies in clarifying issues about individual and social welfare and its implied suggestion that any attempt to improve welfare at the local level on a piecemeal basis is apt to be filled with errors. Thus while economics does rely heavily on individual choice, it does not create an explicit basis upon which to make social decisions. It implies that social decisions should be made on the basis of individual welfare and at the same time demonstrates the "impossibility" of so doing in most instances.

Forming the Problem: Suboptimization toward Programs

In part, then, the problem of goal determination lies in society's inability to provide a final maximizing social welfare function. Since this is the case, we are forced into dealing with welfare problems in the uncomfortable way McKean calls "suboptimization" (see figure 4).[4] The process of suboptimization arises because the welfare function cannot be ascertained, thus criteria must be sought which are "approximate." Instead of attempting to maximize total welfare, the local authority attempts to maximize at lower levels of abstraction. This introduces a number of problems and at the same time eliminates some problems.

As a disadvantage, suboptimization means decision makers may miss the main point. That is, we must depend upon logic and judgment to presume that in attempting to gain a maximizing solution to a subproblem we add to the total welfare. We run the risk of a fallacy of composition in assuming that the path from the subproblem to total welfare is direct.

As an advantage, subproblem solving makes the task somewhat easier simply because decision makers are dealing with lower levels of abstraction and can frame problems more easily. Data becomes more meaningful (but in a less general way) and risks become greater — for example, in having to assume that housing will alleviate human problems. Thus, suboptimizing makes the task easier mechanically but more fraught with cause and effect errors than would have been the case had we had a maximizing scheme for total welfare.

Decision makers must attempt to determine a means of going from an abstract, general goal to specific programs. Once the level is reached at which

[3] Richard B. Lipsey and K. Kevin Lancaster, "The General Theory of the Second Best," *Review of Economic Studies* 24 (1956): 11.

[4] Roland N. McKean, *Efficiency in Government Through Systems Analysis, With Emphasis on Water Resources Development*, a Rand Corporation Research Study, Operations Research Society of America, publications in Operations and Research no. 3 (New York: John Wiley & Sons, 1958), pp. 29–34.

FIGURE 4

SUBOPTIMIZATION ILLUSTRATED

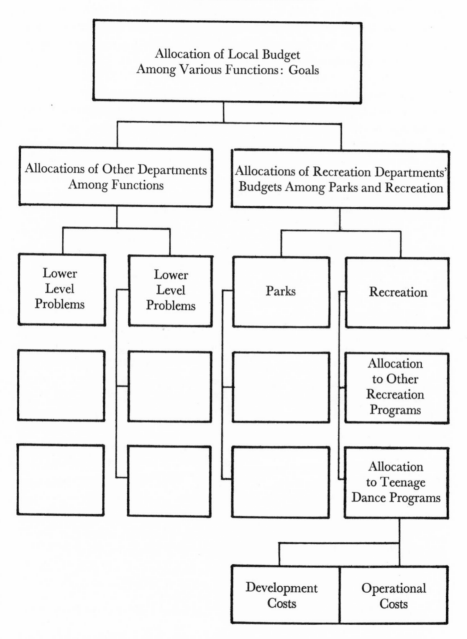

Source: Adapted from Roland N. McKean, *Efficiency in Government Through Systems Analysis* (New York: John Wiley & Sons, 1958), p. 31.

direct questions can be formulated — such as "Who and how many people suffer from what diseases and with what intensity?" — the road to program development will become clear.

Once goals have been translated into suboptimal terms and these subproblems have been detailed, formal proposals for particular programs can emerge. A part of these proposals entails the evaluation of proposed programs in economic terms.

One difficulty mentioned above is defining the population with the "problem" and ascertaining whether or not it is truly the population who has the problem or whether the population in question is representative of the larger society. The translation from goals to programs is the most difficult undertaking in generating effective programs. Managers of existing programs usually know what the outputs of the program are and have some notions of the relative efficiency of the program, but they seldom can logically relate their outputs to community goals. A park administrator, for example, may know that he produces so many units of "recreation days" for the citizens, and he knows something of their likes and dislikes and how to make his operation more effective, but he usually has little idea as to how this output is translated into a community goal except to say that it does make people happy, healthy, etc. — hardly an analytical or logical approach.

The gap in logic between goal and program can be aided significantly by formally writing a narrative which specifically identifies the affected population. Only by first attempting to characterize in considerable detail the population served can links be established from goals to problems to programs. Such narratives become focal points of planners' attempts to generate planning activities at bureau or program levels which are justified in the context of urban goals. Further, by identifying the program participants, unresolved problems may become apparent.

In planned as opposed to ongoing programs, the process is somewhat reversed. The relation to goal is herein established through a consideration of a perceived problem area, a population identified which has the perceived problem, and a program devised which can be defended in explicit terms to generate a solution to the problem.

The detailed narrative is the explicit record of the conception of the goal, the problem, the population, and the program as projected by the program proposer. The narrative requires a considered attempt to plan for perceived individual human beings — as opposed to the "public," the "children," the "poor," or other misleading categories about particular numbers of particular human beings.

Locally Produced Goods

In economics, a distinction is made between various classes of goods. One class of goods is the *pure public good*, a good which, once provided, is available for all. Individuals or groups cannot be excluded from its enjoyment regardless of whether they have contributed to its provision. Samuelson argues that one significant point about public goods is that if they are admitted, then one is admitting the possibility of external effects. If external effects (costs and benefits to persons not accounted for in the economic transaction) are admitted, then price in the private sector cannot generate a competitive optimum.[5] Consequently, the market system of selling for a price cannot be used as a mechanism to make perfectly efficient production and consumption decisions. National defense, law enforcement, space programs, etc., are all examples of public goods.

A second class of goods is that of the *quasi-public good,* a good that could be produced under the private market system or which carries with it important external benefits or costs. The private sector of the economy would not produce the good through the market system in the desired appropriate quantity or quality, so public programs expand its production or change its quality. Such quasi-public goods include neighborhood centers, public education, manpower training, etc.

The third type is the *private good,* a good which is produced in the private sector, a good for which a market price can be set.

Litchfield and Margolis categorize municipal services into a number of kinds of activities and suggest the economic benefits of each.

1. Quasi-private: Where cities conduct enterprises that could readily be in private sectors — parking lots, golf courses, auditoriums. These can be measured by benefit at a value at market prices.
2. Self-financing utilities — gas, water, etc.: These differ because of the monopoly elements. Benefits cannot be measured at the tariff prices. Benefits in imputed prices or physical units.
3. Engineering services — roads, sewers, etc.: Benefits are widely dispersed. Sometimes they can be assigned as cost reductions to users and sometimes they are found in the increases in land values of the benefited property.
4. Social services—schools, health, firefighting, etc.: These beenfits have no market price and while imputed prices can be developed for some, they cannot be for most. Use benefits measures per unit from man hours (effort), performance (physical quantity), result (effect of effort or performance in relation to its objective), and services needs or problem magnitude (number of school children, etc.) as a rough index of need.
5. Police power: Regulative functions which impose costs on individuals to the public benefit. Since cost and benefit fall on different parties, the transaction is outside the market. For programs in this category, we develop costs of the program to the affected group of individuals

[5] Paul A. Samuelson, "Aspects of Public Expenditure Theories," *Review of Economics and Statistics* 40 (1958): 334.

and benefits to the public similar to those costs and benefits in (4) above.[6]

I. Planning, Programming, and Budgeting at the Local Level

Any city is a producer of various classes of these economic goods. With such variety of production how can one begin to evaluate economic efficiency? Normally one would turn to the market and investigate efficiencies using market prices as the test, but in local government there is little direct pricing which is in any way competitive, and there are many outputs for which no price is charged. How do decision makers in the city decide the critical question of what to produce when, without a market mechanism, they have no strong evidence of demand?

The answer to this question lies in part with cost-benefit analysis and its broader complex of systems analysis known as planning, programming, and budgeting systems. PPBS is of limited use in definition of goals, but it can be an aid in evaluating how much to produce once some goal has been stated.

Program Budgeting: An Overview

For the purposes of local government we may consider at least three functions of budgeting. First is the managerial, the management of assets and activities; second, the control activities as undertaken by accountants; and, finally, the planning, programming, and budgeting systems.[7] This latter form is essentially developed by use of economic concepts and is designed for planning purposes and strategies. Local budgets have traditionally been heavily biased towards managerial functions and control functions rather than planning functions. PPBS is developed to make efficient choices among various alternatives in public investment and expenditure decisions and can be defined as a budget which, in economic terms, relates explicitly the costs and gains of various decisions given a particular set of explicit goals of local government.

Historically, PPBS is a later development than the control and managerial functions to local budgeting and, as a result, is not widely accepted yet by local governments. As a functioning set of ideas, it has been used as recently as 1965 with the George Washington University experiment conducted in five cities, five counties, and five states.

Aside from its newness, another aspect of PPBS which one should keep in mind is its incompleteness. It is not a panacea for local decision makers; it is

---

[6] Nathaniel Litchfield and Julius Margolis, "Benefit-Cost Analysis as a Tool in Urban Government Decision Making," in *Public Expenditure Decisions in the Urban Community*, ed. Howard G. Schaller (Washington, D.C.: Resources for the Future, 1963; distr. by Johns Hopkins Press, Baltimore), pp. 130–31. Copyright © 1963, Resources for the Future. Reprinted by permission.

[7] Allen Schick, "The Road to P.P.B.: The Stages of Budget Reform," *Public Administration Review* 26 (1966): 244–45.

simply a form of budgeting which can aid the local decision maker to make more "efficient" decisions if it is properly employed. It is no substitute for decision makers who are involved in complex political considerations where some important ideas may not be quantifiable.

The projected potential of PPBS (although it is not without its critics) lies in the genuine needs of governments to know what they are doing when they make particular output decisions. For example, there is always competition for scarce resources; which programs do we undertake? Further, when is a program productive and when is it not? While PPBS cannot optimize the allocation of resources available to local government, it can, if well done, assist in indicating which programs are likely to be most productive. These are not all of its uses or potentials, however.

A far more significant potential, yet one which PPBS will much less likely be able to acquire with perfection, is the ability of PPBS to begin to bring together several important aspects of government expenditures — namely, the social, the political, and the economic — for a single public decision. Keep in mind that economists, sociologists, and political scientists have worked in isolation from each other, and PPBS, developed well, may allow the disciplines to bring their knowledge into a cohesive and relevant form.

If PPBS is a budgetary system, then it is largely a set of records. It embodies a set of data and leads to larger information systems than current local data systems require. The improved records form the data base for cost-benefit analyses which are developed to facilitate specific objectives of government. The first element of PPBS is a *statement of objectives*. The objective of a waste disposal system is not to maximize the amount of garbage collected, but to provide the level of service which people demand. The related systems of pickups, land fills, and sewers all have the purpose of providing a service for people. No matter what the objective, it must be clearly stated and be related back to a felt need and demand by citizens.

The second step is to *analyze the outputs* of an existing or planned program. There are many benefits, some more important than others, but all need to be specified and the outputs of the program stated in monetary terms if possible. In garbage collection, for example, one would want to know the relevant benefits of that particular service. One benefit is obviously aesthetic; still another is a matter of individual and public health; another is the avoidance of noxious odors; another is the removal of unwanted possessions, etc. In many cases, such as garbage collection, analysts may fall back on proxies for benefits such as tons of garbage removed, etc., but a proxy is only partially useful; one must not forget the reasons people want garbage removed.

Once the outputs of the system have been defined, then analysts must *ascertain the costs* of providing the program. Costs must be determined in a fuller context than the accountant might devise; for example, in a garbage collection program we would want to ascertain not only the costs of collection and disposal, but the external costs to citizens awakened in the early hours of the morning by the banging of garbage cans. While we are interested in the accounting costs of the system or program we plan, we are also interested in appreciating all the social costs or benefits that it might produce. Outputs of a program have therefore both negative and positive aspects.

A fourth step lies in a *comparison of this program with other programs* which might generate the same results. That is, assuming the objective function of the program, are there more efficient means of accomplishing the program than our first plan? In garbage collection, do we provide more collectors and fewer trucks? What are the most efficient mixes of factors of production which will best economize the program? Further, are there alternatives which would provide part or complete substitution for the program planned? Could we, for example, use more garbage disposals in the home instead of expanding a garbage collection system? If we did, then would the increased number of home disposals have cost implications for the sewer system?

Unfortunately, this fourth step is the most difficult of all because, if the thinking is carried far enough, analysts would have to raise questions about the objectives of the proposed use of resources. For example, could the resources used in garbage collection be partially or completely transferred to some other local objective? Not completely, but perhaps in part. Also, could the resources set aside for garbage collection be used in a more desirable way or could garbage collection services be contracted out to the private sector of the local economy? Even in something as initially pedestrian as garbage collection questions arise which make PPBS complex — complex enough, indeed, that we must also consider the efficiency aspects of PPBS itself. If local government spent a high percentage of local budgets on planning expenditures, it would violate the main objective, which is to provide services to citizens.

If alternatives can be considered and the assessments continued to the point where one eliminates all but the most relevant alternatives, then the entire analysis is cast in a form and structure which allows it to be compared to analyses of other local government expenditure programs. By considering alternatives one may use linear and mathematical programming to compare results under varying options. In short, government needs a *systematic process* and a systematic process means a budgeting system which allows comparison of expenditures among various segments of the local government budget.

Formalizing the PPBS

While the foregoing overview statement is useful, some additional specifications are necessary. According to Hatry, the major components of a planning, programming, and budgeting system are:

　　1. An across-the-board governmental structure (a sufficiently descriptive

schematic of government organization and function) to try to identify *the government's basic objectives.*

2. A multi-year *program or financial plan.* The plan is in two parts; the first part is the financial plan where all pertinent costs are developed, including capital costs, noncapital costs, associated support costs, and direct costs. Revenues should be identified and, finally, the expected net cost should be indicated. The program output part of the plan includes details of the major benefit measures and the scope and size of the programs.

3. All *program analysis and evaluation* should, according to Hatry, include:
   a. The fundamental objectives of the agency,
   b. The major feasible alternatives,
   c. The best estimates of total program cost for each alternative,
   d. For each alternative, the best available estimates of the benefits and/or penalties relevant to the objectives for each year concerned,
   e. The major assumptions and uncertainties associated with the alternatives, and
   f. The impact of proposed programs on other programs, other agencies, other levels of government, and private organizations.[8]

4. The fourth explicit requirement of PPBS is some kind of *updating procedure,* or, in other words, an explicit provision for the revision of various types of resource allocation decisions.[9]

Thus, according to Hatry, distinctive characteristics which apply to PPBS are:

1. It calls for an identification of the fundamental governmental objectives
2. It requires explicit consideration of future year considerations
3. It calls for systematic analysis of alternative ways of meeting the governmental objectives[10]

The major components of such a system are:

1. An across-the-board governmental program structure
2. A multiyear program and financial plan
3. Program analysis
4. Program updated procedure[11]

---

[8] Harry P. Hatry, "Criteria for Evaluation in Planning State and Local Programs," in *Program Budgeting and Benefit-Cost Analysis: Cases, Text, and Readings,* comp. Harley H. Hinrichs and Graeme M. Taylor (Pacific Palisades, Cal.: Goodyear Publishing Co., 1969), pp. 95–98. See also the same title published as a Committee Print by the Subcommittee on Intergovernmental Relations to the Committee on Government Operations, U.S. Senate (Washington, D.C.: U.S. Government Printing Office, 1967).

[9] Hatry, "Criteria for Evaluation," in *Program Budgeting,* comp. Hinrichs and Taylor, pp. 95, 96, 98.

[10] Hatry, "Criteria for Evaluation," in *Program Budgeting,* comp. Hinrichs and Taylor, p. 95.

[11] Hatry, "Criteria for Evaluation," in *Program Budgeting,* comp. Hinrichs and Taylor, pp. 95–98.

Introducing PPBS in Local Government

Local governments are usually well-entrenched processes for accomplishing perceived ends. Change is not easy in any large institution, and governments are similarly afflicted. How does one introduce a system of evaluation of existing and planned programs when traditions are strong? Initially, local government must educate itself to the idea of PPBS. Normally, this would demand the hiring of professional consultants and developing in-service training programs. Likewise, no community without access to a reasonably large computer capability can easily enter the PPBS arena. Further, political leadership must be sufficiently convinced that PPBS is advisable and helpful.

In initiating the local government to PPBS, one should note the similarity between normal processes of logic in decision making and PPBS. Much of what now passes for PPBS is simply systematized development of existing ways of doing things. Decisions under PPBS are not radically different, but additional and systematic contexts are introduced.

In the educational process, local government should be aware of the sources of information which it has available to it; included among these sources are various pressures exerted by the public, election results, internal and external records, power structures, political parties, and bureaucrats themselves. How does one systematize this information? Initially each department should attempt to define its own functions carefully and how its activities lead toward specific goals in the city. Operating under some such general goals as those suggested in the previous chapter, existing functions can be identified and related to goals. The process is not so different from the planning a housewife might do, except that when the housewife plans her budget she may not consciously set priorities. If she does not budget with explicit goals in mind and if priorities are not recognized, she may become the impulse buyer instead of the home planner.

Likewise, local government department heads may have a set of operating assumptions which have not been challenged. Traditional modes of doing things take on great force over time, and yet changes in needs may make the "tried and true" decision modes completely irrelevant. Such might be the case of a park director who thinks of parks in a nineteenth-century context of the pastoral stroll. Recreation is an important human activity, and the interrelatedness of parks and recreation programs nowadays is crucial. If goals can be evaluated and challenges developed to generate a viable set of rationales for existing programs, then one is in prospect of producing a framework in which all new programs and plans will be carefully scrutinized to determine if they too fit into defensible patterns of goals and activities directed toward these goals.

More strictly speaking, performance must be predicted in the development of quasi-production functions for each department's activities. What is being produced? How does one value this output? Further, are projected outputs feasible? Strong department heads may overextend their activities while weaker department heads may understate their needs and outputs. Potential conflict demands central coordination of the budgeting process. Once determined, anticipated outputs and their values should be redefined by policy makers whose jobs are to make all departments and outputs comparable.

Internally local government needs a coordinating agency to implement and prepare the formal analyses for PPBS. The quality of various budgets for departments will vary with the skill of the coordinator and the state of the art in PPBS. No great expectations should accompany initial phases of PPBS since considerable time is required to generate a working system, the models, and the data needed to apply the models.

II. Development of the Cost-Benefit Analysis

The essential quality of PPBS depends upon the kind of cost-benefit analysis which is the central analytical core of the PPBS. The analysis of programs is the task of cost-benefit analysis.

According to Prest and Turvey, cost-benefit analysis is a practical way of assessing the desirability of particular public expenditure projects where it is important to take a long view of the expenditure.[12] The technique has developed from the traditional fields within economics of public finance, welfare economics, and resource economics. The purpose of such analyses is to assist in a more efficient allocation of public resources among various alternatives.

The formal analysis of costs and benefits contains a number of ingredients. Certain considerations must be included for the analysis to be complete. One of the first considerations is what do we intend to maximize? That is, what benefits are we concerned with, and how do we measure the welfare generated from them? Some scheme for seeing maximization of welfare is thus required. These concerns are evidenced in the following analytical questions: (1) The objective function—what are the outputs and how are these benefits measured? (2) What are the costs of the program? (3) What are the constraints to the program? (4) What are the externalities? (5) What is the impact of time? (6) What is the impact of risk and uncertainty?

The Objective Function — What Benefits are to be Produced

What benefits are to be sought? Are these benefits to be maximized or are costs to be minimized? Hinrichs summarizes the four possible choices for criteria in resolving these questions.[13] One, you can ignore society's group desires and attach values only to the individual; thus, you junk any kind of organic theory of welfare of the state and you maximize welfare for individuals. A second kind

[12] A. R. Prest and Ralph Turvey, "Cost-Benefit Analysis: A Survey," *Economic Journal* 75 (1965): 683.

[13] Harley H. Hinrichs, "Government Decision Making and the Theory of Benefit-Cost Analysis: A Primer," in *Program Budgeting*, comp. Hinrichs and Taylor, pp. 11–14.

of possibility, as Hinrichs says, is to play the game that everybody can win; that is, all individuals gain in welfare. A third possibility is to follow Pareto optimally: "Somebody wins and nobody loses." Fourth, play the game that the "winners outweigh the losers."

The above logic is of principal importance when one is describing the problem to be solved. If a problem is defined, and an explicit objective function developed, this will be a shorthand statement of the larger objective. It is easy to oversimplify the objective function; problems are not simple, yet most objective function statements typically are. The chief usefulness of the above logic lies in its ability to force the analyst and the decision makers to verbalize a coherent statement of the objective of a program or project within a program.

Whichever criteria or welfare statement is selected, the program design will attempt to improve welfare by either: (1) maximizing benefits given particular cost levels, or (2) minimizing costs given particular levels of benefits. The first category of maximizing benefits is obvious in many cases where alternate programs may bear similar costs but generate different benefits. The second category is what is called cost-effectiveness analysis where a goal is established to be reached and the least costly means of achieving that goal is the most efficient. Cost minimization to achieve fixed objectives has wide applications.[14]

In setting objectives there are certain pitfalls. One is to regard means as ends when it is illogical to do so. For example, if we built a lovely transportation system, that does not necessarily improve the conditions of people's lives unless they use it. A second type of pitfall lies in not regarding means as ends. The means may sometimes be the end. For example, in a participatory democracy the process itself may be more important than any outcome that is generated by it. A third type of pitfall is to measure the wrong thing. Quantification can be a great problem since we may be capable of measuring only a part of what we can conceptualize as the benefit.[15]

In discussing the objective function, no clue has yet been given as to the direction or form that this function might take. The objective function is designed to define the benefits which a program (or its alternatives) is geared to achieve. When we speak of benefits we speak of primary and secondary benefits and of tangible and intangible benefits. By *primary benefit* is meant those measurable benefits which individuals affected by the program receive. By *secondary benefit* is meant those classes of benefits which accrue to society at large. This latter form of benefit is under considerable scrutiny by economists, and arguments over the existence of secondary benefits are common. Practically,

[14] Otto Eckstein, "A Survey of the Theory of Public Expenditure Criteria," in Universities-National Bureau Committee for Economic Research, *Public Finances: Needs, Sources, Utilization*, National Bureau of Economic Research Special Conference Series 12 (Princeton: Princeton University Press, 1961), p. 450.

[15] Hinrichs and Taylor, comps., *Program Budgeting*, pp. 12, 13.

the secondary or social benefits are all those benefits which are indirect and do not accrue directly to the individuals who receive the primary benefit. Secondary benefits are one form of what are referred to as *externalities*, the unaccounted for outcomes of a program or project.

Tangible benefits of either class (primary or secondary) are benefits for which there is a logical means of measurement in dollar terms. If a benefit is known to exist but there is no logical means of measuring it in dollar terms, then such benefits are said to be *intangible*.[16] Tangibility or lack of it is really a condition of whether or not there is an agreed upon means of measuring the benefit. The analyst takes those things which are measurable in dollar terms and calls them tangible.

As might be expected from the term cost-benefit analysis, the analyst is always looking toward the possibility of measuring benefits in dollar terms. One may argue that dollars are not a good indicator or proxy for value, but the economist is uncomfortable with other terms. Dollars are used even for the most sensitive kinds of decisions as in court decisions which "value" a human life by awarding dollars equivalent to lifetime earnings streams to a widow. There can be an economic level to any human act, and while one may argue that the value which economic thinking places on a particular act (such as the death benefit described above) is perhaps not the most important aspect of evaluating that fact, one may not argue that there is no economic significance to the fact. The difficult part of generating logical benefits measures is whether they actually measure the concept intended or whether the benefit measure is wholly or partially irrelevant to the concept of welfare we seek to specify.

Whatever proxy we use, we may have to develop *shadow prices* — prices, as indicated earlier, which do not exist but which are estimated to reflect price if there were a market mechanism which was effective for the benefit we propose. What price would the benefit bring in the hypothetical marketplace? This is the principal question in specifying a shadow price for benefits measures in dollar terms. If we lived in the best of all competitive worlds, prices would allocate resources adequately and the role of government would be limited indeed, but in the real world shadow prices are necessary to develop an economic value to be placed on government outputs of goods and services.

In conceiving the value of goods and services produced by the government, some common practices of shadow pricing are observed. In assessing the value of schooling, the primary benefit is the discounted future earnings streams of those who are schooled as compared to their future earnings streams without schooling. In evaluating urban parks, the value to the user is the cost he bears in coming to the park, mostly in the form of travel costs. In assessing transportation projects, one is concerned with the safety, the time saved, and the comfort

[16] McKean, *Efficiency in Government*, p. 58.

which a street system produces. The value of the street system becomes an economic statement of the value which users place upon safety, time saved, and comfort. In each kind of government production shadow prices can be developed which provide insights into and suggest benefits which are attributable to that particular output.

Margolis discusses three forms of estimation of shadow prices: the intermediate goods approach; the cost-savings approach; and the direct estimation approach. The intermediate goods approach estimates benefits on the basis of treating the public good as an intermediate good which the beneficiary uses as a producer good. Education as a public good is an example. The beneficiary uses the education to increase his income and this income increase becomes a measure of the value of education.[17]

The cost-savings approach is self-explanatory. The benefit is measured as the reduction in costs to individuals in the provision of the public good over what the individual would have to pay without the public good.[18] Transportation and recreation projects may be evaluated in this manner.

The third technique, direct estimation, is based on a comparison of private market prices for services with publicly produced goods.[19] All three of the techniques are fraught with difficulty and subject to much error in estimation.

Cost Measurements

On the surface, devising benefits measures appears more difficult than devising cost figures for a program and the alternatives with which it is to be compared. As noted earlier, the figures used by a cost accountant are not sufficient for the purposes of cost-benefit analysis. Included within the appropriate concepts of cost are the usual accountants' costs covering acquisition, development, and operational costs to the program or project. In addition to these three kinds of costs we must interject an overhead or administrative cost to the program. This overhead cost comes from two sources. First, there is the overhead of general local government such as an allocation of the mayor's salary, etc., which must be made to the program. Second, there is an overhead allocation from the particular agency of local government which must be made to this specific program assuming that the local agency has other functions for which it is responsible.

Other forms of cost which must be assessed include costs to the individual beneficiary — the recipient of the benefits of the program — any factor of cost

[17] Julius Margolis, "Shadow Prices for Incorrect or Nonexistent Market Values," in *Public Expenditures and Policy Analysis*, ed. Robert H. Haveman and Julius Margolis (Chicago: Markham Publishing Co., 1970), pp. 314–29, 323.

[18] Margolis, "Shadow Prices," in *Public Expenditures and Policy Analysis*, ed. Haveman and Margolis, p. 325.

[19] Margolis, "Shadow Prices," in *Public Expenditures and Policy Analysis*, ed. Haveman and Margolis, p. 328.

affected by inflation, and the social costs (externalities) which obtain from the public involvement in the particular form of production examined. There can be capital costs which an individual might bear in participating in a program developed and produced by government; in few instances is the cost of receiving the benefit zero. Likewise *social costs*, another form of externality, are those costs which are born by society at large which may not be reflected in the accounting costs.

The question of social cost is of particular interest because in many government production programs the elimination of some social cost becomes a significant benefit of the program. In juvenile delinquency programs, for example, the social or secondary benefit is the elimination of the harm done by juvenile offenders to society. The elimination of vandalism and its economic costs may be a benefit to such a program. One may venture to say that most law enforcement programs are designed more with secondary benefits in mind than with the primary benefits of aiding "afflicted" juveniles, potential offenders, or felons.

From an efficiency standpoint, social costs may not always demand intervention. As Turvey notes in summarizing the work of Coase, Davis, and Whinston, Buchanan and Stubblebine:

> if the party imposing external diseconomics and the party suffering them are able and willing to negotiate to their mutual advantage, state intervention is unnecessary to secure optimum resource allocation.[20]

The argument is that negotiation can bring about an efficient settlement, thus the case for intervention is made not on the basis of efficiency but on the basis of equity between the bargaining parties.

Constraints

Once the costs and benefits of a government output are conceived, it is necessary to take them out of the theoretical and methodological vacuum and consider them in the light of the realities of the political and social situation. These realities are called constraints and represent limits, the constraining context within which the project or program output must function. Eckstein has described a useful classification of constraints. (1) *Physical constraints*: technology and production possibilities limits. Is it even reasonable to consider a solution where the technological limits are unattainable? Such a constraint might be exemplified by the attempt to use blind workers to work on television sets in a manpower program. (2) *Legal constraints*: where laws constrain what one may do in a program. In some cases a good solution can come only from the change of laws. (3) *Administrative constraints*: in the program devised is there really sufficient talent to administer the program? (4) *Distributional constraints*: a given in-

[20] Ralph Turvey, "On Divergences between Social Cost and Private Cost," *Economica* 30 (1963): 309.

come distribution may make a program unsuccessful. The food stamp program is a case in point in those instances where the poor do not have enough income to purchase the $60 worth of stamps for $20. (5) *Political constraints*: where the program is simply unrealistic because of political considerations as, for example, in the case of a ban on billboards in a city where more than half the city council has an interest in a billboard company. (6) *Budgetary and financial constraints*: where resource scarcity is sufficiently acute relative to the program contemplated and the program cannot be undertaken. Such constraints may also appear in the manner of the budget process itself. (7) *Traditional, social, religious constraints*: under this category one may discover a myriad of obstacles to the projected program. To expect a city council manned by Catholics to easily pass legislation authorizing an abortion information center is naïve. Many innovative programs in urban areas have "bitten the dust" because of failure to consider the impact of the proposed program upon religious and social customs in the community. It is not the fact that such customs cannot be sometimes overcome; it is simply that effective urban policy demands consideration of and some accommodation to strong community views.[21]

The constraints under which policy is derived at the local level could be discussed at considerable length. One might say that the entire field of urban sociology is devoted to analyzing such constraints, as is the case with urban economics and urban political science. The most relevant constraints, however, take the form of questions which are deemed significant. Such significant questions are implicit in the constraints listed by Graeme Taylor.

1. The understanding of, sympathy for, and commitment to the idea of programmed budgeting by the chief executive of the jurisdiction
2. The personality and management philosophy of the executives involved
3. The size and organizational structure of the jurisdiction
4. The constitutional powers and authority of the jurisdiction
5. The ability, size, organizational location, and prestige of the responsible central staff agency[22]

More specifically, Taylor suggests that additional factors will influence the way in which programs are effected:

1. The clarity, precision, and specificity of any guidelines issued by central staff
2. The perceptions by individual agency heads of the degree to which the chief executive is backing the effort

[21] Eckstein, "Survey of the Theory of Public Expenditure," in Universities-National Bureau Committee for Economic Research, *Public Finances*, pp. 450–51. See also Hinrichs and Taylor, comps., *Program Budgeting*, p. 14.

[22] Graeme M. Taylor, "Designing the Program Structure," in *Program Budgeting*, comp. Hinrichs and Taylor, p. 39. Copyright © 1969, Goodyear Publishing Co. Reprinted by permission.

3. The understanding of, sympathy for, and commitment to the principles of PPB on the part of the agency head
4. The personality and management philosophy of the agency head
5. The existing size and organizational structure of the agency; the number of separate bureaus of divisions involved; the degree of centralization or decentralization both geographically and in terms of lower-level autonomy
6. The nature of the mission, or missions, of the agency
7. The homogeneity or lack thereof in the agency's problem mix; the degree to which agency problems are stable or in flux
8. The range of the agency's activities
9. Relations between bureaus or divisions within the agency
10. Inertia and tradition
11. Political popularity of the agency's programs; the personal interest of the chief executive in aspects of the agency's programs
12. Characteristics of the agency's existing data systems (financial accounting, cost accounting, work measurement, performance monitoring, management information, etc.)
13. Appropriations structure
14. Structure of allotments, apportionments, etc.
15. Statutory obligations of the agency
16. Relationship of the agency with key legislators
17. The nature of the agency's clientele groups
18. Reporting requirements of other levels of government (both superior and subordinate)
19. Existence of, and relations with, competitive agencies within the jurisdiction
20. The ability, size, organizational location, and prestige of the responsible staff within the agency.[23]

While all of the items mentioned above can affect the outcome of a given program, they may not all apply. They can be phrased in the form of questions, however, and used as such to frame the program and to later assess the probable success of a given program.

Externalities

The most important forms of externalities are the unaccounted for costs or benefits in economic transactions. Externalities are the spillovers or "spinouts" which are generated by an economic transaction. For example, if A renders a paid service to B and this service "serves" or "disserves" C, then the impact of the service upon C is an externality.[24] In designing our benefit measures, insofar

[23] Taylor, "Designing the Program Structure," in *Program Budgeting*, comp. Hinrichs and Taylor, p. 40. Copyright © 1969, Goodyear Publishing Co. Reprinted by permission.

[24] Hinrichs, "Government Decision Making," in *Program Budgeting*, comp. Hinrichs and Taylor, p. 15.

as possible, we want to "internalize" the externalities; that is, simply include them within the benefits and costs to the extent that it is possible. Such externalities take two forms. First is the pecuniary spillover in which costs or benefits accrue to certain individuals due to a shift in prices as when some person or persons experience a windfall gain. If the gain is a "windfall," that is simply a transfer of income from one to another, then there is no net economic gain to be considered.

McKean cites four pecuniary spillovers common in economic activity. First there is the case of bidding up the factor rates of hire. By this is meant the situation where, for example, one industry in an expanded need for an input bids up the price of that input and causes another industry's production to decline because of the higher price for the input.[25]

A second form of pecuniary transfer is the cutting down of prices of substitute products. This situation occurs when a relatively efficient producer enters the market for a particular good and by expanding his output the price for other substitute goods is reduced in the market.[26]

A third form of pecuniary transfer lies in the possible increases to complementary products. This external affect is exemplified in the situation of a firm's expanded output of say automobiles which causes an increase to the purchase of gasoline and increased profits to petroleum producers.[27]

A fourth form of pecuniary transfer is the case of lowering the price of the output. An example of this pecuniary transfer is similar to the second case, only in this instance an efficient producer expands output and the market price for the goods produced is reduced.[28]

McKean's arguments are based on the premise that if there is not net gain to economic production, then the pecuniary transfer should not be included as costs or benefits. One would have to disagree, not from an efficiency standpoint because in this sense McKean is accurate, but rather from a sense of equity because McKean's analysis implicitly considers all persons as free economic agents. If one perceives income distributions as a matter of public concern, then shifts in income distribution as a result of public production are a necessary consideration.

Some gain and some lose in such situations. Pecuniary spillovers can create significant social costs or benefits if we only momentarily lift the lid of economic efficiency and permit the inclusion of broader questions of social values and problems.

A second spillover or externality which is not a simple transfer of income but is an increase or decrease to production efficiency is called a technological spillover and properly should be included in the analysis.[29]

25 McKean, *Efficiency in Government*, p. 137.
26 McKean, *Efficiency in Government*, p. 138.
27 McKean, *Efficiency in Government*, p. 139.
28 McKean, *Efficiency in Government*, p. 140.
29 McKean, *Efficiency in Government*, p. 136.

Common examples of technological externalities would be the social costs of air, water, and noise pollution. If producer A's smokestack causes laundryman C to produce sooty laundry, then a technological externality of producer A's economic outputs is C's dirty laundry. For cost-benefit analysis technological externalities should be included in the analysis; in fact, all such externalities should be "internalized," i.e., their total economic effect accounted for.

Internalizing externalities is often seen in the pricing of suburban land. In an economic analysis of land, let's say a suburbanite pays a market price for a particular lot. The market price for that lot and the transaction present the basic economics of the matter, but in fact what he is really paying for is more than a lot to build his house on. He is buying a "good" school system and neighborhood, streetlights and garbage collection, and all kinds of things which are not necessarily considered even by him in the whole process. They do affect the outcome; they push him into this one position and keep him from buying a lot in the city where these services may not be available.

Basically, we have to decide what external factors are to be left out in the whole design of the program and its evaluation. In a kind of economy-of-effort thesis we have a number of variables — A,B,C,D,E,F,G — all affecting X. We pick out, let us say, A,D, and E as being crucial and significant economic variables and the others logically inconsequential. We have to make some limiting choices because, in spite of the notion that everything affects everything else, we must retain efficiency in the evaluation process itself.

In sum, economic transactions may involve the following external effects:

1. Production to production: an activity by one producer affects the output of other producers — street maintenance for expensive snow removal in a bad winter may reduce recreation outputs in the summer.
2. Production to consumption: an activity by one producer affects consumers — such as air, water, and noise pollution, etc.
3. Consumption to consumption: an activity by one consumer affects other consumers — such as radio noise in a public park.
4. Consumption to production: an activity by one consumer affects producers — for example, hunting through farm crops.[30]

These represent the basic categories as far as the economist is concerned, but they are oversimplified. Their applications and measurements are difficult.

Economists are generally comfortable in dealing with the economic theory of externalities and the application of externality theory to traditional economic externalities. On the other hand, when faced with costs and benefits which are fundamentally social rather than economic, the economist falters. For example, in assessing the benefits of education, the discounts of future earnings streams of primary benefits are handled well, yet in considering externalities such as the relationship between higher education and the quality of motherhood, the econo-

30 Hinrichs and Taylor, comps., *Program Budgeting*, p. 16.

mist is apt to suggest merely that education may aid in creating a person more effective in carrying out the role of motherhood.

Unfortunately, at this level of generalization, we cannot test such statements. Broad generalizations that suggest that education enhances the quality of motherhood are not hypotheses. What is needed are testable statements that are sufficiently delimited by theory or specification so they can be examined. The point is that economics cannot generate those relevant questions. We need the child development expert, the educational sociologist, and other experts from other disciplines to frame questions for the economist. By this means the economist may take the improved questions and apply economic reasoning to them. This is a fertile field of interdisciplinary study which is, as of this date, very much undeveloped.

Discount Rates and the Impact of Time

Time will affect the final magnitudes of the benefits and the costs in the particular process we contemplate undertaking. Costs may occur over several periods of time and may occur in "lumps." Benefits may occur all at once, only after a period of time, or be evenly or unevenly distributed over the life of the project. An example will prove useful. Imagine two projects which cost $20 and generate benefits of $30; each project is planned for four years. Which is more efficient?

		Year				
		(1)	(2)	(3)	(4)	(Total)
Project A	Benefits	10	10	5	5	30
	Costs	2	4	6	8	20
Project B	Benefits	5	5	10	10	30
	Costs	2	4	6	8	20

Project A is clearly more efficient than Project B because the benefits in Project A occur sooner within the four-year period than do those of Project B, so the present value of benefits from Project A are greater than the present value of benefits from Project B. Further, the present value of the benefits of both projects is less than $30 because $30 worth of benefits in the future is not worth $30 in the present. Costs could be treated by a similar illustration. Discounting the benefits and costs and bringing them both back to present value terms is necessary to provide a comparative basis for the two projects.

Discounting is important, but for most projects by most cities decisions being subjected to a variety of constraints are likely to be in the class of what McKean calls capital rationing with resale of the production process irrelevant.[31] That

[31] McKean, *Efficiency in Government*, pp. 82–87.

is, budget resources are scarce and social, legal, or political constraints make re-sale of the physical assets of the production process unlikely. Intergovernmental transfers also imply limitations. If the state allocates funds to cities, the use of the funds may be limited; thus, discounting would be different than if cities were free to use the money for whatever purposes they chose. Local funds raised by bonding into debt the city's real property are usually passed by voters for specific tasks. Alternative uses for funds may be limited thus discounting is affected. While some communities view the federal pitcher as being bottomless, in most cases projects for urban areas which are funded federally are usually budgeted under some idea of "appropriate size." At the local level, sources of funds are always limited, and, for most purposes, resale of the production process is not relevant.

Under such budgeting constraints, how does discounting work? First, we must imagine the impact of time preference. For public projects a *social time preference rate of discount* (STP) is based on the idea that socially present con-sumption is preferred to future consumption. In the case of dollar benefits, what is the present value of a future dollar benefit? Logically, in most cases, it will be worth less than a present dollar available for consumption.

The difficulty here lies in the translation from individual time preference to social time preference. There is no logical way to translate individuals' time preference functions to a collective time preference. One possibility is a compro-mise which suggests that the planner's perception of time preference be used. The problem is obvious; decision makers are not noteworthy for their attempts to make decisions in the public interest, much less "know" some particular func-tion such as time preference. As Eckstein notes: "The choice of interest rates must remain a value judgment." [32]

Thus, while fraught with possible error, it is likely more correct to discount future benefits with a time preference rate than not to do so at all. The question then becomes at what rate and in what manner?

Market interest rates are probably useful in determining a range of rates, but no particular market rate is valid per se. What society is willing to forego in current consumption to achieve in future consumption must be applied to the discounting of economic benefits. Probably the most useful suggestion in the selection of a discount rate is to determine a relevant range of interest rates and calculate benefits under a "low," a "medium," and a "high" interest rate to see how the three rates affect total amounts of benefits relative to costs. Though use-ful, one might still argue that the same appropriate trio of interest rates in one project are not inherently appropriate to another or an alternative project.

In the case of costs, the same logic holds but in a different set of circum-stances. Time streams of costs are referred to as the *social opportunity costs* of

[32] Eckstein, "Survey of the Theory of Public Expenditure," in Universities-National Bureau Committee for Economic Research, *Public Finances*, pp. 454, 460.

capital. By this is meant that the value of a social choice made is what yield society foregoes in the next best alternative investment by making that particular investment choice. When we are discussing costs, what we usually mean is that we had a number of investment alternatives and having selected one, we forego the others, ergo, the benefits that these other costs would have generated. If one element of cost is the benefit of a foregone opportunity, then we must add to our actual outlays of cost the "net return on alternative investment" which we had to forego. The rate at which we do this is not "established" — rather, argument moves toward setting "appropriate" rates of interest depending upon the kinds of alternatives that were available and the kinds of programs planned. This rate we call the *social opportunity cost rate* (soc).

The social opportunity cost rate is of particular interest because it explicitly demands that decision makers include as a cost the yield that the next best alternative investment would have generated. By so doing there is a rate of return which is a kind of double check on the benefit (return on investment) in the chosen project. No decision maker would select (if he opts for efficiency and that is the sole criterion) a project whose benefits were less than the benefits implied by the social opportunity cost rate.

As in the case of time preference, an soc rate is not widely agreed upon. It is in one sense easier to detail than time preference if decision makers need know only alternative public investments they can make. The question is then one of selecting the appropriate rate of return from alternatives to be used. But as Baumol suggests,

> the correct discount rate for the evaluation of a government project is the percentage rate of return that the resources utilized would otherwise provide in the private sector.[33]

Thus, public decision makers must consider alternatives in the private sector in order to ascertain a genuinely appropriate soc rate. Just as in the case of the stp rate, a range of interest rates for the soc might be calculated to see effects on the costs of the project.

While in the majority of cost-benefit studies reviewed such computations may not actually be made, we should undertake to include both measures in the analysis: namely, the social time preference rate which discounts benefits and the social opportunity cost rate which discounts costs. In essence we imagine two discount rates. stp rate: Discount the future benefits back to present values; a subtraction from benefits. soc rate: Discount (as in above) the yield rate of the next best alternative; an addition to costs, then apply the stp rate to the added costs. In the real world, Hinrichs' summary of practice is suggestive:

1. Do interest rates make a difference in making the decision? Calculate differing interest rates.

[33] William J. Baumol, "On the Discount Rate for Public Projects," in *Public Expenditures and Policy Analysis*, ed. Haveman and Margolis, p. 274.

2. For social welfare expenditures (health, education, etc.) that are deemed inefficient when high discount rates (10%–15%) the error may be in not including enough external effects.
3. In some instances cost effectiveness may be more efficient than cost-benefit analysis.
4. The decision maker should at least use his borrowing cost rates assuming that low rates available to governments reflect a social bias in governments' favor.
5. Interest rates are important but there is no correct one.[34]

Finally, for the STP one might use a range of 5–10–15% for all programs as our low, mean, and high STP factors. As well, experimentation should be made with weighing the STP discount rates with the priorities of the problems. Thus, when we have a project in a high priority problem area, analysts might weigh experimentally with ±2% on our range of three factors. In so doing, high priority projects would have lower than 5–10–15% discount rates and low priority projects would have higher than 5–10–15% STP rates.

Risk and Uncertainty

There are a number of problems related to cost-benefit analysis which raise the question of risk and the uncertainty from which risk arises. One such case lies in the estimate of time for the accrual of benefits. Since benefits are estimated over a period of time, estimates may be considerably off. As a means of determining an estimating device we should attempt to develop a number of likely estimates of the timing and absolute size of benefits. We must attach some notion of our confidence in this range of estimates of benefits. One device might be to estimate an anticipated average amount for an annualized period of time, then strike a high and low estimate on either side of the average estimate.

At any event, major areas of external effects upon outcomes of benefits should be stipulated so that the policy maker has some notion of what kinds of possible conditions might change the structure of benefits. Some major concerns might be the question of whether a long-run program will be funded in a desired sequence or whether funds will be discontinued, cut, or otherwise altered. Still another possibility might be changes in consumer tastes, income, or other elements of demand which could change and cause alterations in the benefits of a given program. This can in part be done by a careful listing of the assumptions under which a program is undertaken.

In some cases, it might be desirable to venture comments on the listed "constraints" which may possibly shift during the program's duration and the circumstances under which this might arise and the possible effects.

Further, if there is the possibility that estimates of benefits cannot be made certain (by comparison with like projects undertaken elsewhere, etc., or by the

[34] Hinrichs and Taylor, comps., *Program Budgeting*, pp. 18–19.

high, low, average estimates) a charge for risk could be included in the estimates to generate a conservative estimate of benefits.[35]

Still another possibility is to estimate break-even points for the economic feasibility of the program undertaken and then estimate the likelihood that the benefits will be "at least" enough to cover the anticipated costs of the program. While this to some degree falls into the area of magic, it might still be useful to anticipate such a break-even point.

The major analytical controversy concerning risk as Hirshleifer and Shapiro suggest is "Does the risk compensation sought by individuals — in the form of a 'risk premium' yield over and above the riskless rate of interest — represent a social as well as a private cost?" [36]

Risk-aversion is a common phenomena in society. Hirshleifer and Shapiro argue that the pooling of risk which is sometimes used to defend social decisions as riskless is not accurate.[37] The pooling argument depends upon market imperfections which hinder trading in the marketplace with the possible result of the elimination of private risk.[38] The importance of the unsettled controversy over the riskiness of social investments lies in the proper discount rate. If risk is not properly included, discount rates should be lower for public projects than for private sector investments. If risk should be included, discount rates would be comparable to the private sector rates.

What Finally to Maximize and the Level of Government Investment

The previous discussion could not come to a definite conclusion on the form of maximization that is specifically relevant to cost-benefit analysis. Until discussions of externalities, discounting, and risk were completed, the maximizing statement for public decisions would be incomplete.

Following McKean's counsel of perfection, governments in making investments should maximize the present value of benefits over the present value of costs.[39] In addition to the maximizing statement, we are also concerned with who gains. The decision maker can precisely see this by developing a table indicating by age, race, and income who receives the benefits. The maximizing statement relates to efficiency, but the distribution of benefits relates to equity. Most economists, while they may disagree on other points, do in fact agree on the maximizing statement above. It may not be certain that public decision makers

[35] Eckstein, "Survey of the Theory of Public Expenditure," in Universities-National Bureau Committee for Economic Research, *Public Finances*, p. 469.

[36] Jack Hirshleifer and David L. Shapiro, "The Treatment of Risk and Uncertainty," in *Public Expenditures and Policy Analysis*, ed. Haveman and Margolis, p. 297.

[37] Hirshleifer and Shapiro, "The Treatment of Risk," in *Public Expenditures and Policy Analysis*, ed. Haveman and Margolis, pp. 302–8.

[38] Hirshleifer and Shapiro, "The Treatment of Risk," in *Public Expenditures and Policy Analysis*, ed. Haveman and Margolis, p. 309.

[39] McKean, *Efficiency in Government*, p. 76.

can do more than try to approximate maximization of benefits, but the point is that to the extent that they work in this direction they may improve the quality and efficiency of government expenditure. Even though the private sector has generated substantial economic benefits in the past, governments will probably be the primary generators of economic gains in the future.

This latter point suggests the possibility of the need to consider the optimum size of the government's productive activity relative to that of the private sector. Further, what does one do about the potentially socially desirable public programs that cannot compete for resources with levels of gain from private investments?

In approaching these questions it is recognized that neither governments nor private firms may undertake all profitable investments. Further, we are faced with choosing between profitable investments in the two sectors but for which there may be different goals. Government should have as a goal the avoidance of displacing more profitable opportunities in the private sector for goods having a similar social priority.[40] Similarly, government should invest as long as its gains are greater than gains in the private sector with the criteria of maximization of the net present value of social benefits evaluated at the marginal social rate of discount.[41] Thus the proper size of government in this context is operational rather than essentially ideal. As long as government can effectively produce goods and services, perhaps it should do so.

Alternatives

Alternatives to the proposed project could not be properly discussed, in this chapter until the reader had approached a basic understanding of cost-benefit analysis. Essentially, alternative projects which decision makers perceive as accomplishing the same objectives must be subjected to an in-depth analysis in the same way as the proposed project under consideration. The latter could hardly have been selected as primary without a comparison of results among several possible means of accomplishing the desired ends. The question of alternatives suggests the necessity to computerize outcomes of each alternative project under a variety of constraining conditions, and mathematical programming may be required to efficiently consider all relevant alternatives.

In reality, many considerations of alternatives may be essentially internal and thereby partial. That is to say that in many projects no other feasible alternative is presented but internally, and the project may have among its planned parts more than one way to accomplish a second-level task. For example, sale-lease decisions may occur in acquiring equipment to undertake the project. In a

[40] Stephen A. Marglin, "The Opportunity Costs of Public Investment," *Quarterly Journal of Economics* 77 (1963): 276.

[41] Peter O. Steiner, "Choosing Among Alternative Public Investments in the Water Resource Field," *American Economic Review* 49 (1959): 913.

significant way cost-effectiveness analysis of particular subportions may be valid even when a comparison among program alternatives may not be feasible.

III. Limitations to Cost-Benefit Analysis and PPBS

Among themes of current interest in the field of public expenditure economics, no subject area is more filled with conflict and criticism than the area of cost-benefit and PPBS. Cost-benefit, while it has tremendous potential usefulness, is still subject to much incompleteness. The following discussion cannot hope to do more than make the reader aware of the many theoretical issues unresolved and to discuss a few of them.

One limitation lies in the difficulty of placing monetary values on all effects of an expenditure decision. If we can place monetary values on some aspects of the public decision we do so, but there is always the possibility that the most important effects are not subject to suitable measures. Is an incomplete measure to a complex situation better than none at all? Proponents would argue that we measure as much as we can and point out the limits to the effects measured and the effects not measured to the decision makers. Opponents might argue, as does Wildavsky, that when there are many diverse types of benefits from a project and many different beneficiaries, it is difficult to list them all and avoid double counting, implying that a poor measure is worse than none.[42] This form of incompleteness is the result of aggregated data. Costs and benefits may differ widely in the minds of the various participants in the decision and among the citizenry. There are, as McKean suggests, discrepancies between individual costs (or benefits) and our conceptions of total costs and benefits. The views that all government decisions are made in complete self-interest of the politician and that all public decisions are made in the public interest are dangerous.[43] Some position between these two extremes is more likely and it will vary according to the particular decision.

Still another fault erroneously laid to the cost-benefit door is that essentially beggar-thy-neighbor policies will result from political jurisdictions attempting to reach solutions without considering adjacent jurisdictions.[44] This is not the fault of the technique; it is the fault of the political boundaries.

Another limitation to cost-benefit analysis lies in comparing one shadow price for one project with the shadow price or proxy for welfare in another totally different kind of program. While we may be satisfied to use a proxy for value (such as travel time in recreational benefits) to compare two like projects,

---

[42] Aaron Wildavsky, "The Political Economy of Efficiency: Cost-Benefit Analysis, Systems Analysis, and Program Budgeting," *Public Administration Review* 26 (1966): 292–310.

[43] Roland N. McKean, "Costs and Benefits from Different Viewpoints," in *Public Expenditure Decisions*, ed. Schaller, pp. 147–62.

[44] Neil W. Chamberlain, "Government Investment: How Scientific Can It Be?" *Challenge*, July/Aug. 1966, p. 34.

what about the case of comparing two unlike projects when we are uncertain of the fullness of our proxies for value? Without price, can we compare soup and nuts? Even with a known market price, while the monetary value is our common denominator, this does not mean that it is as good a measure in one case as another. Comparisons between unlike projects are difficult if not impossible in most instances.

There has also been controversy in the literature over the appropriate rate of discount for public investment decisions. Some have argued for using a market rate; some have argued that since interest rates for capital markets are not competitive, then no existing market rate is appropriate. Many analysts fall back on using high, low, and middle interest rates with which to discount the benefits. This procedure is all well and good if no significant change takes place, but what if it does? What do we tell the decision maker? Perhaps at one rate the project appears economic but at another rate the project appears uneconomic; such situations generally demand a good deal of explanation by the analyst to the decision maker.

In defense of the utility of the analysis, Chamberlain argues that to fault cost-benefit on the basis of not including monetary estimates of all effects amounts to demanding "perfect knowledge." [45] No means are available to us of predicting the future with complete accuracy, and no one would expect to be able to do so.

Chapter 2 Appendix

A Summary of Procedures for Implementing a Cost-Benefit Analysis

Summary of Planning Programs and Using Cost-Benefit to Evaluate the Programs

I. Introduction

   A. General goals — relate project to one or more of the following:

      1. Improve standard of living for all people

         a) Remove social and economic barriers

         b) Develop economic environment

      2. Improve health of all people

         a) Physical

         b) Mental

         c) Environmental

      3. Provide formal education

         a) Preschool

         b) Elementary and secondary

         c) Higher education

         d) Continuing education

[45] Chamberlain, "Government Investment," p. 34.

4. Provide adequate transportation

   a) Water
   b) Air
   c) Urban transit
   d) Motor vehicle transport

5. Provide a satisfactory physical environment

   a) Water supply
   b) Land development
   c) Waste disposal
   d) Conservation and beautification
   e) Drainage and flood control

6. Provide cultural and recreational opportunity

   a) Build and operate facilities
   b) Conduct recreational and cultural programs

7. Safeguard individual, his rights, and his property

   a) Crime prevention and control
   b) Traffic law enforcement
   c) Adjudicate civil disputes
   d) Fire prevention and control
   e) Disaster prevention and control
   f) Control standards of service

B. Recognition of problem — data requirements levels

   1. Survey of need is necessary to detail general problems
   2. Participatory meetings to develop problems and priorities
   3. Problem statements and potential strategies
   4. Other sources of demand

II. Program development

A. Specific statement of the problem to be solved

B. Identify the population which has the problem as stated

C. Identify goal of program and relate to overall goals in narrative
   NOTE: Goal attainment: you cannot maximize total welfare; a problem turned into a program is a suboptimization process.

D. Specify benefits measures — any program will attempt to (for the affected population) either:

   1. Maximize benefits given a fixed level of cost
   2. Minimize cost given a fixed level of benefit

E. Develop alternative programs to gain the same end

   1. Is there more than one way to develop the program?
   2. Is there a more feasible alternative to accomplish the goal?

F. Develop costs for program

G. Rank programs proposed in order of urgency (priority)

H. Design and prepare proposal for program providing costs of the program and specify points A–G above

III. What are the *constraints* under which the program works, and how do they affect the outcome of a program as planned?

   A. Physical constraints

   B. Legal constraints

   C. Administrative constraints

   D. Political constraints

   E. Income constraints

   F. Budgetary constraints

   G. Social, traditional, or religious constraints

IV. What are the impacts of the following general classes of *externalities*?

   A. Production to production

   B. Production to consumption

   C. Consumption to production

   D. Consumption to consumption

V. The impact of time. Since costs and benefits do not occur at the same time we must:

   A. Estimate the useful life of the project

   B. Estimate the time stream of benefits

   C. Estimate the time stream of costs

   D. Discount the benefits and costs back to a notion of the present values of costs and benefits

      1. For benefits: the social time preference rate — a subtraction from benefits

      2. For costs: the social opportunities cost rate — an addition to costs (may or may not be appropriate)

VI. Summary of tables of costs and benefits. Costs and benefits should be developed for each program on a single table which includes:

   A. Program costs

      1. Direct project costs (discounted if applicable)

      2. Direct individual costs (discounted as necessary)

      3. Total resource costs: the sum of points 1 and 2 above

   B. Program benefits

      1. Primary benefits (discounted as necessary)

      2. Secondary benefits (discounted)

      3. Noneconomic variables (externalities and social benefits — not measured but anticipated)

      4. Social costs alleviated (statements of benefits as a result of elimination of some other social costs)

   C. Costs and benefits combined

      1. Total cost

      2. Total benefits

      3. Net benefits or costs

VII. Summary table of costs and benefits over time

    A. Same as above only broken down into years, over the expected life of the project

    B. This can be a flexible kind of table, it should show the time facts clearly and when costs and benefits occur

VIII. Program comparisons (development of total department mix of programs). Assuming a number of alternative program proposals, follow the directions under I–VII above and then:

    A. Prepare a ranking of programs by their anticipated benefits relative to costs. In so doing, develop the following:

        1. Program name

        2. Total costs

        3. Total benefits

        4. Benefit/Cost rates

    B. Prepare a ranking for each of the following:

        1. Ranking in urgency (as developed in the problem areas under Part I, Introduction)

        2. Number of persons affected

        3. Percent of population served

        4. Per person costs

        5. Per person benefits

        6. Expected life of program

    C. Descriptively discuss the relationship between each program and its impact upon the total bundle of problems.

IX. The ongoing cost-benefit evaluation

    A. Once programs are underway, it will be necessary to evaluate them on a regular basis; a six-month evaluation is suggested during the life of the program.

    B. The evaluation should take five forms:

        1. Indices of social change (recapitulation of coefficients of disparity)

        2. Recapitulation of the cost-benefit analysis in which we compare the benefits and costs we anticipated to those which have actually occurred. Thus the initial cost and benefit analysis becomes a standard of measure to evaluate the effectiveness of the program.

        3. The development of feedback questionnaires for the population affected by the program.

        4. Evaluation meeting of staff in programs on a regular basis to determine the effectiveness of the program and its timetable.

        5. A multiple correlation analysis to determine the interrelatedness of various social and economic factors. The coefficients of partial determination then serve as indicators of the percent of change due to specific items. For example, income is a function of education and many other factors. If we have any income increase, how much of it is due to education?

Summary of Program Benefits
Form I

1. Name of committee ....

2. Date of submission ....

3. Program title ....

4. Description of project
   a) Briefly describe the program
   b) Specific statement of the problem to be solved
   c) Identify population to be served
   d) Identify relation of this project to agency goals
   e) Urgency ranking .... of TOTAL of ....
   f) Program attempts with the stated logic to (check one):
       (1) ☐ Maximize benefits given a level of cost
       (2) ☐ Minimize cost given a level of benefit
   g) What alternatives are considered to accomplish the same purpose as this program? Check one:
       (1) ☐ No alternative considered
       (2) ☐ Alternative proposal — title: ....

5. Constraints to the program. Describe each briefly.
   a) Physical constraints
   b) Legal constraints
   c) Administrative constraints
   d) Political constraints
   e) Income constraints
   f) Budgetary constraints
   g) Social or traditional constraints

6. Kind of goods to be produced ....

7. Benefits measures: describe each briefly
   a) Direct or primary benefits
   b) Indirect or secondary benefits
       (1) Production to production
       (2) Production to consumption
       (3) Consumption to production
       (4) Consumption to consumption
   c) Nonquantifiable benefits
   d) Redistribution of income impact

8. Excluded externalities. Describe each briefly.
   a) Pleasures generated by project (intangibles)
   b) Pains generated by project (intangibles)

9. Discount rate: explain basis for social time preference rate

10. Economic life of project
    a) Program funding ....
    b) Program impact ....

11. Benefits computation for project (give title) ....
    ....

12, 13. See pages 92 and 93.

12. GROSS PROJECT BENEFITS

Year	Primary Benefits[1]	Secondary Benefits[2]	Redistribution Impacts[3]	Unquantifiable Benefits[4]	Annual Benefits[5]
1.			±		
2.					
3.					
4.					
5.					
6.					
etc.					
TOTALS			±		

[1] Total annual primary benefits (without discounting) for each year. Should be in dollar amounts of estimated benefits.

[2] Total annual secondary benefits to society (without discounting) for each year. Should be in dollars of estimated benefits.

[3] Redistribution impacts are determinations of whether the benefits derived (primary and secondary) shift the distribution of local income upward toward the rich or downward toward the poor. Determine incomes of beneficiaries of both types and estimate the dollar amounts of benefits which go to recipients who have incomes above the local median family income level and those who have incomes below the local median family income. Indicate for each year. Indicate by a plus sign that amount of benefits for those above and a minus sign for benefits received by those below. Indicate for each year.

[4] Unquantifiable benefits are those impacts which may be significant but are not measured or measurable in dollar terms such as psychic benefits, etc. Denote in table with UB₁ and provide footnoted explanation. Must be included so as to prevent the economics from overshadowing all other aspects, political, social, etc. Not part of formal computation.

[5] Annual benefits are total primary and secondary benefits. Do not include redistribution impacts.

13. DISCOUNTED PROJECT BENEFITS

Year	Annual Benefits with Estimated Rate of Inflation[1] (annual benefits+inflation)	Social Time Preference Rate[2]			Present Value Estimates: Discounted Annual Benefits[3] (with discount rates)		
		High	Middle	Low	High	Middle	Low
1.							
2.							
3.							
4.							
5.							
6.							
etc.							
TOTALS		×	×	×			

[1] Take the estimated rate of inflation and multiply that rate times the annual benefits for each year from section 12. If rate is say 2% per year, then multiply benefits in year one by 1.02 assuming the benefits accrue at the end of the year. For year two, multiply by 1.04 times the annual benefits; 1.06 for year three, etc.

[2] Select a high, middle, and low rate of STP to use for computations; note discussion of this procedure in chapter discussion of discounting. Fill in the rate you intend to use and assume that that rate will be used for each year. If you use a high of 10% then the rate will be 10% of year one, 20% for year two, etc.

[3] Compute the estimate of discounted benefits for each year under the various rates of discount selected, high, middle, and low. Though not completely accurate, the easiest means of doing this discounting is to multiply the discount rate times the annual inflated benefits and deduct that product from the annual inflated benefits. For example, if annual inflated benefits for year one are $100 and you are using a discount rate of 5%, multiply 5% times $100 which will give you $5. Subtract that $5 from the $100 and you have $95, the present value of benefits received at the end of year one. Likewise in year two, the multiplier would be 10% and discounted present value of $100 worth of benefits would actually only be $90. It would be the same with other years, under the three selected discount rates. This is a kind of amateurish discounting technique; for more accurate means, see McKean's *Efficiency in Government Through Systems Analysis* cited in the bibliography.

Instruction Sheet for Summary of Program Benefits Form I

Line

1. Self-explanatory

2. Self-explanatory

3. Self-explanatory

4.   *a*) A brief description
      b) Be specific about problem or problems attacked
      c) Specify particular group of program participants — age, race, condition, etc.
      d) You must be able to identify a broad goal to which the program relates
      e) This ranking refers to program areas under Part I of Summary
      f) You cannot do both
      g) Are you drawing an alternative with which to compare? If so, also prepare summary sheets for its costs and benefits.

5. Under constraints you ought to briefly narrate what problems this program may encounter and what limitations exist. Refer to *Constraints* section in this chapter.

6. Are you producing a public good, a mixed product, or what? Indicate the class of goods and/or services as described under *Locally Produced Goods* in this chapter.

7. Benefits. Briefly describe each category of benefit you choose to use in the analysis. Under item *b*), indicate the spillovers you anticipate from the program under each subheading 1–4. Refer to the discussion on *Externalities* in this chapter. Under *c*) what items are now quantifiable or incapable of being monetized which you think are important? Use the same spillover classifications as in 7 *b*) above. Under *d*) compare the income distribution of this population with the total affected population.

8. Are there externalities which do not fall into benefits? Costs?

9. Select an STP rate which reflects low, middle, and high. Generate benefits under all 3.

10. Self-explanatory

11. Self-explanatory

12. See gross benefits sheet

13. Actual compilations of benefits. See explanatory notes on discounted benefits sheet.

Summary of Program Costs[1]

Form II

1. Name of committee ....

2. Date of submission ....

3. Program title ....

4. Description of project objective: a) purpose, b) population, c) urgency of problem

....

....

[1] Adapted from the Department of Defense Instruction 7041.3 of February 26, 1969, entitled *Economic Analysis of Proposed Department of Defense Investments.*

5. Alternative (next best) ....

....

....

6. Economic life of: *a*) program funding ....

              b) program impact ....

              c) program equipment ....

                  (1) Nonrecurring costs: explain

                      (a) Research and development

                      (b) Investment

                  (2) Recurring costs:

                      (a) Operations

                      (b) Social costs

7. Identify the expected years of cost: from .... to .... (range).

8, 9. See pages 96 and 97.

Instruction Sheet for Summary of Costs Form II

Line

1. Self-explanatory

2. Self-explanatory

3. Self-explanatory

4. Describe briefly the purpose of the program, the population to be served, and the urgency of the program (decision weighted by priority).

5. Describe either an alternative program or an internal alteration of the proposed program. Here be careful to think of the interrelatedness of this to other programs.

6. Economic life includes elements of time including funding period; number of years program will affect population (in other words, are there carry-overs beyond funding period?); physical equipment; economic life. For example, suggest the following unless sound reasons will vary the suggested lives:

    a) EDP (electronic data processing) equipment — 8 years

    b) Buildings — 25 years

    c) Operating equipment — 10 years

7. Identify specific years in which costs will occur.

8.   *a*) Nonrecurring. Break the costs into research and development (R & D) capital and other nonrecurring investments by year. By capital cost is meant plant, equipment, real estate, rehabilitation expenditures, etc. For example, you may rehabilitate a house — this initial investment falls into nonrecurring. Maintenance falls into recurring or operational. Investment costs may not all occur in the first year.

    b) Recurring costs are operational costs including personnel, material costs, travel per diem, etc. Be sure to include support costs of staff, etc. — an overhead of some kind.

    c) Sum of nonrecurring and recurring costs.

9.   *a*) Inflation factor. See notes on cost sheet number 9.

    b) Apply the appropriate discount factor. See note on cost sheet number 8.

    c) Discounted annual cost is the present value of all future annual costs. See note on cost sheet number 9.

8. GROSS PROJECT COSTS

Year	Nonrecurring		Recurring		Measurable and unmeasurable: Individual and Social Costs[5]		Total Annual Costs[6]
	R & D[1]	Capital[2]	Operational[3]	Maintenance[4]	Mc	Uc	
1.							
2.							
3.							
4.							
5.							
6.							
etc.							
TOTALS							

[1] R & D costs are those costs which are generated prior to or during the development of the program, its proposal, and evaluation.

[2] Capital costs include costs for physical equipment and plant.

[3] Operational costs include all costs of operation during each year of the program.

[4] Maintenance costs include all costs for maintaining plant and equipment.

[5] Costs include those costs born by individuals or groups which are external to the immediate cost aspects of the program. Externalities which are measurable social costs should be monetized if possible and included under Mc by type and amount. Social costs which for individuals or the society at large are apparent but not measurable in a monetary form should be measured in whatever unit is appropriate under Uc, or if not measurable in any way, should be included under items Uc_2, Uc_3, etc. Only the monetized costs become part of the formal computation.

[6] Total annual costs include the addition of all forms of monetary cost itemized in the rows for each year.

9. DISCOUNTED PROJECT COSTS

Year	Estimated Rate of Inflation Combined with Annual Costs[1]	Social Opportunity Costs Discount Rates[2]			Discounted Annual Costs[3]		
		High	Middle	Low	High	Middle	Low
1.							
2.							
3.							
4.							
5.							
6.							
etc.							
TOTALS		X	X	X			

[1] Assume a rate of inflation which is specifically relevant to the kinds of costs involved. While in the case of inflation of benefits we could use something like the Consumer Price Index to come to a loose estimate of the impact of inflation, in the case of costs, the rate of inflation is dependent upon the kind of costs incurred. There is little reason to assume that the anticipated rate of inflation over the life of the project for such things as capital expenditures (computers, typewriters, buildings, etc.) will be the same as the cost of living CPI; thus the rate of inflation under costs may differ from the rate used for benefits. If we assume an average of 4%, then we must add to the costs each year the accumulated 4%. If costs each year are $100, then costs will be increased to $104 the first year, approximately $108 the second year, etc.

[2] A social opportunity discount rate may not apply in every case. If the funds are allocated to this project and none other (bond issues for parks as an example), then the SOC rate may not apply. If funds could have been allocated to other uses on the other hand, then the SOC applies as an addition to costs. Selecting a range of 3 rates becomes a judgment of lowest anticipated return of the funds in alternative investments to the highest probable return with a middle range rate which appears most likely. See text for suggestions on rates to use.

[3] The discounted annual costs are the additions of the SOC costs to the inflated annual costs in the second column. Estimates of final discounted costs appear for the high, middle, and low rates. As a final note, it should be added that the summed columns of total discounted costs could be recapitulated to reflect the idea of social time perference for costs which do not have to be made now but can be made in the future. Some STP computations may be desirable.

Total Discounted Costs and Benefits Combined[1]

Form III

Total Discounted Benefits:

High Estimate: ....

Middle Estimate: ....

Low Estimate: ....

Nonmonetized Benefits:

Unmeasurable: explain ....

....

....

Measurable: in appropriate units with

explanation ....

....

....

Total Discounted Costs:

High Estimate: ....

Middle Estimate: ....

Low Estimate: ....

Nonmonetized Costs:

Unmeasurable: explain ....

....

....

Measurable: in appropriate units with

explanation ....

....

....

[1] Combined statement of summary of benefits and costs, monetized, measurable but not monetized and unmeasurable.

Selected Bibliography

Evaluation of Local Government Policy

ACKOFF, RUSSELL L. "Toward Quantitative Evaluation of Urban Services." In *Public Expenditure Decisions in the Urban Community*, ed. Howard G. Schaller, pp. 91–117. Washington, D.C.: Resources for the Future, 1963; distr. by Johns Hopkins Press, Baltimore.

ARROW, KENNETH J. *Social Choice and Individual Values*. Cowles Commission for Research in Economics. Monograph no. 12. New York: John Wiley & Sons, 1951.

BATOR, FRANCIS M. "The Anatomy of Market Failure." *Quarterly Journal of Economics* 72 (1958): 351–79.

――――. "The Simple Analytics of Welfare Maximization." *American Economic Review* 47 (1957): 22–59.

BAUMOL, WILLIAM J. "Informed Judgment, Rigorous Theory and Public Policy." *Southern Economic Journal* 32 (1965): 137–45.

――――. "Urban Services: Interaction of Public and Private Decisions." In *Public Expenditure Decisions in the Urban Community*, ed. Howard G. Schaller, pp. 1–18. Washington, D.C.: Resources for the Future, 1963; distr. by Johns Hopkins Press, Baltimore.

――――. *Welfare Economics and the Theory of the State*. 2d ed. Publications of the London School of Economics. Cambridge, Mass.: Harvard University Press, 1965.

BOHM, PETER. "An Approach to the Problem of Estimating Demand for Public Goods." *Swedish Journal of Economics* 73 (1971): 55–66.

BUCHANAN, JAMES M. "Positive Economics, Welfare Economics, and Political Economy." *Journal of Law and Economics* 2 (1959): 124–38.

BURK [BERGSON], ABRAM. "A Reformulation of Certain Aspects of Welfare Economics." *Quarterly Journal of Economics* 52 (1938): 310–34.

CHAMBERLAIN, NEIL W. "Government Investment: How Scientific Can It Be?" *Challenge*, July/Aug. 1966, pp. 32–35.

COASE, R. H. "The Problem of Social Cost." *Journal of Law and Economics* 3 (1960): 1–44.

DAVIS, JAMES W., JR., ED. *Politics, Programs, and Budgets: A Reader in Government Budgeting*. Englewood Cliffs, N.J.: Prentice-Hall, 1969.

DAVIS, OTTO A., AND WHINSTON, ANDREW. "Externalities, Welfare, and the Theory of Games." *Journal of Political Economy* 70 (1962): 241–62.

――――, AND WHINSTON, ANDREW. "Some Notes on Equating Private and Social Cost." *Southern Economic Journal* 32 (1965): 113–25. Also, Carnegie Institute of Technology. Reprint no. 215. Pittsburgh: Graduate School of Industrial Administration.

DEVINE, E. J. "The Treatment of Incommensurables in Cost-Benefit Analysis." *Land Economics* 42 (1966): 383–87.

DORFMAN, ROBERT, ED. *Measuring Benefits of Government Investments: Papers Presented at a Conference of Experts Held November 7–9, 1963*. Studies of Government Finance. Washington, D.C.: Brookings Institution, 1965.

DOWNS, ANTHONY. *Urban Problems and Prospects*. Markham Series in Public Policy Analysis. Chicago: Markham Publishing Co., 1970.

DUNN, ROBERT M., JR. "A Problem of Bias in Benefit-Cost Analysis: Consumer Surplus Reconsidered." *Southern Economic Journal* 33 (1967): 337–42.

ECKSTEIN, OTTO. *Public Finance*, pp. 20–36. Englewood Cliffs, N.J.: Prentice-Hall, 1964.

ENKE, STEPHEN, ED. *Defense Management*. Englewood Cliffs, N.J.: Prentice-Hall, 1967.

————. "Using Costs to Select Weapons." *Papers and Proceedings of the American Economic Association. American Economic Review* 55 (1965): 416–26.

FELDSTEIN, MARTIN S. "Net Social Benefit Calculation and the Public Investment Decision." *Oxford Economic Papers* 16 (1964): 114–31.

————. "Opportunity Cost Calculations in Cost-Benefit Analysis." *Public Finance* 19 (1964): 117–39.

————. "The Social Time Preference Discount Rate in Cost Benefit Analysis." *Economic Journal* 74 (1964): 360–79.

GEORGE WASHINGTON UNIVERSITY, WASHINGTON, D.C. State and Local Finances Project. *Implementing PPB in State, City, and County: A Report on the 5-5-5 Project.* Washington, D.C.: George Washington University, June 1969.

GEORGE WASHINGTON UNIVERSITY, WASHINGTON, D.C. State and Local Finances Project. *PPB Pilot Project Reports. From the Participating 5 States, 5 Counties, and 5 Cities.* Washington, D.C.: George Washington University, Feb. 1969.

GOLDMAN, THOMAS A., ED. *Cost-Effectiveness Analysis: New Approaches in Decision-Making.* Praeger Special Studies in U.S. Economic and Social Development. New York: Frederick A. Praeger, 1967.

GROSSE, ROBERT N., AND PROSCHAN, ARNOLD. "Military Cost Analysis." *Papers and Proceedings of the American Economic Association. American Economic Review* 55 (1965): 427–38.

HARBERGER, ARNOLD C. "The Measurement of Waste." *Papers and Proceedings of the American Economic Association. American Economic Review* 54 (1964): 58–76.

HAVEMAN, ROBERT H. "Evaluating Public Expenditures Under Conditions of Unemployment." *Monthly Labor Review* 92 (Sept. 1969): 30–33.

————, AND MARGOLIS, JULIUS, EDS. *Public Expenditures and Policy Analysis.* Chicago: Markham Publishing Co., 1970.

HINES, LAWRENCE G. "The Hazards of Benefit-Cost Analysis as a Guide to Public Investment Policy." *Public Finance* 17 (1962): 101–17.

HINRICHS, HARLEY H., AND TAYLOR, GRAEME M., COMPS. *Program Budgeting and Benefit-Cost Analysis: Cases, Text, and Readings.* Pacific Palisades, Cal.: Goodyear Publishing Co., 1969.

HIRSHLEIFER, J. "Investment Decision Under Uncertainty: Applications of the State-Preference Approach." *Quarterly Journal of Economics* 80 (1966): 252–77.

————. "Investment Decision Under Uncertainty: Choice-Theoretic Approaches." *Quarterly Journal of Economics* 79 (1965): 509–36.

JOHNSON, HARRY G. "The Economic Approach to Social Questions." *Economica* 35 (1968): 1–21.

KALDOR, NICHOLAS. "Welfare Propositions of Economics and Interpersonal Comparisons of Utility." *Economic Journal* 49 (1939): 549–52.

KRUTILLA, JOHN V. "Criteria for Evaluating Regional Development Programs." *Papers and Proceedings of the American Economic Association. American Economic Review* 45 (1955): 120–32.

LEVINE, ABRAHAM S. "Cost-Benefit Analysis and Social Welfare." *Welfare in Review* 4 (Feb. 1966): 1–11.

————. "Cost-Benefit Analysis of the Work Experience Program." *Welfare in Review* 4 (Aug./Sept. 1966): 1–9.

LIPSEY, RICHARD B., AND LANCASTER, K. KEVIN. "The General Theory of the Second Best." *Review of Economic Studies* 24 (1956): 11–32.

LITCHFIELD, NATHANIEL, AND MARGOLIS, JULIUS. "Benefit-Cost Analysis as a Tool in Urban Government Decision Making." In *Public Expenditure Decisions in the Urban Com-*

munity, ed. Howard G. Schaller, pp. 118–46. Washington, D.C.: Resources for the Future, 1963; distr. by Johns Hopkins Press, Baltimore.

MAASS, ARTHUR. "Benefit-Cost Analysis: Its Relevance to Public Investment Decisions." *Quarterly Journal of Economics* 80 (1966) : 208–26.

MARGLIN, STEPHEN A. *Public Investment Criteria: Benefit-Cost Analysis for Planned Economic Growth*. Cambridge, Mass.: M.I.T. Press, 1967.

———. "The Opportunity Costs of Public Investment." *Quarterly Journal of Economics* 77 (1963) : 274–89.

———. "The Social Rate of Discount and the Optimal Rate of Investment." *Quarterly Journal of Economics* 77 (1963) : 95–111.

MARGOLIS, JULIUS. "Secondary Benefits, External Economies, and the Justification of Public Investment." *Review of Economics and Statistics* 39 (1957) : 284–91.

McKEAN, ROLAND N. "Costs and Benefits from Different Viewpoints." In *Public Expenditure Decisions in the Urban Community*, ed. Howard G. Schaller, pp. 147–62. Washington, D.C.: Resources for the Future, 1963; distr. by Johns Hopkins Press, Baltimore.

———. *Efficiency in Government Through Systems Analysis, With Emphasis on Water Resources Development*. A Rand Corporation Research Study. Operations Research Society of America. Publications in Operations and Research, no. 3. New York: John Wiley & Sons, 1958.

MISHAN, E. J. "Criteria for Public Investment: Some Simplifying Suggestions." *Journal of Political Economy* 75 (1967) : 139–46.

———. "The Postwar Literature on Externalities: An Interpretative Essay." *Journal of Economic Literature* 9 (1971) : 1–28.

PREST, A. R., AND TURVEY, RALPH. "Cost-Benefit Analysis: A Survey." *Economic Journal* 75 (1965) : 683–735.

ROTHENBERG, JEROME. *Economic Evaluation of Urban Renewal: Conceptual Foundation of Benefit-Cost Analysis*. Studies of Government Finance. Washington, D.C.: Brookings Institution, 1967.

SAMUELSON, PAUL A. "Aspects of Public Expenditure Theories." *Review of Economics and Statistics* 40 (1958) : 332–38.

———. "Diagrammatic Exposition of Theory of Public Expenditure." *Review of Economics and Statistics* 37 (1955) : 350–56.

———. "The Pure Theory of Public Expenditure." *Review of Economics and Statistics* 36 (1954) : 387–89.

SCHALLER, HOWARD G., ED. *Public Expenditure Decisions in the Urban Community*. Washington, D.C.: Resources for the Future, 1963; distr. by Johns Hopkins Press, Baltimore.

SCHICK, ALLEN. "The Road to P.P.B.: The Stages of Budget Reform." *Public Administration Review* 26 (1966) : 243–58.

SCHULTZE, CHARLES L. *The Politics and Economics of Public Spending*. H. Rowan Gaither Lectures, delivered May 1968 at the University of California, Berkeley, under the sponsorship of the Graduate School of Business Administration and the Center for Research in Management Science. Washington, D.C.: Brookings Institution, 1968.

SCITOVSKY, TIBOR. "A Note on Welfare Propositions in Economics." *Review of Economic Studies* 9 (1941) : 77–88.

STEINER, PETER O. "Choosing Among Alternative Public Investments in the Water Resource Field." *American Economic Review* 49 (1959) : 893–916.

———. "The Role of Alternative Cost in Project Design and Selection." *Quarterly Journal of Economics* 79 (1965) : 417–30.

TURVEY, RALPH. "On Divergences between Social Cost and Private Cost." *Economica* 30 (1963) : 309–13.

————. "On Investment Choices in Electricity Generation." *Oxford Economic Papers* 15 (1963): 278–86.

————. "Present Value *Versus* Internal Rate of Return — An Essay in the Theory of Third Best." *Economic Journal* 73 (1963): 93–98.

UNIVERSITIES-NATIONAL BUREAU COMMITTEE FOR ECONOMIC RESEARCH. *Public Finances: Needs, Sources, and Utilization.* National Bureau of Economic Research Special Conference Series 12. Princeton: Princeton University Press, 1961.

WHINSTON, ANDREW B., AND DAVIS, OTTO A. "Welfare Economics and the Theory of Second Best." *Review of Economic Studies* 89 (1965): 1–14.

WILDAVSKY, AARON. "The Political Economy of Efficiency: Cost-Benefit Analysis, Systems Analysis, and Program Budgeting." *Public Administration Review* 26 (1966): 292–310.

3

Work, the Labor Force,
and Manpower Policy

This chapter describes the relation of man to his work and the national labor force in general. Moving through the regional trends in employment, we turn to a brief description of the urban labor force. We then progress to a discussion of unemployment and a description of the current national policy on manpower problems. This is the first of two chapters related to manpower policy. The next chapter goes into more explicit detail about the role and form of manpower policy at the local government level.

One note of caution should be made. The programs discussed in this chapter are example manpower programs. The sharp reduction which the Nixon administration took in manpower programs has reduced the national manpower influence to what one might call a zero level. The student may consider this decline a temporary aberration or may consider it somewhat permanent. This work assumes the former; namely, that manpower programs will return and to some extent be quite similar to the ones which are currently gutted.

I. Work and Mankind

One of the most pervasive characteristics in the history and development of western man has been the association of men and women with work. While it has meant different things in different cultures, work has been synonymous with activity which has changed both human beings and environment. Work has traditionally had some divine connotation associated with it. In fact, working has sometimes been characterized as creation itself. Work has been considered a religious duty; work has been associated with pain — for example, *trabajo* in Spanish and travail in English, both Latin derivatives, suggest the idea of suffering. When we consider the connotations of work, work is an act of man which goes far toward defining him. Through most of history men have been what they did.

Manpower refers to the use of human energy in labor activities which results in the production of marketable goods and services. Manpower planning then becomes the process of generating from within the available population of workers capable of becoming economically productive.

The Potential Danger of Manpower

When we speak of manpower we're not simply speaking of economic man, we're not considering the rational economic machine of pure competition. When we think of manpower we think of something more, in spite of the fact that the term "manpower" or human resource implicitly falls into the economic context. The danger of such a view was best stated by Kenneth E. Boulding when he said:

> The manpower concept is basically, I suspect, an engineering concept, and one of the main problems of society is to keep engineers in a decently subordinate position. Engineers imagine society as having a single well-defined end which is to be pursued with efficiency. Society is conceived as a great machine feeding manpower in at one end and grinding out maximum quantities of the Single Well-defined End . . . . There is no single well-defined end of society measured in bushels or gallons or even dollars. There are a great many different ends of a great many different people, some of which are competitive, some complementary and some independent. Moreover, there is no such thing as manpower, save as a hot abstraction to be handled with long tongs. Not manpower, but men . . . I repeat, not manpower, but men: men in their infinite variety and sacredness, in their complex personalities and unfolding desires. Man as manpower is all very well for a slave society, where man is a domestic animal, to be used for ends which are alien to him. But in a free society, man is not manpower . . . . He is a free-being, the lord of society and not its slave, the creator of demand as well as of supply.[1]

Boulding, in his brief statement, should lead us to suspect that cybernetics and human engineering may have other than desirable consequences. Thus it is as Henry David of the Manpower Council said, "Manpower resources differ from other economic resources."[2]

It is understandable why the seemingly invidious overtones of such terms as demand, supply, shortage, surplus, waste, utilization, and investment suggest mankind as a commodity. Human beings are not commodities even though their skills do bear a price in the labor market on the basis of supply and demand requirements.

> To the extent that the society cherishes individual freedom, the instruments it may use for purposeful and directive manpower development are evidently restricted. To the extent that it values individual fulfillment, however, it must strive to discover the appropriate means for realizing this goal but releasing the potentialities of all its people.[3]

[1] Henry David, ed., *Manpower Policies for a Democratic Society* (New York: Columbia University Press, 1965), p. 7.

[2] David, ed., *Manpower Policies*, p. 8.

[3] David, ed., *Manpower Policies*, p. 11.

While writers on manpower policy allude to the problem of treating human beings as a physical resource in the economic process, most provide the warning but then proceed to treat man as a commodity.

Boulding's warnings are clearly advisable, but it does seem like closing the barn door after the horse has gone. The employers and employment agencies, both public and private, have for years treated man as a commodity. This is evident in the limited approach to manpower in the past. The typical agency operation simply sifts through its openings and presents the prospective employee with the question, "What category do you wish to be placed in?" The alternatives are distinctly meat-like — you can be a "computer operator" (the bobbin on the sewing machine) or perhaps some other equally economic but subhuman category.

The problem of "commodity man" suggests an even more interesting possibility, namely that perhaps as the economy progresses and the society enlarges, industrial civilizations find that there are an increasing number of unsatisfying jobs. That is, there are more persons doing routinized and meaningless tasks.

Satisfaction with Work

There appear to be common elements which determine worker satisfaction. Chamberlain has developed a list which is applicable to the urban worker:

1. Wages
2. Physical working conditions
3. Interest in the work itself
4. Relations with peers
5. Economic security of work
6. Fair treatment by employers
7. Amount of independence in work
8. The quality of immediate management (the authority or supervisor immediately above the worker)[4]

Modern satisfactions derived from work have historical origins. We have always associated mankind with work, even to the extent that we name ourselves after our work. For example, names like Smith, Cooper, Farmer, and Mason all refer to occupations. In the medieval city with the idea of a hierarchy of men in social and economic positions, it was easy to confer value (i.e., status) on the occupational roles of persons. Further, in spite of language barriers even among Middle English dialects, it was not difficult for the citizen of one city to comprehend that the kind of work he performed existed elsewhere in his world. Historically, smaller numbers of occupations and constricted mobility created a

---

[4] Neil W. Chamberlain, *The Labor Sector: An Introduction to Labor in the American Economy* (New York: McGraw-Hill, 1965), p. 69.

world perspective of the working man as one satisfactorily fulfilling his particular allotted task and finding value in its universality, its permanence, and its relative status.

It was not only the constricted world, but also the small numbers of specialized occupations that accounted for the status satisfactions of men and women with their work. In the majority of instances, work, no matter what its nature, was widely understood — masons cut and fit stone, coopers made barrels, cordwainers made rope, smiths cast and shaped metal, etc. Only when we go into somewhat esoteric occupations does the identification and understanding of occupations by the general citizenry diminish; thus while the citizen might have understood the role of the barber, he was not likely to understand the scholarly role of the cleric or the activities of the castle quartermaster. Fortunately, with a well-ordered set of social and occupational classes, it was never necessary for the citizen to wonder too long about the role of persons much higher in status and authority.

What can we conclude from this discussion of medieval work? First is the concept of universality of occupation; second, the small numbers of different kinds of occupations; third, the constricted world picture as defined by limited mobility; fourth, a hierarchical world order which placed individuals in a particular role by dint of social class; and, finally, a value which could readily be placed upon work because of the general understanding of what that work consisted. From this picture, it would appear that within the limits of his culture and his economy, the medieval citizen had solid reasons for respecting a vocation. He held, understood, and was accepted for his occupation; in short he had status.

Compare this with modern men and women. They may work at IBM, which simply means being employed in some capacity by that company. When asked what one does for a living, the employees are forced in the majority of cases to reply, "I work at IBM," because only a few people would know what they did if they mentioned a particular job. Put yourself in the same situation. Do you when asked the above question say, "I work at . . ." or do you say, "I am a . . ." indicating the actual job you perform? Further, do you have to explain the nature of your position? Or, is it generally understood? If you cannot easily identify (define) your work, then perhaps you have a position which is less satisfying to you because fewer people can comprehend (identify) it. It does appear likely that specialization in our modern society has reduced the universality of occupations, increased the number of (kinds of) occupations, and generated the possibility that work status has been removed from the particular job itself.

If the above discussion is in any sense accurate, then job satisfaction has declined. Class distinctions are now based on income rather than work or other class potential with the result that the intrinsic importance of work in our minds may have diminished. Also there is some truth to the argument that to the extent that a worker is removed from the "total" production or creation of a good — that is, he works on only a part of the final product — there is an alienation from work which might cause him to seek satisfactions in things other than work. We have probably come to value work in the abstract rather than work in reality since we still demand that all people work, whether the work means anything or not and no matter what the nature of the work.

Worker satisfaction with jobs is complex, yet economic theory simplifies the motivation, stating that man seeks to maximize satisfaction from income (utility in the case of the consumer and profit for the producer). An interesting challenge to this idea is contained in motivator-hygiene theory. Motivator-hygiene theory posits that man has separate and independent need systems that do *not* interact. The motivator aspect defines man's need for psychological growth and is met by intrinsic job factors such as achievement, responsibility, recognition, opportunity for growth, and work enjoyment. Thus, the motivator factors provide job satisfaction. Hygiene refers to freedom from pain in man's environment, namely, extrinsic factors such as salary, status, company policy and administration, good interpersonal relationships, etc. Hygiene thus is essential to keep the worker from states of dissatisfaction.[5]

Satisfaction and dissatisfaction are thus posed as separate and independent aspects of job attitudes. Satisfaction is not the opposite of dissatisfaction. Rather the opposite of satisfaction is no satisfaction and the opposite of dissatisfaction is no satisfaction.[6]

Nickson and Karp in empirically applying this theory to a group of working poor blacks discovered among other things that the sampled persons changed jobs when motivator and/or hygiene factors were low.[7] Measuring the person's perceptions of deprivation in the two areas of need is the significant aspect. It relates the idea that the worker's perception of his job is the principal source of understanding satisfaction and that deprivation in either area of need is independent of the other. The motivating factors are the source of *satisfactions* while the hygiene factors keep man from a state of *dissatisfaction*.

If you are poor, then hygiene factors in jobs may be inadequate. Likewise, the poor may be poor in motivation, deprived in this area of need as well.

The implications of this study for policy makers are rather clear. Take the case of an income guarantee program which provides good incomes, salaries, or benefits, but neglects the possibilities for responsibilities, opportunities for growth,

[5] Jack W. Nickson, Jr., and H. B. Karp, "An Application of Motivator-Hygiene Theory to Motivational Patterns and Economic Variables Among the Black, Working Poor," paper presented at the Southern Economic Association Meeting, Washington, D.C., November 10, 1972, pp. 1–2. This paper is based on the work of Frederick Herzberg, Bernard Mausner, and Barbara Snyderman, *The Motivation to Work*, 2d ed. (New York: John Wiley & Sons, 1959).

[6] Nickson and Karp, "An Application of Motivator-Hygiene," p. 2.

[7] Nickson and Karp, "An Application of Motivator-Hygiene," pp. 9–10.

etc. — it eliminates dissatisfaction but does little that is satisfying. Piecemeal policy tends to concentrate on one aspect or the other but does not emphasize both aspects. Neglected need is therefore common in public programs of many kinds.

The foregoing discussion serves only to qualify what we might think about job satisfactions and to force a recognition that job and work satisfactions are complex. Considerable elaboration is required to develop a useful set of categories. One means of developing categories is to attempt to analyze motivations by observing behavior rather than attempting to fathom satisfactions.

Motives for Labor Force Participation

Why do people work? That sounds like a naïve question, but it is one which we are rather uncertain of answering in light of our discussion in the previous sections. Fundamentally, people work in order to live, but many may well live in order to work. The man who retires early and spends his remaining days happily engaged in some form of personal activity is an indication of a balanced existence between work and leisure which most of us never develop. The ordinary situation (which we do not see on television very often) is the man who, upon retiring, is dead within the year from loss of status, justification, or simply loss of meaningful activity. Few males live beyond the first few years of retirement.

Perhaps the principal reason for working, aside from economic survival, is the compulsions which modern urban society forces upon us. In the previous section we discussed satisfaction with work, while in this section we are talking about reasons for working. The pressures are constant, daily, and vigorous. We are required to be nearly compulsive consumers. We are required to work full time; part-time jobs are punitively low paying. It is usually a case of work full time or no work. Even women, who in this society have until recently seldom been in the pay-for-work labor force, are now regularly employed, and the pressure for all women, particularly educated women, to work is enormous. A woman who graduates from college is asked, "What are you going to do?"; an answer of "nothing" is not usually acceptable.

With great pressures to work we never stop to ask would we work if we did not have to in order to live? For many people the answer is that they would continue to work even if they had independent means. What is more curious is the previously mentioned idea that some of us may well have jobs to which we attach little pleasure or that we heartily dislike. Even so, most of us would keep our jobs because free time hangs heavily on us. As a man's work life comes to an end, isn't it ironic that the company gives him a gold watch? It is adding insult to injury to remind a man that he has spent numerous years of his life performing a routine task for which he received little else than pay and then suggest to him that he can carry this golden dictator home with him. Our society is still work dominated; of that there is no question.

In their analysis of labor force participation rates, Bowen and Finegan noted several causal factors which affect positively (those marked with +) or negatively (those marked with –) participation in the labor force. Broadly conceived, these factors present the key forces which lead to greater or lesser amounts of labor force participation within households. Included as factors were:

I. Tastes [of potential or actual workers]
  A. Tastes for money income [+] [depend on:]
    1. Number of persons in the household [+]
    2. Differential between "permanent income" and current income: negative transitory income caused, e.g., by unemployment of a regular worker [+]
    3. Amount of fixed obligations such as interest payments, debt obligations, property taxes, etc. [+]
    4. Anticipated expenditures on such items as education, as approximated by number of children nearing college age [+]
  B. Tastes for market work per se [+] [depend on:]
    1. Health: poor [–]
    2. Education [+]
    3. Color and sex combined: Negro male [–], Negro female [+]
    4. Marital status and sex combined: married male [+] married female [–]
  C. Tastes for "home" goods [–] [depend on:]
    1. Number of young children [–]
    2. Size of house [–]
  D. Tastes for unpaid work in the home [–] [depend on:]
    1. Sex: Females [–]
  E. Tastes for additional schooling [–] [depend on:]
    1. School enrollment status: enrolled [–]
  F. Tastes for leisure [–] [depend on:]
    1. Location of residence: good climate [–]
  G. Family rules and decision-making processes [?]

II. Expected market earnings rates: substitution effects [+] [depend on:]
  A. General job prospects [+]
    1. Average market wage rates [+]
    2. Cost of getting to jobs in local labor market as affected by such factors as availability, convenience, and cost of public transportation [–]
    3. Unemployment rate in local labor market [–]
  B. Group job prospects [+]
    1. Demand for the particular market skills possessed by family members as affected by the industrial and occupational mix of the area [+]

    2. Supply of persons in the area with skills and job preferences similar to those of family members [−]

  C. Personal job prospects [+]
    1. Age [+ up to some age level and then −]
    2. Sex: males [+]
    3. Health: poor [−]
    4. Education [+]
    5. Experience [+]
    6. Color [generally −]
    7. Proximity of residence to job opportunities [+]

III. Expected nonmarket earnings rates: substitution effects [−] [depend on:]

  A. Productivity of family members in "home" tasks [−]
    1. Sex: females [−]

  B. Costs of having non-family members perform essential home tasks [−]
    1. Wages of domestic servants [−]
    2. Prices per unit of output of home appliances such as dishwashers [−]
    3. Cost of nursery schools or "child-care centers," including elementary schools [−]

  C. Expected rate of return on the education of family members [−]
    1. Average rate of return on education [−]
    2. Expected rates of return for particular family members, as affected by age, sex, color, aptitude [−]

IV. Family resources [−] [are a function of:]

  A. Potential labor supply [−]
    1. Number of potential earners in the household [−]

  B. Expected market earnings rates: income effects [−]
    [Same as II, with signs reversed.]

  C. Expected non-market earnings rates: income effects [−]
    [Same as III.]

  D. "Other (non-labor) income" and wealth of the household [−]
    1. Assets [−]
    2. Earnings on assets [−]
    3. Gifts, inheritances, and windfalls [−]
    4. Pensions and welfare payments [−] [8]

---

[8] From William G. Bowen and T. Aldrich Finegan, *The Economics of Labor Force Participation* (Princeton: Princeton University Press, 1969), pp. 20–21. Copyright © 1969 by Princeton University Press. Reprinted by permission of Princeton University Press.

Let us take an example of how one might further understand Bowen's and Finegan's derived motivations. Consider adult males not in the labor force. How do we account for their situation? Obviously, if it is a matter of choice there are more negative forces operating than positive ones.

Susan Holland points out that the extension of retirement benefits and private pension plans to men in their early 60's has continued the downward trend in their rate of participation in the labor force.[9] Some proportion of male workers have been squeezed out of the labor force by economic factors beyond their control.

Of course, nonparticipation in the labor force means different things to men of different age groups. For younger men the main reason would be school attendance while in an age group which approaches 65, retirement is contemplated by some and others are disabled by ill health or disability. But in the ages between 18 and 65, work is still an economic necessity for the majority of males, and Holland argues that "nonparticipation is frequently an evidence of deprivation." While it is not altogether possible to determine the real degree of deprivation, we do know that as of 1966 at least 10% of the men between the ages of 18 and 64 were not in the labor force. With such a high percentage of persons in the adult man's age group not in the labor force, some special consideration should be given to the nonparticipant.[10]

With regard to older men in the ten years between 1956 and 1966, nonparticipation rose among men age 55 to 64 from 11.5 to 15.5% of the population. The largest amount of this increase took place among men between the ages of 60 and 64 and partially could be attributed to voluntary retirement and mandatory or forced retirement. The greater tendency of men with low educational attainment, low earnings, and poor work histories to withdraw from the labor force indicates why the proportion of nonparticipants in this older group is higher for nonwhites than for whites — 19% as opposed to 15%. At the same time, we should note that the principal amount of withdrawal from the labor force among these older men comes almost entirely among those with the lowest educational attainment. We cannot perceive early retirement as being, in any real sense, a voluntary attribute on the part of the workers.

Within the central ages 25 to 54, the labor force has traditionally been stable and the proportion not in the labor force has been low, under 4% annually. In the decade 1956 to 1966 there was little change in this statistic.

Among the 2.1 million nonparticipants ages 18 to 24, 1.8 million of them were attending school. Another quarter of a million were out of the labor force for other reasons such as waiting to go into the armed forces or recovering from a short-term illness.

[9] Susan S. Holland, "Adult Men Not in the Labor Force," *Monthly Labor Review* 90 (Mar. 1967): 5–15.

[10] Holland, "Adult Men," p. 5.

II. The Labor Force

To the economist, labor represents one of the four basic factors of production (land, labor, capital, entrepreneurship), factors which are combined in a variety of ways to produce the goods and services which represent the outputs of the economy. Labor productivity can be improved by the acquisition of skills, training, and education and by the use of improved capital and tools. Unlike the other factors of production, labor cannot be separated from people — it is the animate factor. Also, as the human resource, labor represents the only factor capable of buying outputs. Relative to the other factors of production, another characteristic of labor is its inelastic demand; this inelasticity is caused by lack of mobility of labor and the time necessary for labor to learn and acquire new skills.

The National Labor Force

By definition (and somewhat arbitrarily so) the labor force contains almost 88 million Americans, or about 59% of our total population. Within the civilian labor force one of the most relentless trends is the decline in agricultural workers. From 1950 to 1972 agricultural workers declined from 7.1 million to 3.3 million. Nonagricultural employment rose over the same time from about 62 million to 85 million employed workers. While this comparison relates to major changes in the labor force, it is also an indicator of continuing urbanization in the United States labor force.[11]

A further characteristic of our civilian labor force is the rising number of women who are working. In 1950 there were 17.3 million women employed, and by 1972 this figure had grown to 30.7 million. Male employment over the same time period increased from 42 million to 50 million. While female employment relative to male employment is rising, the unemployment rates continue to be nearly 25% greater among women.[12]

A third aspect of the labor force is the age distribution over time. There appears to be a decline in the number of persons in the labor force who are 65 years or older. In 1950, persons in the labor force over 65 represented 4.8% of the total while in 1971 this figure had dropped to 3.6%. Further, there appears to be a trend in recent years toward greater numbers of persons 16 to 24 years of age in the labor force. This trend is apparent among both males and females and is supported by the decline in average age of the population.[13]

The labor force is widely dispersed among a variety of occupations. Among nonagricultural workers, the largest number work in manufacturing — about 18.7 million in 1972. Not too far below comes wholesale-retail trade with 15.4

[11] U.S. Bureau of the Census, Department of Commerce, *Statistical Abstract of the United States, 1973* (Washington, D.C.: U.S. Government Printing Office, 1973), table 340, p. 216.

[12] U.S. Bureau of the Census, *Statistical Abstract*, table 340, p. 216.

[13] U.S. Bureau of the Census, *Statistical Abstract*, table 341, p. 217.

million workers, government with 13.4 million, and service industries with 12.2 million workers.[14]

When other occupational categories are considered, the largest single category is white-collar workers which in 1972 numbered 39 million. Blue-collar workers are next with 28 million, followed by service workers and farm workers. While farm workers are declining in number, and blue-collar workers are relatively constant, white-collar and service workers are increasing relative to total. The area which has evidenced the greatest growth within white-collar employment has been professional and technical workers.[15]

A further feature of the American labor force is its productivity. Using 1967 as the base and measuring productivity by output per man hour, productivity has increased by about 60% from 1950 to 1971.[16] Compensation increased by about the same amount over the same period. Wages and output have gone up over the years as workers sought to gain pay increases to match productivity increases.

Earnings, while higher for males than for females, vary considerably in the economy, with a range extending from farm laborers and foremen with median annual earnings of $779 to physicians and surgeons with median earnings of nearly $25,000. Median earnings for all male workers in 1970 was $7,152, for females $2,730.[17] Groups included in these medians are operatives and kindred workers, clerical and kindred workers, service workers, laborers and farm laborers, as well as some categories of workers such as self-employed people in retailing and farm workers who are not self-employed.

Before we turn to an examination of the local labor force it should be recognized that cities exist in regions, and regional economic differences are quite significant. If one is to study an individual city and its labor market, one must place that city in the context of the region into which it falls. The unemployment rate in the Pacific region in 1971 was 8.7% of the total regional labor force, while only 4.3% of the West-North-Central regional labor force was unemployed (table 1). Since the relation between city growth and development is keyed to the region in which the city exists, such differences in employment will suggest the likelihood of success of a city's attempts to deal with unemployment problems.

Regionally, unemployment among minorities is greater than among whites. Usually twice as high as the white unemployment rate, rates for minorities range from a low of 7.4% in the South Atlantic region to a high of 16.2% in the New England region.

The Urban Labor Force

When we turn to the characteristics of the urban labor force, we should be aware that the urban labor force is essentially a mirror of the nonagricultural

[14] U.S. Bureau of the Census, *Statistical Abstract*, table 361, p. 225.
[15] U.S. Bureau of the Census, *Statistical Abstract*, table 366, p. 230.
[16] U.S. Bureau of the Census, *Statistical Abstract*, table 369, p. 232.
[17] U.S. Bureau of the Census, *Statistical Abstract*, table 379, p. 237.

TABLE 1

REGIONAL UNEMPLOYMENT, 1971
(PERCENTAGE UNEMPLOYED OF LABOR FORCE)

Region	Percentage of Total Labor Force Unemployed	Percentage of Minority Races Unemployed
New England	6.9	16.2
Middle Atlantic	6.6	8.5
East-North-Central	6.0	13.3
West-North-Central	4.3	10.4
South Atlantic	4.5	7.4
East-South-Central	5.2	10.1
West-South-Central	5.3	11.0
Mountain	6.1	11.5
Pacific	8.7	10.6

Source: Modified from U.S. Bureau of the Census, Department of Commerce, *Statistical Abstract of the United States, 1973* (Washington, D.C.: U.S. Government Printing Office, 1973), table 352, p. 222.

regional or national labor force. Within cities, however, there can be great differences, and among cities there are widely differing patterns of employment and economic activity.

The most obvious principal difference in the urban labor force is the insignificant amount of agricultural work. A second difference is that wage levels and incomes tend to be higher in urban areas than in the nation. For example, national median family income in 1970 was estimated to be $9,867 and for all urban families the median was higher at $10,006. On the other hand, prices are not much higher in urban areas than for the nation as a whole.

Some further characteristics of the labor force in Standard Metropolitan Statistical Areas (a compilation of data from the largest cities) are noted in table 2.

Employment by industrial type varies among cities. Some cities have relatively more manufacturing employment than others. Some have more government employment than others. What appear to be the kinds of employment which are proportionally similar among cities and what kinds vary widely among cities?

A coefficient of variation calculated for the above employment categories and reproduced in table 2 shows just how wide relative variation can be among cities. The interpretation one should place on the coefficients is as follows: as a measure of relative variation, a coefficient by itself shows little, but when compared with other coefficients of variation it can be interpreted to mean that the higher the value of the coefficient, the greater the variation, or, in other words, the greater the relative amount of dispersion. Our interest in the value is in

TABLE 2

LABOR FORCE CHARACTERISTICS FOR 106 SMSAs
WITH POPULATIONS OF 250,000 OR MORE*, 1969

Employment	Mean of Total Urban Labor Force	Standard Deviation (in %)	Coefficient of Variation V
Manufacturing	28.6%	14.6	.51
Wholesale/retail	21.6	7.9	.36
Services	15.4	5.8	.37
Transportation and public utilities	6.7	3.0	.44
Contract construction	5.5	2.4	.43
Finance, insurance, and real estate	5.0	2.3	.46
Government	17.0	8.6	.50
Total	98.8†		

* Excludes the 5 largest, New York, Boston, Philadelphia, Chicago, and Los Angeles.

† Excludes categories for which data are not available. Differences due to rounding.

Source: Compiled from U.S. Bureau of the Census, Department of Commerce, *Statistical Abstract of the United States, 1971, Metropolitan Area Statistics* (Washington, D.C.: U.S. Government Printing Office, 1971), table 1, p. 836.

comparing the relative dispersion among the forms of employment noted in table 2. The result provides some indication of the variation in the relative proportion of employment in various categories among these large Standard Metropolitan Statistical Areas (SMSAs). A low coefficient of variation (relative to others) would indicate that city size appears to make less difference to proportions of employment within a category. In other words, these large cities have similar proportions of employees in the employment category in question. Looking at table 2 we see that two categories of employment fall into this latter category. Wholesale and retail trade and Services employment appear to be more nearly proportional among these large SMSAs. On the other end of the spectrum, Government and Manufacturing employment vary widely in proportion among these same urban areas. The other three categories, Transportation and public utilities, Contract construction, and Finance, insurance, and real estate, exhibit a kind of middle range of variation in proportions. Such data reflect the variation in structure of the economies of various SMSAs and would appear to indicate that government and manufacturing employment is likely to be a less predictable form of employment among cities than would be the case for wholesale-retail or service occupations.

Urban Unemployment

While unemployment rates in Standard Metropolitan Statistical Areas in 1971 were estimated to be an average of 6.3%, unemployment rates nationally were lower at 5.9% (table 3). Unemployment rates in SMSAs were higher

TABLE 3

LABOR FORCE, EMPLOYMENT, AND UNEMPLOYMENT IN SELECTED AREAS, 1971
(IN MILLIONS OF PERSONS 16 YEARS OLD AND OVER, EXCEPT PERCENTAGE)

| | | | Percentage Unemployed | | |
| | | | | (% of Total %) | |
Area	Civilian Labor Force	Employed	Total	White	Negro and Other
United States Total	84.1	79.1	5.9	5.5	9.9
All SMSAs	55.1	51.6	6.3	5.7	10.2
With 250,000 inhabitants or more	47.2	44.2	6.3	5.7	10.1
Urban poverty neighborhoods	6.0	5.5	9.7	8.0	12.4
Other urban neighborhoods	41.1	38.7	5.8	5.5	8.7
20 largest metropolitan areas	27.8	26.0	6.4	5.8	9.9
Central cities	11.9	11.0	7.2	6.3	9.8
Suburban rings	15.9	15.0	5.8	5.6	10.6
With less than 250,000 inhabitants	7.9	7.4	6.1	5.6	11.2
Nonmetropolitan areas	29.0	27.5	5.3	5.0	8.8
Nonfarm	25.4	24.0	5.7	5.4	9.2
Farm	3.6	3.5	2.5	2.2	6.2

Source: U.S. Bureau of the Census, Department of Commerce, *Statistical Abstract of the United States, 1973* (Washington, D.C.: U.S. Government Printing Office, 1973), table 355, p. 233.

than the national average for both whites — at 5.7% as compared to the national figure of 5.5% — and nonwhites — at 10.2% as compared to 9.9% nationally. These figures represent a change in unemployment rates between large city-regions and the nation. Until recently the city-region was favored with lower than national rates of unemployment. Whether the city will continue to suffer higher rates of unemployment is not known, but at least during recent years of relatively high unemployment, the large urban area has suffered more than the nation as a whole.

Major differences in unemployment rates of urban areas lie not in comparisons with national data, however, but within urban areas themselves. Greater disparities exist within urban areas as exemplified by analyzing the 1971 unemployment rate in SMSAs of 6.3%. In the suburbs, the rate of unemployment was 5.8%, while within the central city the rate was higher at 7.2% (table 3). Arbitrarily selecting as urban poverty neighborhoods those with family incomes in the lowest 20%, the unemployment rate among citizens of these low income neighborhoods was 9.7% compared to a 5.8% rate in the other urban neighborhoods in large cities (table 3). A difference can be seen between the white-nonwhite unemployment rates in the two classes of urban neighborhoods. In the low income or poverty neighborhood the unemployment rate for whites was 8.0% as compared to the nonwhite rate of 12.4%. Even in the other urban neighborhood category, the rate of unemployment among nonwhites was 8.7% compared to 5.5% for whites. Thus another disparity is that nonwhites in non-poverty neighborhoods have the same unemployment rate as whites in the poverty neighborhood. Following this point, the same data suggest that whites fare better in the city than nonwhites.

Additional evidence of metropolitan disparities exists when we consider age groups in the city. In poverty neighborhoods of large cities, the unemployment rate among youth ages 16 to 19 years is high at from 20 to 38%; even in other white urban neighborhoods, the unemployment rate for this age group is 16 to 32% (table 4). Adding dimension to this point is the idea that females in low-income or poverty neighborhoods fare better than males. For the males over the age of twenty who live in poverty neighborhoods the unemployment rate is 10.2% for nonwhites and 7.1% for whites. In the same two racial categories, the rates for females are lower than for males. The reverse is normally true; that is, in other urban neighborhoods, the unemployment rate is higher among females than among males.

In summarizing unemployment in cities, let us analyze unemployment rates presented in table 5. The data are fragmentary and rates are lower than is currently true, but the analysis serves to reveal the wide differences in urban unemployment among the ninety-six largest metropolitan areas. Seven of the SMSAs had unemployment rates in 1969 of less than 2% while twenty-nine SMSAs had unemployment rates which were similar to the national rate of 3.5% for that year, a rate which was also the mean rate for SMSAs in this class size.

TABLE 4

UNEMPLOYMENT IN URBAN NEIGHBORHOODS
BY RACE, 1971

Race	Urban Low Income	Other Urban
White	8.0%	5.5%
16 to 19 years old	20.0	16.0
20 years and over:		
Male	7.1	4.1
Female	6.6	5.3
Nonwhite	12.4	8.7
16 to 19 years old	38.0	32.0
20 years and over:		
Male	10.2	6.7
Female	10.0	7.5

Source: U.S. Bureau of the Census, Department of Commerce, *Statistical Abstract of the United States, 1973* (Washington, D.C.: U.S. Government Printing Office, 1973), table 356, p. 223.

TABLE 5

UNEMPLOYMENT RATES AMONG 96 SMSAS
WITH POPULATIONS IN EXCESS OF 250,000 FOR 1969*

Annual Average Unemployment Rate	Number of SMSAs	Percentage
1.0–1.9	7	7.3
2.0–2.9	41	41.5
3.0–3.9	29	36.2
4.0–4.9	14	14.5
5.0–5.9	5	5.2
Total number	96	

* Excludes SMSAs where data is not available, including Orlando, Florida; Tucson, Arizona; Bakersfield, California; Columbia, South Carolina; Duluth-Superior; Ft. Lauderdale-Hollywood; Hartford and Knoxville, Tennessee.

Source: U.S. Bureau of the Census, Department of Commerce, *Statistical Abstract of the United States, 1971* (Washington, D.C.: U.S. Government Printing Office, 1971), table 1, p. 837.

In our concern with urban unemployment, aside from a recognition of the personal suffering which afflicts unemployed persons, we should recognize that unemployment of persons in the city creates significant economic waste. Growth of the local economy depends upon utilizing resources effectively. Efficiency and growth cannot be achieved when large segments of the labor force are unemployed. Unemployment therefore is quite costly to the city.

The Economic Costs of Unemployment[18]

Until recent years the notions about the costs of unemployment were analyzed by economists in a limited way. Such costs as the loss of productive activity were of primary concern. Today we recognize that the costs of unemployment are numerous and of considerable variety. Understanding unemployment is made more difficult because of its interrelationships with underemployment, delayed entrance into the job market, premature exit from the labor market, individual family incomes, absence of employment rights and benefits, poverty, and limited or nonexistent savings; in addition, the longer a worker is out of the labor force, the more difficult it is for him to find a position.[19] Being out of work generates barriers to reentry for many people. In particular, Ginzberg notes three groups:

> Those out of the labor force who want to work, those in the labor force who would prefer to remain at work but are forced out, and those who are underemployed and who want and need a job which will enable them to support themselves and their dependents.[20]

[18] This section is based on Eli Ginzberg's *Manpower Agenda for America* (New York: McGraw-Hill, 1968).

[19] Ginzberg, *Manpower Agenda for America*, p. 107.

[20] Ginzberg, *Manpower Agenda for America*, p. 107.

People are expected to support themselves in our society, and when one does not there is the very real belief that there is something seriously wrong with the person. Once fallen from grace, particularly during times of tight labor markets, many persons find themselves in continually worsening situations in which even if they regain employment, it is at a lower status job with reduced pay which eventually lands the erstwhile self-supporting family in poverty.[21] Trying to "hold body and soul together" puts the family in the position of merely seeking any income, even part-time income, thus forcing family members into low-paying jobs simply out of desperation. Once in these low-paying jobs, many people find it difficult if not impossible to gain something better.

If the local economy suffers from relatively high unemployment rates, there may also occur the phenomenon of delayed entrance into the local labor market. Students may stay in school merely because there are no jobs available.[22]

Another aspect of a loose labor market can be found in the pressure of others for jobs, a pressure which may force the early exit of some workers from the labor force.[23] Almost impossible to measure, this fact is obvious in situations where older workers may be considered by employers to be doing a marginal job and are replaced when there is an abundance of persons seeking jobs; it is common to note this among persons above 60 years of age.

A further feature generating costs for unemployed persons and social losses is the situation of loss of benefits and rights in social security. Persons who become unemployed may lose social security benefits at a later date; they may lose pension rights and in many cases not qualify for unemployment compensation due to the loss of a job.[24] One should not overlook the loss of such things as hospitalization insurance which ceases when the position is lost. Even when such persons gain new employment they may lose benefits like pensions from former jobs since most pension funds are not vested.

Another form of loss to society comes in the voting patterns of the unemployed. Ginzberg notes that in the 1964 election 73% of the employed voted while only 58% of the unemployed voted.[25] Loss of job may result in the failure to participate in the electoral process. Unemployed persons in the society may withdraw from that society; persons who have never been adequately employed may never have truly belonged to the society.

Chronically unemployed persons are often a loss to society and a loss to themselves. The problems of the inner city are primarily problems of poverty from unemployment and all the implications which that fact suggests. One should not discount racial bias in urban ferment, but even part of the racial bias is merely economic competition for too few jobs.

[21] Ginzberg, *Manpower Agenda for America*, p. 111.
[22] Ginzberg, *Manpower Agenda for America*, p. 109.
[23] Ginzberg, *Manpower Agenda for America*, p. 109.
[24] Ginzberg, *Manpower Agenda for America*, p. 113.
[25] Ginzberg, *Manpower Agenda for America*, p. 113.

While some may argue that mobility is what is necessary to match workers up with available jobs (e.g., migrant workers), some studies show that during times of unemployment mobility between city and farm slows down considerably.[26] Mobility as policy may not aid unemployment problems but may simply aggravate them since the costs of searching for jobs can be considerable.

Another form of cost which Ginzberg notes is the destruction of family life.[27] Broken families are common among low-income or irregularly employed families. When the head of household is unemployed, his status may be lost, his self-esteem reduced, and the consequent results for his family can be disastrous — often a separation. Under such circumstances, the problem of unemployment for the household head is measured in terms of lost opportunities for his children.

Unemployment can also lead to reductions in the quality of education received and even withdrawal from the educational process. While it may not be necessary for middle-class children to remain in school to have later opportunities at desirable employment, the educational system still represents one of the few opportunities out of poverty for children in poor families.

There are other forms of unemployment costs. The military represents an opportunity but one which is not available to many deprived persons because of poor health, illiteracy, and mental tests which require an eighth-grade education. The family which has uneven support will in many instances live in substandard housing. Medical care may be inferior and health may interfere with normal functioning. Low incomes contribute to mental retardation since a high percentage of women who do not receive prenatal care have premature births, which in turn is a primary cause of retardation. Rates of infant and maternal mortality are highly associated with prenatal and postnatal care, which in turn depends upon income for quality and quantity. Emotional problems appear to be associated with low income and unemployment: suicide rates are higher and psychoses appear generally higher.[28]

The costs of unemployment are considerable and the list of costs of this type is nearly endless. Relatively high degrees of unemployment are associated with almost every significant social problem. Whether the problem be medical, criminal, educational, a problem of age or housing, unemployment lies as root cause or effect leading to other causes.

III. The Idea of Manpower Policy

Traditionally we have depended heavily on the so-called free market to allocate resources, including labor resources. Shifts away from a reliance on the market are few but come from an increasing knowledge of the limitations of the capitalistic economy. We recognize that there will always be situations in our

[26] Ginzberg, *Manpower Agenda for America*, pp. 115–16.
[27] Ginzberg, *Manpower Agenda for America*, p. 116.
[28] Ginzberg, *Manpower Agenda for America*, pp. 119, 121.

economy which demand policy intervention by government. The private market may allocate most resources in a reasonably efficient manner, but for a black man living in the ghetto the labor market mechanism is a bus which passes him by, leaving him standing on the street corner. The economic system does not include places or positions of employment for all who wish to work. With the labor market not always responsive to changes in wage levels, fluctuations in the labor force do not occur. In recent periods of high and increasing wages, the labor market has failed to provide a smooth flow of labor and consistent employment for many.

The traditional theory of competitive economics assumes a relatively free man. This economic man has a number of characteristics which make it possible for him to move through the economic system with a kind of surety. If, for example, we had a perfectly competitive labor market on the supply side, workers would have full knowledge of the market including information on wages and opportunities available to them. Secondly, workers would be entirely rational and respond to different wage and salary considerations in such a way as to maximize their opportunities. A third characteristic of a perfect labor market would make every worker completely mobile. That is, he would have his choice (with perfect knowledge) of a variety of jobs in a variety of locales and the ability to get to them. Finally, as far as workers are concerned, there would be no artificial constraints operating upon their behavior. In other words, there would be no labor unions, and each worker or laborer would decide among the opportunities at the wage levels offered.

The above characteristics describe competition on the supply side of the market. In order to complete the picture we must consider the demand conditions or, in other words, the conditions in a perfectly competitive labor market as far as the employers are concerned. On the demand side of the market, employers would act individually; they would not respond to what their competitors were doing in the offering of wages and fringe benefits. Secondly, the employer would have as a requirement in all short-run cases to maximize profit. Third, just as in the case of employees, the perfectly competitive employer would have a thorough knowledge of the market rates of pay and the other necessary information to be completely knowledgeable about the markets in which he functions. A fourth characteristic of the employer, again similar to that of the employee, would be that he undertakes no concerted action; that is, he would act independently of all of his competitors and his share of the market in which he functions would be small enough so he cannot control the prices he pays for labor.

If we have perfect competition in labor markets, then the barter in the marketplace determines wages. In this manner the market mechanism allocates resources in an optimal way. What this essentially means is that, in theory, the competitive market provides us with the most that we can gain from available economic resources.

How would such a market operate? In economics we ordinarily imagine that a market is a place where, dependent upon the laws of supply and demand, exchange of goods takes place. By this we do not mean necessarily a specific geographic market such as a stock exchange. Rather, we can think of a market for labor as largely being a time and a situation in which many exchanges of the same type take place. For example, there is a market for new cars; there is also a market for tool and die makers; many markets exist for many kinds of occupational talents. Finally, another way in which we might perceive a market or describe its characteristics is to suggest that the extent of the labor market depends upon the degree to which the competitive economic conditions apply — that is, the degree to which markets are constrained whether it be by the unwillingness of a laborer to move from one town to another, or the actions of a monopolist in a particular geographic area. The limits of the market can in some sense be characterized by the constraints or imperfections under which the market functions.

The need for manpower policy results from essential failures in the marketplace. Imperfections arise which do not permit efficient allocation of resources. Monopolists appear, labor unions arise, or other imperfections become apparent. Unfortunately, eliminating one imperfection does not make the market more competitive. Thus manpower policy arises because of market failure, not in order to create competitive markets, but as a substitute for the market.

Active Manpower Policy

The purpose of manpower policy is to provide a smooth flow of labor, but it has not typically been designed to deal with social problems. This rather cold-blooded approach to people out of work essentially says, "All of you poor or unskilled who are capable of working, given some improvements in your skills, (and indeed, somewhat moralistically, your attitudes) we will attempt to ready you for the labor market. For those of you who for one reason or another are disqualified (because of handicap, intelligence, illness, age, etc.), don't call us, we will call you." In a more moderate vein, we may return to manpower and distinguish between active manpower policies and redundancy policies.

Active manpower policies are redeployment and retraining measures designed to generate economic gains for the economy and society. Redundancy policies are redeployment policies which have as their purpose the alleviation of hardships of individuals or social problems more broadly.[29] A redundant worker is one who is no longer required in the economy. Given the level of his skills and the demand for them in the market, he is an obsolete factor of production. Unlike active manpower, redundancy policy is related to social policy rather than to economic effect.

[29] A. D. Smith, "Active Manpower and Redundancy Policies: Their Costs and Benefits," *International Labour Review* 95 (1967): 51.

We have seen a rise in active manpower policies over recent years. An example of an active manpower policy is the case of any unemployed worker successfully completing a retraining course and being reemployed. As well, certain redundancy practices have become entrenched. An example of such a redundancy policy is the internal transfer negotiated between management and unions where the worker is simply transferred to another job rather than lose employment. In this case, it is likely that the efficiency of the output of that economic unit is reduced to the extent that the internally redeployed worker does not have the skills necessary to undertake his new activity.

Active manpower policy is gauged to stimulate economic growth which promotes social well-being. As well, it is increasingly recognized that the society has a responsibility to protect individuals from hardships they may suffer as a result of economic progress. An acceptable approach to both the economic and social problems accompanying these structural adjustments would be to promote an efficient economic distribution of the labor force by means of active manpower policy and to deal with any social problems by means of the appropriate redundancy policies.[30] The point is clear enough: if society benefits from the economic fruits of active manpower policy, then it must bear the costs of redundancy policy as well. Too often in the economy we have promised to the strong that they may exercise their strength, but for the weak we have only suggested that perhaps they should become stronger.

When economic progress generates benefits and structural changes occur, the benefits are spread throughout the society; workers, capitalists, and consumers enjoy some of the benefits of economic change, but when a person becomes obsolete or unemployed redundancy policies may obtain. Unemployment compensation is one form of redundancy policy which has immediate appeal, but a policy which is limited in scope. Likewise, the WPA was essentially redundancy policy rather than active manpower policy.

Active manpower policy is designed to overcome short-term adjustment problems in the economy, but it also has long-run implications. In a short-run sense, should we train workers to work in a plant which has a government contract which, upon its completion of the contract, will close its doors? Should we train people, in other words, for positions which may not long exist? Given the costs of training, it is likely that most manpower policy of the active variety will tend to make a trade off between training for long-term flexibility and permanence of skills and short-term, immediate employment. The only problem with this trade off (to the extent that it occurs) is that when we see the "success" of immediate employment, we are more apt to cheer than when we see a group of persons trained in anticipation of some slightly more distant future positions, or for positions which demand more adjustments on the part of the trainee such as moving to another city. Redundancy policy, on the other hand, should be per-

30 Smith, "Active Manpower Redundancy Policies," p. 53.

ceived with immediate short-run interest in its social parameters rather than its economic ones. Necessarily, however, such policies are apt to be temporary as they are currently perceived; the suggestion from this idea is that redundancy policies will largely fail in dealing with persistent social problems or individuals' hardships which demand more rigorous action.

IV. National Manpower Policies for Urban Areas[31]

The interest in manpower resource development, other than by laissez-faire economic policy, really began with the 1946 Employment Act. Congress reflected public opinion (developing since the 1930s) that

> it is the continuing policy and responsibility of the Federal Government . . . to foster and promote conditions under which there will be afforded useful employment opportunities to those who are able, willing, and seeking to work . . . and to promote maximum employment, production and purchasing power.[32]

This legislation, implying that the federal government should be responsible for the high human social cost of unemployment, represented an increasing sophistication over earlier bills such as the 1933 Wagner-Peyser Act establishing the United States Employment Service (USES). Legislation prior to 1960 emphasized the symptoms of unemployment; it never concentrated on the reasons for both underemployment and unemployment among the nation's labor force.

Area Redevelopment Act

Under the Kennedy administration Congress began to focus on the causes of unemployment. The Area Redevelopment Act (ARA) of May 1961 was formulated to combat widespread unemployment in depressed areas, especially in Appalachia. This program, however, strengthened the employer rather than the employee. Low interest rates on loans were promised to businesses which would locate in the depressed areas. Financial aid was provided to improve public facilities so as to attract business. Technical assistance was sent to help mobilize resources in planning, construction, and training programs which were to help equip the unemployed and the underemployed to obtain jobs. The Public Works Acceleration Act (PWAA) of 1962 extended the ARA philosophy by granting temporary aid in the form of federally financed projects to be built in areas of chronic labor surplus. This program, unfortunately, proved to aid the construction industry and its skilled labor rather than to provide jobs for the unskilled workers who constituted most of the unemployed.

---

[31] The material in this section comes from the U.S. Department of Labor's *Manpower Report of the President*, 1969 and 1972. Special appreciation goes to Mrs. Suzanne Page for her help in the development of this section.

[32] Ginzberg, *Manpower Agenda for America*, p. 223.

Manpower Development and Training Act

The 1962 Manpower Development Training Act (MDTA) broke away from treating the unemployed individual; the individual, his family, and the private enterprise system were now to be the primary determinants of manpower development. While the National Defense Education Act of 1958 hinged on a labor scarcity within strategically needed occupations, the MDTA began by emphasizing the need to instruct adults who suffered from obsolete skills. It later took up the cause of training all unemployed labor. Also provided for was an annual assessment and report to the president on the state of manpower resources and for the Department of Labor to have the authority to contract for research in manpower fields.

The MDTA at first provided a modest stipend of $35 per week to enrollees in its institutional (school) program; the other job trainees were to work for pay (provided by the government).[33] As first conceived, the program was directed toward an On-the-Job Training (OJT) program as a joint effort of business, corporate groups, trade groups, community organizations, and government in employing the unemployed by providing specific training in particular job areas. However, confusion and apprehension on the part of both government, which subsidized businesses who participated in OJT, and of the sponsoring groups, especially the labor unions who feared competition for jobs, reduced the size of the OJT program.

Initially, only "those with a reasonable expectation of employment" were allowed to participate in the MDTA. A 1963 amendment extended the program to youth training, providing a basic literacy program and liberalizing the stipends. Training the unemployed entailed considerably more than just vocational education. Further amendments in 1965, 1966, and 1968 provided for limited health, legal, and "employment oriented" aid, and remedial education for upgrading the working and health habits of the enrollees. Within the Manpower Training Skill Centers, instruction was provided in both vocational and remedial educational fields. By 1969 goals were set for MDTA training to be directed so that 65% of the enrollees came from the ranks of the hard-core unemployed and 35% were to be trainees for skill-shortage fields. The benefit-cost ratio of the institutional program measuring direct and indirect benefits to society exclusive of increased tax revenues was shown to be 1.78/1.00 within one year after training.

Statistics of the program show the change in emphasis from classroom to OJT programs. In 1963 the enrollment of the classroom program was 32,000 and 2,000 for OJT trainees. By 1971 the classroom enrollment increased to 155,000 and the OJT program increased to 99,000 (table 6). The amendments

---

[33] Clair Wilcox, *Toward Social Welfare: An Analysis of Programs and Proposals Attacking Poverty, Insecurity, and Inequality of Opportunity* (Homewood, Ill.: R. D. Irwin, 1969), p. 319.

TABLE 6

Enrollments, Completions, and Post-training Employment for
Institutional and On-the-Job Training Programs Under the MDTA,
Selected Fiscal Years, 1963–71
(In Thousands)

Item	Total for All Years	FY 1971	FY 1969	FY 1967	FY 1965	FY 1963*
Total:						
Enrollments	1,706.2	254.8	220.0	265.0	156.9	34.1
Completions	1,123.1	135.9	160.0	192.6	96.3	20.1
Post-training						
Employment	878.5	105.1	124.0	153.7	73.4	16.1
Institutional training:						
Enrollments	1,134.0	155.6	135.0	150.0	145.3	32.0
Completions	742.0	90.3	95.0	109.0	88.8	19.2
Post-training						
Employment	550.2	65.9	71.0	80.0	66.9	15.3
On-the-Job Training:						
Enrollments	572.2	99.2	85.0	115.0	11.6	2.1
Completions	381.1	45.6	65.0	83.6	7.5	.9
Post-training						
Employment	328.3	39.2	53.0	73.7	6.5	.9

* Program became operational August 1962.

Note: Completions do not include dropouts. Post-training employment includes persons employed at the time of the most recent follow-up. (There are 3 follow-ups with the third occurring one year after completion of training.)

Source: U.S. Department of Labor, *Manpower Report of the President* (Washington, D.C.: U.S. Government Printing Office, 1972), table F-4, p. 264.

resulted in youths and the hard-core unemployed becoming a larger percentage of the participants.

Ninety percent of the OJT enrollees were placed in jobs, many continuing in the same job in which they were trained. A slightly lesser figure of 70% from the classroom groups found jobs. From 1963 through fiscal 1971, 1.7 million were enrolled in MDTA of which 1.1 million completed training. An average benefit-cost ratio for fiscal years 1963 to 1968 revealed that the relation of direct and indirect benefits to society, exclusive of increased tax revenues, was estimated to be 3.28/1.00 within one year following OJT training.

The failure of continuous support of MDTA programs in recent years is evidenced by the decline in the growth of enrollments following 1967. Had the growth of MDTA been continued, fiscal year enrollments might have been closer to an estimated 500,000 as opposed to the 255,000 actually enrolled in 1971.

The Smith-Hughes federal aid to occupational education of 1917 was updated with the Vocational Education program in 1963. In cooperation with uses, which was to place the trainees and to inspect the curriculum's relevancy, the act allowed federal aid to all occupations except those requiring four years of college or more. Office skills proved to be one of the most popular fields offered. Amended in 1968, and costing $250 million a year, the emphasis of the program changed to place added importance on the expansion and improvement of vocational education for the physically, mentally, and socially handicapped, regardless of their age. Presumably most of the classes were given at public schools. Again the disadvantaged were the last to be attracted, possibly due to the continued emphasis on teaching agriculture and home economics which had little salability to urban youth.

In 1963 the federal government, continuing in the philosophy of the ARA and PWAA, approved loans and grants to workers in depressed areas who wanted to move. Unemployed human labor characterized by immobility was a waste to the national economy as well as to the individual. For as little as $400 per move, the unemployed and their families could be moved elsewhere in hopes of finding a job. However, the high default on loans made by this bill was undesirable to many public officials even though the moving cost might be considerably less than continued welfare payments.

During the 1960s, the United States Employment Service, established by the Wagner-Peyser Act of 1933, was reactivated and reoriented. Operating under a federal-state arrangement, its 1,900 local offices placed approximately 15% of all hirings done in any year's time. Its main function has been traditionally to handle applications for unemployment benefits of which has been said, "...the close relationship of the unemployment service with the payment of unemployment benefits obscures the clear image of its own proper functioning." [34] In times of severe unemployment, uses employees spent more time in administering the unemployment benefit than in trying to find jobs for the unemployed.

> The uses which has been subject to much criticism is hampered from fuller effectiveness because of business' failure to list job vacancies with it. Edward R. Chase suggested a tax cut incentive to firms hiring the marginal worker through uses.[35]

Recently the service has tended to be of special asset in establishing programs for the handicapped, inexperienced youths, migrants, and veterans.

In 1971, with high unemployment around the nation, Congress passed the Emergency Employment Act authorizing the federal support of approximately 145,000 temporary public service jobs for unemployed and underemployed persons. In addition, amendments to the 1971 Social Security Act provided for

[34] Joseph M. Becker, William Haber, and Sar A. Levitan, "Program to Aid the Unemployed in the 1960's" (Kalamazoo, Mich.: The W. E. Upjohn Institute for Employment Research, January 1965), p. 61.

[35] Eli E. Cohen and Louise Kapp, eds., *Manpower Policies for Youth* (New York: Columbia University Press, 1966), p. 61.

public employment opportunities under the Work Incentive Program (WIN) for welfare clients. "Workfare" programs (the requirement of presumed able-bodied persons on welfare to be trained and/or to work) do not appear to be particularly effective in aiding persons and may be largely designed to reduce welfare rolls rather than provide opportunities for welfare recipients to work. In 1971, 112,000 persons were enrolled in WIN.

The War on Poverty

The ideologies of the manpower programs as pointed out by Eli Ginzberg are:

1. Every American has the right to the opportunity to develop his potential to the full.
2. Investment in human beings can yield a high rate of return.
3. The federal government has the responsibility to take the lead in shaping national employment policies.[36]

These concerns took form with the passage of two important bills in 1964.

The first act was the tax cut, sponsored by President Johnson, employing fiscal measures to expand the demand for goods and services, and, hopefully, expanding employment opportunities. The second and more revolutionary act was the Economic Opportunity Act (EOA). This legislation, which avoided the training and educating approach of earlier programs, launched the "War on Poverty." The new philosophy was represented in the Community Action Program (CAP) which aimed at providing jobs for the poor by utilizing them in planning for their own betterment. This approach recognized the need for government to provide jobs for the poor and the necessity of the poor to assert themselves in their own struggle. Nine hundred million dollars was spent by the program in 1965, and this was extended to $1,800 million in 1966 in hopes of helping about three million people.

Among the more famous programs begun under the EOA were the Job Corps and the Neighborhood Youth Corps (NYC). These programs, while attempting to increase the employment of youths, approached the problem from two different philosophies. The Job Corps' ideology was that the youths were not able to find jobs since they lacked "salable skills." Therefore, occupational training was the solution to this problem, particularly since the number of unskilled jobs was declining due to the changing nature of the national economy. The NYC professed that youths were unemployed because of their "inherent unemployability" (poor work habits), lack of experience, and etc. Surely the most effective way to correct this deficiency was to provide jobs in the public sector in order to give the teen-agers some practice at holding a job.

The divergent philosophies — efforts to find a panacea for the high unemployment among youth — were manifested in different approaches to the solu-

---

[36] Ginzberg, *Manpower Agenda for America*, p. 232.

tion. The Job Corps, small relative to the NYC, required that teen-agers be removed from the home environment for one year by being sent to either one of the eighty-two Civilian Conservation Centers or one of the twenty-seven urban centers for training. Of the youths enrolled during the period 1965 to 1968, the mean age was 17.5 years. Although they had completed an average of nine years of schooling, they read and computed on the fifth-grade level. Sixty-three percent of the males could not qualify for the armed services due to either educational or physical defects.

A great many problems surrounded the Job Corps Programs, not the least of which was the high cost of training each enrollee ($8,470 a year in 1966, reduced to $6,300 in 1969), the lack of time to process test data, and hostility among the citizens of the town in which the centers were located. The towns-people objected to having a large number of "delinquent" youths brought into their social environment. Those male youths who showed no vocational orientation were sent to the Conservation Centers for prevocational training and remedial education. While at the Centers, they planted trees and did agricultural-type work which had little relevance to these urban youths who comprised the majority of the corpsmen. The Urban Corps training centers attempted to teach vocational skills. Once graduated from the training program, many of the corpsmen who were looking for jobs were assisted by the Graduate Aid to Employment Houses (GATE), located in several cities to provide professional services needed by the youths during the transitional period. Statistics of June 1968 have shown that 79% of former corpsmen held jobs, 10% were in school, and 11% were in the armed forces. Most of those employed found jobs in the construction industry. Those unable to find jobs claimed that lack of transportation, racial discrimination, or lack of a high school diploma was their chief obstacle.

The NYC neither attempted to remove the low-income youths from their homes nor to provide vocational education. By focusing on the bettering of teen-age working habits and offering remedial education and counseling, it provided part-time jobs for those corpsmen still in school, full-time jobs for those out of school, and summer jobs for those who were returning to school in the fall. It was centered around the recognition of a need to provide material needs for kids who had police records or encounters with the law. The jobs provided them with money which, hopefully, would reduce the corpsman's propensity toward illegal behavior and encourage him to stay in school or go back to school. Generally speaking, the program did a better job at encouraging kids to stay in school than it did in providing meaningful jobs for dropouts. In a few studies researchers have shown a decrease in the crime rate in an area which had contributed corpsmen to the program. Criticism of the Job Corps caused its removal to the Department of Labor in 1969.

The NYC, with an enrollment in 1971 of over 740,000 young people, is composed of three programs in a sweeping effort to reach all lower-income youths. For example, the 2,000 corpsmen in school in 1968 were provided with part-time jobs of no more than fifteen hours a week, paying $1.25 an hour. The 160,000 out-of-school participants were located in jobs of forty hours per week and were given remedial education and supportive services (medical, legal, etc.) necessary to keep them in their jobs. These two groups were employed by non-profit organizations and public agencies. The summer program for youths returning to school were jobs provided by sixty-six private firms who had agreed to participate.

Another program initiated under EOA was the Adult Basic Education Program. This was an attack on the meager education of many of the hard-core unemployed which kept them from holding jobs. In the first four years free classes were given to 1.3 million adults (one in five was on public aid, previous to enrollment). The federal government paid 90% of the expenses, leaving only 10% to be covered by state and local authorities. In 1968 the Adult Education Act shifted the control of this program to the United States Office of Education.

Recent programs for manpower resource development include the Apprentice Outreach Program to encourage young men of minority group status to become apprentices. Statistics show that by late 1971, 13,000 youths were credited as bona fide apprentices in the construction industry. Operation Mainstream, a small NYC program for adults of 50 years and over, employs these people in neighborhood beautification programs. As of 1971 about 1,100 persons were enrolled.

In 1968 Job Opportunities in the Business Sector (JOBS) was founded to provide immediate employment to hard-core unemployed. It differs from Job Corps by servicing only the disadvantaged in the fifty largest urban areas and by relying on business to provide not only the jobs but all supportive services to the new workers. The National Alliance of Businessmen (NAB) was formed to assist this program. The costs essential to recruitment and training are paid by the business with the government covering the other costs through Department of Labor contracts. The AFL-CIO developed the "buddy system" among its rank and file to help acclimate the workers whom they sponsored, and 100,000 were put in jobs by June 1969. Aiming for a goal of 500,000 by 1971, the program enrolled only 92,600 in that year. Statistics on the type of individuals involved in JOBS show 75% were black and 10% had Spanish surnames. The median education was less than eleventh grade and the average unemployment for workers in the last year was 23.7 weeks. Mean family income was $2,790 (below the federal poverty level), and 66% were between 20 and 40 years, 23% were under 20, and 11% were over 40. Interestingly enough, only about 17% of the enrollees were public assistance recipients.

Summary: Work, the Labor Force, and Manpower Policy

In western society work has been associated with religious duty, pain, suffering, and satisfaction. Economics has not treated all the significant aspects of men working. One danger of government intervention in the form of manpower policy is to treat man simply as a "factor of production" or a commodity. Manpower problems are not strictly labor problems but must be viewed in the larger sense of man working in a particular world.

Satisfaction with work is conditioned by wages, physical working conditions, worker interest, relation with peers, economic security, fair treatment by employers, amount of independence in work, and the quality of immediate management. Specialization has been much responsible for reducing a general understanding of specific occupations, increasing the variety of kinds of jobs, and reducing work status.

Motivations to work include tastes for money income, expected market rates, expected nonmarket rates (substitution effects), and family resources.

The labor force in the United States numbers about 85 million persons. Trends in employment reveal declines in agricultural and increases to nonagricultural employment. Women in the labor force represent an increasing proportion of the total. When age is considered, fewer persons over 65 are participating and more young people are entering the labor force. In nonagricultural employment manufacturing accounts for the largest numbers followed by wholesale-retail and government employment. White-collar workers are more numerous than blue-collar workers. Wages are increasing and labor productivity is increasing.

In the United States, regionally, employment levels vary widely and according to regional growth patterns. Essential differences between the national and urban labor forces include the higher wages of urban areas and the smaller numbers of agricultural workers in SMSAS. Unemployment rates in cities are no longer generally less than national rates. National nonwhite unemployment is relatively greater than urban nonwhite unemployment.

In the urban labor force central city workers suffer from relatively greater unemployment rates than their counterparts in the suburbs. Poverty neighborhoods have higher unemployment rates than the rest of the central city. The economic costs of unemployment arise from many sources and have widespread effects. Age, marital status, sex, color, education, and skills affect employment rates.

In large cities manufacturing accounts for about 29% of total employment, followed by wholesale-retail trade at 21.6%, government at 17%, and services employment at 15.4%.

Within occupational categories and among large cities wide variation exists. Large cities have similar proportions of employees in wholesale-retail trades and in-service occupations, but there are great differences in manufacturing employment and government employment.

Active manpower policy is designed to provide a smooth flow of labor, not specifically for social purposes. Manpower policy consists of retraining and redeployment of the labor force. Redundancy policy refers to labor force members who are obsolete in the labor market. Both active manpower and redundancy policies are required because of problems of persons in and out of labor markets, problems in which the private sector has little interest.

National manpower policies, which are currently in a state of flux, fall into three basic areas of government activity. The Area Redevelopment Act of May 1961 was designed to combat unemployment in certain disadvantaged regions of the nation. The Manpower Development and Training Act of 1962, along with its amendments, centered first on job training of adults who have suffered from obsolete labor skills and has been extended to all unemployed labor. Support of a modest amount was made available to participants in MDTA programs. The third manpower element has been the so-called war on poverty through the Economic Opportunity Act. Concentrating on local citizens' participation, programs under this act included the Job Corps and the Neighborhood Youth Corps. The latter program trained and employed youths in government in hopes of increasing their private sector employability. The Job Corps removed youths from their homes to one of eighty-two Civilian Conservation Centers or twenty-seven urban centers for remedial education and work training. A third war on poverty measure was the Adult Basic Education Program, later removed to the United States Department of Education. The Adult Basic Education Program was designed to attack the problem of low adult educational skills through remedial programs. Most manpower programs have been developed to make unemployed persons employable in the private sector.

Selected Bibliography

Work, Labor Force, and Manpower Policy

BECKER, JOSEPH M.; HABER, WILLIAM; AND LEVITAN, SAR A. "Program to Aid the Unemployed in the 1960's." Kalamazoo, Mich.: The W. E. Upjohn Institute for Employment Research, January 1965.

BOLINO, AUGUST C. Manpower and the City. Cambridge, Mass.: Schenkman Publishing Co., 1969.

BOWEN, WILLIAM G., AND FINEGAN, T. ALDRICH. The Economics of Labor Force Participation. Princeton: Princeton University Press, 1969.

CARLSSON, ROBERT J., AND ROBINSON, JAMES W. "Inflation and Moonlighting." Mississippi Valley Journal of Business and Economics 6 (1971): 75–84.

CHAMBERLAIN, NEIL W. The Labor Sector: An Introduction to Labor in the American Economy. New York: McGraw-Hill, 1965.

CHAPIN, GENE. "Unemployment Insurance, Job Search, and the Demand for Leisure." *Western Economic Journal* 9 (1971) : 102–7.

COHEN, ELI E., AND KAPP, LOUISE, EDS. *Manpower Policies for Youth.* New York: Columbia University Press, 1966.

DALE, EDWIN, JR. "The Great Unemployment Fallacy." *New Republic*, Sept. 1964, pp. 10–12.

DAVID, HENRY, ED. *Manpower Policies for a Democratic Society.* New York: Columbia University Press, 1965.

DEUTERMANN, WILLIAM. "Educational Attainment of Workers, March 1969, 1970." *Monthly Labor Review* 93 (Oct. 1970) : 9–16.

ENGLAND, GEORGE W.; AGARWAL, NARESH C.; AND TRERISE, ROBERT E. "Union Leaders and Managers: A Comparison of Value Systems." *Industrial Relations* 10 (1971): 211–26.

FAIR, RAY C. "Labor Force Participation, Wage Rates, and Money Illusion." *Review of Economics and Statistics* 53 (1971) : 164–68.

FERGUSON, C. E. "Wages, Productivity, and the Guidelines." *Economic Record* 47 (1971): 217–29.

GALLAWAY, LOWELL E. *Manpower Economics.* The Irwin Series in Economics. Homewood, Ill.: R. D. Irwin, 1971.

GINZBERG, ELI. *Manpower Agenda for America.* New York: McGraw-Hill, 1968.

———. "The Outlook for Educated Manpower." *The Public Interest*, no. 26 (Winter 1972) : 100–11.

GOODSTEIN, M. E. "A Note on Urban and Non-urban Employment Growth in the South, 1940–1960." *Journal of Regional Science* 10 (1970) : 397–401.

GRONAU, REUBEN. "Information and Frictional Unemployment." *American Economic Review* 61 (1971) : 290–301.

HALL, R. E. "Why is the Unemployment Rate So High at Full Employment?" *Brookings Papers on Economic Activity* 3 (1970) : 369–410.

HAMERMESH, DANIEL S. "White-Collar Unions, Blue-Collar Unions, and Wages in Manufacturing." *Industrial and Labor Relations Review* 24 (1971) : 159–70.

HAMILTON, DAVID. "The Paper War on Poverty." *Journal of Economic Issues*, Sept. 1971, pp. 72–79.

HERMAN, ARTHUR S. "Manpower Implications of Computer Control." *Monthly Labor Review* 93 (Oct. 1970) : 3–8.

HOLLAND, SUSAN S. "Adult Men Not in the Labor Force." *Monthly Labor Review* 90 (Mar. 1967) : 5–15.

IDEN, GEORGE. "Wage Increases in the Construction Industry." *Western Economic Journal* 8 (1970) : 431–36.

KALECKI, MICHAL. "Class Struggle and the Distribution of National Income." *Kyklos* 24 (1971) : 1–9.

KATONA, GEORGE. *The Mass Consumption Society.* New York: McGraw-Hill, 1964.

KLITGAARD, ROBERT E. "The Dual Labor Market and Manpower Policy." *Monthly Labor Review* 94 (Nov. 1971) : 45–48.

KREPS, JUANITA M. "Youth Unemployment and Minimum Wages: Some Further Questions." *Nebraska Journal of Economics and Business* 10 (Winter 1971) : 14–21.

LONG, L. H. "On Measuring Geographic Mobility." *Journal of the American Statistical Association* 65 (1970) : 1195–1203.

MABRY, BEVARS D. "An Analysis of Work and Other Constraints on Choices of Activities." *Western Economic Journal* 8 (1970) : 213–25.

MAYHEW, ANNE. "Education, Occupation, and Earnings." *Industrial Labor Relations Review* 24 (1971): 216–25.

McGUIRE, TIMOTHY W., AND RAPPING, LEONARD A. "The Supply of Labor and Manufacturing Wage Determination in the United States: An Empirical Examination." *International Economic Review* 11 (1970): 258–68.

MILLER, ROGER LeROY. "The Reserve Labour Hypothesis: Some Tests of Its Implications." *Economic Journal* 81 (1971): 17–35.

MOORE, THOMAS GALE. "The Effect of Minimum Wages on Teenage Unemployment Rates." *Journal of Political Economy* 79 (1971): 897–902.

NACHMAN, LARRY. "Strategies for Radical Social Change." *Social Policy* 2 (1971): 52–57.

NEWHOUSE, JOSEPH P. " A Simple Hypothesis of Income Distribution." *Journal of Human Resources* 6 (1971): 51–74.

NICHOLS, DONALD A. "Growth and Unemployment in the United States: 1947–64." *Yale Economic Essays* 11 (1971): 145–80.

PERRY, G. L. "Changing Labor Markets and Inflation." *Brookings Papers on Economic Activity* 3 (1970): 411–48.

REES, ALBERT, AND SHULTZ, GEORGE P. *Workers and Wages in an Urban Labor Market.* Studies in Business Society. Chicago: University of Chicago Press, 1970.

ROOSEVELT, FRANK. "Market Socialism: A Humane Economy?" *Journal of Economic Issues*, Dec. 1969, pp. 3–20.

ROSEN, SHERWIN. "Unionism and the Occupational Wage Structure in the United States." *International Economic Review* 11 (1970): 269–86.

————, AND WELCH, FINIS. "Labor Supply and Income Redistribution." *Review of Economics and Statistics* 53 (1971): 278–82.

SACKLEY, A., AND GAVETT, T. W. "Analysis of Occupational Wage Differences." *Monthly Labor Review* 94 (June 1971): 5–12.

SHANAHAN, JAMES L. "Spatial Isolation and Job Opportunities for Lower Skilled Core Residents in the Detroit SMSA." Ph.D. dissertation, Wayne State University, 1972.

SIEGEL, I., AND BELITSKY, A. H. "The Changing Form and Status of Labor." *Journal of Economic Issues* 4 (1970): 78–94.

SMITH, A. D. "Active Manpower and Redundancy Policies: Their Costs and Benefits." *International Labour Review* 95 (1967): 49–60.

TUCKMAN, HOWARD P. "Determinants of College Student Migration." *Southern Economic Journal* 37 (1970): 184–89.

U.S. Department of Labor. *Manpower Report of the President, and a Report on Manpower Requirements, Resources, Utilization, and Training.* Washington, D.C.: U.S. Government Printing Office, 1972.

VANDERKAMP, JOHN. "The Effect of Out-Migration on Regional Employment." *Canadian Journal of Economics* 3 (1970): 541–49.

WILCOX, CLAIR. *Toward Social Welfare: An Analysis of Programs and Proposals Attacking Poverty, Insecurity, and Inequality of Opportunity.* Homewood, Ill.: R. D. Irwin, 1969.

4

Problems and Policies
of Manpower
for Local Government

Manpower policy is designed to deal with problems of unemployment in the society. While the role of the local government is severely limited in this problem area, there are distinct areas of policy in which the local government can become effectively involved. This chapter starts with a brief overview of manpower problems to which the society is heir followed by a brief discussion of the limited present roles of both the private and the public sectors. A discussion of cyclical, frictional, and structural unemployment is based on the premise that the primary role of local government lies in the area of structural or chronic unemployment. An expanded bureau of local government employment services is discussed followed by a description of the stages of a local manpower process. From a description of some of the most serious cases of structural unemployment in the city, we turn to a consideration of the data necessary to effect a viable local manpower policy. The concluding section provides a conceptual framework in which manpower programs may be evaluated.

I. An Overview of Problems

Manpower problems can be summarized broadly. Richard A. Lester, in developing a profile of major manpower problems, suggested the following:

1. Our largest labor increases will be in categories that experience high rates of unemployment. The growing addition of youths and non-whites to the labor force will aggravate our unemployment problems.
2. The United States is the first country to experience a pronounced shift in employment from goods manufactured to a predominantly service supplying economy. In part that shift is the result of increased demand for services like education, medical care, recreation, and finance. In part it is the consequence of the declining demand for physical labor that stems from automation and other labor-saving

advances in industry. These shifts are characterized by the decline in blue-collar employment and an expansion in white-collar employment.

3. Manpower problems in the United States are complicated by the size and diversity of the country and by a scattering of manpower responsibilities among federal, state, municipal, and school district agencies. Inadequate coordination of manpower policy and programs, poor interstate communication and placement, and low average quality of state employment service personnel are serious problems for manpower planning and operations in the United States.[1]

Labor shortages create problems for manpower policy. Arthur Ross suggests: "Short of a general depletion of manpower reserves, labor shortages are usually localized in specific occupations, industries, and geographical areas." These specific shortages are usually caused by one or more of the following:

   a) Rapid increase in demand
   b) Chronic occupational insufficiencies
   c) Concentration of employment increased in certain areas or industries
   d) Unresponsiveness of the wage structure
   e) Inadequate personnel policies.[2]

Manpower problems in America are enormously complicated as evidenced by the above characteristics. For the American city to begin to deal with the varieties of problems requires something just short of a revolution in thinking. Local governments have seldom demonstrated an interest in the problems. State governments have traditionally provided weak employment services in which civil servants sat behind desks waiting for the "unemployed" to present themselves. Few alternatives were available for unemployed in cities, and they have included little beyond unemployment compensation and some minor job counseling.

It is important at the outset that we recognize the expenses involved in the revolution. The costs of adequate local manpower agencies are enormous, and the current financial structures of cities are not sufficient to do the task. Limitations in tax gathering capacity enlarge the problem. It should be apparent that the total unemployment problem which may reside in a given city cannot be completely dealt with at the local level. Manpower policy demands a mix of local, state, federal, and private actions.

[1] Richard A. Lester, *Manpower Planning in a Free Society* (Princeton: Princeton University Press, 1966), pp. 10–22.

[2] Arthur M. Ross, "Theory and Measurement of Labor Shortages," *Critical Issues in Employment Policy*, a report of the Princeton Manpower Symposium, May 12–13, 1966 (Princeton: Industrial Relations Section, 1966), pp. 17–21.

The Local Private Sector

Recognizing that manpower policy must be cooperative between the private and public sectors of the economy, there are a number of questions about the quality of services of the local private sector which must be raised:

1. "Information." How is job information disseminated?
2. "Counseling and motivation." Do any counseling programs exist among large firms?
3. "Unemployment." Are there private sector attempts to reduce it?
4. "Discrimination in employment." How extensive is discrimination?
5. "Adaptability of compensation." What are the wage levels and their flexibility?
6. "Elimination of shortages." How do firms attempt to solve labor shortages?
7. "Areas of greatest effectiveness." In what ways does the private sector appear to function effectively?[3]

Tentatively, the above questions lead one to the limitations of the private sector in the allocation of labor resources. Information to the private firm is simply the dissemination of information regarding positions within that firm. Counseling and motivation consist of counseling within the context of the firm and motivation to work up through the firm. There are no neutrals in the field of information and counseling in the private sector. The needs of the worker are always subservient to the needs of the firm, and the needs of the local economy are seldom considered. While there is a good deal of vocational counseling and there are various incentive programs for motivation, all are highly specialized and in no sense neutral.[4]

Historically the market has done little to prevent widespread discrimination in employment. Further, for wages to be adapted to alterations in the skills of worker groups, the private market has to be effectively competitive. Unless we have competitive labor markets as defined by good information among workers as to job opportunities, mobility of workers to gain the opportunities, and competitive firms to pay competitive wages, there is little likelihood that the private market can generate a valid and socially desirable level of wages. Monopolistic elements on both sides of the labor market create wage rigidity. Monopolistic elements close the doors to proper evaluation for adjustments in compensation. A persistent problem is the failure to be able to measure the productivity of workers, a failure which results in continued misallocations. Also, there appears to be no close relationship between compensation and labor supply, and the market is limited in terms of what it can do to accommodate the labor shortages.

[3] Lester, *Manpower Planning*, p. 34.
[4] Lester, *Manpower Planning*, p. 35.

Market forces appear to operate most effectively for professions, graduating seniors in high schools, vocational schools, and colleges and universities. While these constitute a large part of the labor force, the lack of competition within the market precludes adequate allocation of most labor resources.[5] We cannot view the role of the private sector as neutral; we cannot view the private sector as competent to undertake local manpower policy with the best interests of the worker and the local economy in mind. This is not necessarily an indictment; firms should be understood to be principally involved in the production of goods and services. While we cannot develop manpower policy locally without the cooperation of private firms, we can anticipate that conflicts of interest will undoubtedly arise. The same can be said of unions. Like private firms, unions tend to be most concerned with their primary task — maintaining good wages and working conditions for their members — and therefore tend to be cooperative with local policy but will have distinctly different priorities.

The Limited Public Commitment

Lester raises the question of the amount of resources governments devote to manpower planning. He compared employment service personnel in the United States with figures in other countries. In 1965, for every 10,000 persons in the work force, there were 12.5 persons engaged in labor placement and vocational guidance in Sweden, 7.3 persons in Germany, and only 3.3 persons in the United States.[6] The United States lags far behind in terms of staff for employment service work. When public expenditures for training and retraining adults for jobs are considered, the United States devoted about 2/100 of 1% of the working population to training under MDTA where Sweden in 1963 had about 1% of its working population.[7]

Another type of comparison is in the size of total expenditures on labor mobility which includes expenditures for manpower information, replacement, counseling, adult training, and mobility. In Sweden in 1963, 1% of all government expenditures were used in this direction. In Germany in 1963, the figure was 1.4% and in the United States in fiscal 1964 to 1965, the figure was about .2%.[8] Such comparisons can be made among state and local authorities and would be desirable manpower research in the United States. Federal manpower policy is a recent phenomenon which would today alter these comparative figures, but likewise it can be argued that this recent federal manpower activity has done little to create permanent manpower agencies at the local government level.

[5] Lester, *Manpower Planning*, p. 35.

[6] Lester, *Manpower Planning*, p. 173.

[7] Lester, *Manpower Planning*, p. 174.

[8] Lester, *Manpower Planning*, p. 174.

II. Forms of Unemployment and the Local Manpower Role

The central issue in manpower policy for local government lies in defining the local role in alleviating unemployment. Since most manpower programs currently undertaken are initiated at the federal level and since local government institutions do little more than administer federal programs, no broad based local manpower services exist. We discussed in the previous chapter the dimensions of unemployment, but we have not yet differentiated between the three main kinds of unemployment: cyclical, frictional, and structural. The local manpower role will be seen to emphasize structural unemployment over the other two forms.

Cyclical Unemployment

Cyclical unemployment is unemployment that arises from regional or national business cycles. Such unemployment is generally conceived under Keynesian analysis as arising from inadequate demand. The fiscal policy prescription under cyclical stress relates to the government acting during times of recession and depression to stimulate the economy by increasing government spending, reducing taxes, or both. Such stimuli expand aggregate demand in the economic system and reduce unemployment. It is normally thought that only the federal government is sufficiently large to engage in counter-cyclical fiscal policy since business cycles are usually nationwide or at least regional in scope.

Local economies can little react to the problems of cyclical unemployment. With the large national movements of economic rise and fall, local economies and their governments tend to swing with the inflation or recession. We have no tools at the local level which would allow us to undertake counter-cyclical fiscal policies affecting the national economy.

While it is customary to disclaim the local economy's positive role in cyclical unemployment, we should note that the policies of the primary actors in cities — namely large local governments, private firms, and labor unions — can certainly aggravate a given condition. Pressure for high wages locally can, in a city the size of New York, affect its total economy and call forth higher prices during times of inflation. Likewise, price increases by large firms producing for the markets of a large city can raise the cost of living substantially. Local government also affects local stability by cutting back on spending programs when there is a short fall in revenues.

Frictional Unemployment

A second form of unemployment is referred to as frictional unemployment which occurs through normal frictions in the economy as persons change jobs. In a dynamic economy, short-run changes in demand for particular goods may create expansions of employment or unemployment. If the labor market does not function perfectly, then workers who are unemployed may not immediately find alternative positions. If the employment situation is truly frictional, then any unemployment of the worker is due merely to the time it takes for available workers to find available jobs. If a worker is not out of work for a long period of time we presume his unemployment is frictional. The local role under such situations should be thought of in terms of improving the local labor flows through job placement, information about jobs, and counseling.

Structural Unemployment

Basically a person is structurally unemployed when changes in the economy render him unemployable; when a worker is available and there are no jobs available to him for which he is qualified, he is structurally unemployed. This occurs when labor skills do not match available jobs, labor is immobile due to aging or other restrictions, restraints are put on wages due to racial discrimination, and in other similar situations. Imagine the structurally unemployed person as having a number of barriers around him preventing him from being employed. Most such persons have not a single problem from the employment standpoint, but more than one problem. For example, the structurally unemployed person is apt to lack necessary marketable skills and be uneducated, or old, etc.

While we may ascertain that total unemployment is made up of those who are cyclically, frictionally, and structurally unemployed, actual measurement to distinguish among the forms of unemployment is difficult. For example, if a woman is laid off from a manufacturing plant and then becomes ill for a period of time before she can find another position, was she frictionally or structurally unemployed? Presumably duration of time is important in distinguishing between frictional and structural situations, but how do we account for the illness? Was she seeking work while ill? If so, she may not have found work immediately because of her illness rather than because of her lack of skills. Employers may have viewed her as subject to high absenteeism and rejected her even though her skills presumably were adequate. At any event, she is out of work for an extended time, and, when accounted for in labor statistics, she would likely be considered structurally unemployed. In short, on the surface the definitions appear satisfactory, but in practice there is considerable overlap.

Another aspect of structural unemployment which is difficult to measure is hidden unemployment. The "discouraged worker" is one who stops seeking employment. If we could discourage all structurally unemployed persons from ever seeking employment, could we then claim to have eliminated such unemployment simply because these people would no longer be part of the labor force? In a survey of six cities conducted by the United States Department of Labor in 1969, people who wanted jobs were asked why they had stopped looking for work. For males the reasons most commonly given were retirement, old age, school, or health (table 7). For women over 15 years of age the most notable reasons were the same with the addition of family responsibilities. How would you judge these people? Were they truly out of the labor force? Were they structurally unemployed? Were they frictionally unemployed? The only way we would know for certain would be to consider each case separately. No aggregate measure or limited definition will tell us satisfactorily, at least not for the purposes of local manpower policy.

What then is the appropriate role for local manpower policy? Primarily, a local manpower service should be interested in alleviating structural unemployment. Secondarily, the local manpower service should seek to improve the flow of jobs through consideration of diminishing the time of unemployment for those who are frictionally unemployed.

Possible Avenues of Local Policy

According to Wilbur Thompson, the principal attack on structural unemployment rests on three basic tactics: information, retraining, and relocation.[9] The ability of the local government to have a significant impact on this problem has been largely untapped except in the peripheral activities of job placement through the National Alliance of Businessmen (NAB), the Urban League, and other quasi-public agencies.

One of the characteristics of an effective labor placement market is informational: information about opportunities and alternatives must be readily

TABLE 7

WHY PEOPLE WHO WANT JOBS ARE NOT LOOKING FOR WORK:
PRINCIPAL REASONS OFFERED BY THOSE NOT IN THE LABOR FORCE
(IN PERCENTAGES)

	Atlanta	Chicago	Detroit	Houston	Los Angeles	New York
Males over 15:						
Retirement, old age, or school	29	46	33	39	47	41
Health	47	36	40	35	37	41
Females over 15:						
Retirement, old age, or school	14	13	13	15	16	13
Health	30	29	28	22	27	31
Family responsibilities	29	38	33	31	34	41

Source: Committee for Economic Development, *Training and Jobs for the Urban Poor: Employment and Income Data for the Poor Areas of Six Cities, July 1968–June 1969* (New York: Committee for Economic Development, July 1970), p. 26. Reprinted by permission.

9 Wilbur R. Thompson, *A Preface to Urban Economics* (Baltimore: Published for Resources for the Future by Johns Hopkins Press, 1965), p. 214.

available so workers may know at all times of positions available to them and can shift to these employments if they desire. Exactly what, however, beyond job information is necessary for local manpower policy to make the local labor market more effective? First we need active solicitation on the part of local manpower authorities; the task of manpower development does not end with the structurally unemployed. Regular campaigns are required to make manpower programs known in the community, and referrals from all cooperating sources should be enhanced. A manpower staff attuned to public relations and media is necessary for such activities to bear fruit.

In the retraining of displaced workers, the local educational establishment has considerable sophistication and the capacity to undertake this role. This is particularly true when we consider the fact that general education will not be undertaken by private firms. In any urban community there are educational institutions available which could be used for retraining displaced workers who do not have the educational qualifications to compete with other workers.

Financing these retraining programs need not be undertaken out of strictly local funds. Indeed, the federal government has entered the picture of manpower retraining, and its role is going to increase. On the other hand, the financial burden attendant on displaced workers must to a great degree be born by local resources. Perhaps the most important factor of local manpower training in dealing with the problem of structural unemployment is the necessity of managing the program locally since in most instances we cannot force the worker to remove himself from the city.

A further argument for the role of local government is the necessity of developing programs on a case basis — person by person. The importance of this cannot be overstressed. When we consider that the unemployment rate among low income groups within the city, as Thompson points out, is seldom less than 20%, we recognize the near catastrophic results for communities faced with increasing numbers of migrating middle-class and prosperous blue-collar workers.[10]

How should we use educational institutions to undertake retraining of workers? It is logical that they do so since local educational institutions could in some cases simply expand their vocational training activities. While this is necessary, it is not sufficient. One aspect of persons who make up the lists of the structurally unemployed is that they lack both specific skills and general education. The role of the educational establishment lies in both areas. Local schools can undertake programs in general education along with specific job training. Basic mathematics, English language, and reading skills are all part of the deficiencies characteristic of most persons who are persistently unemployed. Thus the local schools may have some impact on both specific training through

[10] Thompson, *A Preface to Urban Economics*, p. 220.

their vocational capability and on general education through their remedial activities.

But school systems cannot undertake such programs alone. While the school system can undertake the retraining of many, local employers must also undertake job training programs wherever possible. As well, the local employer has an obligation to learn of available programs and to tailor his hiring and employment policies to accommodate to needs of the unemployed. Significant among these accommodations is the elimination of discrimination in employment, low wages or wage levels not commensurate with skills, etc. The problem with the local employer's role is that government must require that he undertake it. Imperfections in the market which account for these difficulties demand intervention by government. Thus the principal role of the local employer is to tailor his policies toward local needs and to undertake specific job training programs where relevant.

The essence of retraining is to provide a full circle of services for the person being retrained. Retraining for nonexistent jobs is self-defeating. Retraining without the cooperation of local employers is meaningless, if we assume that the retrained workers will be engaged locally. On the other hand, local employment may not be possible. For example, in the training of teachers (where a state educates teachers and they leave that state) there is a problem of reciprocity, and the local community has little choice but to accept the fact of losses through migration. Workers must be able to move where the employment possibilities exist since given skills may not be required in the local economy.

If educational institutions undertake retraining of workers, then it is necessary that they, in cooperation with local, state, and federal employment authorities, design programs which will provide for determinate needs in local employment. Further, public employment may be expanded with the local government becoming the employer of last resort, guaranteeing employment to the urban unemployed. If central city revenues are insufficient to expand its own employment, increases in taxes and subsequent revenues should be undertaken as well as subsidy from the national government. With local services seriously undernourished, there is a rich field for local government employment of retrained workers.

One possibility for expanded employment lies in the local health field, and health services in the United States is one of our fastest growing industries. Since 1940, employment in this area has increased immensely. In most communities mental and medical care is a rapidly growing industry with the potential for becoming a double-edged attack on manpower problems. In the first instance, expanded medical care can improve employment and productivity possibilities for an urban labor force. Second, the expansion of this industry in itself creates new employment possibilities in the urban community. Skill levels within this industry vary from the low skills to the very high; among the low and middle skill levels there are many additional opportunities for urban employment. Carol A. Brown has suggested a number of requirements to expand the structure and aid in the development of health services industries in the urban community.

1. To develop new organizational forms using new forms of manpower to provide service to urban populations.
2. To encourage the use of, and to staff adequately, outpatient facilities.
3. To increase the flexibility of the municipal hospitals with respect to their personnel policies.
4. To support nursing homes and mental hospital facility construction which will enable citizens to receive such services within the community.
5. To expedite the translation of research findings into practice by providing public and private firms to assist workers in acquiring new emerging skills.
6. To bring hospital workers' wages, especially those of nurses and technicians, to a level competitive with wages in other industries.
7. To increase the training opportunities available in the city for various health services, professions, and occupations.
8. To increase the opportunities for effective mobility at all levels of the health service structure.[11]

From the above illustration and the foregoing discussion we can see that local manpower problems are subject to some form of local control and intervention. The limitations of the role of local government are numerous but not overwhelming.

In response to local unemployment problems it might be suggested that local governments establish offices of local employment services designed to take a major role in dealing with local unemployment. A significant part of any city budget ought to be allocated for such problems since they are in a considerable way more basic to the well-being of the community than many service functions the city now undertakes. The expansion of these city services would be through the civil service and personnel operations of local government, and they should have considerable authority and funding to implement programs.

An Outline of Organizational Role

In table 8 major organizations are indicated with their contributions to a local manpower program. Local government has a major role in three distinct areas: coordinating the entire set of programs, gathering data for the research and information collection system, and functioning as a counseling agent. Also

---

[11] Carol A. Brown, "The Expansion of Health Service," in *Manpower Strategy for the Metropolis*, ed. Eli Ginzberg and the Conservation of Human Resources Staff, Columbia University (New York: Columbia University Press, 1968), p. 109. Copyright © 1968, Columbia University Press. Reprinted by permission.

TABLE 8

COMPONENTS OF A LOCAL MANPOWER PROGRAM WITH RANKING OF RESPONSIBILITIES

Organization	Employment	Training — Vocational	Training — General	Counseling	Information, Research, and Follow-up	Coordination	Health and Clinical
Local government	x†	x‡	x	x*	x*	x*	
State government	x	x		x†	x†	x	
Private firms	x*	x†			x		
Educational institutions		x*	x*	x‡	x	x	
Federal government	x‡				x‡	x†	
Medical services		x			x		x*
Courts				x	x		
Private service agencies, U.F., unions, etc.	x	x			x		x

* Priority among other agencies for function.

† Second priority among other agencies for function.

‡ Third priority among other agencies for function.

important in the local government role is employment and, in some specific ways, training; training is largely limited to occupational requirements of local government itself.

The chief object of state government, while it holds no primary responsibilities, should be to assist local government in collecting information, coordinating employment, counseling, and training. As in the case of local government, state government should be responsible for undertaking training for occupational categories within its own employment capabilities. Before we leave state government we should indicate that funding of manpower programs is the responsibility of all three levels of government. Since manpower programs cannot be limited to a city itself, but must be expanded to include at least the SMSA, the coordination, funding, and development of manpower programs should largely be a cooperative venture between the city and state. The regional (SMSA) bureau of employment for manpower should be housed in the largest city government since large city governments tend to be the most capable of planning to undertake such a role.

The role of private firms is highest in the responsibility for employment and quite heavy in vocational and specific job training. Information gathering among groups of firms is an essential part of the total process and should include the private employment agencies as well. No large-scale manpower program can be fully successful without the cooperation of both major and minor business firms in the geographic area.

Educational institutions, both public and private, should be chiefly responsible for general and specific training. A major function for local schools can be as a counseling agent so that potential manpower problems for specific individuals are diagnosed early in the schoolchild's career, probably beginning in the seventh grade or at some point in the process where it is possible to isolate children who may present manpower problems in the future. No set of institutions in a community are so well equipped to begin the process of training as are schools. Their function in this area has been distinctly limited historically, relative to the needs of a modern city.

Uncle Sam has his usual role: money. Initially, federal funds are definitely required to make local programs function; however, national manpower policies should be tailored as much as possible to local needs. A vast array of consulting services should be available for local governments to establish meaningful local programs in addition to interarea mobility subsidies for surplus local labor.

Least equipped of the necessary institutions to impact upon local manpower problems is the health establishment. At the same time, no set of services is more needed to insure the success of many individuals participating in manpower programs. Not only physical health, but also mental health problems tend to prevent many from functioning adequately on job performance. Again it would appear that federal assistance is needed on a broad scale. It is necessary that a substantial medical care program sponsored by the federal government be developed so that the medical services complement of manpower programs can be satisfactorily met.

Courts can serve two needed functions in cooperating with manpower programs: first, counseling and, second, information and referral. Likewise, many private agencies can and do make available services which enable a manpower program to function. Indeed some, such as the Urban League, make programs possible and operate them. Family services and other agencies are ready sources of contractors to be hired by local government to develop and provide certain necessary services in the manpower sphere. There is no need to expect local government to develop the expertise to attempt to accommodate to all structural unemployment problems when competent service organizations can be hired to provide many services the local government may be incapable of undertaking.

While the above are merely suggestions and any or all of the points are open to argument, these are at least possible avenues of attack. The problems are many and the services necessary are complex. Two additional points should be made with regard to manpower programs under a structure as suggested above. Manpower programs have been established largely with the assumption that many, if not all, could be made productive, without any real questioning of the idea that perhaps we do not need as many people working in cities as we have had in the past. A guaranteed family income of decent proportions would eliminate the need for much manpower planning: to train people to deal with unnecessary and meaningless jobs would be criminal when economically it might be more feasible to attempt to educate people to use their time profitably, but not in the economic system. The above points are ones that we will eventually face, but our social mores appear to demand everyone working even though we be like lemmings marching to the sea.

The Stages of the Local Manpower Process

The local manpower process can be seen as a series of stages much in the same manner as any other formal system.

STAGE 1: IDENTIFICATION. Imagine a man sitting in a motel room on the afternoon of July 8, 1979, after spending most of the past three days looking for work. He has just moved to Akron, Ohio, from Dryprong, West Virginia, where the mill was closed and he was suddenly out of a job. Think of him as having a sixth-grade education, and for the past fifteen years he has worked as a common mill hand. He has a wife and three children, ages 7, 10, and 12. He has been in Akron for three days and has had no luck in finding a job. At that moment the phone rings . . .

The identification stage should be sufficiently coordinated and effective so that a person looking for work should be referred to, or should be contacted by, a local manpower representative as soon as it is known that he is seeking employment unsuccessfully. The first place that he applied should have told him of the manpower office and who to see or should have called the manpower office in his behalf.

He should have been invited immediately for an interview to the local employment service and an attempt should have been made to fit his skills to an available job. If no jobs were open and none likely to be for his skills, then the manpower service should have discussed alternatives with him including the possibilities of available manpower programs for retraining.

STAGE 2: COUNSELING. This should be full and complete in the sense of aiding the individual in caring for his family immediately, dealing with the problems of housing, and providing whatever services are required to aid his relocation to the city.

STAGE 3: TRAINING. This should, after due consideration of alternatives, be the stage in which training takes place. During this time, some support payments or part-time on-the-job activity would provide a person with sufficient income to make ends meet.

STAGE 4: JOB PLACEMENT. Upon successful completion of the training, he enters the fourth stage, or job placement, in which, just as with the training, he is provided with some alternatives to the extent that they are available. This placement period is essentially a probation period for him as a trainee, and an evaluation of his work is made at the end of a specified period with him, his employer, and the manpower service. At this point, discussions will center on his interest, job satisfaction, income level, and the employer's satisfaction level with his work. If the job has been unsatisfactory, then steps should be taken to make other arrangements with the aid of the manpower service.

STAGE 5: PERIODIC REEVALUATION AND FOLLOW-UP. Reevaluations and follow-ups insure that the individual and job are indeed suited to each other and they keep the individual apprised of alternatives in employment which may be open to him.

As we can see from the previous discussion, policy proposals for local manpower development are characterized by their costliness, their comprehensiveness, and their persistence. Halfway measures in manpower tend to reach out to those who can most easily benefit, such as the young, intelligent man who needs some additional basic educational and skills training. The scope of manpower programs suggested here has been of a broader and more permanent nature than current programs. Just as welfare policy has had an impact only on certain of the poor, manpower policy has impacted largely on the most promising among the structurally unemployed. In a more encompassing concept we are concerned with the total local labor market, while simultaneously our principal thrust is with the structurally unemployed.

III. Some Structural Unemployment Problems for the City

Manpower policy in the city can be developed to aid specific persons solve specific problems. What follows is a brief discussion of some of the groups whose pressing problems of employment in the city are critical.

Female Employment

The labor force participation rate among women is rising during the twentieth century. For example, in 1940 the rate was only about 5%; by 1950 it had risen to 15%; by 1960 to 24%. In 1967 it had reached 37%.[12] The working woman in the urban complex finds herself suffering from a number of discriminatory practices. First, women are typically paid less for the same job than are men. Second, women are discriminated against relative to men in finding jobs. Third, women have a narrower range of jobs open to them than do men; some jobs are virtually taboo for women in society. Fourth, women who seek employment in many cases are required to be temporary and part-time employees rather than full time and permanent. Discrimination by sex is a serious problem of the local community. The situation of women who are heads of households is a particularly acute problem. Because wages are low, turning to

[12] William G. Bowen and T. Aldrich Finegan, *The Economics of Labor Force Participation* (Princeton: Princeton University Press, 1969), p. 88.

the labor market for employment in order to support children is not a very inviting situation for women. Among families headed by women in 1969, 21% had incomes of less than $2,000 (table 9). Further evidence of the economic stress upon such families is the fact that only 28% of these families had incomes in excess of $6,000 for 1969. If we set the poverty level at $4,000 income, half of all the families headed by women in the United States are impoverished.

There are a number of characteristics affecting the labor force participation rates of women. Female participation (among married women) in the labor force is conditioned by forces which push participation rates down:

1. Increase in the proportion of married women who have preschool aged children
2. The increased level of real income leading to increased demands for leisure
3. Increase in the cost of domestic services

and forces which tend to push up participation:

1. General increase in female wage rates
2. Rise in educational attainment of women
3. Increase in femininity in the industrial mix (more jobs open)
4. Decline in length of work week
5. Increase in part-time jobs
6. Changes in the methods of producing home goods
7. Rising income aspirations[13]

Since the woman in the labor force suffers job discrimination at virtually all higher status job levels, local manpower policy must intervene in such discrimination.

TABLE 9

PERCENTAGE OF FAMILIES WITH CHILDREN
HEADED BY WOMEN WITHIN 1969 INCOME LEVELS

Family Income	Families Headed by Women
Under $2,000	21%
$2,000 to $2,999	15
$3,000 to $3,999	14
$4,000 to $4,999	12
$5,000 to $5,999	10
$6,000 and above	28

Source: Robert L. Stein, "The Economic Status of Families Headed by Women," *Monthly Labor Review* 93 (Dec. 1970): 5.

[13] Bowen and Finegan, *The Economics of Labor Force Participation*, p. 240.

The Peripheral Worker

Peripheral workers are defined as those persons in the labor force who have intermittent or part-time employment for part of the year, part-time employment on a continuing basis, or intermittent full-time employment. As Dean Morse points out, since the peripheral worker is not part of the regular full-time work force little attention is paid to his particular problem. The most common groups of peripheral workers are found among women, workers under 24 years of age, nonwhites, and laborers over 55. Such workers are employed in low skill, low pay, and low status occupations, generally in service industries. If local manpower policy does not consider the role of the peripheral worker, these people may well lose desirable employment, or, if employed, they may suffer poor working conditions, little job security, and exploitive pay levels.[14]

The distinguishing characteristic of peripheral workers is the degree to which workers in this group would choose to secure full-time employment if available. Manpower policies must be flexible enough to develop strategies enabling peripheral workers to improve their wages and working conditions in the urban area.[15] The intermittent nature of employment among these workers might provide a valid source of training time for improvement of skills.

The Hard to Employ

The "hard to employ" are workers who fall between the employable or the unemployable.[16] Such a worker tends to be difficult to employ during periods of surplus labor, but when the economy is operating at full employment or near it, these people may find job opportunities.

People who fall into this category include those who lose their jobs through aging or deterioration of their skills and health and who find difficulty in regular employment thereafter. Hard to place persons sometimes fall into this category meaning that the attitude of the employer about the person's past performance, appearance, or race may affect the person's finding employment.

The hard to employ is a catchall; perhaps the best way to describe it is by characterizing more of the people who fall into this class: a man of 41 who was rejected from several jobs because he was a known homosexual; an attorney disbarred for using his client's money and who could not obtain any work he felt to be appropriate to his social or economic status; a man of 42 with eleven children who could work only irregularly because of a slight physical disability which kept him from securing permanent employment. Further examples include a 20 year old who had dropped out of school and by the time he was 20 had changed jobs seventeen times, seeking seasonal and overtime pay to cover the cost of a too

14 Dean W. Morse, "The Peripheral Worker," in *Manpower Strategy*, ed. Ginzberg, pp. 157, 158.

15 Morse, "The Peripheral Worker," in *Manpower Strategy*, ed. Ginzberg, p. 182.

16 Beatrice Reubens, "The Hard to Employ," in *Manpower Strategy*, ed. Ginzberg, p. 185.

expensive car; a boy of 18, the product of a broken home, turned freak and who looked so dirty he could not be sent for job interviews; the self-employed picture frame shop owner aged 59 who could find no employment after giving up his dying business.[17]

In general, a great number of the hard to employ suffer from a variety of pathologies. To imagine a single kind of employment program to assist such people seems unlikely. Programs would have to be developed to handle case by case problems. An intimate working relationship between employment services, medical services, psychiatric social work, corrective educational programs, and other services is necessary.

Reubens suggests that a comprehensive large-scale program for the hard to employ should have provisions for creating jobs. It should include outreach, intake, testing, counseling, basic education, prevocational training, work experience, occupational training, job development, placement, and follow-up. Supportive services for health, education, social work, transportation, and day care of children are usually needed. Overhead functions would include administration, research, program planning, and evaluation.[18]

One cannot be optimistic about the "hard to employ." In America, we do not appear to be very forgiving. We demand that people be self-supporting but work itself has little other definable value for many of us. Recognition of human problems and regard for all types of manpower as a valuable resource is required to generate programs for the "hard to employ."

Youth

In cities throughout America, the position of youth in the labor force is critical. Persons ages 16 to 19 accounted for between 16 and 30% of all unemployed between 1955 and 1969 (table 10). Persons ages 20 to 24 also accounted for a

TABLE 10

PERCENTAGE OF TOTAL UNEMPLOYMENT IN THE UNITED STATES
ACCOUNTED FOR BY YOUTH, 1955–69

	1955	1960	1965	1969
Age 16–19 (1,000s)	450	711	874	853
Percentage of total unemployed	15.8	18.5	26.0	30.1
Age 20–24 (1,000s)	396	583	557	560
Percentage of total unemployed	13.9	15.1	16.5	19.8

Source: U.S. Bureau of the Census, Department of Commerce, *Statistical Abstract of the United States, 1971* (Washington, D.C.: U.S. Government Printing Office, 1971), table 335, p. 214.

[17] Reubens, "The Hard to Employ," in *Manpower Strategy*, ed. Ginzberg, pp. 187, 188.

[18] Reubens, "The Hard to Employ," in *Manpower Strategy*, ed. Ginzberg, p. 205.

large portion of total unemployment over the same fourteen-year period, from 14 to 20%. Even if we assume that the data included persons only partially committed to seeking employment, and even if the data included many college students, the rates of unemployment are three to six times the rates of unemployment for the total labor force.

The staggering dimension of the problem is shown by the absolute numbers. Nearly 1.4 million youths were unemployed as of 1969. Employment opportunities for youths, whether males or females, are not very attractive. Among persons in that age group not enrolled in school, nearly 70% of the males held blue-collar jobs (compared to about 49% of males of all ages) while among women 64% of them held white-collar jobs (as opposed to about 59% of all females) (table 11). The evidence suggests that young males obtain poorer jobs relative to all males, while young females are more able to get white-collar jobs compared to all women workers. Many young women hold positions which are also held by older women; males, on the other hand, appear to take the shank end of jobs traditionally open to males. One should not surmise that the youthful female is better off than the youthful male. The male has the opportunity to gain advancement to a much greater degree. In an economy demanding a highly skilled and specialized labor force, youths typically fail to have sufficient education and skill to offer.

TABLE 11

PERCENTAGE DISTRIBUTION OF EMPLOYED PERSONS 16–21 YEARS OLD,
NOT ENROLLED IN SCHOOL, BY OCCUPATIONAL GROUPS, SEX, AND COLOR

Occupation and Sex	Total Percentage	Percentage of Total Percentage	
		White	Nonwhite
*Men**			
White collar	18.6	20.0	11.6
Blue collar	69.8	69.1	73.2
Service	6.5	5.8	9.8
Farm workers	5.2	5.1	5.4
Women†			
White collar	64.0	66.3	45.5
Blue collar	16.0	14.9	24.8
Service	19.6	18.4	28.8
Farm workers	.4	.3	.9

* Total number of white men: 2,021,000; total number of nonwhite men, 387,000.

† Total number of white women: 2,847,000; total number of nonwhite women, 2,530,000.

Note: Because of rounding, sums of individual items may not equal totals.

Source: Modified from Anne Young's "Employment of School Age Youth," *Monthly Labor Review* 93 (Sept. 1970): 9.

Nonwhites

The Civil Rights Act of 1964 under Title VII specifically forbids discrimination in any feature of employment on the basis of race, color, sex, religion, or national origin. The Age Discrimination section in the Employment Act of 1967 added age to the list of forbiddens. What have been the results of these and other acts to eliminate discrimination in hiring against ethnic minorities and other minority groups? In summary, the major points appear to be as follows:

1. Among minority groups, Indians and then blacks are still in the poorest economic condition.
2. Minority groups suffer occupational discrimination in all six of the highest paid occupational groups: crafts, professions, managerial, technical, clerical, and sales.
3. A larger proportion of minority persons are found in the lowest occupational categories than their numbers would suggest, namely, operative, service, and laborer occupations.
4. Wages within categories appear to be lower for minority group members.
5. Part-time, seasonal, or "dead-end" jobs are many times more common among members of minority groups than proportionally among whites.
6. Unemployment rates among minority groups are several times higher than among whites.

Evidence of these points is born out in table 12 where the unemployment rate among nonwhites is almost never less than two times that of whites. Efforts toward improving opportunities among nonwhites are not revealed in this data. Covering a nineteen-year period, the unemployment rate has consistently been twice as high as that of whites, and, as a percent, it has been as high as 10.2% and never lower than 6.4%. Prejudice and discrimination in American manpower development have sustained what Myrdal calls the vicious circle of cumulative

TABLE 12

Unemployment Rates Among Whites and Nonwhites,
And the Ratio of Nonwhite to White Unemployment Rates,
For Selected Years, 1955–69

Unemployment Rate	1955	1960	1965	1966	1967	1968	1969
White percentage	3.9	4.9	4.1	3.3	3.4	3.2	3.9
Nonwhite percentage	8.7	10.2	8.1	7.3	7.4	6.7	6.4
Ratio of nonwhite to white	2.2	2.1	2.0	2.2	2.2	2.1	2.1

Source: U.S. Bureau of the Census, Department of Commerce, *Statistical Abstract of the United States, 1971* (Washington, D.C.: U.S. Government Printing Office, 1971), table 321, p. 216.

causation — namely that discriminatory forces within the economic system tend to force a constant circle of poverty on nonwhites.

In 1969 data for employed persons classified by occupational category and white and nonwhite revealed: professional, technical, and kindred workers; white — 14.5%, nonwhite — 8.3%: farmers and farm managers; white — 2.5%, nonwhite — 1.0%: manager, officials, and proprietors except farm; white — 11.1%, nonwhite — 3.0%: sales workers; white — 6.5%, nonwhite — 2.0%: craftsmen, foremen, and kindred workers; white — 13.6%, nonwhite — 8.5%: operatives and kindred workers; white — 17.8%, nonwhite — 23.9%: private household workers; white — 1.3%, nonwhite — 8.5%: service workers, except private household; white — 9.2%, nonwhite — 18.2%: farm laborers and foremen; white — 1.7%, nonwhite — 3.2%: laborers, except farm and mine; white — 4.0%, nonwhite — 10.5%.[19] In spite of prohibitions against segregation in employment it is still a widespread practice.

While local manpower policy cannot eradicate all of the discrimination that exists against nonwhites, an effective local policy for the urban area must explicitly deal with enforcement of civil rights.

The Aged

The problems of the aged present a particularly difficult situation for local manpower policies. Among older persons who are unemployed, it is necessary to determine whether the unemployment is voluntary or involuntary. There is another pertinent subdivision — those who wish to be and are capable of being employed but cannot find employment and those who wish jobs but for one reason or another are incapable of being employed. For persons who want jobs and can be trained to have skills which the market may profitably use, there is no reason why local manpower policy should not serve them. Involuntary retirement is a cruel result of private capitalistic economies. While the older worker may no longer be as productive as the younger worker who replaces him, productivity and the need to work do not end when one reaches 65.

Many would argue that with the aged it is inefficient to invest manpower funds, but the problems of the aged can't be viewed only through economics or simply through redundancy policies. Manpower programs should be designed not simply from the standpoint of the efficiency of the urban economy, but from the economic desires of individuals as well. For example, how would you evaluate a program designed to train elderly men to make chairs, a task enormously satisfying for these elders, when the program itself generates greater costs than it does economic output in terms of the sales of the chairs? Does one view it as inefficient? Such questions must be dealt with for it is obvious that not all desirable

---

[19] U.S. Bureau of the Census, Department of Commerce, *Statistical Abstract of the United States, 1971* (Washington, D.C.: U.S. Government Printing Office, 1971), table 335, p. 226.

activities for the elderly undertaken in the city will be efficient in the market sense; yet they may still be socially desirable.

Such illustrations suggest the difference between work and employment. Employment carries the connotation of "approved," that is, paid work; work is a broader term. Work may be of great importance to the individual but not to the society. If you are learning to play a banjo or talk to geese, it may be in every respect work; that is, it is satisfying, challenging, productive to you, and even creative, but in spite of its meeting every test of work, it does not bring you a wage. Thus it is not gainful employment. Such is the case of the elderly working; many of their activities are work in every sense save that of having that work valued in society. Such situations should caution the student who thinks that all work in the society must pass a market test to be valuable. Thoreau's better work was certainly not the work for which he was paid as a surveyor, it was in the production of his *Journals* which in his day had no economic value.

There has been a consistent decline in the number of workers in the labor force who are over 65 years of age. As of 1969, persons 65 and over accounted for only 3.8% of the labor force, but as retirements continue to occur at an earlier age, the number of "elderly" will not diminish.

The Problem of Underemployment

Many people in cities are essentially poor but working. That is, they are performing useful jobs, but, for one reason or many, they do not receive a decent income for their work. In a Department of Labor study of six cities conducted in 1968 and 1969, a range of 31 to 41% of the families in the cities were earning less than $5,000 per year (table 13). From 15 to 23% of the families in these six cities earned less than $3,500 for that year. Statistics like these suggest at least two possibilities. First, the private market may not find it economical to pay some workers a living wage; second, some of these people may reflect workers who, with additional education and training, could increase their earnings in other occupations.

TABLE 13

FAMILIES OF 4 OR MORE RECEIVING LESS THAN $5,000 PER YEAR
IN 6 CITIES, JUNE 1968–JUNE 1969
(IN PERCENTAGES)

Annual Money Income	Atlanta	Chicago	Detroit	Houston	Los Angeles	New York
$0–$3,499	23	18	19	21	15	18
$3,500–$4,999	18	14	13	17	16	18
Total below $5,000	41	32	32	38	31	36

Source: Committee for Economic Development, *Training and Jobs for the Urban Poor: Employment and Income Data for the Poor Areas of Six Cities, July 1968–June 1969* (New York: Committee for Economic Development, July 1970), p. 25. Reprinted by permission.

Further evidence of this problem of employment without a living income among workers in these same six cities shows that males earning less than $65 per week made up from 10 to 22% of all males working (table 14). Among females working in these same cities, from 30 to 72% were earning less than $65 per week.

These data do not suggest that all of the persons included are essentially underemployed. Certainly many of them are, and, at the present time, there are no serious efforts in our cities to attack this problem. For persons who are not underemployed, that is, those who cannot earn higher incomes even with training, something other than manpower programs is needed. The data, however, present a shocking possibility when we consider that in the national labor force there are 30 million women and 70% of them earned less than $100 per week in 1969. Likewise, when we consider that there are 55 million males in the labor force and at least 30% of them make less than $100 per week, the idea staggers the myth that we are indeed a wealthy nation.

TABLE 14

EMPLOYED PERSONS EARNING LESS THAN $100 PER WEEK
(IN PERCENTAGES)

Employed Persons	Atlanta	Chicago	Detroit	Houston	Los Angeles	New York
All persons with earnings						
Male:						
$0–64	22	11	15	21	10	12
$65–99	37	22	14	36	21	37
Female:						
$0–64	63	30	48	72	33	30
$65–99	27	43	31	20	43	47
Persons employed fulltime						
Male:						
$0–64	12	6	7	12	3	7
$65–99	41	22	13	38	22	38
Percentage of all persons with earnings	78	86	79	81	82	87
Female:						
$0–64	50	22	33	62	19	16
$65–99	35	46	38	26	52	55
Percentage of all persons with earnings	65	78	66	67	79	65

Source: Committee for Economic Development, *Training and Jobs for the Urban Poor: Employment and Income Data for the Poor Areas of Six Cities, July 1968–June 1969* (New York: Committee for Economic Development, 1970), p. 25. Reprinted by permission.

Education and Job Requirements

In an article entitled "Education and Work," Ivar E. Berg suggests that the conventional wisdom operative among planners is that the supply of labor is conceived to be amenable to substantial manipulation while the demand for labor is held to be best influenced by interventions only "at the margins." [20]

Since most of our traditional economic theory demands that the economic system can best function with only limited restraints, we have traditionally accepted the businessman's assessment of his own problems. This has led to what Berg would appear to see as an excessive amount of interest in and emphasis on the inadequacies of the unemployed as defined by the job requirements of the employer, and that the solution to this unemployment in part at least lies in anti-poverty and other programs designed to upgrade those who do not function in the economy. Thus it is, as Berg argues, we spend most of our time attempting to alter the supply of labor and give little consideration to the characteristics of the demand for labor.[21]

There is a great deal of evidence leading to the conclusion that we must alter the labor supply. The findings of economists that there is a relationship between education and income, the fact that sociologists talk about upward social mobility as a function of education, all lead, as Berg argues, to the popularization of the idea that as a society we have more options in dealing with the supply side.[22]

Recent studies in the rate of return on investment in education have indicated that there is very little real difference in our economy between the earnings of the high school and the college graduate. A close examination of education and unemployment data reveals that the large increase in job opportunities is among middle-level jobs, those held by high school graduates. Berg argues that there is a shortage of high school graduates and a surplus of college graduates, especially among female members of the work force.[23]

IV. Aspects of Manpower Information for Policy

In the United States today, the question of information held by large organizations continues to be a problem. Many believe that the amount of information about you held by credit bureaus, government agencies, insurance companies, and others may be a dangerous threat to privacy. For manpower planning at the local level we need a great deal of information about citizens. Is it possible that the work histories and the analytical results of manpower program data research would be made available to private individuals and firms? Probably there would be great pressure for such information to be made avail-

[20] Ivar E. Berg, "Education and Work," in *Manpower Strategy*, ed. Ginzberg, p. 117.

[21] Berg, "Education and Work," in *Manpower Strategy*, ed. Ginzberg, pp. 119–24.

[22] Berg, "Education and Work," in *Manpower Strategy*, ed. Ginzberg, p. 121.

[23] Berg, "Education and Work," in *Manpower Strategy*, ed. Ginzberg, p. 125.

able for one reason or another. Would manpower records be open to law enforcement agencies? Could a firm seeking to hire you determine information about you which you would not want them to know? Yes, probably. We have a difficult dilemma in a sensitive society that idealizes democracy but has a very low tolerance toward dissidents or critics. Information in a repressive state can be dangerous for individuals, and some policy must be developed which allows the individual to determine which information held by the agency may be kept confidential. At the same time we must recognize that no effective manpower program can be developed which does not gather great amounts of information about individuals.

Probably the first requirement of an effective manpower data system is solid employment, wage, and hour data for the urban region. The fundamental employment series which duplicates the national series on wages, hours, and employment by sector is necessary from a planning point of view. Series might be developed not only by sector but by occupational classification as well. While not going into all aspects of the national labor statistics gathered by the Department of Labor, we should recognize the necessity of examining them to see which should be duplicated at the local level.

It is likely that cities must develop some form of continuing analytical manpower data series to view the complexities of urban structural unemployment. Initially we might recall the factors developed by Bowen and Finegan and discussed in the preceding chapter to determine if it is possible to construct a series on both positive or negative factors affecting labor force participation.

First there is the matter of *taste* for money income. As for taste for money income, we can distinguish small differences for the structurally unemployed (as opposed to the cyclically or the frictionally unemployed) except in the context of the factor of differentials between permanent and current income. Structurally unemployed persons would tend to have less disparity between current income (current in the sense of recent periods prior to unemployment) and permanent income.

A second factor determining labor force participation is *expectations*. With regard to expectations, the structurally unemployed person will likely earn (when working) below average wages. Transportation will be more difficult to acquire. He will have few marketable skills. All other things equal, he will usually fall out of the desirable age range for employment. He will typically have less suitable experience for the current market. As a result of these factors, his expectations of earnings will be quite low.

Structurally unemployed persons are also commonly below average in health and education; higher numbers of them (relatively) are black and female. Marital status may be a factor but this is not easily determined. Structurally unemployed persons are likely to have a higher than average number of children at home, a smaller house, lower tastes for additional schooling, and poorer residence locale.

A third factor affecting labor force participation is *the substitution of non-market work for market work* and mainly lies with the skills of homemaking in which the female, due to social forces and tradition, is typically better equipped. People are kept out of the labor force by home exigencies and home requirements. The cost of labor-saving devices is inversely related to the number of working housewives. The cost of nursery schools and day care is inversely related to employment of family members.

A fourth factor is *other family resources*. The number of structurally unemployed persons may increase with the per household number of potential earners. Incentives to work for the individual may be less among extended families.

No matter how we define the structurally unemployed, we must investigate the above factors. Once enumerated, evaluation of individuals who are unemployed could provide means for looking at the urban structural unemployment picture in any city. At present no city has this research capacity.

With the above conceptual framework we can develop a set of descriptive categories of problems which people have. While to some degree overlapping, since a person may have one or more of these problems, Wilbur Thompson's suggested classifications are instructive:

1. Self-sufficient unemployed: those willing and able to find new jobs unaided;
2. Personal placement problems: those with low intelligence, poor work habits (e.g., absenteeism, rebelliousness), alcoholics; part-time jobs for working mothers with little or no skill;
3. Information problems: those unrealistically holding out for jobs that do not exist, jobs that have ceased to exist, or jobs that they could never get;
4. Occupational placement problems: those with highly specialized skills and advanced age, where replacement without substantial downgrading will be difficult because an equivalent amount of occupational training in a new skill is impractical;
5. Retrainees, vocational: divided between those whose retraining requirements are minor and could be handled by the potential employer and those who need a new or first skill imparted under a major (public) training effort;
6. Retrainees, general education: those who must undergo substantial (public) education in English, arithmetic, and so forth before they would qualify for a private apprenticeship program, for example, rural in-migrants and long-time residents of urban slums;
7. Victims of discrimination: Negroes, females, school dropouts, and older workers illustrate social groups which constitute more of an employer than an employee problem; these three groups are dis-

tinctive in that reconversions on the supply side are impossible, the pattern of demand must be changed; our knowledge here should include the effect of firm size and the nature of the industry on willingness to employ these groups;

8. New entrants: the recent graduates and especially the school dropouts; the problem of identifying the kinds of jobs that not only do not require experience but also produce experience — enrich the worker;

9. The locationally mobile: bachelors and renters and others for whom the job market is truly national; the group is especially valuable in adjusting total supply in the local labor market;

10. High-level reconversions: professional and technical workers who are either unemployed or more likely underemployed in jobs less demanding than their capabilities justify and who pose problems in advanced education, such as aeronautical engineers who need postgraduate university work in mathematics and physics to qualify for missile work.[24]

Still another role of local manpower research should be to develop trends which affect unemployment levels. Such data might be in the form of a trend of employment for varieties of job types with wage rates over time in order to determine the problem areas in the future as well as potential growth areas of employment.

V. The Evaluation of Manpower Programs[25]

While it is certainly desirable to establish manpower services for the local government to undertake, means of evaluating the effectiveness of these programs are required. While the chapter on the evaluation of local government production contains greater detail, some special consideration must be given here to cost-benefit analysis as it relates to manpower programs. The problem with a general discussion of cost-benefit applied to manpower programs lies in the great differences between programs. Manpower programs can be designed to deal with a variety of problems, thus we can only describe some of the general considerations.

The Benefits of Training

First, all training programs have objectives they are designed to attain, and these objectives should be made quite explicit. Normally the purpose of any such program is to increase the productivity and earnings of the person who is trained. We should not forget that training programs may have adverse effects upon other workers. The principal benefit can be stated in terms of increased income and increased employment experience for the person trained.

[24] Thompson, *A Preface to Urban Economics*, pp. 232–34.

[25] This section is based on Burton A. Weisbrod's "Conceptual Issues in Evaluating Training Programs," *Monthly Labor Review* 89 (1966): 1091–97.

How could we develop a measure to show an increase to earnings? Ideally we need to know the earnings the person could achieve with and without training. What we usually must settle for is income or earnings data before and after training. Further, it may not be valid to compare earnings of a trained group to earnings of an untrained group since circumstances differ so widely.[26]

We might compare training this particular group of people with training another group of people or spending the funds in another investment alternative. In fact, we never know for certain that a program is the "best" investment the local government can make among its economic alternatives, but we must be certain that the program as designed is logically connected to the long-run goals of welfare in urban communities.

In addition, when we measure benefits and develop concepts about them, we should recognize that our measures are never more than estimates. Certainty is not a part of the benefit analysis. Our thinking should at all times be explicitly verbalized so that policy makers may have the benefit of a clear understanding of the limits of the analysis.

Let us turn now to some problems with our primary benefit measure. Since training takes time, we must be aware of differences in income that would have accrued to the trainees if they had not undertaken training. Second, we must be concerned with attempting to project the anticipated increase to earnings over very long periods of time, normally the lifetime of the workers less the anticipated number of workers who will, for one reason or another, not earn incomes until they reach a retirement age. This latter point is probably the greatest single weakness in our measure. Projections for even a short period of time are fraught with error. Further, how do we know that the immediate increase to earnings will be a continuing pattern?

In order to deal with this problem we may have to recast our thinking about our initial concept of benefits to enable us to establish a control group for comparative purposes. Even then we are evaluating the program ex post because the explicit purpose of the control group is to compare over time the earnings of the trained with the untrained control group. Perhaps our best efforts lie in an anticipation of benefits carefully compared to similar evaluations in other studies to at least sense the "reasonableness" of our own estimates.

A third possible problem in the analysis of benefits is the question of the impact that this program has on employment among other workers. If we disregard this problem, we can only do so when the program is relatively small compared to total employment in the community. If the program is large, then it can have major impact on local employment of others not engaged in training. Do we "shuffle the persons in the job queue," or do we generate employment with the training? Since our primary concern was with a particular group of structurally unemployed, to the extent that we reduce structural unemployment in

[26] Weisbrod, "Conceptual Issues," p. 1092.

this group we are generating beneficial activities in the community. But, if we do not increase aggregate local employment, then we have possibly shuffled the queue.

Finally, we should be concerned that cyclical effects and frictional effects do not enter the estimates of benefits or costs to the program. Since training time may be long, an analysis begun at the bottom or trough of a business cycle and examined through a period of recovery and expansion would yield widely differing results compared to an analytical time period which started with a peak and examined a period through a decline and recession. Our problem really lies in the fact that the cycle affects different industries in different ways, and, if we are comparing a control group to a group of trainees, it is unlikely that they will all be employed in the same industry. Further, during times of recession there would be relatively less opportunity for the untrained to remain employed than the trained group. In times of expansion, however, both groups would have better opportunities to maintain employment. The effect on the cost-benefit analysis is thus a kind of employment effect which is essentially cyclical and may have nothing to do with the training per se.

Weisbrod mentions a further consideration in his concern with distributional effects. Normally we consider the benefits in aggregate and the costs in aggregate, not distinguishing among individuals who receive the benefits or bear the costs. Weisbrod suggests that information should be presented in the evaluation that details a matrix or cross classification of the kinds of individuals who gain what particular levels of benefits.[27]

Cost of Training

When we turn our attention to the costs of training we should consider at least the following kinds of costs: (1) project costs, broken down into capital and operational costs; (2) costs born by individuals in the training program; i.e., direct costs plus incomes foregone by being in the program. This latter cost may be offset by a payment to the trainee, but in this case the differences in payment and income foregone should be noted, and the payment included under operational costs, with the net difference, positive or negative over income foregone, shown under costs to the individual.

Time Consideration

A further aspect of the evaluation of training programs lies in the impact of time on cost and benefit estimates and the necessity of considering time explicitly in the computation of these costs and benefits. Since in any investment program costs and benefits occur over different periods of time, we cannot compare costs and benefits unless we develop a common time point for valuation. The most logical point in time is the present, and our comparison of costs and benefits thus

[27] Weisbrod, "Conceptual Issues," p. 1096.

should become a comparison of the present value of costs as compared to the present value of benefits. Let us imagine a program in which we expend costs in one year and do not derive benefits until two years later. Are the costs dollars and benefits dollars comparable? Not without the inclusion of some means of bringing both costs and benefits back to present value.

Our means of assessing the present value of benefits is in the examination of the time value of dollars. A simple illustration will serve: Would you prefer to have a $1 now or a $1 one year from now? Obviously, most would prefer the $1 now, since present income is valued more than future income. We continue to ask about such comparisons until we strike an amount of future dollars which one values the same as a $1 now. Would you prefer to have $10 one year from now as opposed to a $1 now? Chances are one would prefer the $10 in the future. At this moment then, his time preference for the present $1 is within a range of more than a $1 and less than $10 in the future. That is, he values a $1 now comparable to something more than a $1 a year from now yet something less than $10 a year from now. Let us imagine that by asking additional comparative questions one finally decides that he is indifferent as to whether he has a $1 now or $1.10 a year from now. We have now equated the value of dollars in the future with dollars in the present.

Turning again to the evaluation of the training program, our task is to discount future dollars of benefits to make them comparable to dollars valued at the present time point. Our $1 in the future is worth less than a $1 now, so we must discount by some rate the dollars in the future. The problem now, however, is that we must aggregate these dollars in the future and jump from one as an individual to the social time preference rate; that is, we are concerned with a time preference function for money which tells us how society values dollars in the future. We do not know what that rate ought to be so we usually settle for a rate greater than zero and less than the higher rates of interest in markets. The usual procedure is to investigate the benefits from the standpoint of a high, a low, and a middle discount rate to see if various rates of interest have significant impact on benefits relative to costs. These discounts have the effect of lowering benefits, a subtraction from benefits. For a fuller treatment of discounting, refer to Chapter 2.

When we turn to costs, we also have a discounting problem. If costs all occur in the immediate time period then we have no problem with social time preference (which would suggest that dollars of cost in the future would be worth less than costs undertaken now). However, we have a discounting problem which lies in the fact that had we not invested in the training program, we could have invested the money in some other economically advantageous investment. A social opportunity cost rate is that rate of discount which equates the lost yield or profit of another investment that could have been undertaken with the investment actually undertaken. This discounting has the effect of raising the present value of costs, and an appropriate rate is again not possible to ascertain definitely. Typically we might use some market rate of interest, but there are limitations to this due to imperfections in market rates. The choice of an individual social opportunity cost rate is never completely logically satisfying, yet to fail to select a rate is possibly a greater error than picking a wrong one.

The Decision Rule

In short, we are concerned with comparing the present value of benefits to the training program with the present value of costs. This brief discussion has left out a large number of other necessary computations and inclusions in the analysis. It is not the purpose of this section to provide the reader with a working model to be applied to particular programs, but to present some of the major ideas for the evaluation of training programs and the development of such specific models. If the present value of the benefits exceeds the present value of the costs, then we say the program is efficient, but even the program that generates losses may still be socially desirable.

Summary: Manpower Policy for Local Government

The concerns of this chapter have been directed toward denoting an effective role for local government in dealing with manpower problems. One of the manpower problems in the city rests in labor force increases among youths and non-whites, traditionally high unemployment groups. Other problems exist as a result of the decline in blue-collar employment, the scattering of policy responsibility among various levels of government, the limited public commitment to labor policy, and the narrow concerns of the private sector for social policy.

The local authorities are limited in the kind of manpower policy with which they can work effectively. Cyclical employment is beyond the scope of the city to control, and frictional unemployment, if truly so, is not a major concern. Structural unemployment is a matter of concern and an area in which local policy may intervene.

Major thrusts of local manpower policy fall into the categories of information, retraining and relocation, and some form of guaranteed employment. Any manpower policy moving toward a solution of local problems is of necessity a cooperative venture in which private and public agencies in the city are coordinated by local government. The major stages of manpower policy consist of identification, counseling, training or retraining, placement, and follow-up.

Some special manpower problems for the city include the problems of high unemployment rates among females and the low wage rates of working women. The peripheral worker, one who seeks occasional or part-time employment, is a vital part of the city's work force and should be protected. The hard to employ, persons who because of prior experience are socially unemployable, could include, for example, disbarred lawyers, homosexuals, and any person who is unemployed because of criminal or antisocial acts. Another problem area is city youths who are numerous among those chronically unemployed. Nonwhites add another dimension to local manpower concerns. The aged, many suffering from involuntary retirements, represent a particularly difficult problem group because we tend to think more in terms of social programs for them than employment or manpower programs. However, for the aged there are direct benefits to be achieved by maintaining their social, if not their strictly economic, productivity. The problem of underemployment is demonstrated by the large quantities of people in cities who do not earn a living wage. Finally, job requirements for education go up simply because of the number of people who are educated.

A viable local manpower policy demands extensive information about residents in the city. There needs to be sufficient information on wages, work hours, employment by sector, and changes anticipated within and among sectors. Personal data, though sensitive to collect, is necessary to define the extent of, and the individuals who compose, the structurally unemployed in the city. Tastes and preferences, expectations, family situations, nonmarket substitutions, education, and health are all factors affecting labor force participation. External costs, such as child care, clothing, and transportation costs, affect participation. Number of children, unfavorable housing conditions, and the number of working members in the household are related to the number of structurally unemployed. Solid labor force data in the city, combined with intensive analysis leading toward the definition and identification of the structurally unemployed, is necessary for effective local policy.

In the evaluation of local policy, cost-benefit analysis is applied. The primary benefit connected with manpower programs lies in a comparison of discounted future earnings streams of individuals with and without the training. The benefit measures must be compared to the costs of the training and the supportive programs to ascertain if the benefits exceed the costs.

Selected Bibliography

Manpower Policy for Local Government

MANPOWER

APPEL, GARY L., AND SCHLENKER, ROBERT E. "An Analysis of Michigan's Experience with Work Incentives." *Monthly Labor Review* 94 (Sept. 1971): 15–22.

BERG, IVAR. *Education and Jobs: The Great Training Robbery.* New York: Praeger, 1970.

BOLINO, AUGUST C. *Manpower and the City.* Cambridge, Mass.: Schenkman Publishing Co., 1969.

BORUS, MICHAEL E., AND BUNTZ, C. G. "Problems and Issues in the Evaluation of Manpower Programs." *Industrial and Labor Relations Review* 25 (1972): 234–45.

————. "The Economic Effectiveness of Retraining the Unemployed: A Study of Benefits and Costs of Retraining the Unemployed Based on the Experience of Workers in Connecticut." *Yale Economic Essays* 4 (1964): 371–429.

BOWLBY, ROGER L., AND SCHRIVER, WILLIAM R. "Nonwage Benefits of Vocational Training: Employability and Mobility." *Industrial and Labor Relations Review* 23 (1970): 500–9.

COMMITTEE FOR ECONOMIC DEVELOPMENT. *Training and Jobs for the Urban Poor: A Statement on National Policy by the Research and Policy Committee of the Committee for Economic Development.* New York: Committee for Economic Development, 1970.

CONLEY, RONALD W. *The Economics of Vocational Rehabilitation.* Baltimore: Johns Hopkins Press, 1965.

GARMS, WALTER I. "A Benefit-Cost Analysis of the Upward Bound Program." *Journal of Human Resources* 6 (1971): 206–20.

GINZBERG, ELI, AND THE CONSERVATION OF HUMAN RESOURCES STAFF, COLUMBIA UNIVERSITY, EDS. *Manpower Strategy for the Metropolis.* New York: Columbia University Press, 1968.

HAMERMESH, DANIEL S. *Economic Aspects of Manpower Training Programs: Theory and Policy.* Lexington, Mass.: Heath Lexington Books, 1971.

HARDIN, EINAR, AND BORUS, MICHAEL E. *The Economic Benefits and Costs of Retraining.* Lexington, Mass.: Heath Lexington Books, 1971.

HOLT, CHARLES C., ET AL. *The Unemployment — Inflation Dilemma: A Manpower Solution.* Washington, D.C.: Urban Institute, 1971.

LESTER, RICHARD A. *Manpower Planning in a Free Society.* Princeton: Princeton University Press, 1966.

NORTHRUP, HERBERT R., ET AL. *Negro Employment in Basic Industry: A Study of Racial Policies in Six Industries.* Studies of Negro Employment, vol. 1. Philadelphia: Industrial Research Unit, Wharton School of Finance and Commerce, University of Pennsylvania Press, 1970.

PERLMAN, RICHARD. *Labor Theory.* New York: John Wiley & Sons, 1969.

RAWLINS, V. L. "Job Corps: The Urban Center as a Training Facility." *Journal of Human Resources* 6 (1971): 221–35.

RUTTENBERG, STANLEY H., AND GUTCHESS, JOCELYN. *The Federal-State Employment Service: A Critique.* Policy Studies in Employment and Welfare, no. 5. Baltimore: Johns Hopkins Press, 1970.

SMITH, A. D. "Active Manpower and Redundancy Policies: Their Costs and Benefits." *International Labour Review* 95 (1967): 49–60.

SOMERS, GERALD G., AND STROMSDORFER, ERNST. "Benefit-Cost Analysis of Manpower Retraining." In "Manpower and Welfare Programs: Benefit-Cost Analysis," Proceedings of the 17th Annual Meeting, Industrial Relations Research Association, Dec. 28 and 29, 1964, Chicago, Ill., pp. 172–85.

U.S. CONGRESS, SENATE COMMITTEE ON LABOR AND PUBLIC WELFARE, SUBCOMMITTEE ON EMPLOYMENT, MANPOWER, AND POVERTY. *The Manpower Revolution: Its Policy Consequences,* ed. Garth L. Mangum. Garden City, N.Y.: Doubleday, 1965.

POVERTY

ALLEN, ROBERT L. *Black Awakening in Capitalist America: An Analytical History.* Garden City, N.Y.: Doubleday, 1970.

BANFIELD, EDWARD C. *The Unheavenly City: The Nature and Future of Our Urban Crisis.* Boston: Little, Brown and Co., 1968.

BECKER, GARY S. The Economics of Discrimination. 2d ed. Chicago: University of Chicago Press, 1971.

CAPLOVITZ, DAVID. *The Poor Pay More: Consumer Practices of Low-Income Families.* New York: Free Press of Glencoe, 1967.

CENTER FOR POLICY STUDY. *The Social Impact of Urban Design.* Chicago: University of Chicago Press, 1971.

DOWNS, ANTHONY. *Urban Problems and Prospects.* Markham Series in Public Policy Analysis. Chicago: Markham Publishing Co., 1970.

————. *Who Are the Urban Poor?* Supplementary paper no. 26. New York: Committee for Economic Development, 1970.

GANS, HERBERT J. "The Uses of Poverty: The Poor Pay All." *Social Policy,* July/Aug. 1971, pp. 20–24.

GINSBURG, HELEN, ED. *Poverty, Economics, and Society.* Boston: Little, Brown and Co., 1972.

GLAZER, NATHAN, ED. *Cities in Trouble.* Chicago: Quadrangle Books, 1970.

HARRINGTON, MICHAEL. *The Other America: Poverty in the United States.* New York: Macmillan, 1962.

HELLER, WALTER W. "Economics of the Race Problems." *Social Research* 37 (1970): 495–510.

KAIN, JOHN F. "Coping with Ghetto Unemployment." *Journal of the American Institute of Planners* 35 (1969): 80–83.

————. "The Distribution and Movement of Jobs and Industry." In *The Metropolitan Enigma: Inquiries into the Nature and Dimensions of America's Urban Crisis,* ed. James Q. Wilson, pp. 1–43. Garden City, N.Y.: Doubleday, 1970.

MYRDAL, GUNNAR. *Challenge to Affluence.* New York: Pantheon Books, 1965.

ORNATI, OSCAR. "Poverty in the Cities." In *Issues in Urban Economics,* ed. Harvey Perloff and Lowdon Wingo, Jr., pp. 335–62. Baltimore: Published for Resources for the Future by Johns Hopkins Press, 1968.

ORSHANSKY, MOLLIE. "How Poverty is Measured." *Monthly Labor Review* 92 (Feb. 1969): 37–41.

PIVEN, FRANCES FOX, AND CLOWARD, RICHARD A. *Regulating the Poor: The Functions of Public Welfare.* New York: Pantheon Books, 1971.

SACKREY, CHARLES. "Economics and Black Poverty." *Review of Black Political Economy,* Winter/Spring 1971, pp. 47–64.

————. *The Political Economy of Urban Poverty.* New York: W. W. Norton, 1973.

SELIGMAN, BEN B. *Permanent Poverty: An American Syndrome.* Chicago: Quadrangle Books, 1968.

SIEGEL, IRVING H. *The Kerner Commission Report and Economic Policy.* Kalamazoo, Mich.: The W. E. Upjohn Institute for Employment Research, 1969.

TABB, WILLIAM K. *The Political Economy of the Black Ghetto.* New York: W. W. Norton, 1970.

TAYLOR, WILLIAM L. *Hanging Together: Equality in an Urban Nation.* New York: Simon and Schuster, 1971.

THOMPSON, WILBUR R. *A Preface to Urban Economics.* Baltimore: Published for Resources for the Future by Johns Hopkins Press, 1965.

WEISBROD, BURTON A., ED. *The Economics of Poverty: An American Paradox.* Englewood Cliffs, N.J.: Prentice-Hall, 1965.

5

Urban Education

The fate of cities lies clearly with the maintenance of sophisticated educational establishments. The value of education in general, and in training specifically, is central to continuous economic development. Since the economist necessarily runs the risk of treating men as objects or commodities (because the capitalistic unit treats men as resources), we must assert at the outset that this chapter is a narrow treatment of education and its relation to human development. In education we are interested in the following: what is the nature of the economics of education, and what is the relation of education to urban economic development?

I. A Statistical Summary of Schools

Education in the United States is big business, a business which takes place largely in urban areas. According to the *Statistical Abstract*, in the United States in 1971 there were an estimated 112,000 educational institutions consisting of public and private elementary and secondary schools, and public and private colleges and universities. About 66,000 of these were public elementary schools, 14,000 were private elementary schools, and, at the secondary level, about 25,000 were public high schools and 4,000 were private. Among colleges and universities, nearly 1,100 of them were public and about 1,500 of them were private.

School Enrollments

Total enrollments during 1972 were estimated to be in excess of 60 million persons. Of the 60 million, about 32 million were elementary school children, and slightly more than 3.1 million were kindergartners. In grades nine through twelve, there numbered some 15 million students, while there were about 8.3 million students enrolled in colleges and universities.

In cities, white school enrollments totaled 22 million in 1960, and by 1969 enrollments had jumped to 27 million, a change of almost 21% (table 15). Likewise, nonwhite enrollments jumped in cities from 3.4 million to 5.1 million, an even larger increase, 51%, than among whites. Around the United States the percentage increase of nonwhite over white enrollments was substantial, 32% as compared with a white increase of 17% for the same nine-year period.

Median school years completed has risen slowly but steadily and by 1972 had reached 12.2 years. The slight improvement in nonwhite educational status can be seen by the fact that among nonwhites in 1972 who were 55 years and older, the median school years completed was only 7.2 years, while among people ages 25 to 29, the rate was 12.3 years. Over time for both whites and nonwhites the median number of school years completed is rising.

School Finance

Turning from enrollments to finances, as of 1969 combined public and private school expenditures totaled $61.4 billion of which nearly $50 billion was for public school expenditures. Operating expenditures accounted for about $54 billion and capital expenditures the remaining $8 billion. This total investment of $61.4 billion on education in the United States was 7.1% of the gross national product for 1969.

When local public school expenditures are separated from state and federal expenditures in 1969, towns and cities in the United States were spending $20 billion on education, or roughly 32.6% of all local expenditures. How this $20 billion was allocated among the levels of schools reveals that most, about $19.4 billion, went to primary and secondary schools while the balance went to publicly supported institutions of higher learning.

TABLE 15

SCHOOL ENROLLMENT OF PERSONS 5 TO 17 YEARS OLD,
BY RACE AND RESIDENCE: 1960, 1965, AND 1969*

Residence	White				Negro and Other			
	1960	1965	1969	Percentage Change 1960–69	1960	1965	1969	Percentage Change 1960–69
Total	36,750	40,928	43,116	17.3	5,549	6,554	7,334	32.2
Metropolitan	22,279	26,309	26,915	20.8	3,378	4,344	5,106	51.2
In central cities	9,645	9,806	9,398	−2.6	2,615	3,433	3,898	49.1
Outside central cities..	12,634	16,503	17,517	38.6	763	911	1,207	58.2
Nonmetropolitan	14,471	14,619	16,200	11.9	2,171	2,210	2,229	2.7

* Enrollment in thousands.

Source: U.S. Bureau of the Census, Department of Commerce, *Statistical Abstract of the United States, 1971* (Washington, D.C.: U.S. Government Printing Office, 1971), table 155, p. 109.

Support for local public elementary and secondary school comes largely from local sources. As of 1968 about 52.7% of local school support came from local sources (table 16). The trend appears to suggest that local sources of revenues are decreasing since, in 1940, local sources accounted for 68% of the funding. The federal government is increasing its support of local schools from only 1.8% of the total funding in 1940 to almost 9% in 1968. Likewise, state support of local schools is increasing but more slowly than federal — moving from 30.3% in 1940 to 38.5% in 1968.

Expenditures by local public schools have increased dramatically since 1950 when total expenditures were only $5.8 billion while, by 1968, this total had grown to nearly $33 billion (table 17). The major amount of this public money is spent by school authorities on current operating expenses, which in 1968 represented in excess of $27 billion or 84% of the total. Of this nearly $27 billion, about $18.3 billion was spent on instruction, including teachers' salaries, books, clerical assistance, and supplies. Table 17 provides a breakdown of these expenditures for selected years.

A part of the educational expenditure which should be analyzed in more detail is teachers' salaries. As of 1972, it has been estimated that there were 2.1 million teachers in public elementary and secondary schools. According to the *Statistical Abstract*, there were approximately 1.1 million elementary teachers and 967,000 secondary teachers. The average salary for all teachers was esti-

TABLE 16

PUBLIC ELEMENTARY AND SECONDARY SCHOOLS —
REVENUE, BY SOURCE OF FUNDS: 1940–68
(IN MILLIONS OF DOLLARS, EXCEPT PERCENTAGE)

School Year	Total Revenue for Public Schools	Federal		State		Intermediate and Local Sources*	
		Amount	Percent	Amount	Percent	Amount	Percent
1940	$ 2,261	$ 40	1.8	$ 684	30.3	$ 1,536	68.0
1950	5,437	156	2.9	2,166	39.8	3,116	57.3
1956	9,687	441	4.6	3,829	39.5	5,416	55.9
1958	12,182	487	4.0	4,800	39.4	6,895	56.6
1960	14,747	652	4.4	5,768	39.1	8,327	56.5
1962	17,528	761	4.3	6,789	38.7	9,978	56.9
1964	20,544	897	4.4	8,078	39.3	11,569	56.3
1966	25,357	1,997	7.9	9,920	39.1	13,440	53.0
1968	31,903	2,806	8.8	12,276	38.5	16,821	52.7

* Includes receipts from gifts and from tuition and transportation fees paid by patrons.

Source: U.S. Bureau of the Census, Department of Commerce, *Statistical Abstract of the United States, 1971* (Washington, D.C.: U.S. Government Printing Office, 1971), table 178, p. 121.

TABLE 17

PUBLIC ELEMENTARY AND SECONDARY SCHOOLS —
EXPENDITURES, BY PURPOSE, 1950 AND 1968
(IN MILLIONS OF DOLLARS, EXCEPT PERCENTAGE)

Purpose	1950		1968	
	Total	Percentage	Total	Percentage
Total expenditure, all schools	5,838	100.0	$32,984	100.0
Total current expenditure, all schools	4,723	80.9	27,750	84.1
Current expenditure for day schools	4,687	80.3	26,886	81.5
Administration	220	3.8	1,260	3.8
Instruction	3,112	53.3	18,376	55.7
Plant operation	428	7.3	2,164	6.6
Plant maintenance	214	3.7	701	2.1
Fixed charges	261	4.5	2,386	7.2
Other school services	452	7.7	2,000	6.1
Other current expenditure	36	.6	865	2.6
Capital outlay	1,014	17.4	4,256	12.9
Interest	101	1.7	978	3.0

Source: U.S. Bureau of the Census, Department of Commerce, *Statistical Abstract of the United States, 1971* (Washington, D.C.: U.S. Government Printing Office, 1971), table 178, p. 121.

mated for 1972 to be $9,700 per year. For secondary teachers this average was in excess of $10,000, and for elementary teachers the figure was lower at about $9,400. About 20% of the teachers in the United States make less than $7,500 and almost 80% make in excess of $7,500. These salary figures all indicate that probably school teachers are paid less well than others with comparable education. The teacher in the United States had a median number of eight years taught in 1972, a decline from the 1964 median of eleven years. It would appear that the number of teachers of young age is increasing, and the average level of education of teachers appears to be increasing. While salaries rise, the teacher on the average is making an income which is slightly below the mean income in the United States.

II. Economics of Education

To the economist, the school system at the local level looks considerably like a private firm producing a diversity of products. The analogy does not hold throughout, but the models of economics have relevance for analyzing the educational system.

The School as Producer

Rather than discuss the broad term education, economists refer to units of schooling. We define schooling as the output of the production process; organized education then refers to the process which produces schooling. A year of schooling means a year of going through the process of organized education.

There is little doubt that when we define schooling in such a limited way we are open to much criticism. The value of education in our lives is so great that its economic aspects may be of little consequence. Critics might argue that we debase the process to so limitedly conceive it; as Schultz points out:

> What is the value of schooling? A babel of voices will respond to this query. It is moral, refines taste, and gives people real satisfactions. It is vocational, develops skills, increases earnings, and is an investment in man.[1]

While the economic level of urban education is only one conceptual level, there is little doubt that understanding economic behavior is relevant to understanding the process of education.

Returning to the application of economic terminology, the total of local school systems represents an industry.[2] The problem with the output of this industry has already been suggested above, namely that it is multi-dimensional and has various levels of value to those concerned. The value of the output is not easily measured because it is not readily sold in the marketplace as a single commodity. Further, schools (except for a few private schools) do not operate at a profit. If the output is not directly sold in the market by the producer, then who gains the value of this output? Generally we imagine that the individuals who go through the process capture the majority of benefits of the process, but it is too limited to say that only those direct participants benefit from the educational process. As we shall see, the values to others than the direct recipient can be quite high.

When we speak of benefits derived from education, we consider the individual benefits, the personal profit complement, and the national productivity orientation or social benefits. According to Bowen, the personal profit orientation looks at differences in net earnings of people with various amounts of education, this net difference being profit. The national productivity orientation considers the same net income differences as partial evidence of the effects that educational investments may make upon the output of the economy. To consider the profitability of investing in education by either the individual or the state, we are concerned with attempting to determine the rates of return to these investments. As Bowen points out, the individual is concerned with his own direct costs, out-of-pocket and opportunity costs. It is not merely the direct costs to the individual that are important, it is important as well to consider foregone income (income not gained because of being in school) and any other opportunity costs. To the state, all costs are relevant including direct costs of schools,

---

[1] Theodore W. Schultz, *The Economic Value of Education* (New York: Columbia University Press, 1963), p. 6.

[2] Schultz, *Economic Value of Education*, p. 4.

costs of subsidies, and opportunity costs. The individual rate of return and the social rate of return become statements of primary benefits and secondary or social benefits respectively.[3]

Before turning to a discussion of some results of studies, it should be noted that there are significant difficulties in measuring the economic returns of educa-cation. Central to this difficulty is the problem of measuring returns and deter-mining if they are strictly the result of education, rather than products of family background, sex, age, income, and other characteristics. Another problem lies in using wages as proxies of productivity in the economic system. As long as wage levels are not competitive, there are difficulties in using net earnings differences as a measure of contribution to the output of the economy.

The Economic Value of Education: Returns to the Individual

Economists for many years have been aware of the close association between education and economic well-being. As Adam Smith noted:

> When any expensive machine is erected, the extraordinary work to be per-formed by it before it is worn out, it must be expected, will replace the capital laid out upon it, with at least the ordinary profits.
> ... A man educated at the expense of much labor and time to any of those employed, which require extraordinary dexterity and skill, may be compared to one of those expensive machines. The work which he learns to perform, it must be expected, over and above the usual wages of common labor will replace to him, the whole expense of his education, with at least the ordinary profits of an equally valuable capital. It must do this too in a reasonable time, regard being had to the very uncertain duration of human life, in the same manner as to the more certain duration of the machine.[4]

Smith supported public education as a desirable investment for the community to undertake.

Schultz, noting the ideas of early economists, suggested that both Ricardo and Malthus thought of education as an instrument for promoting the well-being of the masses through increasing capital and checking the growth of population. John Stuart Mill advocated "an effective national education of the children of the laboring people," with a view to inculcating in them "common sense, habits of prudence, economy, temperance, and self-government." Alfred Marshall saw education as a "national investment." He stressed the need for general education for every man, "for it makes him more intelligent, more ready, more trustworthy in his ordinary work; it raises the tone of his life in working hours; it is thus an

---

[3] William G. Bowen, "Assessing the Economic Contribution of Education," in *Economic Aspects of Education: Selected Readings,* comp. Mark Blaugh, vol. 1 (Harmondsworth, Eng.: Penguin Books, 1968), p. 78. Also in "Higher Education Report," Report of the Committee Under the Chairmanship of Lord Robbins, 1961–63, London, H.M.S.O., 1963, appendix 4, pp. 73–96.

[4] Adam Smith, *An Inquiry into the Nature and Causes of the Wealth of Nations* (New York: Modern Library, 1937), p. 101.

important means to the production of material wealth . . . ." This is not to suggest that early economists believed in treating man as a portion of capital or as a commodity. There has been resistance to such treatments right up until today. Investments in human capital is strictly a modern concept.[5]

Beginning with early studies, procedures have evolved for measurement of the returns to the individual. Such procedures today have three common threads:

1. The computation of expected *additional lifetime earnings* concomitant with a certain attained educational level based on the number of years of schooling. This has been the primary *benefit* or return.

2. The computation of the *costs* of the education. The costs of education to an individual consist of the *direct costs* to him of attending (tuition, supplies, transportation, etc.), the income which he has given up by devoting his time to education, and the *indirect costs* in the form of taxes or costs to the community.

3. The application of a *rate of discount* to the returns. Since there may be the assumption that the individual could have invested his money in an alternative manner, this discount rate will be that interest rate which is equal to the rate of return which the individual could have realized by that alternative investment.[6]

The problem with discounting lies in trying to determine what rate of interest to use. Borrowing costs for education vary, and the rate of return from alternate uses of capital is not uniform since the rate depends on the degree of risk and on imperfections in the capital market.[7]

An early and largely ignored paper was done by Walsh in 1935. In considering the returns to education of professionals, he concluded that while he could not separate the impact of education on income from other income determinants, there were significant returns to education among professionals. This paper is usually credited as being the first application of the capital concept to human beings.[8]

It was not until much later that the thread was picked up in the now classic study done by Friedman and Kuznets published in 1946. Among other things, Friedman and Kuznets in their study of independent professional practice concluded that the time spent by doctors in additional education generated sufficient income over incomes of dentists to justify the longer education of doctors.[9]

[5] Schultz, *Economic Value of Education*, pp. 4, 72.

[6] Shane J. Hunt, "Income Determinants for College Graduates, and the Return to Educational Investments," *Yale Economic Essays* 3 (1963): 305.

[7] H. S. Houthakker, "Education and Income," *Review of Economics and Statistics* 41 (1959): 27.

[8] J. R. Walsh, "Capital Concept Applied to Man," *Quarterly Journal of Economics* 49 (1935): 255–85.

[9] Milton Friedman and Simon Kuznets, *Income from Independent Professional Practice*, no. 45 (New York: Publications of the National Bureau of Economic Research, 1946), pp. 147–48.

A study by Glick and Miller used data from the 1950 census and generated the conclusion that a college education was worth $100,000 to an individual. Based on the 1950 census data, these were the average lifetime earnings to be expected from various schooling levels:

Schooling	Lifetime Incomes
Elementary	
None	$ 58,000
1–4 years	$ 72,000
5–7 years	$ 93,000
8 years	$116,000
AVERAGE	$113,000
High School	
1–3 years	$135,000
4 years	$165,000
College	
1–3 years	$190,000
4 years	$268,000[10]

The difference, therefore, in lifetime earnings between the average high school graduate and the average college graduate is $103,000.

In consideration of costs, Glick and Miller took an average 4.5 years for completion of a college degree and adjusted their estimated cost of $7,000 for 4 years to generate a total out-of-pocket cost to the individual of $8,000, less $2,700 for tax deductions, leaving a net figure of $5,300.

In the case of costs due to foregone income (income lost during the stay in college), average annual income of males ages 18 to 21 with high school diplomas was used. Estimating this figure to be $1,200 per year and income earned by college students at $400 per year, the foregone income for 4.5 years amounted to an opportunity cost of $3,600. Thus a college degree was estimated to cost a total of $3,600 plus $5,300 or $8,900.

Comparing the yield that one would gain from $8,900 invested securely to the yield of a college education and degree, Glick and Miller found that the lifetime interest earnings on the investment were only $24,000 while the lifetime earnings of the investment in a college education generated $103,000, leaving a net benefit or differential of $75,000, in favor of the college degree.[11]

An empirical examination of the Glick and Miller study was significant in drawing forth further work to point out errors in the original study. Houthakker

[10] Paul C. Glick and Herman P. Miller, "Educational Level and Potential Income," *American Sociological Review* 21 (1956): 310.

[11] Glick and Miller, "Educational Level and Potential Income," p. 311.

added to the Glick and Miller computations the impact of adjusted federal taxes, mortality rates, and discounted the returns at an 8% discount rate so that the estimated present value of the differential between high school and college educations was not worth $75,000 but only about $3,300. Reducing the monetary value difference to only $3,300 certainly raises serious questions about the validity of college educations as an economic investment.[12]

Other studies have shown different results. Morgan and David analyzed earnings differentials and concluded that the bachelor's degree generated a larger income than the high school degree with a return on investment in the neighborhood of from 4 to 6%. Likewise, Carol and Parry suggested that some occupational categories paid well enough that if the student left school and invested what would otherwise be the costs of graduate school education, at returns of 5%, he would be financially better off to quit and invest than to continue in college.[13]

It may be that the degree makes the real difference in increasing incomes rather than the number of years of schooling. "Many employers prefer or hire only college graduates . . . only because a college degree serves them as a credential for the diligence and intelligence of the applicant." "The applicant who has graduated gets the better job and the better pay because the degree *identifies* him as the better man, not because higher education has necessarily added to his skill." [14]

Gary Becker refined the measurement process. He is credited by Hunt with improving on the work of his predecessors in three ways:

1. He shifted the emphasis of analysis from that of an individual investment to that of social policy by comparing the returns from education to the returns obtained by business investment in physical capital.

2. He did not compute the excess of returns over costs at an arbitrarily chosen discount rate, but instead computed the discount rate which equated costs and returns.

3. He not only made allowances for mortality, race, and unemployment, but also contrived an adjustment which allowed for ability differences between groups of diverse educational levels.[15]

Using this improved methodology, Becker quoted a rate of return of 12% from an investment in a college education for an urban white male in 1940. By 1950, this rate had slipped to 10%, mostly as a result of increased income tax

[12] Houthakker, "Education and Income," p. 38.

[13] James Morgan and Martin David, "Education and Income," *Quarterly Journal of Economics* 77 (1963): 434–35.

[14] Fritz Machlup, *The Production and Distribution of Knowledge in the United States* (Princeton: Princeton University Press, 1962), pp. 114–15. André Danière, *Higher Education in the American Economy* (New York: Random House, 1964), p. 41. (Emphasis in the original.)

[15] Hunt, "Income Determinants," p. 305.

rates. However, since the student pays only ⅔ of the total costs of his college education, Becker adjusted this rate to a figure of 9% for both 1940 and 1950 students. He concluded that this is not an especially high return and that it may not be better than the return from tangible capital. This 9% rate of return, incidentally, was for urban whites only. For nonwhites the rate was 7%, and for all whites slightly less than 9%. Roger Freeman noted that "attending college or high school for less than the full four years seems to bestow little advantage." [16]

Using a cost-benefit approach, Werner Hirsch and Morton Marcus found that attendance in college for two years for a male yields a net cost of $44 or a return of $.99 for every $1.00 invested. The return for a female for the same period was $.47 on a $1.00 with a net cost of $2,405. Their analysis included only incremental benefits.[17]

A recent study revealed that returns to noncollege bound graduates of vocational high schools were higher than were those of noncollege bound graduates of comprehensive high schools.[18]

Studies of the value of education have been deficient in that economists do not agree on the many variables or qualifications that affect a cause and effect relationship of income and education. More consideration needs to be given to the influence of such things as intelligence, attitude, personality and emotional make-up; health; sex; race; age; religion; self-education; armed forces training; on-the-job training; experience; degree of competition in the labor market; rate of unemployment and supervisory status; number of hours worked; quality of education; geographic area; socioeconomic level of parents; educational level of parents; occupation of father; mental, social, and physical stresses; and, perhaps, most important of all — motivation.

Other Values to the Individual: External Effects

In addition to the principal measures of the value of education to the individual, i.e., the direct monetary returns, there are also additional nonmonetary benefits which are in essence externalities. These spillovers from the educational investment can be significant for many persons and have economic value.

One significant externality for the person educated is that of the "option" to buy further education. The value of additional education must be thought of, in terms of monetary returns, as having two components:

1. The additional earnings resulting from completion of a given level of education.

[16] Gary S. Becker, "Underinvestment in College Education?" *Papers and Proceedings of the American Economic Association, American Economic Review* 50 (1960): 346–54. Roger A. Freeman, *Crisis in College Finance? Time for New Solutions* (Washington, D.C.: Institute for Social Science Research, 1965), p. 29.

[17] Werner Z. Hirsch and Morton J. Marcus, "Some Benefit-Cost Considerations of Universal Junior College Education," *National Tax Journal* 19 (1966): 51.

[18] Teh-Wei Hu, Maw L. Lee, and Ernst W. Stromsdorfer, "Economic Returns to Vocational and Comprehensive High School Graduates," *Journal of Human Resources* 6 (1971): 25–50.

2. The value of the "option" to obtain still further education and the
rewards accompanying it.[19]

To this point we have been discussing only the actual monetary returns for
education. The option to buy further education, however, adds additional value
to the investment. One cannot go on to college, for example, without first having
completed high school.

A second related monetary value of education is the opportunity it presents
for "hedging" against the vicissitudes of technological change. This value is still
monetary in nature because it reduces the chances of the worker's skills being
replaced by technological advancement.[20]

A third related monetary value is the wider range of desirable employment
choices which are available to the individual as a result of increased schooling.
In general, this range widens as the educational attainment level increases.

Intangible benefits also include the possibilities of personal pleasure to the
individual and the sharing of cultural and aesthetic pleasures with parents and
children, a pleasure which may provide a more stable and happy home life. This
may be a benefit for the individual both with the present family and with his own
future family.

III. Education and Urban Development: Benefits of Investing
in Human Capital

Education has an impact on the political and social structure of a nation.
Education determines, in part, how well a society is managed and how wise will
be its economic and political decisions, ranging from tax cuts to nuclear war.
Ackoff, for example, states:

> Education provides the information and skills necessary for the continua-
> tion and expansion of scientific effort, for economic development, and for
> health. It attempts to produce well-adjusted, ethical and moral individuals.
> It creates artists and appreciators of art, and it instructs in recreational
> activity.
> Education, then, may be thought of as an accelerator, an activity which
> affects the rate of development of each function necessary for continuous
> progress toward the ideal of mankind: the ability of every individual to
> satisfy each of his expanding sets of desires.[21]

The line between external benefits to the individual and external benefits
to the society is indistinct. These externalities may in some instances be primarily

---

[19] Burton A. Weisbrod, *External Benefits of Public Education: An Economic Analysis*
(Princeton: Princeton University Press, 1964), p. 20.

[20] Weisbrod, *External Benefits*, p. 21.

[21] Russell L. Ackoff, "Toward Quantitative Evaluation of Urban Services," in *Public Expenditure Decisions in the Urban Community*, ed. Howard G. Schaller (Washington, D.C.:
Resources for the Future, 1963; distr. by Johns Hopkins Press, Baltimore), pp. 110–11.

social and only partially beneficial to individuals and vice versa. Also, some of the external effects of education may be individual and social costs as opposed to benefits, depending upon the interpretation one places on the idea considered. Some of the more frequently mentioned external benefits to society as a result of education include:

1. More efficient consumption
2. Higher taxes resulting from higher incomes
3. Educated persons are less prone to antisocial behavior
4. Students learn acceptable ways of behavior
5. Increased demands for goods and services imply economic growth
6. Advances in science
7. Transmission of cultural heritage
8. More politically active citizens, ergo, better citizens
9. Education creating social mobility
10. Value of literacy to an advanced society
11. Intergenerational benefits in the form of children learning from their parents and the continuity that this implies
12. Employer related benefits, benefits to the employers of educated persons
13. Reduced social costs

A benefit ascribed to *more efficient consumption* may occur or it may not. Normally, one would imagine that a better educated person would make more "educated" choices thereby reducing waste, but this depends largely upon the source of taste and preference in the individual. If such choices arise from an individual set of values, then one may approve their quality and yet recognize that such benefits are not necessarily measurable. On the other hand, if such a taste and preference function is "administered," as are prices, then there are several implications. By administered taste is meant tastes and preferences of individuals controlled by producers through advertising. Administered prices are prices set by producers instead of prices set in competitive markets. The first implication of administered taste is that wasteful consumption results by the fact that producers will be able to generate demands for whatever is produced and, within limits, at whatever prices they choose. The second implication might be that while such a system would show "net gains" in economic growth it might do so at the cost of social control and manipulation. To suggest that education generates more efficient consumption on the part of consumers requires that the individual make careful, reasoned choices from a set of values which are personal as opposed to exclusively administered. Such a requirement casts considerable doubt upon the efficacy of this benefit.

The spillover to society from the increased earnings of educated people results in *higher taxes* for a particular community, state, or nation. This means a reduction of the burden on other taxpayers or an increase in public services output. This is only a benefit if the consumption of public services by the educated is reduced or held constant.[22]

Weisbrod suggests, "The real benefits of education are the real costs of non-education." A more educated population is presumably *less prone to antisocial action* due to the inculcation of acceptable attitudes and behavior patterns. Consequently, there would be a direct saving in social outlays on police, courts, prisons, welfare, etc. A nonmonetary benefit may be the personal satisfaction and freedom from fear enjoyed by those who live in a more secure environment.[23]

This benefit is truly a loaded concept. While our society may be given to gradualism and peaceful life in viewing social change, antisocial behavior may be quite desirable and necessary for groups to achieve desired ends. If the action is legal, then one may question whether it is really beneficial to socially manipulate people through education to guide them toward less antisocial behavior for in so doing we may stifle individuals in such a way that the costs of education to the individual are greater than the presumed benefits to society. Any consideration of this benefit should be carefully conceived and not automatically applied.

The related value of *students learning acceptable ways of behavior* may not be measurable because there are many views of what constitutes acceptable behavior. The role of the school as a purveyor of social attitudes and cultural beliefs is undoubtedly true, but whether this is a benefit or a cost depends upon the attitudes and the conditions. People in reformatories learn acceptable ways of behavior, but this may mean nothing more than the reformatory is easy to administer. The results on the inmates may be quite undesirable.

The extent to which education calls forth *increased demand for goods and services* depends on the incomes generated from education. This benefit relates to economic growth.

The question of *advances in science* is provisionally acceptable in concept but no means of measuring this kind of innovation has yet arisen. Likewise, the benefit assumed in *transmission of the cultural heritage* is on the surface acceptable but largely not possible to measure or place value upon.

People with more education may become more involved in community activities and appear on the surface to be better citizens. Besides joining civic organizations, educated people are more *politically active*. Weisbrod cites the correlation of voting records and schooling in support of these statements. However, Philip E. Jacob, in his analysis of the influence of college on student values, says that with the exception of their voting record, college graduates "are politically irresponsible and politically illiterate." Jacob further states that "their college ex-

[22] Weisbrod, *External Benefits*, p. 69.

[23] Weisbrod, *External Benefits*, pp. 80, 95, and John Vaizey, *The Economics of Education* (London: Faber and Faber, 1962), pp. 48–49.

perience barely touches their standards of behavior, quality of judgment, sense of social responsibility, perspicacity of understanding, and guiding beliefs." Weisbrod does admit, "it is possible the people who go to school longer would be more public spirited even if they had not obtained the additional education."[24]

That formal schooling is a predominant factor in *social mobility* is questioned by C. Arnold Anderson. He considers ability and motivation as the two most powerful factors in generating vertical mobility. He also observed that much of the mobility occurring served to compensate for "incorrect placement" among the occupations of the fathers.[25]

Paul Goodman even questions the concept of the benefits of *literacy* to society. He asks "Why should most people bother to learn to read seriously?" He suggests, "Because in our society serious literacy is of no practical importance whatever . . . we should be as well off if it were socially acceptable for large numbers not to read."[26]

The future family beneficiaries of a student's education are primarily his children. This produces what are called *intergenerational effects*. Children learn from their parents and an investment in the education of one generation establishes a base for the next. A study conducted by the Survey Research Center of the University of Michigan concluded, "The education of the spending unit (household) head is far more important than any of the other variables in predicting educational aspirations." A similar study in 1960 by Harvey Brazer and Martin David indicates the same thing, although their analysis did not explicitly control for the influence of the child's ability or his educational attainment. George Bugbee of the Health Information Foundation suggested that education produces another intergenerational benefit insofar as education reduces infant mortality, because parents become aware of the proper procedures and basic requirements of sanitation and nutrition.[27]

Employer related benefits are important where production involves the cooperative effort of workers. The flexibility and adaptability of one's work is an advantage to others. The productivity of each member of a group influences the productivity of other members. This statement rests on the assumption that education develops the properties of flexibility and adaptability. Weisbrod believes further study is necessary to determine the validity and significance of

[24] Weisbrod, *External Benefits*, pp. 38–39, 95–98; Philip E. Jacob, et al., "Does Higher Education Influence Student Values?" *NEA* (National Education Association) *Journal* 47 (1958): 36.

[25] Arnold C. Anderson, "A Skeptical Note on the Relation of Vertical Mobility to Education," *American Journal of Sociology* 66 (1961): 560–70.

[26] Paul Goodman, "The Universal Trap," in *Social Foundations of Education: Current Issues and Research*, comp. Dorothy Westby-Gibson (New York: Freedom Press, 1967), p. 62.

[27] Charles S. Benson, *The Economics of Public Education* (Boston: Houghton Mifflin, 1968), p. 26. William J. Swift and Burton A. Weisbrod, "On the Monetary Value of Education's Intergeneration Effects," *Journal of Political Economy* 73 (1965): 643n, 644.

this assumption. The following benefits may accrue to employers as a result of widespread schooling:

1. Better quality of industrial training programs not only related to the knowledge and skill of the instructors but also to the quality of the trainees' previous schooling
2. An alert work force with stable work habits
3. Better communication between employers and employees as economic relationships become more complex
4. Function of personnel departments and screening personnel are performed for the employer[28]

The *reduction in social costs* due to education exists in the form of savings to society by education's role in preserving employment. The cost savings then become savings in welfare costs and unemployment compensation costs.

Having discussed the individual benefits to educational investments, how are cities "developing" from an educational standpoint? Education related to manpower requirements is the key to the economics of urban development and education, yet manpower planning and educational planning in cities have been conducted by different persons for different reasons. Education is planned by the local educational authorities while manpower planning, to the extent that it is pursued, has been somewhat narrowly conceived by its concentration on job training activities.

Harbison and Myers characterized problems of human resource development in two broad categories: (1) the problem of shortages of high-level manpower with critical skills, and (2) the problem of an excessive supply of labor or underutilized manpower. When we discuss high-level manpower we can speak of the generation of skills and the utilization of these skills in economic terms as the process of formation and investment of strategic human capital. While the market economy will generate reasonably efficient markets for existing labor skills, it may not be capable of providing all of the strategic skills necessary. In other words, strategic human capital may be efficiently employed or it may be wastefully underutilized. Harbison and Myers define strategic human capital in terms of educational level and occupation. Their essential occupational categories of high-level manpower are:

1. Entrepreneurial, managerial, and administrative personnel in both public and private establishments including education institutions
2. Professional personnel such as scientists, engineers, architects, economists, doctors, veterinarians, lawyers, accountants, journalists, artists, etc.

[28] Charles S. Benson, *The School and the Economic System* (Chicago: Science Research Associates, 1966), pp. 62–63.

3. Qualified teachers
4. Subprofessional technical personnel, such as nurses, engineering assistants, technicians, senior clerks, supervisors, skilled craftsmen, skilled clerical workers
5. Top-ranking political leaders, labor leaders, judges, and officers of the police.[29]

Hitherto, the institutions of education which have been discussed have been local elementary and secondary schools, the basic educational components of a city. Yet from a developmental standpoint, the most critical class of workers are the college graduates who make up strategic manpower. Local public schools may provide category 4, above, the subprofessional group, but for other elements of strategic manpower, the community must attract college graduates. The necessity for universities to exist in large cities satisfies this need to attract — that is, train the manpower locally. A significant aspect of urban development lies in the need for universities providing manpower and innovation to the development process.

Other manpower requirements which become apparent revolve around the needs of an increasingly sophisticated technological society. As Assistant Secretary of Commerce Holloman noted during the Clark hearings:

> (1) Not enough of our bright young people are learning the practice of engineering and the technique of developing and applying knowledge to crucial needs of society. The pursuit of science or research alone is not enough; knowledge must be applied, put to use if the society is to get tangible benefit. . . . (2) The technologically rich are becoming richer and the technologically poor are becoming more so. This is a trend that must be halted in the national interest.[30]

While Secretary Holloman's comments under item one are reasonably self-explanatory, what he means in point number two is that technological innovation is increasingly falling to the very largest companies. He points out that technological activity in companies with fewer than 5,000 employees has stagnated at a fairly constant level in recent years. Secretary Holloman goes on:

> (3) A third problem of importance is the role of the university in advancing the economy of the nation. Whereas the need for greater university participation in the economic development of the regions in which they are located is growing, the gap between the need of industry and activity of the university, with some exceptions, is widening. Most of the nation's universities carry on programs that are unconnected with local industrial problems,

29 Werner Z. Hirsch, "Quality of Government Expenditures," in *Public Expenditure Decisions*, ed. Schaller, p. 174.

30 J. Herbert Holloman, "Scientific and Technical Manpower: A Key to Economic Growth," in *The Manpower Revolution: Its Policy Consequences*, U.S. Congress, Senate Committee on Labor and Public Welfare, Subcommittee on Employment, Manpower, and Poverty, ed. Garth L. Mangum (Garden City, N.Y.: Doubleday, 1965), pp. 274–75.

and too many industries fail to draw upon the intellectual resources of nearby academic institutions. . . . (4) The transformation and adaptation of knowledge to meet a practical need in society requires a particular skill that is not science nor research but yet which has to be developed to the professional levels we have come to expect only of top scientists.[31]

What Holloman speaks of here is the concentration of scientific activity into basic research without providing a sufficient number of scientists to work in applications.

Harbison and Myers developed some quantitative indicators of human resource development which fall into two general categories:

1. Those indicators which measure the stock of human capital, and

2. Those which measure the additions to the stock or the rate of human capital formation over a given time period.[32]

For comparison of urban areas we can make use of the following indicators of the human capital stock:

1. Levels of educational attainment.

2. The number of persons in relation to the population and/or labor force who are in high-level occupations as defined in our occupational categories above.[33]

With regard to the rate of accumulation it is suggested that the best measure would be the net addition to the number of persons in high-level occupations. Further, net additions to the stock of persons as measured by educational attainment would be useful. Since neither of these measures are readily available for changes over short periods of time, we might make use of what Harbison and Myers refer to as second-best measures of available human resources:

1. Number of teachers (by class) per 10,000 population

2. Engineers and scientists per 10,000 population

3. Physicians and dentists per 10,000 population

4. Pupils enrolled in primary education as a percentage of the estimated population ages 5–14

5. The adjusted school enrollment ratios for first- and second-level schools combined

6. Pupils enrolled in second-level schools or secondary education as a percentage of the total estimated population ages 15–19

7. Enrollment in higher education as a percentage of the age group 20–24.[34]

[31] Holloman, "Scientific and Technical Manpower," in *The Manpower Revolution*, ed. Mangum, pp. 276–77.

[32] Frederick Harbison and Charles A. Myers, *Education, Manpower, and Economic Growth: Strategies of Human Resource Development* (New York: McGraw-Hill, 1964), p. 24.

[33] Harbison and Myers, *Education, Manpower, and Economic Growth*, p. 25.

[34] Harbison and Myers, *Education, Manpower, and Economic Growth*, p. 27.

The first three items can be classed as stock measures, while the last four can be conceived as additions to the stock.[35]

Two additional indicators of human resource development involve the orientation of higher education: (1) the percentage of students enrolled in scientific and technical faculties in a given time period, (2) the percentage of students enrolled in faculties of humanities, fine arts, and law in the same year of the same time period. It should be cautioned that the above indicators are developed by Harbison and Myers principally from the standpoint of available information on an international basis. Data within the urban area of the American economy should be more complete and additional indicators could be developed. Obviously in the urban context a number of these indicators would have to be adjusted for in-migration and out-migration purposes so as to become the basis of a partial score of development of the urban economy and its immediate future. Borrowing from Harbison and Myers, we conclude the following:

1. There is some degree of correlation between enrollments in education and a city's level of economic development. It is possible for a system to emphasize the wrong kinds of education, however.
2. A balance of human resource development is crucial.
3. The magnitude of subsequent investments in education is a function of the economic development and growth of the area.
4. In all cities, people look at education as a means of job opportunity and advancement in career, thus among other things, systems should equip people for jobs.
5. The proportion of local income devoted to resource development is likely to rise in growing cities due to demands, high-level manpower requirements, etc.[36]

A Caveat on Education and Economic Development

One problem with education and economic development which must be considered is the fact that the school is essentially a product of the state and, as such, aims to serve the community goals. There is no problem as long as the goals of the school are consistent with those of the individuals in the community. But what if social welfare aims differ from individual aims? What, indeed, if the school system damages development of the individual human being by thrusting him toward a narrow "marketable skills" form of existence? What is good for development in the economic sense may not necessarily be good for development of the city or development of the individual.

It must therefore be recognized that urban economic development is not the same as urban development, and while it is customary in making such distinctions to suggest that economics is one aspect of the larger notion of development, one must also recognize that economic development may come in conflict with other

---

[35] Harbison and Myers, *Education, Manpower, and Economic Growth*, p. 27.
[36] Harbison and Myers, *Education, Manpower, and Economic Growth*, pp. 185–86.

aspects of urban development. A sense of high quality urban life may moderate the current exclusive evaluation of city life based on the goal of higher and higher incomes.

If we educate well, provide high quality health and recreation services, and provide solid manpower services in cities, we may well expect that, individually, citizens of the city will have more profitable lives. On the other hand, we may not at the same time assert that the successful provision of these urban services necessarily leads to more economic growth and development in the sense of increases to real per capita income. Indeed, such "improved" citizens may opt for something other than economic growth (affluence) and maintain only that level of economic development which serves these other ends. Normally, one would anticipate that such options would generate economic growth, particularly in the long-run sense, but such long-run economic development may not be assured. Rather, higher quality urban development may mean relatively less economic growth, if quality becomes a higher priority item than quantity. Consequently, one may view the development of good educational institutions as ultimately in conflict with the current kind of economic growth we see in cities.

Turning once again to the short-run questions of the relation of current investments in human capital to urban economic development, it is possible to say that "wishing makes it so" — that is, if economic development is deemed desirable, then there are powerful forces which press for the realization of growth. One may ask, "Who says we need what kind and what quality of labor force?" The answer lies in several directions. First, large corporations demand particular strategic manpower persons. Second, government presses for particular labor skills and promotes some over others. Thirdly, educators themselves promote and create demands for particular kinds of high-level manpower. The result is that powerful economic groups which dominate economic activities in the society pressure schools and colleges into producing certain types of labor skills for economic growth purposes.

This almost automatic growth is accomplished by means of social control through economic domination. The business-government complex is considerably more successful in our society than the military-industrial complex. Such a complex creates growth through the private corporate domination of both the production and the consumption sides of markets and through domination of most social institutions, accomplished with the approval of governments. The same is true in the city, though different cities may have different economic power structures. The domination of cities' social institutions, such as education, is accomplished through the power exercised by corporations and unions and strong individuals over local governments. The end result is that in a narrow sense one may say that all schools are essentially "schools of business" generating not well-equipped individuals, enlightened in the arts of living fully, but economic producers and consumers.

Even when the school teacher or the college professor has the best of intentions and senses the importance of liberal, individualized education, the image of this ideal is translated to a mass (a classroom full) of students, and students are not considered individually but as a group under that one perceived image. This kind of distortion due to aggregation is in evidence in every college and lower school in the city. Thus, even when the teacher chooses another course, the result is largely the same — homogenized laborers with a false impression of their individuality.

Finally, then, the caveat lies in whether or not it is possible to opt for less affluence and more quality in urban life. Perhaps we cannot. Perhaps we will merely continue to have growth in local economies of the same form and in the same way simply because the system is capable of nothing else.

IV. A Summary of the Benefits of Education

The educational process is so complex that one cannot anticipate any system of logic which will be sufficient to analyze it with perfect accuracy. The economics just discussed ignores many real questions and problems of education in the city. Each aspect of urban education demands an intensive analysis. Numerous assumptions are implicit in the previous discussion, and many more are deeply imbedded in our ideas about education. Economics is in somewhat of a quandry since it must take an institution like education at face value. Educational goals become the assumptions of most analysis because economics is not designed to set goals, simply to attempt to analyze the effectiveness of the economic aspects of an institution moving toward its goals. Thus, great caution should be exercised in attempting to use the previous discussion on any single school or aspect of a school. Rather, attempt to use the foregoing discussion as a means of asking questions about the economics of urban education. The following summary may be of some help in this direction:

A Summary of Possible Economic Benefits of Education

Primary Benefits to Individual

1. Discounted increased earnings streams over working lifetime
2. Psychic incomes: satisfaction of personal pleasures of education, status, etc.
3. Imputed incomes: ability to do tax, etc., negative costs

External Benefits Gained by Individual

1. Option value: the value of being able to obtain more education
2. Hedging benefit: ability to hedge against technological change
3. Employment options: wider choice of employment

Possible External Benefits to Society: Many are Suspect

1. More efficient consumption, less waste
2. Higher tax revenues
3. Persons less prone to antisocial actions
4. Students learning acceptable ways of behavior
5. Increased consumption of goods and services (growth)
6. Advances in science
7. Transmission of cultural heritage
8. More politically active citizens
9. Greater degree of social mobility
10. Literacy
11. Intergenerational effects
12. Employer related benefits
13. Reduced social costs

Having discussed some of the possible benefits of education, what are the quality aspects of education? In previous discussions of benefits it has been implicitly assumed that no significant differences in quality exist. If schooling is the product, then we need to recognize some dimensions of the quality of the good.

V. Quality Dimensions of Education

According to McKean and Kershaw, the education that pertains to a student per day (or per year) has a number of dimensions of quality:

1. knowledge in standard subjects
2. knowledge in special and optional subjects
3. ability to reason
4. intellectual curiosity
5. creativity
6. social poise
7. emotional stability
8. physical health[37]

All of these items can be measured on some basis; current school programs account for some systematic accumulation of progress of students in some of these areas. Current costs per pupil can be assessed for a given level of quality and then compared to other levels in order to obtain a supply curve which will reveal to some degree the costs involved in improving education.

[37] Joseph A. Kershaw and Roland N. McKean, *Systems Analysis and Education* (Santa Monica, Cal.: Rand Corporation, 1959), pp. 8–9.

In breaking down these per pupil costs for an average level of quality, Hirsch suggests that we need to look at the quality of the supply inputs, namely:

1. *Caliber of teaching staff and teaching load:* Important characteristics are percent of experienced teachers, percent of teachers who are graduates of stong liberal arts colleges with majors in the field in which they teach; number of outside-the-area candidates interviewed for each teacher hired; number of students per counselor, librarian, and other specialists; number of college hours the average teacher has taken; and percent of teachers with more than ten years' teaching experience. Average teacher salary is likely to reflect some of these factors. Teaching load is another indicator. In many schools, twenty hours a week of teaching, and dealing with about 175 students, is considered normal. One measure would be the average teaching load of a given school in relation to the national average.

2. *Caliber of school administration:* The leadership and ability of the school superintendent and his principals cannot be neglected. Number of superintendents, principals, and consultants per 100 pupils could prove a useful measure.

3. *Grouping and class size:* Many educators maintain that within limits good education requires students of common ability and interest to be grouped together. The result is small classes, which generally indicate a more intensive education effort that can thus be measured by the pupil-teacher ratio.

4. *Teaching Program:* The scope and quality of the teaching program can be measured in terms of the number of high school instruction units offered by the school. Other measures might be percent of college bound students who carry four courses a year in English, mathematics, science, history, or foreign languages; percent of students who have taken mathematics courses beyond a second year of algebra and one year of plane geometry, or four years of foreign languages.

5. *Length of school year and day:* Schools differ in the number of hours in a given year in which a child participates in formal education.[38]

According to Hirsch, these characteristics combine in various ways and result in many different qualities of public education and a wide variation in costs.[39]

We begin by relating cost per student to a given improvement in quality within the education system. Further, we are not interested merely in the fact of graduation; we are concerned with the quality of education of the student who graduates. While incomes may increase for average graduates, what additional gains are available to the student who has had a better than average education? Relating net gains in quality per pupil to net gains in income requires

[38] Werner Z. Hirsch, "Quality of Government Expenditures," in *Public Expenditure Decisions in the Urban Community*, ed. Howard G. Schaller (Washington, D.C.: Resources for the Future, 1963; distr. by Johns Hopkins Press, Baltimore), p. 174. Copyright © 1963, Resources for the Future. Reprinted by permision.

[39] Hirsch, "Quality of Government Services," in *Public Expenditure Decisions*, ed. Schaller, p. 174.

estimates about the deviation of incomes given quality differences within particular age-education levels. In addition, we can relate the earnings of high school graduates to college graduates and compare the rates of college completion among high schools of varying quality inputs. If the education in high school is of high quality, then the rate of those entering and completing college will be higher.

VI. Problems and Policies for Urban Education

While we have discussed some of the formal economics related to urban education, we have not discussed possible existing barriers which may serve to reduce education's effectiveness or, if you will, its efficiency. The following discussion is in no sense the "full story"; rather, it is a potpourri of problems for which, in many cases, there may be no satisfactory answer.

Distortions of Aggregation

Lumping all urban schools together is fallacious. After all, schools are different and more importantly students are different. While schools may be largely successful, they may also be very unsuccessful. For example, it has been estimated that in the fifteen largest cities in recent years:

1. 31% of the children who completed the ninth grade did not graduate from high school
2. At least 6% of children who start the fifth grade never start the tenth grade
3. 40 to 48% of the welfare applicants, age 16 to 21, even with high school educations, were unemployed
4. About 88% of the applicants for welfare in Chicago in a recent six-week period had not completed high school.[40]

Thus, while schooling may be necessary for urban development, it is certainly not successful for all of those who enter the system. The problem here has two dimensions: (1) public schools are designed more for an average person than for the mix of the existing population, or (2) public education is not an effective instrument to bring people "up." Sizer comments that the prime purpose of some inner city schooling is definitely not to enhance the learning process but to maintain order.[41]

The Interrelatedness of Urban Problems

An additional barrier to the efficient performance of schools in cities lies in the outside influences and environments which prevent schools from functioning.

[40] Theodore R. Sizer, "The Schools in the City," in *The Metropolitan Enigma: Inquiries into the Nature and Dimensions of America's Urban Crisis*, ed. James Q. Wilson (Garden City, N.Y.: Doubleday, 1970), pp. 343–44.

[41] Sizer, "The Schools in the City," in *The Metropolitan Enigma*, ed. Wilson, p. 347.

One cannot say definitely, but it appears that, particularly in the case of inner city schools, the environment thwarts any prospect of success in schools. Problems of hunger, broken homes, and other urban situations reduce any effectiveness which schools may have.

Further evidence of the impact of the interrelatedness of urban problems upon schooling is suggested by the fact that we cannot say with certainty that schooling accounts for increases to incomes. Certainly some part of the additional earnings may be accountable in this manner, but some estimates have determined that as little as 10% of the increases to incomes are due to educational increases. This is reasonable when we compare two students of equal intelligence who come from totally different backgrounds. One may be black, the other white; one may be from a wealthy family, one may be from a poor family. The Coleman Report tends to substantiate the idea that black children perform less well on entrance tests to first grade. Also, there is some evidence to suggest that no matter what the situation of the school, the black student on the average tends to perform at about a fourth-grade level when he is in the sixth grade.[42] In short, external barriers appear to be of overwhelming significance in the impact which schools may have on future earnings.

Racism

Other barriers to a smooth functioning school lie in the problems of racism and its many manifestations. We see a decline in the number of black principals; we see widespread racism implicit in our colleges and universities, not perhaps because of particularly high entrance requirements, but simply because many colleges tend to seek a particular client so the student body has similar cultural backgrounds, similar tastes, etc. The obvious manifestation of racism in local schools is demonstrated by the flight to the suburbs, the resulting Balkanization of inner city schools, and the variance in quality between outer city and inner city schools.

Licensing Barriers

Instead of a variety of teachers in local schools we are faced with a barrier which allows, through state legislation, the control of teacher certification by college professors of education whose interests are served by increasing the requirements for an education degree and subsequent certification. The result is that a teacher is a standardized product. Check your own college bulletin and you will see that the education majors have practically no free electives. If this higher echelon of the educational establishment continues its way, we can look forward to little change in educational institutions or reform of schools at the

---

[42] U.S. Office of Education, "Equality of Educational Opportunity," (Washington, D.C.: U.S. Government Printing Office, 1966). This study, headed by James Coleman of Johns Hopkins University, covers a wide variety of issues.

local level. Most importantly, there will be few choices available at the local level for students in city schools.

The Taxpayers' Revolt: Distribution of Benefits

Evidence of dissatisfaction with local schools can be readily seen in the increasing number of local school systems which are going broke. These situations occur in states where local resources are relatively more important than other sources of finance. For example, in Ohio school districts have been voted out of existence, school years have been shortened, courses dropped, extracurricular activities curtailed, and school districts absorbed by other school districts.

There are numerous explanations for such problems. One might be related to spatial dimension; that is, local taxpayers do not believe they are gaining the benefits from the educational investments they are making. As youths leave small towns this may certainly be the case.

Likewise, there are time dimensions to the taxpayers' revolt. While we may blithely assert that there are social benefits to be gained from education, these benefits are not in any real sense distributed in local communities so that citizens recognize them. Obviously, when the local resident refuses to vote in favor of an educational levy on the grounds that his children are already educated and away from home, he does not perceive a benefit from educating other peoples' children.

Confusion over Who Controls Schools

Local schools are undergoing some particular stress in the overlapping control mechanisms under which they are forced to function. Federal regulations, state regulations, and local policy all combine, hopefully in harmony, to generate a viable local school system. The issue of local control has been with us for many years and appears to be moving toward more neighborhood control of districts within large cities; that is, a decentralization of power from a big city school board to the local school neighborhood on the presumption that such a move generates a more responsive school system. On the other hand, many inner city schools continue to be run from the view of maintaining tight in-house control on the part of principals and teachers; this tightening is seen by the staff as necessary to survival.

There are more than a few problems to neighborhood control of schools. One such problem is the quality of the schools. Proponents of neighborhood control argue that if schools are not more responsive to the needs of the neighborhood quality cannot exist. They argue that local schools fail to provide legitimate quality for their particular children because the system is designed for sameness. People opposed to neighborhood control argue that quality of local schools is better when higher-level governments exert control over the schooling process. Such opponents might also argue that neighborhood control would result in an even more dictatorial school policy than currently exists. Conflicts over authority always result in disruption of the operation of a school system, but that is not to say a short-run disruption is undesirable, particularly if it brings a long-run change which is desired.

A Few Policy Suggestions

Any listing of policy suggestions which has been proposed for the improvement of local education will be partial and tentative, but some suggestions seem to have considerable merit. One suggestion for improvement of local schools has been the voucher system. Though starting from somewhat suspicious origins in the South during the period of "massive resistance" to the 1954 Brown decision of the Supreme Court, the voucher system can be adapted to local schools to some degree. The idea is simply that each child's education is paid by voucher by the state no matter where he goes to school. The attractiveness of this device is that it could serve to aid both religious institutions, which perform a large educational task in cities, and secular private schools. The voucher system might adversely affect the local public school system to some degree, but it would stimulate the development of other forms of local schools, experimental schools, as well as existing schools.

Another suggestion for policy which has been proposed is related to higher education, but could be related to high schools as well. A student could borrow the costs of his education to be paid back after the completion of his education. Such a plan, attempted at Yale, allowed the student to borrow up to the full cost of his schooling and then begin paying off the loan upon graduation, based more on the amount of income he earns than upon the loan itself. Thus, graduates who earn greater incomes would pay relatively more than students who earn less upon graduation. Such notes could be used by schools to form the basis for borrowing from banks to maintain their present operations — borrowing in short on these future incomes.

Another interesting policy experiment has come from Gary, Indiana, where the Behavioral Research Laboratory contracted with the city of Gary to run an elementary school in the city for four years with a money-back guarantee. The Laboratory group contracted to bring all students up to the national norms for particular grade levels within the four-year period at a cost of $800 per year per pupil (current costs per pupil in Gary). For students not brought up to national norm levels within that time, the money was to be refunded to the city. Such experiments are possible with great potential merit, but they do not consider the fact that skills available in the Behavioral Research group may not be available generally for school systems. The experiment has apparently failed, but if successful, perhaps the only conclusion to be reached is that with a staff of superior skill, an elementary school may be vastly improved. No matter what the outcome, there is reason to believe that additional quality would occur in local schools if contracting of some services was expanded.

Summary: Education

The period of the late fifties and sixties saw large increases in the urban expenditures for education. During this same time period, educational attainment increased with notable increases in the numbers of people going to college and graduate schools. The seventies will probably see a relative decline in both public school and higher education expenditures as a result of slowed population growth, poor economic conditions, and growing public disenchantment with schooling. In addition, court cases in California and New Jersey have challenged the use of the property tax as a means of local school support, and drastic changes in educational finance will be sought.

To the economist the school can be seen as a plant which is engaged in producing schooling. The total of schools thereby represents the educational industry.

Because schools are not run for profit and prices of a direct nature are not charged (at least for public schools), there has been considerable discussion in economics as to the value of schooling. Early studies of the value of education were characterized by attempts to estimate the lifetime earnings streams of individuals who were educated and compare these earnings streams with individuals who were not educated in an attempt to estimate the net gains of education, ergo, its value. Such studies as those done by Glick and Miller estimated the value of a college education to be about $100,000. Houthaker, using the same 1950 data, came to different results by discounting the future earnings streams and applying mortality figures to the data.

Recent studies in the economics of education have attempted to refine the process of valuing education and have included results which question the value of education beyond some less than college point. Given the costs of education it has sometimes been argued that the student would be wise to leave high school and invest the money with a consequent higher return than if he stays in school. Some have argued that it is not the years of schooling that are important, it is the college degree. Other studies have generated results which tend to suggest education is not as valuable economically as was once thought.

Becker, for example, turned the analysis of education into a comparison of investments in human as opposed to physical capital. Becker's results tended to show a very slight decline in the net returns from a college education from 1940 to 1950. It would appear that returns have been declining because of increases in the cost of education and the increase to incomes foregone which persons could have acquired rather than going to college. Weisbrod developed the notion of negative costs applied to education and argued that some costs to the individual can be eliminated if the individual acquires certain levels of education.

Externalities appear to be important in assessing the value of education. External benefits to the individual include the option to purchase more education and the ability to hedge against the problems of technological change. A third form of externality is found in the wider range of employment choices for the college graduate than for persons with less education. Intangible benefits include the personal advantages of accessibility to a wider variety of social and cultural outputs.

The value of education in economic growth and development has two major human resource development problems. One problem is the necessity of maintaining a sufficient supply of high-level manpower while the second problem centers around the possible excessive supply of labor or underutilized manpower. Harbison and Myers discuss strategic human capital in terms of entrepreneurial and professional talents which a nation or a community must have in order to develop or maintain a desired level of development. Harbison and Myers developed means of measuring the strategic manpower levels which are useful in assessing such manpower in urban areas.

In considering the quality of education, a number of measures of quality of a school were suggested. Being primarily concerned with the quality of the education of the student, one begins to examine the student for his knowledge of standard subjects and special subjects, his ability to reason, his creativity, his intellectual curiosity, his social poise, his emotional stability, and his physical health. Measures of these quality outputs can be compared to the quality of inputs, primarily the quality of the teachers, but also the administrative quality, the class size, the scope and quality of the curriculum, and the length of the school year and school day. Such quality evaluations would lend themselves to estimates of the cost per unit of quality in education.

Problems in the consideration of urban education include the distortions that arise when one lumps all schools together. Another barrier to efficient local schools or universities is accounted for by the interrelatedness of urban problems. Racism is a prominent barrier to quality education. Teacher licensing barriers may well curtail quality in education. The taxpayers' revolt of the later years of the sixties generates instability in school finance. Overlapping controls on schools create both hostility and confusion in administering schools.

Policy suggestions for improving school systems may lie in the use of the voucher system in local schools and the use of a college financing system which requires the graduate to repay, over time, the costs of his college education. Another policy possibility is in the subcontracting of education by local authorities to private contractors.

Selected Bibliography

Education

ACKOFF, RUSSELL L. "Toward Quantitative Evaluation of Urban Services." In *Public Expenditure Decisions in the Urban Community*, ed. Howard G. Schaller, pp. 91–117. Washington, D.C.: Resources for the Future, 1963; distr. by Johns Hopkins Press, Baltimore.

ANDERSON, C. ARNOLD. "A Skeptical Note on the Relation of Vertical Mobility to Education." *American Journal of Sociology* 66 (1961): 560–70.

ASHENFELTER, ORLEY, AND MOONEY, JOSEPH D. "Graduate Education, Ability, and Earnings." *Review of Economics and Statistics* 50 (1968): 78–86.

BECKER, GARY S. *Human Capital: A Theoretical and Empirical Analysis, with Special Reference to Education.* New York: National Bureau of Economic Research, 1964; distr. by Columbia University Press.

———. *Investment in Education.* New York: National Bureau of Economic Research, 1965.

———. "Underinvestment in the College Education?" *Papers and Proceedings of the American Economic Association. American Economic Review* 50 (1960): 346–54.

———, AND CHISWICK, BARRY R. "Education and Distribution of Earnings." In "Economics of Education," *Papers and Proceedings of the American Economic Association. American Economic Review* 56 (1966): 358–69.

BENSON, CHARLES S. "Teaching Methods and Their Costs." *International Social Science Journal* 14 (1962): 676–84.

———. *The Economics of Public Education.* 2d ed. Boston: Houghton Mifflin, 1968.

———. *The School and the Economic System.* Chicago: Science Research Associates, 1966.

BLAUG, MARK. "Approaches to Educational Planning." *Economic Journal* 77 (1967): 262–87.

———, COMP. *Economics of Education: Selected Readings.* Vols. 1 and 2. Harmondsworth, Engl.: Penguin Books, 1968.

BOWEN, WILLIAM G. "Assessing the Economic Contribution of Education." In *Economic Aspects of Education, Three Essays*, William G. Bowen, pp. 3–40. Industrial Relations Section, Research Report no. 104. Princeton: Department of Economics, Princeton University, 1964.

———, AND FINEGAN, T. ALDRICH. "Educational Attainment and Labor Force Participation." *Papers and Proceedings of the American Economic Association. American Economic Review* 56 (1966): 567–82.

BOWMAN, MARY J. "Schooling, Experience and Gains and Losses in Human Capital Through Migration." *Journal of the American Statistical Association* 62 (1967): 875–98.

———. "Social Returns to Education." *International Social Science Journal* 14 (1962): 647–59.

CAMPBELL, ROBERT, AND SIEGEL, BARRY N. "The Demand for Higher Education in the United States, 1919–1964." *American Economic Review* 57 (1967): 482–94.

CAROL, ARTHUR, AND PARRY, SAMUEL. "The Economic Rationale of Occupational Choice." *Industrial and Labor Relations Review* 21 (1968): 183–96.

CHANCE, W. A. "Long-term Labor Requirements and Output of the Educational System." *Southern Economic Journal* 32 (1966): 417–28.

COMMITTEE FOR ECONOMIC DEVELOPMENT. *Education for the Urban Disadvantaged: From Preschool to Employment.* A Statement on National Policy by the Research and Policy Committee. New York: Committee for Economic Development, 1971.

CONLEY, RONALD W. *The Economics of Vocational Rehabilitation.* Baltimore: Johns Hopkins Press, 1965.

DANIÈRE, ANDRÉ. *Higher Education in the American Economy.* New York: Random House, 1964.

DEITCH, KENNETH. "Some Observations on the Allocation of Resources in Higher Education." *Supplement: Aug. 1960. Review of Economics and Statistics* 42 (1960): 192–98.

HANSEN, W. LEE. "Total and Private Rates of Return to Investment in Schooling." *Journal of Political Economy* 71 (1963): 128–40.

―――, AND WEISBROD, BURTON A. *Benefits, Costs, and Finances of Public Higher Education.* Chicago: Markham Publishing Co., 1969.

HANSON, NELS W. "Economy of Scale as a Cost Factor in Financing Public Schools." *National Tax Journal* 17 (1964): 92–95.

HARBISON, FREDERICK, AND MYERS, CHARLES A. *Education, Manpower, and Economic Growth: Strategies of Human Resource Development.* New York: McGraw-Hill, 1964.

HARRIS, SEYMOUR E. "Economics of Higher Education." *American Economic Review* 43 (1953): 344–57.

―――, ED. *Higher Education in the United States: The Economic Problems.* Cambridge, Mass.: Harvard University Press, 1960.

―――. "Some Economic Problems of Education Expenditure on Education and Income Levels." In *Public Policy,* ed. John D. Montgomery and Arthur E. Smithies, pp. 221–35. Cambridge, Mass.: Harvard University Press, 1965.

HIRSCH, WERNER Z. "Fiscal Impact of Industrialization on Local Schools." *Review of Economics and Statistics* 46 (1964): 191–99.

―――. "Quality of Government Expenditures." In *Public Expenditure Decisions in the Urban Community,* ed. Howard G. Schaller, pp. 163–79. Washington, D.C.: Resources for the Future, 1963; distr. by Johns Hopkins Press, Baltimore.

―――. "Regional Accounts for Public School Decisions." Paper presented to the Conference on Regional Accounts, 1964. Los Angeles: University of California, 1964.

―――, AND MARCUS, MORTON J. "Some Benefit-Cost Considerations of Universal Junior College Education." *National Tax Journal* 19 (1966): 48–57.

―――, AND SEGELHORST, ELBERT W. "Incremental Income Benefits of Public Education." *Review of Economics and Statistics* 47 (1965): 392–99.

―――; SEGELHORST, ELBERT W.; AND MARCUS, MORTON J. *Spillover of Public Education: Costs and Benefits.* Los Angeles: University of California, 1964.

HOLTMANN, A. G. "A Note on Public Education and Spillovers Through Migration." *Journal of Political Economy* 74 (1966): 524–25.

HOUTHAKKER, H. S. "Education and Income." *Review of Economics and Statistics* 41 (1959): 24–28.

HU, TEH-WEI; LEE, MAW L.; AND STROMSDORFER, ERNST W. "Economic Returns to Vocational and Comprehensive High School Graduates." *Journal of Human Resources* 6 (1971): 25–50.

HUNT, SHANE J. "Income Determinants for College Graduates, and the Return to Educational Investments." *Yale Economic Essays* 3 (1963): 305–57.

KATZMAN, MARTIN T. *The Political Economy of Urban Schools.* Publications of the Joint Center for Urban Studies. Cambridge, Mass.: Harvard University Press, 1971.

KIESLING, HERBERT J. "Measuring a Local Government Service: A Study of School Districts in New York State." *Review of Economics and Statistics* 49 (1967): 356–67.

LEVIN, MELVIN R., AND SHANK, ALAN, EDS. *Educational Investment in an Urban Society: Costs, Benefits, and Public Policy.* New York: Teachers College Press, 1970.

MAYHEW, ANNE. "Education, Occupation, and Earnings." *Industrial and Labor Relations Review* 24 (1971): 216–25.

McMahon, Walter W. "An Economic Analysis of Major Determinants of Expenditures on Public Education." *Review of Economics and Statistics* 52 (1970) : 242–52.

Merrett, Stephen. "Student Finance in Higher Education." *Economic Journal* 77 (1967) : 288–302.

———. "The Rate of Return to Education: A Critique." *Oxford Economic Papers* 18 (1966) : 289–303.

Morgan, James, and David, Martin. "Education and Income." *Quarterly Journal of Economics* 77 (1963) : 423–37.

Mushkin, Selma J., ed. *Economics of Higher Education.* U.S. Office of Education Bulletin no. 5, pp. 69–169. Washington, D.C.: U.S. Government Printing Office, 1962.

Owen, J. D. "The Distribution of Educational Resources in Large American Cities." *Journal of Human Resources* 7 (1972) : 26–38.

Schultz, Theodore W. *The Economic Value of Education.* New York: Columbia University Press, 1963.

Sizer, Theodore R. "The Schools in the City." In *The Metropolitan Enigma: Inquiries into the Nature and Dimensions of America's Urban Crisis,* ed. James Q. Wilson, pp. 342–66. Garden City, N.Y.: Doubleday, 1970.

Swift, William J., and Weisbrod, Burton A. "On the Monetary Value of Education's Intergeneration Effects." *Journal of Political Economy* 73 (1965) : 643–49.

Tuckman, Howard P. "High School Inputs and Their Contribution to School Performance." *Journal of Human Resources* 6 (1971) : 490–509.

Vaizey, John. *The Economics of Education.* London: Faber and Faber, 1962.

Walsh, J. R. "Capital Concept Applied to Man." *Quarterly Journal of Economics* 49 (1935) : 255–85.

Weisbrod, Burton A. "Education and Investment in Human Capital." *Supplement: Oct. 1962. Journal of Political Economy* 70 (1962) : 106–23.

———. *External Benefits of Public Education: An Economic Analysis.* Princeton: Princeton University Press, 1964.

———. "Geographic Spillover Effects and the Allocation of Resources to Education." In *The Public Economy of Urban Communities,* ed. Julius Margolis. Washington, D.C.: Resources for the Future, 1965; distr. by Johns Hopkins Press, Baltimore.

———. "Investing in Human Capital." *Journal of Human Resources* 1 (1966) : 5–21.

———. "Preventing High School Dropouts." In *Measuring Benefits of Government Investments: Papers Presented at a Conference of Experts Held Nov. 7–9, 1963,* ed. Robert Dorfman. Washington, D.C.: Brookings Institution, 1965.

Welch, Finis. "Measurement of the Quality of Schooling." *Papers and Proceedings of the American Economic Association. American Economic Review* 56 (1966) : 379–92.

Wiseman, Jack. "Public Finance and Education: A Summary of the Issues." In *Public Finance and Education, Public Finance* 21 (1966) : 316–24.

6

Urban Recreation

The cities of America provide a variety of public recreation programs. Depending upon the size of the city and the locale and climate, cities emphasize certain seasons of activity. Since most of the clientele of urban parks and recreation programs are children, the summer becomes for many communities the focal point of the program design. Most programs for summer activities include the hiring of large numbers of part-time personnel to administer the activities. The recreation programs are the actual planned social services, and these programs, to the extent that they are formal, are typically offered in the city's existing park systems. The emphasis on most recreational activity appears to be geared to physical recreation in an outdoor setting, but additional passive recreational pursuits are planned as well: picnicking facilities, arboretum displays, zoos, aquariums, museums, and even the operation of stadiums, outdoor theatres, and educational classes are common features of recreational planning.

The purpose of this chapter is to discuss some of the more significant aspects of urban recreation and parks programs. Little attention is given to the organization of commercial recreation, but the reader should be aware of the fact that there is significant overlap between what cities may provide and what the private market provides.

I. Recreation Expenditures and Participation

Local Government Expenditures

Recreation as an item in the typical community's budget is not large. On the average, communities in the United States in 1967 spent only about $7.85 per person on recreation services and parks. Table 18 reflects the level of expenditures by a sample of communities of various size. Expenditures in the largest cities run fully $5 per capita less than for cities of between 500,000 and 1 million. Likewise, cities of smaller size appear to spend less per capita on public recrea-

TABLE 18

PARK AND RECREATION EXPENDITURES: PER CAPITA AND AS PERCENTAGE
OF GENERAL EXPENDITURE, FOR SELECTED CITIES, ALL FUNCTIONS,
BY CITY SIZE, 1967–68

Cities by Population Size (1960)	Per Capita Expenditures	Percent of Total General Expenditures
1,000,000 or more	$ 9.89	2.62%
500,000 to 1,000,000	15.16	5.75
400,000 to 499,999	13.13	6.65
300,000 to 399,999	13.13	6.65
200,000 to 299,999	11.35	6.39
100,000 to 199,999	10.35	5.60
50,000 to 99,999	8.99	5.31

Source: U.S. Bureau of the Census, Department of Commerce, *City Government Finances, 1967–68* (Washington, D.C.: U.S. Government Printing Office, 1969), series GF 68, no. 4.

tion budgets. How does one explain the expenditures patterns? What likely occurs in the less than average expenditures among large cities is that loss of the tax base, lack of responsiveness of government, and pressure for expenditures in other directions create a downward pressure on recreation budgets. In smaller communities, the lowered budget may simply reflect a tradition of low budgets, less organized demand for recreation and parks, and greater availability of open space. Demand in the small community may not be as strong as in the middle-sized city, and demand in the large city may simply go unmet.

Consumer Expenditures for Recreation

The average family, consisting of 3.2 members, spends $200 for recreation per year.[1] The recreation expenditure occupies ninth position in the family budget preceded by expenditures for housing, food, transportation, clothing, medical care, household operation, home furnishing, and utilities, and is succeeded by personal care, other, alcohol, tobacco, education, and reading.[2] This order of rankings would seem to indicate that recreation is the most important consideration after basic family needs are met. If we could extract from the preceding categories those expenditures related to recreation, the ranking would be even higher.[3] For example, the family car is used for pleasure trips part of the time.

[1] U.S. Bureau of the Census, Department of Commerce, *Statistical Abstract of the United States, 1968* (Washington, D.C.: U.S. Government Printing Office, 1968), pp. 35, 325, 316.

[2] U.S. Bureau of the Census, *Statistical Abstract, 1968*, table 461, p. 316.

[3] Sebastian De Grazia, *Of Time, Work, and Leisure* (New York: Twentieth Century Fund, 1962), pp. 101–2.

The ambiguity of recreational expenditures is even more pronounced when the figures are viewed according to net income groupings for 1960–61 (table 19). It does not seem likely that families with incomes of $15,000 or more spent less than $700 for recreation. High income is related to increased education: the more education, the more likely the recreational pursuits chosen will be expensive. There is little variation in the percentages between income classes. Perhaps the similarity indicates a sociological force which operates to control the amount of recreational expenditures in relation to total income; however, there is a very real difference in the amount of recreation that can be purchased. That the highest percentage (5%) is expended by the lowest income group illustrates the disadvantaged position of anyone in that category. Even if recreational expenditures are minimal, they still comprise a larger portion of meager incomes.[4]

Nationally, trends seem to reflect increased recreational expenditures during recent years with the proportion of total expenditures increasing to about 6.3% of expenditures in 1969 (table 20).

Leisure and recreation have been accepted by the general population as desirable. People express a desire for more recreational activity if they have the time and money. Yet, when it appears that people have more of both, their behavior changes very little. Recreation may still be valued in terms of the Protestant ethic: Work is good, play is bad — and the latter is acceptable only to the degree to which it facilitates work. This was a necessary attitude during

TABLE 19

RECREATION EXPENDITURES AND
RECREATION EXPENDITURES AS A PERCENTAGE OF INCOME
BY INCOME CLASS, 1960–61

Income Range	Average Income	Recreation Expenditures	Percentage of Income
0 to $999	$ 535	$ 27	5
$1,000 to 1,999	1,521	38	2
$2,000 to 2,999	2,507	73	3
$3,000 to 3,999	3,515	121	3
$4,000 to 4,999	4,504	161	4
$5,000 to 5,999	5,491	190	3
$6,000 to 7,499	6,707	254	4
$7,500 to 9,999	8,554	327	4
$10,000 to 14,999	11,723	471	4
$15,000+	21,926	665	3

Source: Modified from U.S. Bureau of the Census, Department of Commerce, *Statistical Abstract of the United States, 1968* (Washington, D.C.: U.S. Government Printing Office, 1968) table 116, p. 128.

[4] De Grazia, *Of Time, Work, and Leisure*, pp. 101–2.

TABLE 20

TOTAL PERSONAL CONSUMPTION EXPENDITURES
AND TOTAL RECREATION EXPENDITURES, FOR SELECTED YEARS, 1960–69

	1960	1965	1969
Total personal consumption expenditures (in billions)	325.2	433.1	577.5
Recreation expenditures (in billions)	18.3	26.4	36.3
Percentage of recreation expenditures of total personal consumption expenditures	5.6%	6.0%	6.3%

Source: U.S. Bureau of the Census, Department of Commerce, *Statistical Abstract of the United States, 1972* (Washington, D.C.: U.S. Government Printing Office, 1972), table 490, p. 308.

the early formation of this country, but it is no longer justified in our hyper-productive society.[5] We work hard but we also play hard. Death can come from "over play" as easily as from overwork.

That leisure is not a pure blessing has been suggested by a study which involved 390 steel employees who received a thirteen-week vacation for the first time. Most reported they did not feel any compulsion to return to their jobs and enjoyed relaxing and recreating with their families. But during the thirteen weeks the majority did not develop any new interests or hobbies; and more than one-third reported no increase in recreation or entertainment expenditures. Unless these are peculiarities related to an initial extended vacation experience, the responses might suggest that people must learn to fill their leisure more imaginatively.[6] More and varied recreational activity does not automatically correlate with leisure and financial availability.

Judging from expenditures alone, the passive entertainment of television is preferred by far to any other type of leisure activity (table 21). If the dollar amounts of radio and television expenditures are combined, the figure would be almost twice that of the next major expenditure, "nondurable toys, sports supplies." When combined with radio and records, the dollar expenditures on television correspond to the heavy time use of people in these pursuits. Comparable to the expenditures of money, the amount of time citizens consume viewing television has been estimated to be almost equal to the time they work. Most significantly, affluence has generated increased expenditures for recreation and made possible wide participation in various recreational pursuits for Americans. Recognize that the expenditures are purely private and do not include government expenditures on the supply side for such items as parks, reservoirs, etc.

[5] Roger Revelle, "Outdoor Recreation in a Hyper-Productive Society," *Daedalus* 96 (Fall 1967): 1173–74.

[6] W. J. Klausner, "An Experiment in Leisure," *Science Journal* 4 (June 1968): 81–85.

TABLE 21

Personal Consumption Expenditures for Recreation, 1960, 1965, 1969,
(In Millions of Dollars)

Recreation Items	1960	1965	1969
Radios, TV, records, instruments	$3,412	$6,110	$8,085
Nondurable toys, sports supplies	2,417	3,408	5,213
Wheel goods, sports equipment, and average boats	2,106	2,985	4,219
Magazines, newspapers, sheet music	2,193	2,844	3,778
Books and maps	1,304	2,049	3,226
Spectator amusements	1,606	1,811	2,263
Movies	(951)	(927)	(1,097)
Theatre, concerts	(365)	(495)	(679)
Sports	(290)	(389)	(487)
Commercial recreation	1,161	1,512	1,719
Flowers, seeds, potted plants	641	976	1,361
Radio, TV repair	801	1,032	1,266
Clubs, fraternal organizations	733	879	1,108
Parimutuel receipts	517	734	952
Other*	1,404	2,046	3,118

* Includes pets and supplies, hobby equipment, etc.

Source: U.S. Bureau of the Census, Department of Commerce, *Statistical Abstract of the United States, 1972* (Washington, D.C.: U.S. Government Printing Office, 1972), table 317, p. 200.

Outdoor Recreation Participation

In 1965, the Bureau of Outdoor Recreation tabulated participation in various outdoor activities to determine what recreational facilities would be needed during the next thirty-five years. Participation figures were collected for major activities in 1965 (table 22).

Increased participation in outdoor activities in general, and more select pursuits in particular (boating, skiing, etc.), is related to increases in the youth population, family activity, incomes, technical and professional occupations, and educational levels — all of which influence outdoor recreation selection and participation.

Based on reports from 57% of the museums (history, live, science, art, and related organizations) attendance increased from 83 million in 1952 to 184 million in 1962; attendance in each category either doubled or tripled. Attendance at concerts performed by major orchestras has only slightly increased; 5 million in 1950 to 6 million in 1965.[7]

[7] U.S. Bureau of the Census, *Statistical Abstract, 1968*, tables 303 and 304, p. 208.

TABLE 22

OUTDOOR RECREATION PARTICIPATION FOR 1965

Activity	Number (In Millions)	Percentage of Population	Percentage of Increase (1960–65)
Picnicking	80.5	57	16
Pleasure driving	77.7	55	14
Sightseeing	69.2	49	26
Swimming	67.8	48	15
Walking	67.8	48	57
Group games	53.7	38	37
Fishing	42.7	30	12
Spectator sports	42.4	30	35
Motorboating	33.9	24	18
Bicycling	22.6	16	92
Nature walks	19.8	14	8
Sledding	18.4	13	55
Hunting	17.0	12	1
Outdoor concerts	15.5	11	32
Camping	14.1	10	35
Ice-skating	12.7	9	38
Horseback riding	11.3	8	44
Hiking	9.9	7	26
Water-skiing	8.5	6	8
Bird-watching	7.1	4	8
Snow skiing	5.7	4	115
Canoeing	4.2	3	62
Sailing	4.2	3	62

Source: Bureau of Outdoor Recreation, U.S. Department of the Interior, *Outdoor Recreation Trends* (Washington, D.C.: U.S. Government Printing Office, 1967), p. 20.

II. The Nature of Recreation and Leisure

Before we can approach some of the economic aspects of urban recreation, we need to specify what is meant by leisure and recreation. Each person may believe that he has a reasonably good understanding of what the terms recreation and leisure mean, since we appear to have somewhat rigid classifications describing expenditures. But as we move to a more detailed discussion we recognize the blurred lines and inadequate conceptualization underlying the expenditure classifications.

One useful classification of our individual time has been to distinguish between work time and leisure time. Work time is defined as that time in which the individual is devoted to some form of economically productive activity; leisure time is defined as that time which is essentially free from work. While one may argue that most of us have definable work time, we may not all be certain to have "free" time, since even our nonwork or leisure time is largely bound up with obligations of various sorts. Nonwork obligations include civic duties, clubs, and any other forms of activity which are obligations we assume, but for which we are not economically rewarded in a direct way. Nonwork obligations fill a good deal of our leisure time, thus are really a third time classification.

Having defined leisure as nonwork time, let us analyze the relation between work and leisure. In this era of high mass urban consumption and the continual production of a surplus beyond minimal needs, many urbanites find themselves free from compulsory labor. As Lewis Mumford points out, "Without compulsory labor civilizations would not originally have produced enough spare energy to maintain their higher activities. Without freedom from compulsory labor, man cannot enjoy these higher activities. . . ." [8] He means by higher activities the capacity to create. In this context the function of work is to provide man with a living in order to stimulate and liberate his capacity to create. The purpose of making a living is not simply to put one's self in a position of consuming more and more goods, but to be able to extend one's energies toward more successful enjoyment of social, spiritual, and personal existence.

While the increased security of affluence may be desirable, it adds to the problem of man dealing with leisure time. In an era of increased leisure, Karl Mannheim notes that the average citizen is not fully capable of inventing new uses for his leisure. According to Mannheim:

> Comparative studies in the use of leisure show at first glance that a higher position, larger income, and increased security do not necessarily lead to culture. Unless material advancement is combined with personal example and the persuasion exercised by the presence of intelligent standards for the use of leisure, it may end in boredom, neurosis, and general decadence. . . . Security alone is no guarantee that surplus energies will be turned in any particular direction, unless they are guided by personal influence and education. . . . [The average citizen is unable to invent new uses for his leisure . . .] [9]

Thus, while it is true that we do appear to be generating additional amounts of leisure time, there is no certainty that this leisure time will be used in any socially or personally desirable way.

In line with the above fear that individual citizens may not know how to use increased leisure time, Nels Anderson suggests a number of trends in the use of leisure time.

1. *Nonwork Obligations.* Definitions of leisure often include categories of activities, but many off-the-job activities turn out to be nothing like

[8] Lewis Mumford, *The Condition of Man* (New York: Harcourt, Brace and Company, 1944), p. 5.

[9] Karl Mannheim, *Man and Society in an Age of Reconstruction*, Studies in Modern Social Structure (New York: Harcourt, Brace and Company, 1944), p. 317.

paid work nor yet like leisure. One works in the garden, helps around the house, does favours for the neighbors, works for the trade union, the political party, the church, the community centre, and so on. These are often called nonwork obligations and they often yield leisure-like satisfactions. The more the individual is integrated into family life, organized group life, and community life the more of his free time is likely to be given to such activities, and often the less interest he has in leisure. There is good reason to believe that as people become more identified with nonwork activity the less need they have for leisure and the more their leisure is linked with these activities.

2. *Family and Home Leisure Centredness.* Contrary to fears about family disintegration, studies of leisure indicate that most family members spend half or more of their leisure-activity time at home where they can be reached by telephone and where they have world contact by radio and television. This is in addition to time at home spent on nonwork obligations. It seems that even this so-called one-generation family is very much concentrated on living, and for each family member the home is the accumulation of leisure-use things, and of prestige things essential to social living, a phase of leisure.

3. *Declining Worker Interest in the Job.* It is generally recognized that most workers who sell their time seem to have little interest in the job or in the enterprise. This is often regretted and experts have designed various methods for reviving worker interest. Some of the experts, including industrial sociologists, are asking what the worker has to gain and how would industry benefit by drumming up a 'company consciousness', that being what management is paid for. As far as I know, there is no evidence that this worker attitude is detrimental to his efficiency; productivity increases and worker efficiency does not decline. The worker sells his time and skill, a business transaction; the transaction complete, at quitting time he puts work out of mind. He is no longer the slave of a routine job, but has worked out a sensible relationship with it. He is not bored with his job; he has come to terms with it. He will strike to hold his job and he will give an honest day's work. He can take pride in his work but still he leaves thinking about it at the plant.[10]

In addition Anderson challenges the idea that man may have trouble dealing with his leisure time.

4. *Passivity and the Cultural Level.* Here it is necessary to take issue with a great many intellectuals who complain that the great mass of people are helpless when faced with leisure. They settle into meaningless dull routine, floating with the tide, lacking a zest for life, surrounded by opportunity but developing no special interests. This adds to the conclusion that the level of culture is doomed to decline. Actually the level of culture (however measured) is not declining. We need but step back in imagination to 1850 or even 1900. The answer is a long-perspective look at things.

[10] Nels Anderson, *Work and Leisure* (New York: Free Press of Glencoe, 1961), pp. xii, xiii.

This final thesis is not sheer optimism. I would add that while we are looking at the changes in the lowest level of culture we examine some of the present trends in uses of leisure. I find it hard to share the view that the mass of people is incapable of using leisure, that they stand helpless before a great emptiness. This is arguing that a people who continue to be experimental in their work cannot be experimental in their leisure.[11]

On passivity and the use of leisure time, it could be argued that both Mannheim and Anderson are in some sense accurate. Not all people have difficulty in their use of leisure time, but it is certain that many urban dwellers evidence this difficulty. If one accepts the argument that people have difficulty in using their leisure time and tend to fall into a kind of boredom, then it is difficult to see the choice of watching television as being a positive one. Further, increased numbers of people are engaged in watching spectator sports. Can we then argue that the high rise in attendance at sporting and other public events is a result of creative use of leisure time or are these activities pursued simply to escape boredom? It would seem that the optimum would probably be a balance of leisure activities. To the majority of citizens, it would seem undesirable to devote all of their time to passive leisure, but it might be considered equally undesirable if citizens spent all of their leisure time in vigorous physical activity. In short, there must be some kind of balance between active and passive pursuits, but the exact balance for any individual human being is apt to be the result of his total background of experience and therefore difficult to unequivocally predict.

The Industrial Setting of Leisure

The setting in which our fundamental concepts of leisure might apply is distinctly industrial. That is, we live in a complex city which is more than simply machines and factories. The city is a composit of techniques, mechanisms, skilled labor forces, and social organizations which are adapted to carrying on an industrial society. Further, an industrial society is distinctly urban, as suggested by Anderson when he discusses the traits which an industrial society possesses:

1. Man no longer lives in cherished isolation, as in the oldtime village, but must live in contact with large agglomerates, co-ordinating his interests and efforts to the wider group. This is a new form of collective living. The city man is extremely collective in both work and play.

2. The mass production needed to keep industry vigorous demands mass consumption; that is, behaviour and taste uniformities over wide areas. Millions sleep on the same sort of mattresses, own the same kind of radio sets, and listen to the same programmes, read the same newspaper, wear the same kind of shoes, etc. Yet with all the conformity and uniformity one can achieve variety.

[11] Anderson, *Work and Leisure*, pp. xiii, xiv.

3. In the mechanized man-made environment one must be acquainted with the use and potentialities of hundreds of mechanisms and be alert to them every waking hour. Being alert and informed is to co-operate in their proper use, whether the mechanism be an automobile, a street traffic control, a building elevator, a vending machine, a juke box, or gadgets in the home.[12]

Man no longer lives in isolation but in continued coordinated contact with other persons in a collective city. The industrial production which demands high mass consumption generates widespread uniformities, yet the very extent of the productive capacity makes variety possible. Further, mechanized man must be aware of literally hundreds of machines and mechanisms, and he must learn to use them in a cooperative way. The complexity under which urban man lives today demands the greatest degree of cooperation that men have ever had to pursue.

In order to work efficiently in this cooperative necessity, man necessarily becomes disciplined by his machines if they are to effectively serve him. This discipline requires that man be confident in at least three different respects:

1. Modern man must keep on learning; skills, habits, and manners of yesterday may not suffice for today. As he must learn new work ways, so he must learn new play ways. Falling behind the procession is a mark of aging. He must know the latest gadgets as he must also know about the latest songs.

2. He must be able to adjust to increasingly complex situations, since innovation tends to move from the simple to the complex. We see the complexity trend in the automobile; how it introduces variety in the work spheres, how it changes the use of leisure, how it introduces innovations in family and individual life (courting practices, for example). Similarly we can see this complexity trend with the introduction of mechanisms in offices and in the household.

3. With the greater integration and development of the industrial order its area of contact and influence widens. People must learn to think in wider terms. Where the grandfathers were amazed that words could be telegraphed from San Francisco to New York in the 1860s the grandsons are not impressed at all to hear voices radioed from the South Pole. We think casually both about global communication networks as well as of global transportation networks. Different industries, oil, automobiles, metals, and many more are linked in global markets. Basketball has become a world game, and, like boating and other sports, is uniformly so. As one becomes associated with the thinking that matches this global trend his mental reach must widen.[13]

As a result of the foregoing, life in an industrial city is highly nontraditional; that is, great flexibility is required. Further, urbanization is highly sophisticated

---

[12] Anderson, *Work and Leisure*, pp. 3–4.

[13] Anderson, *Work and Leisure*, pp. 4–5.

and consequently more demanding. Since life in modern urban centers is highly dynamic, change and expansion are rapid. The complexity of the city makes life in the city largely anonymous. We live together as a mass, but it is a faceless mass, cooperating together not because of personal identifications with one another, but because of the necessities which complexity demands of us.

A Tentative Definition of Leisure in an Urban Context

In the modern city each day we see literally hundreds of people we do not know. We see persons at work, on the streets, on the freeways, in the shops, and in the schools who are only identifiable to us by a set of assumptions and perceptions about them. Human relationships become mere instrumental relationships. It is logical, therefore, that leisure time be used for personal development. According to one definition, "leisure is activity to which the individual may freely devote himself outside the needs and obligations of his occupation, his family, and society, for his relaxation, diversion, and personal development." [14]

In the pursuit of leisure we need to realize that different kinds of leisure activities have different kinds of value. These values may be so varied among people that for a given activity no person will have precisely the same value attachment as others. The result is that we are forced to assume that, with a wide variety of choices open to him, a person can generally find the values he wants from his leisure time. Studies of leisure have revealed that leisure values probably depend more upon personality than upon age, sex, or social class characteristics. Thus, while we may specifically plan activities for different age groups, different sexes, or people of different social classes, the underlying understanding must be largely in personal terms.

Though leisure activity is difficult to measure, we recognize that leisure represents time and time is opportunity. If an individual has leisure time, it means that he has free time in which to exercise choices about how he uses that time. Leisure choices are guided by educational and social values that influence the individual; these choices do not provide just simple "play" time, nor is leisure merely that time in which a person is not working. Leisure time is effectively free time sandwiched in-between work obligations and the nonwork obligations such as political party work, church work, fixing things around the house, helping children with their lessons, etc.

A Tentative Definition of Public Recreation

What is the relationship of recreation to leisure? Recreation (literally, to re-create), we now see, is a use of leisure time. Recreation suggests the actions of an individual re-creating himself or putting himself back together. Recreation is a leisure activity which the individual engages in purely by choice because of the enjoyment and satisfaction which it brings him. Indeed, we can imagine

[14] Anderson, *Work and Leisure*, p. 36.

recreational activity as being performed for its own sake, not for any external reward. One definition of recreation suggests that recreation should mean active participation, adapted to strength and age, but participation: "Rocking-chair sitting before the radio and television is not enough. Motion pictures, where others act, is not enough. Sitting in the stadium watching sports is not enough. Getting second-hand thrills in race track gambling is not enough. Recreation means staying in the game." [15] Recreation can also be characterized as a movement which is designed to engage people in more active participation. It implies movement to promote activities for the use of leisure time; it also means administration and organization — both public and private.

While all of these comments on recreation are instructive, we should recognize that recreational activity is an expansive activity. We move away from the traditional notion of simple physical activity into the larger sphere of participation. Thus, we might require recreation, whether it is active or passive, to provide sufficient stimulus to participate and to provide people with genuine alternatives in using leisure time.

In the context of our discussion, public recreation is the provision of programs and participation opportunities for citizens to use their leisure time in ways which are meaningful both personally and socially. If we can assume that there is any deficiency in the way in which people make personal choices to creatively use their own leisure time, then one principal responsibility of the public recreation program is to lead the community in terms of innovative and creative programming and to provide those services which are thought to be significant for personal and social development in combination with the stated preferences of the population. It should be the responsibility of the public recreation authorities to have an ever-expanding view of what constitutes proper programming. Ideally, the only limitation that the responsible public authority would consider is the amount of leisure time available to citizens and what citizens would be willing to pay.

Recreation programs must meet certain conditions to be effective for citizens in communities. Sutherland suggests six such fundamental conditions.

> A first condition for the enjoyment of leisure during time not sold for pecuniary reward is *integrity of purpose*. Leisure is an inward activity and the genuineness of its expression lies in the absence of propaganda or constraint. A use of leisure has value *per se* for the very reason that its end exists for creative expression. An old Chinese proverb states the case: "Life is not a vessel to be drained, but a cup to be filled."
>
> A second fundamental concept of leisure is the *liberty to review goals*, to explore possible avenues of experience, to choose, and to agree upon the ends and purposes of activity. Teamwork comes from agreement.
>
> A third concept is *objectivity*. Within the context of action, human relationships are free from personal feelings, personal prejudices, and personal

15 Anderson, *Work and Leisure*, p. 43.

imperialisms. No participant seeks either to achieve ulterior ends or to accomplish hidden plans.

A fourth concept is *equality in fellowship*. Persons enjoy their fellowship with others in objective enjoyment of the common activity. In the association on the bowling team, for example, it makes little difference that one man is employer and the other employee; that one man is a physician and another a freight agent; that one man is rich and the other poor.

A fifth concept is *common command of skills*. There is something defective in the character of the experience when participants lack capacity and competence to participate. They must both *understand* and have the *know how* of the game.

A sixth concept is *growth*. Because men enjoy doing what they do well and increasingly better, there exists within the creative use of leisure an organic thrust toward depth and quality. In the field of photography, for example, mere activity in taking and collecting pictures can move into a study of aesthetics or into a detailed record of rose culture. Personal development places new responsibilities upon recreation leaders because it is entirely possible for "growing participants" to move beyond the competence of the leader. Hence constant inservice training is essential for the maintenance of the leadership position.[16]

If a person is instructed in the use of recreational time, that means that he has acquired skills of a game, a hobby, or other leisure activity. Throughout the literature it seems that persons who have acquired intensive education in sports find no problem in dealing with their leisure time. The same would be true of the person who has acquired skills in drama, music, art, or any other personally satisfying leisure activity. Skills are necessary to enjoy any activity, and it seems that the most important single act that recreationists should perform is that of effectively teaching skills in such a way that the person acquires them for their own sake and learns them well. While we require proficiency in math in schools, our requirements for recreational pursuits are less demanding and less effective. Therefore, if a person has not attained a high degree of skill in learning a recreational pursuit, then it is the obligation of the society to provide opportunity to be so instructed. Undoubtedly the problem lies in the manner of instruction, the limited choices, and the intensity of instruction which would enable an individual to attain a self-generating level of skills. If our parks are empty of people, then the quality of instruction may be poor and the local recreation department must accept some responsibility.

One final but significant point is that the public should be made aware that when school is out the public parks and summer recreation programs are the most important social institutions operating for children. Public recreation is more important than we have in the past thought.

[16] Willard C. Sutherland, "A Philosophy of Leisure," *Annals of the American Academy of Political and Social Science* 313 (Sept. 1957): 2.

III. The Value of Urban Public Recreation:
Demand and Supply

In valuing urban public recreation, we speak of the goods and services which are offered to residents by the local government in the form of programs of recreation at recreation sites or parks. First, we need to know something about the economic demands for recreation in order to be able to generate an efficient output of these goods and services in the city. Second, we need to know something about the effects that recreational programs and parks have on the local residents and the local economy. Further, due to increased interest in public recreation since World War II, citizens' demands for increased public expenditures in more sophisticated directions have forced local recreation authorities to more carefully understand their role as producers. Finally, trends in urban participation appear to continue to rise as incomes continue to rise, and a slackening in urban recreational participation does not appear likely to occur in the near future.

An important reason for our interest in recreation sites in particular is the fact that such uses for land come into direct competition with private market demands for land, and, until recently, those who chose to preserve parks had little economic argument to present. The private user of land could argue increased incomes and jobs and other apparently tangible benefits to cities. In line with this competition for available land comes the necessity on the part of local recreational authorities to price the goods and services they produce. Without knowledge of the economic value which these outputs have in the minds of citizens, pricing cannot be undertaken.

Factors of Demand for Recreation

When one considers demand for the recreational outputs of a city it is necessary to think in terms of combining the demand for a particular program with the fact that this demand is met at a particular recreational site. A recreation program must be offered somewhere, and the demand for the site is a part of the demand for the program. A park, for example, is essentially a receptacle in which numerous activities are possible, whether they be passive or active pursuits.

Broad aspects of demand are associated with income, taste and preference, the price of other goods and services, and the number of consumers in the market. In general, demand for recreation increases with a rise in incomes; demand for recreation rises with increasing recreation; demand may even rise in cities where residential densities are actually greater. Further, the demand for some recreational activities may be class oriented; for example, tennis has only recently filtered into the inner city.

Demand factors for a particular recreation site, as noted by Clawson and Knetsch, include factors related to users and potential users; factors related to the recreation area itself; and the relationships between the potential users and the recreation area.[17] Two elements related to potential users are their total number in the surrounding area and their geographic distribution within the area. Socio-economic characteristics such as age, sex, family size and composition, educational status, and race also appear to be significant. Income level, the time available for leisure, the time distribution of that leisure, and specific knowledge and education as to the recreational activities are additional factors of demand.

Elements related to the recreational site itself include its attractiveness to the consumer, the management of the area, the capacity of the area to accommodate recreationists, and the climatic and weather conditions of the area. Those factors which are significant to the interrelationships between consumers and recreation areas include the time required to travel to the site and return, the comfort or discomfort of that travel, the monetary costs involved, and the extent to which demand is stimulated by advertising or notice.

While Clawson and Knetsch drew this list of factors to relate to regional, state, and even national recreation sites, the same characteristics appear to hold for urban areas. Cities to some extent can be viewed as microcosms of a region or a state when recreational demand is considered.

The Supply of Recreational Outputs

Recreational outputs are a mix of goods or services; what people do with their recreational time is to consume a variety of recreational goods and services. The basic public unit in the city where this consumption takes place is the public recreation site.

Although all public recreation facilities are not the same, they appear to have a number of common characteristics. First, all are utilized: that is, visitors come to the specific site to consume the recreational goods and services. Second, all recreational sites are spaces in the total urban space. Significant spatial characteristics involve internal design and proximity to other similar and competing recreational facilities. A third characteristic of importance is that recreational sites do not function in a timeless world. The dynamics of parks and other facilities consist of the short-run use in which consumers "spend time" and the long-run aspects of the impact of parks upon property values and other urban development, as well as the aging process of the particular site.

Supply of recreational services is similar to the supply of recreational sites. Facilities and programs are in a sense competitive since in operating under scarce resources the proper product mix must be considered. One may allocate too much budget to parks and not enough to programs or vice versa.

The recreational site as a unit of production in the city is subject to similar locational concerns as is any commercial or industrial site. For example, parks are located either near a unique topographical feature or they are located near

[17] Marion Clawson and Jack L. Knetsch, *Economics of Outdoor Recreation* (Baltimore: Published for Resources for the Future by Johns Hopkins Press, 1966), p. 60.

the market, i.e., in neighborhoods. When considering the condition of location in proximity to the market — that is, near those who will use the park — one must consider the social and physical boundaries and barriers within a city which diminish the service area of a park, and one must take account of densities. One must think in terms of the spatial efficiency of the location of parks. We could have too many parks too close together, or we could have too few parks located too far apart. In either case the city is served less efficiently.

With locational problems park administrators have learned to develop standards of location. These standards tend to be somewhat arbitrary and ignore the economics of parks, but they reflect the experience and best judgment of practitioners who, though influenced by particular biases, draw heavily upon sound background and experience. One such man is Charles Doell, former head of the Minneapolis park department and a kind of congenial dean of park administrators. In his book on park administration, Doell cites a useful set of standards as employed by the city of Dallas, Texas (table 23). Within this listing there is reference to service zones which indicate to the park director how far apart to place his parks. These standards may be arbitrary. The point is that such standards reflect a kind of unsupported ideal which is not unrelated to the concept of optimum in economics. Location of parks in an urban space depends largely upon the distances significant numbers of persons will come to use a particular park facility or attend a particular recreation program.

Such standards should be viewed with caution. A natural resource for recreation purposes exists only in the case of a site for which there is the possibility of or an actual early use for recreation purposes.[18] Since demands are so complex, it is difficult to identify useful standards for the provision of park and recreation programs.

A further complication in the provision of an efficient supply of programs and recreation sites is peak loading. Seasonal variations in urban recreation create some peak usage which in turn creates diseconomies of congestion that tend to press the public supplier to respond to the seasonal peak rather than to the normal usage level. An illustration will clarify the concept of peak loading. If one were to use price to ration the use of a swimming pool, users would be charged different prices at different times. Slack morning hours might show a very low fee while heavy afternoon hours (or whenever the peak loading occurred) would bear a higher fee. But if the facility is already in operation, how would one justify such a fee, and, indeed, how much would the relative fee increase be? The problems of developing a fee or user charge which would be effective in rationing use would be largely a matter of trial and error. The justification of any price discrimination might be difficult to argue, and, finally, there is little doubt that the consumer would yell about such discriminatory pricing. If the consumer were edu-

[18] Clawson and Knetsch, *Economics of Outdoor Recreation*, p. 145.

TABLE 23

PARK AREA AND SERVICE STANDARDS

Type of Park Area	Size	Recommended Area per 1,000 Persons	Service Area
Playlot	Less than 1 acre	Special facility	Usually limited to single block or project
Playground (neighborhood park)	6 acre minimum, additional for parking and natural science areas desirable	1 to 2 acres per 1,000 persons depending upon shape & intensity of development	Approximately ½ mi. or 1 sq. mi. Neighborhood same as elementary school
Playfield (includes athletic field)	15 to 25 acres, may be part of larger scenic area if location provides convenient service	1 to 2 acres per 1,000 persons with at least 1 acre active play area per 1,000 people	Approximately 1 mi. or 4 or 5 neighborhood units. Similar service area to high school
Large park	Minimum of 100 acres, preferably several hundred acres	Approximately 5 acres per 1,000 persons	3 mi. or more with good accessibility by auto
Parkways, ornamental areas, special parks	Size varies depending on conditions and nature of area	Approximately 2 acres per 1,000 persons	No specific service areas as most facilities serve entire urban area
Reservations and preserves	Several hundred to a thousand or more acres	10 acres per 1,000 persons. May include some close in regional recreation areas	Entire urban area
Regional recreation areas	Several thousand acres	No specific standard. May be partially included in area of reservations and preserves	Entire region

Source: Charles E. Doell, *Elements of Park and Recreation Administration* (Minneapolis: Burgess Publishing Company, 1963), p. 16. Reprinted by permission from *Elements of Park and Recreation Administration*, 1963, Charles E. Doell, Burgess Publishing Company.

cated to be aware that it is sometimes the peak hour user who accounts for some higher costs then differential charging might be possible.

Other factors significant to the supply of recreation programs and parks are the budget constraints under which most communities operate. The modern city, if it has no large backlog of recreational land acquired in an earlier time, has little opportunity to catch up. To start an acquisitions program which will enable it to secure sufficient land holdings for just minimal standards is usually too costly even with the present possibilities of some federal aid. Recreation sites must be developed before programs can be effected, and costs for land have risen more rapidly than most city recreational budgets. This prompts the city to turn to more mobile unit programming such as "fun mobiles." As another alternative, the city may turn to the local school system for aid in using school facilities for recreational programs. Today multiple use facilities have a definite cost advantage over earlier separate park and school facilities.

IV. Models for Evaluating Parks and Recreation Programs

As one might suspect from the previous discussions, the economic value of parks and recreation programs lies largely in the value of the participation of people in the goods and services. As they exist, public programs are generally limited in scope and provide only a small number of the total recreational activities people actually pursue. The public response to this point has at best been partial. Models are designed to deal with what is rather than what should be.

In all current models participation is the key. Participation can be thought of as active or passive—that is, people who participate in programs do so actively while those who are spectators are passively engaged. The aesthetic pleasure of an attractive park also falls into the passive category. How are we to evaluate such participation, active and passive? What value does it have to those who do participate, and what monetary price can we develop for this value? One thing is certain, we need not separate the good, or parks, from the service programs. They are not the same things certainly, but they have interrelated and only occasionally separable values.

There have been numerous models developed for assessing the benefits of a recreation area or more properly a recreation resource. Few of the available models are designed for urban recreation, in particular urban parks, but most are adaptable to the urban scene. None are complete models; all fail in some particular way, but the efforts have at least provided means of raising questions about the economic value of recreation.

As Burton and Fulcher have pointed out:

> Ideally, one would like to be able to measure the total social benefit derived from these recreation facilities. For normal goods, this benefit can be divided into three components; (1) appropriated benefit — i.e., what one actually pays for the use of the facilities; (2) consumer surplus — i.e., the difference between what one actually pays and what one would be prepared to pay; and (3) the indirect benefit to society for which there is no charge.[19]

The Trice and Wood Model

Trice and Wood developed their model for calculation of benefits to water-based recreation, but with little modification the model can be adapted to the

[19] T. L. Burton and Margaret N. Fulcher, "Measurement of Recreation Benefits: A Survey," *Journal of Economic Studies* (May 1970), p. 35.

urban park. Basically the model depends upon travel cost as a proxy for value since the benefits of recreation are assumed to be largely intangible.

The method outlined bears the following characteristics:

1. It is in terms of a standard unit of time and is expressed in dollars.
2. It is representative of recreational enjoyment for which there is no expenditure by the recreationist and for which the state is not directly reimbursed.
3. It is separately derived and independent of costs of providing recreational facilities.
4. It consists of a single figure which applies to recreationists . . . as a group without regard to the form of recreation being enjoyed or to differences among individuals as to capacity to enjoy recreational benefits.
5. It is peculiar to the area under consideration, even though similar areas may have similar values.
6. It is reasonable in amount and subject to tests based upon judgment values by informed people.[20]

According to Trice and Wood, the above characteristics must hold for the model to have usefulness in measuring economic benefits.[21]

The model is one based on travel costs under particular assumptions. Imagine a series of zones bounded by rings around a given recreation site which represent distance zones around the site. For our purposes the outer zone might be a city boundary. The average travel cost to the site would be multiplied by the number of users of the site from that particular zone. The assumption made is that the "market price" of the recreational visit has been established by the outer ring visitors, the visitors who come from the greatest distance zone. Thus, market value is the maximum price consumers would be willing to pay. The proxy for this market price which people are willing to pay is the travel cost from the most distant zone. Thus, any person visiting the park or recreation site from a distance less than the average travel cost from the most distant zone gains a benefit or consumer surplus. This hinges on the assumption that all people value recreation to the same degree; thus, the surplus occurs because people from lesser distances do not have to pay the maximum price.

Figure 5 illustrates the analysis. A person coming from Zone C has a travel cost of $3. This is set as the average travel cost from Zone C and is thus the maximum price consumers are willing to pay. If a person coming from Zone B bears only $2 in travel cost, then his net benefit is $1. If the person from Zone A goes to the park, then his cost is $1 and his net benefit becomes $3–$1 = $2. Thus the consumer is locationally subsidized in his recreational enjoyment by the government and its expenditures through tax revenues.

[20] Andrew H. Trice and Samuel E. Wood, "Measurement of Recreation Benefits," *Land Economics* 34 (1958): 195–207.

[21] Trice and Wood, "Measurement of Recreation Benefits," p. 201.

FIGURE 5

Hypothetical Park with Service Zone
And Costs of Transportation to Park

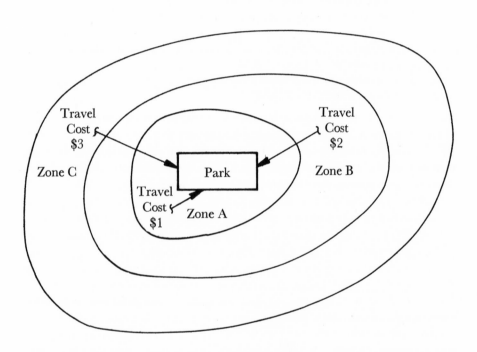

Source: Adapted from Andrew H. Trice and Samuel E. Wood, "Measurement of Recreation Benefits," *Land Economics* 34 (1958): 202.

In evaluating the method it should be mentioned that at the time of its development it was probably the best available. The greatest limitation was assuming that everyone in a given zone valued recreation in the same way. This method did, however, provide a device which could measure recreation benefits. It provided, under its limiting assumptions, a separation from governmental cost; it also expressed the value of the benefit in dollar terms, and, obviously, if we assume its validity, it presented a method which could be generalized upon and used in numerous investigations of different recreational sites.

The Clawson Demand Curve Model

Marion Clawson developed a method for assessing benefits which is also based on travel costs as a proxy for price. Taking data from users and place of origin, Clawson develops a demand curve which, by using travel cost as the price ⁎and evaluating the area under the demand curve, develops a notion of the value of the recreation site.

Knetsch elaborated and extended the Clawson approach. Assume we have three neighborhoods whose populations represent the total potential visitors to the given park. Assume the neighborhoods are of different population sizes and different distances from the park. Further assume that all costs of travel (car, gas, food, etc.) over and above those necessary if the trip were not taken are included in the concept of travel cost. With distances to the park differing from the various areas, costs will be different.

Neighborhood	Population	$ Cost of a Visit	Visits Made	Visits per 1,000 Population
A	1,000	$1	400	400
B	2,000	$3	400	200
C	4,000	$4	400	100

From the above data we discover that the rate of visits per 1,000 population declines as distance (cost) increases.[22]

The second step in the computation leading to the Clawson demand curve is to develop particular points along the hypothetical curve . Assuming that there were 1,200 visits at zero charge (not total cost, but addition to cost), this becomes one point on the demand curve.

If a charge were levied on the visit, then we would expect the quantity demanded to decline. If we assume a charge of $1 then we can determine what would happen to quantity demanded by investigating the relationship between the data for the cost of a visit and the visitation rate per 1,000 population (figure 6). The present cost of a visit from neighborhood A as $1 with a rate of 400 visits.

[22] Jack L. Knetsch, "Outdoor Recreation Demands and Benefits," *Land Economics* 39 (1963): 388–90. Marion Clawson's original paper, "Methods of Measuring the Demand for and Value of Outdoor Recreation," was published in 1959 by Resources for the Future, Washington, D.C., as reprint no. 10.

FIGURE 6

HYPOTHETICAL RELATION BETWEEN
COST AND VISIT RATE

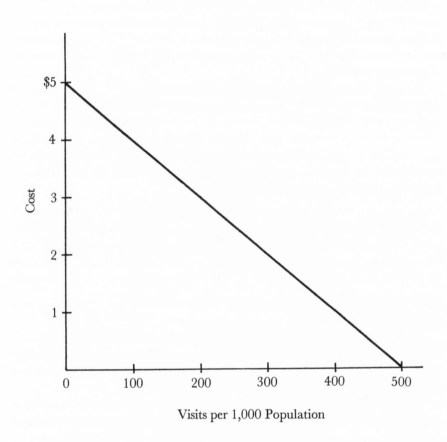

Visits per 1,000 Population

Source: Adapted from Jack L. Knetsch, "Outdoor Recreation Demands and Benefits," *Land Economics* 39 (1963): 389.

If we add $1 to the cost (the fee), the visitor rate from each neighborhood declines. The visitation rate from area A would reduce to an estimated 300 per 1,000 population. Since population is 1,000, visitors from A would now number 300. Similarly, the rate for area B drops from 200 to 100 per 1,000 population with the visitors from B now numbering 200. Finally, the rate from area C drops from 100 to zero so no visitors come from C. The visits then totaled from the above (for an additional charge of $1) would be 500. In figure 6 the rate is developed, but remember that the numbers refer to visits per 1,000 population. Thus we have an additional point on the demand curve when the additional charge of $1 is levied, indicating that 500 persons will visit the park given those conditions.

In a similar manner, the other points on the demand curve are developed. In Knetsch's illustration they are as follows:

Price (added cost)	Quantity (total visits)
$0	1,200
1	500
2	200
3	100
4	0 [23]

In the above context, the value of the resource (park) is defined as the capitalized net profit resulting from imposing the maximizing added cost. Factor costs would be subtracted from the total revenue method developed, and for the sake of illustration net benefit would be the difference between cost and $500 since that would be the maximum revenue if we assume costs as zero. This model, the derivation of the demand curve, is currently the most widely accepted evaluation device for recreation.

An Alternative Model

The analysis of economic benefits accruing to an urban park's users depends upon somewhat unconventional means. In the ordinary economic sense, benefits are measured by the total of prices people are willing to pay; it is assumed that the user or consumer of the service is willing to pay the price. Normally this estimate would be derived from a demand curve. The following model is based on the idea of the inappropriateness of demand curves for publically produced goods.

Unfortunately the use of urban parks (except in the case of special facilities such as swimming pools) implies no direct price payment. In order to ascertain user utility or gross benefits to users, some measure of consumer behavior other than direct price derived from demand curves must be used.

[23] Knetsch, "Outdoor Recreation," p. 389.

THE SPATIAL BENEFIT. Transportation costs are real in the sense that they represent actual costs to users of parks. If the consumer pays the price of the transportation, his costs can be ascertained and his benefit assumed to be in excess of cost. Thus, real costs of transportation become a "cost" element in the cost-benefit analysis, and the hypothetical cost (cost to the most distant user) would be a measure of gross benefit. To calculate the net benefit for a given user, actual cost would be subtracted from the hypothetical cost.

This method measures the consumer surplus by taking real parks and determining where the consumer would have to go if the present park were not available. Thus, the consumer surplus in this case is based on the notion of the next best alternative park.

At this point it would be logically necessary to consider the various types of parks. The next best alternative would be one which provided the facilities and services of the existing park. For example, imagine that the user at X can enjoy the facilities provided at Park A which is a neighborhood park with certain characteristics (figure 7). Compute his real cost of transportation which we might imagine to be zero since he can and does walk to the park. Now take that park away. Since Park A no longer exists, the consumer at X would have to go to the next best alternative, which in this case might be Park B. The hypothetical cost of going to Park B for the consumer at X is calculated to be $.15. Since in fact he does not have to go to Park B, but can go to Park A instead, the net benefit or consumer surplus in this case is $.15 less the cost of going to Park A. The computation of the benefit for a given period will be the addition of all such surpluses among all consumers of the Park A's services. In making use of this form of benefit we gain only a partial expression of total economic net benefits of the urban park.

THE ACTIVITY BENEFIT. The kind of benefits discussed previously dealt with a location or spatial benefit based on the transportation savings. A second benefit of a primary nature is the economic benefit of the park service when the activities offered in the park are examined. In a strict economic sense, any activity which is offered in the park adds economic benefits in the same way as an equivalent service offered in the private sector of the economy. For example, group dancing lessons are available in the private sector as well as at many recreation centers. An examination of the two services as to comparable quality and cost and extent to which there is price differentiation leads to the suggestion that if the service offered by the park is of comparable quality and if the fee for the service is less, then the net difference between the private price and the public price is a benefit. It is a benefit if the price charged by the park is less than that of the private studio; or, if higher, then it is a net cost to the park. Other examples abound: swimming pools which are publicly owned, concerts, art and music classes. Insofar as these services are provided by the parks, then there will likely be benefits which are measurable.

FIGURE 7
Alternative Cost Transportation Model

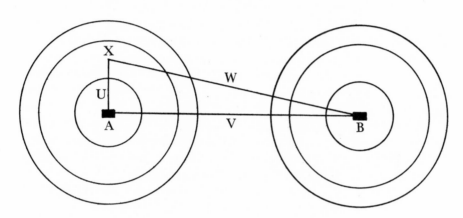

Cost for an individual, X, to go to Park B is (g_1) (w_1).

where: $g_1 =$ cost per unit of distance for X to go to Park B

$w_1 =$ length of line W for X

Net benefit of being able to go to Park A (for X) is then:

(g_1) $(w_1) - (u_1)$ (g_2)

where: $g_2 =$ cost per unit distance for X to go to Park A

$u_1 =$ length of line U for X

For a homogeneous distribution of park users around Park A, the average value of w_1 will be v (where v is the distance from Park A to Park B). If X has to drive to Park B then g_1 will have a positive value, but assuming he can walk to Park A the value of $g_2 = 0$. Therefore, total net benefit (of Park A) is $[(n)$ (g) $(v)]2$

where: n = number of users of Park A

g = average cost per unit distance to drive from home (near Park A) to Park B

2 = round trip.

One issue might hinge on whether the service is provided in the private sector or not. It could be argued that if the service is not provided in the private sector, then the park service has no economic benefit. This is fallacious; in fact, if the activity provided by the park is not offered in the private sector, it can mean one of three things. First, the lack of the private counterpart could be a result of the fact that the park service is sufficient and competitors in the private sector cannot economically compete. Or, the lack of a private counterpart might mean that the market for the service is limited. Thirdly, the park service, if demand for the activity is indeed limited, may be offering a variety of services which, though uneconomical in isolation from each other, may collectively be economically provided. In any event, the existence of an immediate private counterpart is not logically necessary. Computationally, however, a private counterpart *somewhere* is necessary in order to compare a private fee or charge with the park fee (if there is one) for the same service.

Benefits for activities can be assessed in a variety of ways. Generally speaking, activities for which a fee is charged demand suitable records, and the extent of use over a given period of time can be ascertained. Other activities offered by the park may not have records of sufficient quality, however.

In the case of some activities there will be no economic counterpart in the private sector. For example, baseball which is played in the park may also be played with no charge in the yard, in vacant lots, or in the street. As an activity benefit, baseball may not be a measurable economic item. Still it should be noted that baseball may fall into an assessable item under transportation or time. In any event, activities for which good records are available make the assessment quite easy, while activities which are economic services can be assessed on a sampling basis.

The Measurement of Public Costs

Recognizing that the benefits to users thus far described are net to the consumer, but gross benefits to the community, costs must also be considered in order to derive net social benefits. Costs to the community can be conveniently divided into costs of acquisition, costs of development, and operational costs. Acquisition costs consist of those costs related to the acquiring of land. The acquisition price, however, is generally insufficient. The acquisition cost of the park is the current capitalized value of the land. This, of course, includes a rate of interest. It does not matter whether the land was given or purchased; the value it has is its current market value under conditions of relevant use. If residential land, the costs are determined by subdividing the park property into residential lots, then developing the number and expected market price of these lots. Of course this is only an approximation since the value of the land around the park may partly depend on the existence of the park. Nevertheless, an estimate gives a notion of the economic value of the land.

Time enters in because it is necessary to allocate to a time period studied a certain portion of the acquisition cost. For these purposes we associate the cost of the land to a particular time period. This is arbitrary because the total time period involved should be the common life expectancy of the park under its present useful service. Probably twenty years is not outrageous in this regard, but studies should be made to arrive at the period of time it takes for a given neighborhood to follow a transition pattern. If the character of the neighborhood changes, then the character of the park changes as well, so the park should properly be conceived of as a different unit. Once the life expectancy of the park has been determined, it is a better period for capitalization than the period of time the property is held. Obviously, a newly acquired land parcel would have an unrealistically high value associated with the park's early assessment. In dealing with such fixed costs, capitalization allows a more reasonable approach.

Once the acquisition cost is allocated to a relevant time period, then the question of development costs enters. Again, the capitalization involves an interest amount, and the time period for capitalizing the value is the life expectancy of all the facilities, equipment, and buildings in the park. The allocation to the time period studied is then possible.

Operation costs can be developed directly from accounting data for the city parks. The only problem in these cases is the allocation of joint costs, such as administration, which sometimes include the maintenance costs and supervision costs. These cost figures can be developed easily for maintenance and supervision, but care must be taken in the case of administrative costs. One convenient manner might be to divide total administrative costs for the year by the number of parks of given sizes. Though arbitrary, larger parks generally demand greater administrative time than smaller parks and an allocation could be developed. Once costs are developed then the total costs and total benefits are discounted to present value terms.

The Mack and Myers Model: A Nonmonetary Evaluation Device

While conceding that more work can be done with some form of a dollar measure in terms of what people are willing to pay for recreation, Mack and Myers see little gain in relying on the various dollar schemes that have been proposed to date as means to measure the benefits derived from outdoor recreation. Taking the Outdoor Recreation Resources Commission's definition (in Report number 21) of outdoor recreation as "leisure time activity undertaken in a relatively nonurban environment characterized by a natural setting, for the primary purposes of enjoyment and physical or mental well-being," [24] a theory based on the merit of a recreational service is implied — the merit of a recreational service is equal to the utility it provides and its contribution to social welfare.

[24] Ruth P. Mack and Sumner Myers, "Outdoor Recreation," in *Measuring Benefits of Government Investments: Papers Presented at a Conference of Experts Held November 7–9, 1963,* ed. Robert Dorfman (Washington, D.C.: Brookings Institution, 1965), p. 73.

Mack and Myers see outdoor recreation as providing a "good" (note: the term "service" is not used) characterized by three utilities:

1. Immediate enjoyment to the participant.
2. Long-run physical and psychological benefits to the individual (alleged to be provided from "wholesome" outdoor activity).
3. Benefits to the nation as a whole.
    a) Third-party benefits resulting from residing in a country where outdoor recreation opportunities and education in the "ways of the out-of-doors" exist for all regardless if they choose to use them or not.
    b) Conservation of outdoor recreational resources.[25]

These three utilities highlight the premise that outdoor recreational opportunity is meritorious, and, therefore, a bias already exists to provide recreation. It can also be concluded that these utilities follow logically from their original statement of the merit of outdoor recreation.

Mack and Myers rationalize the public interest in outdoor recreation, and, in particular, why the private market cannot be expected to maximize recreational benefits. First, they credit the "government's paternal interest in the individual's general well-being" and suggest that the inherent bias of the system in providing recreation is a reason for public consideration of outdoor recreation. Secondly, the government has a "third-party interest in outdoor recreation and conservation" since there is no well functioning private mechanism of supply and demand. This is a valid statement due to the externalities and spillovers (secondary benefits and costs) that are not directly accounted for in the market price system for a recreational service. Lastly, the government is said to be interested in the efficient supply of resources especially where government control might be more efficient than private. This follows from the government's past and present interest in public utilities such as TVA.[26]

As utility here is a function of *what kind* of recreation is provided and *for whom*, obviously some form of weighting is necessary. This method presupposes that certain people in certain situations receive more benefit from their recreational experience than do other people.[27] Mack and Myers employ the term "user day" as the unit of output for recreation services provided by government. Mack and Myers deduce five criteria to help weight the relative user utilities and thereby provide a basis for comparison of the "user days" with the cost of providing them. They say that weighting would have to be done on the basis of a criterion formulated by the political process and the government. (The implication is that this is to be done by the federal government.) No doubt Mack and

25 Adapted from Mack and Myers, "Outdoor Recreation," in *Measuring Benefits*, ed. Dorfman, pp. 73–74.

26 Mack and Myers, "Outdoor Recreation," in *Measuring Benefits*, ed. Dorfman, p. 75.

27 Mack and Myers, "Outdoor Recreation," in *Measuring Benefits*, ed. Dorfman, pp. 89–90.

Myers see this as the only method for establishing some national standards in weighting and, consequently, some consistency in measurements.

First of all, Mack and Myers state that a definition of the relationship between the public and private sector is necessary.[28] This encompasses the entire range of private and public services plus the role government will play in setting standards for private initiative in outdoor recreation. Areas in which policy criteria must be developed include:

1. Conservation as a public purpose. . . .
2. Government policy with respect to providing recreation where public supply price is markedly lower than private. (Linked with problems under point 5 below concerning appropriate user-prices.) . . .
3. Government provision of recreation as a method of setting standards for private provision. . . .
4. Public policy with respect to encouraging private recreation. . . .
5. The charge of a total or partial price for some sorts of recreation to, perhaps, some sorts of people. (The dollars received as user-payments would potentially provide a larger yield of benefit when applied to services of other kinds for other sorts of people.) . . .
6. Public provision of a "modest but adequate" standard for people unable to pay for it. . . .
7. The maintenance of a designated standard of care for grounds and equipment. . . .
8. The development of recreational facilities and program as a method of expanding and deepening use. . . .
9. Physical standards of use and adequacy including the control of overcrowding of what are, by definition, low density facilities. . . .
10. The maintenance of a well-conceived and well-balanced variety of recreation facilities which takes the differential merit and tastes into account. . . .
11. The geographic distribution of areas with respect to accessibility for after-work, weekend, and vacation use. . . .
12. Distribution among people of different ages, education, and previous experience. . . .
13. Distribution among people of different incomes and, consequently, different opportunities to use private facilities. . . .
14. Meeting the requirements of the future by a variety of means appropriate to the uncertainty that surrounds prediction.[29]

Policy areas 9 and 10, above, concern the character of the recreation offered in assigning a weight to the opportunity. Numbers 11 through 14 attempt to provide some ways of judging adequacy and distributive justice to the members (present and future) of the society.

[28] Mack and Myers, "Outdoor Recreation," in *Measuring Benefits*, ed. Dorfman, p. 90.
[29] Mack and Myers, "Outdoor Recreation," in *Measuring Benefits*, ed. Dorfman, pp. 90–93. Copyright © 1965, Brookings Institution, Washington, D.C. Reprinted by permission.

This merit-weighted user day system is essentially useful for estimating the number of people that each park under examination will probably attract under a given design specification. One then classifies the users on the basis of the performance criteria which are applicable to a specific choice. If the planners feel more people of a certain "type" should be using a facility, they will compare the actual level of service provided by that park with the desired level of service (for example, 10,000 actual to 15,000 desired user days) and determine the merit factor in that situation (1.5) as a proportion of both.[30] The reasons for giving this facility a higher merit factor might be the high density of living conditions or poor private alternatives for recreation, or it might be due to the fact that mostly large families with low incomes reside in the area. A merit factor of unity indicates that the actual use level equals the desired (weighted) use level. In short, this shows that the actual number of user days equals the desired number of user days. A factor less than unity suggests that the marginal utility of additional recreation decreases as more recreation is made available, and, therefore, the weighted user days (desired level of service) is less than the actual use of the park. This factor is then used for comparison of dollars to be spent on recreation thereby facilitating examination of future expenditures.

Mack and Myers propose a four question test for any method of measuring benefits.[31]

1. What is the portion of the total benefit it adequately measures? Here they decide that this form of shadow pricing is fairly good. If it were to be formulated as a tightly structured scheme it can do an excellent job in measuring whatever benefits the government foresees providing to the nation as a whole. It can also be used to estimate the long-run physical and psychological benefits to the individual, given a standard of judgment. However, in attempting to measure immediate enjoyment, the merit-weighted user day can only assume it indirectly (example, less overcrowding increases enjoyment). Also, it must be noted that while this criterion could prove to be quite illuminating by measuring "utilities," it is limited by the biases and abilities of the political process and government in determining government policy and the extent of the standards, especially for whom certain ones should apply. Even a poorly situated facility might be deemed accessible if certain standards are not tightly formulated and pursued.

2. What good is the merit-weighted user day in revealing the aspects of total benefits that it is unable to measure?[32] Mack and Myers decide it does a better job than any of the dollar measures because it considers changing conditions of supply and demand. The future orientation of this method is admirable and utilitarian in terms of bringing long-run considerations into play with immedi-

30 Mack and Myers, "Outdoor Recreation," in *Measuring Benefits*, ed. Dorfman, p. 94.

31 Mack and Myers, "Outdoor Recreation," in *Measuring Benefits*, ed. Dorfman, p. 99.

32 Mack and Myers, "Outdoor Recreation," in *Measuring Benefits*, ed. Dorfman, p. 99.

ate decision making. However, since they propose no stringent formula, future concerns could easily be forgotten in determining the weighting of the user day.

3. What is the method's general acceptability?[33] Here Mack and Myers admit the method, although it may be conceptually excellent and feasible, is of little value if it is not generally accepted. The method's acceptance, no doubt, will be delayed by the inertia and predisposition of government agencies to use the "tried and true" methods of the past. Also, it might be rather difficult to set rigid standards (especially for overcrowding) applicable to facilities in different areas which are tempered by varying physical, social, and political climates.

4. Does the measure have any way of improving either legislative or administrative processes by its emphasis on "well considered notions of public weal"? [34] This last test is an extremely relevant addition made by the merit-weighted user day. Unlike other methods, including user fee questionnaires, projective methods, resistance points, and travel and time studies, this method forces the political process to decide its position on matters of public gain from recreation opportunities. The vast majority of other methods never consider the setting of standards or the future benefits to be had from a recreational endeavor. It, above all, narrows thinking on determining the values that can be derived from outdoor recreation, the role of government, and the extent of involvement of the private sector, which the other methods tactfully avoid.

Additional Possible Values

While all of the foregoing models make an attempt to measure the economic value of recreation, they do so with only limited success. There are additional value potentials which we might suggest as being relevant to a value attributable to recreation in the city.

HEALTH. The relationship of physical activity to maintaining good health is a well-known benefit. Medical authorities concur that sensible participation in physical recreation is healthy; it improves muscle tone, controls weight, reduces tensions, and improves the efficiency and capacity of heart and lungs.

RELIGION. For many the philosophies of religion and recreation are harmonious and complement each other; both seek to prolong the life, to promote the well-being, and recognize the worth of the individual; to some, recreation expresses the morality of religion in that both desire justice, fair play, truth, faith, and joy to strengthen and enrich life.

MENTAL HEALTH. Recreation agencies have unrealized potential in promoting emotional health within metropolitan areas. They often have more contact with children than the parents, and the contacts are during the formative years under the most natural conditions of childhood — play activity.

[33] Mack and Myers, "Outdoor Recreation," in *Measuring Benefits*, ed. Dorfman, p. 99.
[34] Mack and Myers, "Outdoor Recreation," in *Measuring Benefits*, ed. Dorfman, p. 99.

A lack of suitable recreational facilities to help dissipate boredom and frustration in the ghetto has been suggested as a cause contributing to recent riots. There are many forms of recreative activity which would permit acceptable outlets for expressions of violence and hostility, but they are unavailable to the ghetto resident for reasons of cost and social exclusion.[35]

THE IMPACT OF PARKS ON PROPERTY VALUES. In addition to potential values which recreational goods and services may have for individuals who make use of public programs and facilities, parks may exert an influence upon property values, particularly residential property values. If a park is aesthetically pleasing, it may enhance the values of nearby properties; conversely, if parks are unsightly or generate nuisance values, it is possible that they may deter from nearby property values. In any event, it would appear that studies have shown that the effect of parks upon property values is seldom neutral.

One such study made in Dallas, Texas, revealed that in thirteen neighborhood parks certain conclusions could be reached and inferences drawn:

1. Normally, parks exert either a positive or a negative influence upon property values of parcels near the park.
2. Either positive or negative values may be seen in the value of improvements to the lot.
3. The park impact on property value appears to be greater upon the land value than upon the total value of the property.
4. The degree of impact varies among residences of particular economic classes. The impact appears to be relatively greater among properties of high value than among properties of low value.[36]

In addition, the impact of parks upon property values appears to be related to their use as well as their appearance. It may be that the zone of property impact around a given park is similar to the zone of use of the service area of the park.

The implications of the possible impact of parks upon residential property values lies in several areas. First, if such is the case, parks may be significant stabilizers of neighborhoods, not only from a social but from an economic standpoint. Second, to the extent that the park can aid in stabilizing a neighborhood, the property tax base in a city is stabilized. It certainly seems logical that if people value recreation and parks in a city, this sense of value may well be seen in the enhancement of residential property values.

Possible Benefits to Urban Recreation and Parks: A Summary List

1. Immediate enjoyment of activity to user.
2. Anticipation.

[35] Richard Kraus, "Riots and Recreation," *Journal of Health, Physical Education, Recreation* 38 (Mar. 1967): 42–45.

[36] William S. Hendon, "The Park as a Determinant of Property Values," *American Journal of Economics and Sociology* 30 (1971): 296–97.

3. Recollection.
4. Preservation of natural resources.
5. Stabilization of property values.
6. Possible impact upon juvenile delinquency.*
7. Aesthetically pleasing environment.
8. Provides means of social interaction.*
9. Accessibility of activity or site (saving of time and transport cost).
10. Community involvement in decisions.*
11. Savings in collective over private fees.
12. Physical well-being.*
13. Learning process, educational function of socialization.*
14. Social control aspects, positive and negative.
15. Psychological aspects, positive and negative.*
16. Source of out-of-house family activity.*
17. Option value of having the facilities available.
18. Human relations aspects — positive or negative.

* Skills learning elements

V. Problems in Urban Recreation

In assessing the current state of urban public recreation one is continually reminded of a particular set of problems.

Lack of Professionalization of Administration

Generally speaking, the academic disciplines (planning, geography, economics, sociology, political science, and urban studies, etc.) have not had sufficient impact upon recreational planning and administration. Universities and park authorities themselves are combining to initiate college level training. Basic training in the development of two-year programs leading to associate degrees in recreation leadership are increasing. Likewise, four-year programs in physical education are moving toward more public recreation administration, and degrees in park administration are in evidence. Such programs enhance the communication between academics and professionals.

Inadequate Knowledge of Demand

A major indicator of the lack of analytical procedure and social science knowledge necessary to conduct urban recreational research is that few park administrators have adequate knowledge of the demands of citizens for services and facilities. Few regular recreation censuses or samples are conducted; participation estimates are usually inadequate and park administrators, as public employees, are very subject to pressure. Six phone calls may be sufficient, in the administrator's mind, to reflect massive public opinion. Adequate contact and knowledge of community demands could counter such problems. Some dispersal of authority in recreational planning to the neighborhood would enable city authorities to pursue their tasks less easily but with more recognition that what was planned was wanted.

Likewise, with no knowledge of the economic models of demand, the administrator is in a poor position to make the decisions on the margin which small increments to budgets require. How does one improve a particular system and its function when scarce resources are the rule? One should take the most efficient course available given the constraints under which the system operates.

Cheap Land and Expensive Land

In the process of the development of parks, land acquisition usually appears to be the first order of business. Indeed, one may not develop a park if the land is not available, but the real issue lies in the fact that land costs over the life of an operating park are a very slight cost factor. Operational and developmental costs are all much higher. Since land is a prerequisite, however, many park land acquisition programs tend to look for vacant land to be had at low cost, failing to recognize that locational factors for the ultimate efficiency of the park may make the cheap land ultimately the most expensive. If one selects a land parcel which is locked in by natural or man-made barriers on one or more sides, the practical effect is to cut down on the ultimate use of the park since utilization depends upon a service zone around the park. The upshot is that the present purchase of very expensive and developed land may be more efficient than purchasing or accepting gifts of less useful land.

Does Equity Mean Equal?

Many park and recreation systems in the country are in a kind of inefficient lockstep of providing similar activities for each neighborhood. Different neighborhoods may have different demands, thus similar programs conducted throughout the city may discriminate against persons. Do low income neighborhoods require more, less, or the same level of recreational activity as more affluent neighborhoods? Usually, it would appear most efficient to provide a greater budget allocation to low income areas than to higher income areas. Persons of middle to higher income have more recreational choices than do low income persons. If the typical tract provides spacious yards and the inner city block is without yards, it does seem desirable to discriminate in favor of the poorer resident of the city.

Boundary Problems

One form of boundary problem arises when the city provides a recreational facility which is paid for by the city but which is used as a regional facility. An example might be a museum which attracts people from all over a region. The problem comes in the financing of such facilities. In many cases the user charge has merit to deal with the financing of such facilities. It becomes a price which the user must pay to gain entrance.

The Question of Race

Central to the political pressures brought to many community recreation programs and site location plans is the question of race. White neighborhoods have turned down park facilities where there was fear that the black child would come into the neighborhood to play in the park. Blacks may not meet happily city plans for a new park in their neighborhood because of feelings that the black community is being "gamed" to death by the white power structure. In both cases, recreation programs and park developments may be impaired.

Competition with Privately Produced Recreation

The typical urban public park and recreation programs are limited by scarce resources and lack of imagination in providing somewhat nontraditional programs and parks. Private developers of parks and commercial recreation entrepreneurs are not limited by anything except demand. Thus, commercial recreation competes for the public's leisure time with the public agencies, and the latter, without benefit of venture capital, advertising budgets, or resources for effective planning, are left out of the profitable aspects of recreation. There is little reason to assume that city park authorities should not seek some profitable activities if such profits are used to subsidize unprofitable but equally desirable programs.

The use of concessionaires (licensing or contracting a service) by public recreation authorities developed for two reasons: social pressure by private profit seekers and lack of management sophistication on the part of park authorities. One can see little need for this situation to continue in the future.

Summary: Urban Recreation

Local governments provide a modest amount of recreational programming and parks for their citizens. Conservatively, most families spend about 3% of their disposable incomes on recreational goods and services. As a percent of personal consumption expenditures, recreation represents in excess of 6% of the total. Participation in outdoor recreation activities increases significantly each year with picnicking, pleasure driving, sightseeing, swimming, and walking heading the list of these activities.

Recreation is part of leisure. Leisure time is defined as time which is free from work. To an increasing degree, we appear to allocate a larger amount of leisure time to nonwork obligations. Recreation is that time spent on the pursuit of skills, pleasures, and learning for personal satisfaction and development.

Arguments occur among sociologists over whether modern man is increasingly or decreasingly capable of using his leisure time. Trends in the use of leisure time appear to show an increase to nonwork obligations, an increase to family and home centered leisure time, and a decline to the worker's interest in his job.

If people do experience difficulty in using their leisure time, then the role of a public recreation program should be to provide expert training in the use of leisure time.

Recreation programs are not provided in a vacuum. They are provided in parks and schools in modern, industrial cities. The discipline of a machine age requires a continuing education and development of skills for urban residents. Life in cities is nontraditional, sophisticated, and complex. In an industrial society we see an increasing need for leisure time to be used for man's relaxation, diversion, and personal development.

Public programs for recreation should function under a set of concepts which support the enjoyment of the programs. First, the program should provide an integrity of purpose. Second, enjoyment demands a liberty to review the goals of a program. Third, within the context of human feelings, programs should exhibit objectivity. Equality in fellowship is a fourth requisite. Fifth, a command of skills which is common to the participants is required. Sixth, enjoyment depends upon the potential for growth in the skills used in the program. Public recreation, then, requires the provision of goods and services which support active diversions and personal skill development by the provision of the training necessary to acquire skills and the opportunity to use these skills.

Factors which affect the demand for urban recreation include factors related to particular users and their preferences, factors related to the recreation site, and the interrelationships of demand which exist between users and a particular recreation site.

Supply of recreational outputs is concerned with use, internal design, spatial distribution in the city, competition with alternatives, and the determination of the efficient mix of recreation sites and programs.

In locating recreational sites, the local authorities must be concerned with locating near the population and/or near the particular resource. Location efficiencies are hindered by the uneven distribution of populations and resources and the barriers which exist in cities. Park administrators have developed standards for the location and development of recreation sites.

Peak loading is a continuing problem in efficient supply. For most public recreation sites, price is not used as a rationing device.

Long-run elements include the increasing difficulty of gaining recreational land in areas of the city where demand is great. Most recreation budgets do not include sufficient funds to meet demands for programs and sites.

Several models of evaluation were examined. The Trice and Wood Model calculates benefits on the basis of a series of zones in which nearby consumers of the park site and its services gain a consumer surplus. The Clawson-Knetsch Model derives a demand curve to develop an estimate of the value of the site. The alternative model posits two benefits to users — a saving in transportation costs and a saving in possible fees. The Mack and Myers Model rejects the monetary models and derives benefit based on a merit-weighted user day; this latter model would be a cost effectiveness model in that it minimizes cost given a desired quantity and quality of output. Additional aspects of benefits include physical health, religious values, mental health, impacts of parks on property values, and numerous other benefits.

Problems in the provision of parks and recreation programs include lack of professional administration, inadequate estimates of demand, minimizing costs and minimizing benefits, treating populations as exactly similar, boundary problems, racial problems, and competition with the private sector.

Chapter 6 Appendix

Operation of a Recreation System: Examination of Needs and Research*

As in the case of most urban services, there is a significant need for research on urban recreation systems. Some of the following suggestions for research are useful:

Resources Allocation and Activities Development in Relation to User Preferences

1. Develop the meanings of and the demands for a wide variety of recreational activities: development of index needs.

2. Resource inventories.

3. From an analysis of needs and resource inventories, design experimental programs, combining resources in different ways, and then evaluate their effectiveness.

Potential for Expanding the Supply of Recreational Resources

1. New technologies: snow making, lighting technologies.

2. Reclamation projects: dysfunctional park lands; polluted waters, land fills, etc.

3. Introduction of recreational activity which is not too space consuming, so as to be able to use things like small areas, rooftops, etc.

4. Combined private and public sector activities: coffee shops in downtown parks, flea markets, etc.

5. Multiple use activities: schools, and combined recreation and education programs.

Quality Maintenance and Management of Irreplaceable Resources

1. Devising means for identifying high quality sites for given types of recreation activities by consideration of the activity related to the site in means of light intensity, temperature, relative freedom for locomotion, and vision.

* Adapted from the National Academy of Sciences, *A Program for Outdoor Recreation Research*, publication no. 1727 (Washington, D.C.: National Academy of Sciences, 1969), pp. 48–60. Reprinted by permission.

2. Devising means for assessing impacts on ecology by use.

3. Devise means of assessing consumer response to sites for a measure of the "effectiveness" or preference for various sites and various activities.

4. Establish standards for quality of sites given 1, 2, 3, above.

5. Establish policy to maintain high quality resources use by price rationing, restrictions, or whatever to reduce utilization or expand utilization by means of access by transport, special programming, time restrictions, etc., to attain some standard of optimum usage.

To summarize, research should be undertaken on recreation resources in order to:

a. Measure quality factors that are dependent upon both environmental attributes and the availability of facilities and services, and correlate these factors with user preferences;

b. Establish standards for site factors, discrimination of which will permit yields of varying quality, for factors considered either individually or in combinations;

c. Determine the impact of varying levels of use density on the quality of recreation experiences, in particular the carrying capacity that can be sustained without loss of quality;

d. Explain user behavior in recreational environments including the sociopsychological causes of misuse, and explore ways of modifying such behavior in the interest of environmental quality.

e. Develop means of preventing overuse of resources, such as pricing and rationing — e.g., offering incentives for users to engage in alternative forms of recreation, controlling access, or staggering the discretionary time of major user groups.

f. Develop criteria for the selection, management, and preservation of unique irreproducible environments.

Planning, Coordination, and Administration Systems

1. Historical studies and comparative analyses of the structures and policies of governments and governmental agencies, and of planning and decision-making processes affecting natural resources allocation. These studies might logically be divided into two parts: one focusing on areas of direct governmental responsibility; the other on areas in which governments perform only regulatory or promotional functions. Particular stress should be placed upon instances in which jurisdiction and interests are shared by several governmental agencies with each other or with private organizations.

2. Analytical reviews of jurisdictional congruence, or lack thereof, affecting the exercise of overlapping or interrelated functions, such as zoning, environment control, and recreation planning.

3. Examination of the legal problems involved in the acquisition and assembly of public land for outdoor recreation, including patterns of land ownership and land-use control (zoning and public access) and tax mechanisms that discourage speculation.

4. Comparative analysis of and experimentation with alternative intergovernmental arrangements for planning, developing, and managing recreation services.

5. Analysis and development of alternative budgetary strategies for the allocation of resources to recreation services and supporting functions.

6. Identification and amelioration of common administrative problems, such as employee morale and motivation, headquarters — field relationships, and interpersonal difficulties encountered in working with specialists from a variety of disciplines.

7. Experimentation with instruments for monitoring the results, both intended and unanticipated, of new or modified procedures.

8. Analysis of information flow among administrators, especially their access to management data and to new developments in the management and policy sciences.

Access-Systems Research

1. The manner in which the inconvenience or high cost of transportation prevents various categories of users from satisfying their preferences for outdoor recreation or leads them to substitute other forms of recreation. The forms that such substitutions take should also be studied.
2. The effects on patterns of outdoor recreation use of advances in transportation technology, including the design of completely new modes of transportation.
3. The conflict between the public interest in access to recreation sites and existent patterns of private ownership of lands and waterways, including legal techniques that might be developed to accommodate both interests.
4. The psychological and technical considerations essential to the safety and enjoyment of travel.
5. Alternative modes of low-cost transportation for transporting urban residents to recreation facilities outside their immediate neighborhoods.

Information Services for the Public

1. To determine the type and quantity of information needed to maximize enjoyment of a given recreation experience, including the effect of public information and promotional activities on motivation patterns in outdoor recreation.
2. To assess the psychological impact of environmental education and nature appreciation on users of resource-based recreation facilities, especially the effect on their perceptions of the value of the experience.
3. To analyze the response of various segments of the population to recreation rules, guidelines, and instructions. . . .
4. To analyze recreation users' needs for information in order to identify the conditions required for its favorable reception, such as the most appropriate times for its delivery.

Outdoor Recreation Data Bases and Information Analysis

1. Develop standards based on appropriate units of measurement, along with the necessary checklists and manuals, to guide the conduct of recreation surveys on a neighborhood, municipal, regional, or national scale, to be used in the planning, design, management, and operation of recreation services.
2. Establish linkages between recreation data and other data series, especially the national census.
3. Promote systems-design and systems-analysis efforts aimed at improving measurement, sampling, and predictive capabilities. . . .
4. Undertake design and cost-effectiveness studies for data-handling systems to meet user requirements for information storage, retrieval, and dissemination.

Education and Training to Meet Manpower Needs

1. Predict future changes in personnel requirements and determine generally the types of skills and other attributes required in recreation managers.
2. Indicate the kinds of competence that should be given priority in training programs — that is, those in shortest supply for which there is a projected need.
3. Establish the organizational requirements and training prerequisites for professional, as opposed to management, personnel. . . .
4. Develop imaginative programs to train or attract personnel to fill the needs identified above.

Selected Bibliography

Recreation

ANDERSON, NELS. *Work and Leisure.* New York: Free Press of Glencoe, 1961.

BOYET, WAYNE E., AND TOLLEY, GEORGE S. "Recreation Projection Based on Demand Analysis." *Journal of Farm Economics* 48 (1966) : 984–1001.

BURDGE, RABEL J. *Outdoor Recreation Studies: Vacations and Weekend Trips.* Agricultural Economics and Rural Society, no. 65. Department of Agricultural Economics and Rural Sociology, Agricultural Experiment Station. University Park, Pa.: The Pennsylvania State University, Aug. 1967.

CICCHETTI, CHARLES J. "Some Economic Issues in Planning Urban Recreation Facilities." *Land Economics* 47 (1971) : 14–23.

————; SENECA, JOSEPH J.; AND DAVIDSON, PAUL. *The Demand and Supply of Outdoor Recreation: An Econometric Analysis.* New Brunswick, N.J.: Bureau of Economic Research, Rutgers, The State University, 1969.

CLAWSON, MARION, AND KNETSCH, JACK L. *Economics of Outdoor Recreation.* Baltimore: Published for Resources for the Future by Johns Hopkins Press, 1966.

DAIUTE, ROBERT J. "Methods for Determination of Demand for Outdoor Recreation." *Land Economics* 42 (1966) : 327–38.

DARLING, A. H. "Measuring Benefits Generated by Urban Water Parks." *Land Economics* 49 (1973) : 22–34.

DAVID, E. L. "Lakeshore Property Values: A Guide to Public Investment in Recreation." *Water Resources Research* 4 (1968) : 697–707.

————. "The Use of Assessed Data to Approximate Sales Values of Recreational Property." *Land Economics* 44 (1968) : 127–29.

DAVIS, ROBERT K. "Recreation Planning as an Economic Problem." *Natural Resources Journal* 3 (1963) : 239–49.

DE GRAZIA, SEBASTIAN. *Of Time, Work, and Leisure.* New York: Twentieth Century Fund, 1962.

DEVINE, E. J. "The Treatment of Incommensurables in Cost-Benefit Analysis." *Land Economics* 42 (1966) : 383–87.

ECKSTEIN, OTTO. *Water-Resource Development: The Economics of Project Evaluation.* Cambridge, Mass.: Harvard University Press, 1958.

FREEMAN, A. MYRICK. "Income Distribution and Planning for Public Investment." *American Economic Review* 57 (1967) : 495–508.

GRUBB, HERBERT W., AND GOODWIN, J. T. *Economic Evaluation of Water Oriented Recreation in the Preliminary Texas Water Plan.* Report no. 84. Austin, Tex.: Texas Water Development Board, Sept. 1968.

HAVEMAN, ROBERT. "The Federal Rivers and Harbors Program: An Analysis of Regional Impact." *Papers and Proceedings of the American Economic Association. American Economic Review* 54 (1964) : 568–79.

HENDON, WILLIAM S. "The Park as a Determinant of Property Values." *American Journal of Economics and Sociology* 30 (1971) : 289–300.

————. "Property Values, Schools, Park-School Combinations." *Land Economics* 49 (1973) : 216–18.

HOTELLING, H. Letter to Roy A. Prewitt. In *The Economics of Public Recreation — An Economic Survey of the Monetary Evaluation of Recreation in the National Parks.* Mimeographed. Washington, D.C.: National Park Service, 1949.

JAMES, L. D. "Evaluating Recreation Benefits from Visitation Prediction Equations." And "Reply" by W. E. Boyet and G. S. Tolley. *American Journal of Agricultural Economics* 50 (1968): 437–42.

JOHNSON, B. M. "Travel Time and the Price of Leisure." *Western Economic Journal* 4 (1966): 135–45.

KALTER, ROBERT J. *The Economics of Water-Based Outdoor Recreation: A Survey and Critique of Recent Developments.* U.S. Army Engineer Institute for Water Resources. Publication Report no. 71–8. Washington, D.C.: National Technical Information Service of the Department of Commerce, Mar. 1971.

KNEESE, ALLEN V. *The Economics of Regional Water Quality Management.* Baltimore: Published for Resources for the Future by Johns Hopkins Press, 1964.

KNETSCH, JACK L. "Economics of Including Recreation as a Purpose of Eastern Water Projects." *Journal of Farm Economics* 46 (1964): 1148–57.

———. "Land Values and Parks in Urban Fringe Areas." *Journal of Farm Economics* 44 (1962): 1718–29.

———. "Outdoor Recreation Demands and Benefits." *Land Economics* 39 (1963): 388–96.

———, AND DAVIS, R. K. "Comparison of Methods for Recreation Evaluation." In *Water Research*, ed. Allen V. Kneese and Stephen C. Smith, pp. 125–42. Baltimore: Published for Resources for the Future by Johns Hopkins Press, 1966.

MACK, RUTH P., AND MYERS, SUMNER. "Outdoor Recreation." In *Measuring Benefits of Government Investments: Papers Presented at a Conference of Experts Held November 7–9, 1963*, ed. Robert Dorfman, pp. 71–101. Washington, D.C.: Brookings Institution, 1965.

MARGOLIS, JULIUS. "The Economic Evaluation of Federal Water Resource Development." *American Economic Review* 49 (1959): 96–111.

NORTON, G. A. "Public Outdoor Recreation and Resource Allocation: A Welfare Approach." *Land Economics* 46 (1970): 414–22.

PEARSE, P. "A New Approach to the Evaluation of Non-Priced Recreational Resources." *Land Economics* 44 (1968): 87–99.

REGAN, M., AND GREENSHIELDS, E. "Benefit-Cost Analysis of Resource Development Programs." *Journal of Farm Economics* 33 (1951): 866–78.

ROBINSON, WARREN C. "The Simple Economics of Public Outdoor Recreation." *Land Economics* 43 (1967): 71–83.

SECKLER, DAVID W. "On the Uses and Abuses of Economic Science in Evaluating Public Outdoor Recreation." *Land Economics* 42 (1966): 485–94.

TOLLEY, GEORGE S., AND HARRELL, CLEON. "Extensions of Benefit-Cost Analysis." *Papers and Proceedings of the American Economic Association. American Economic Review* 52 (1962): 459–68.

TRICE, ANDREW H., AND WOOD, SAMUEL E. "Measurement of Recreation Benefits." *Land Economics* 34 (1958): 195–207.

TURVEY, RALPH. "Optimization and Suboptimization in Fishery Regulation." *American Economic Review* 54, Part I (1964): 64–76.

U.S. OUTDOOR RECREATION RESOURCES REVIEW COMMISSION. *Outdoor Recreation for America, A Report to the President and to Congress.* Washington, D.C.: U.S. Government Printing Office, 1962.

———. "Private and Public Provision of Outdoor Recreation Opportunity," Marion Clawson, Arthur L. Moore, and Ivan M. Lee, contributors. Economic Studies of Outdoor Recreation. Outdoor Recreation Resources Review Commission Study Report no. 24. Washington, D.C.: U.S. Government Printing Office, 1962.

WEICKER, JOHN C. AND ZERBST, TROBERT H. "The Externalities of Neighborhood Parks: An Empirical Investigation." *Land Economics* 49 (1973): 99–104.

7

Urban Health

We all recognize that the good health of the residents of a city determines the level of continuous development of that city. Beyond this point there is very little agreement because health care means different things to different people. When we discuss the term health, we are confronted with a wide variety of goods and services produced in the city. Since no single definition exists, we begin to think of the medical care industry rather than health. The medical care industry consists of the personnel, facilities, and organizations which produce goods and services in the health field. Physicians, dentists, and other medical employees make up a labor force operating to produce medical goods and services. The goods and services of which we speak include the services of physicians, dentists and technicians, hospital services and the various support systems, the activities of public health services, the health insurance industry, and finally drugs and medical goods production including medical machinery and supplies, the producer goods of the medical care industry.

The industry as it operates in cities has not been widely studied by economists. As Klarman has pointed out, part of the difficulty is due to some of the unique characteristics of the industry.[1] For example, health care is seen as a need so basic that there is widespread belief that a person is entitled to it whether or not he can pay. In addition, for the individual consumer, health care expenditures are largely unpredictable, thus a good deal of pooling of risk occurs as evidenced by health insurance. Furthermore, health care is rife with externalities and to some extent is a collective good. Vaccination programs are beneficial to the public at large just as the shot is to the individual. Each person who is innoculated against contagious disease reduces the risk for others. Consumer ignorance in the health care market is not totally different than in other markets, but there are few markets in which the consumer is so completely ignorant. Another market char-

[1] Herbert E. Klarman, *The Economics of Health* (New York: Columbia University Press, 1965), pp. 10–19.

243

acteristic which makes analysis difficult is the large nonprofit tradition in medical services. Finally, there is a mixture of consumption and investment elements in medical care. Medical care for the elderly is largely a consumer good, but medical care for a worker is both a consumption good and an investment good.

Health care in cities is available, but we are uncertain for whom it is available. We do not have health care for all. Many are excluded from the market on both the consumption and production side. Inefficiencies exist in the market. Prices and costs may be monopolistically derived. In spite of the fact that health care is increasingly thought of as a basic human right, we have not yet been able to create a health care delivery system which serves most of the population well.

This chapter surveys some of the basic questions of health care in cities. The sections on demand and supply of physicians' and hospitals' services are derived from the work of Herbert Klarman in *The Economics of Health* published by Columbia University Press in 1965. We then turn to an examination of some specific problems of health care, and, finally, we examine some elements of urban health care policy and its evaluation. As to policy, we are concerned only with local policy, not state or nationally operated programs.

I. Demand for Medical Services

In order to understand the economic aspects of health and medical care services, we must consider the determinants of demand. With the production of most economic goods we can assume a negative slope to the demand curve and a consequent inverse relation between price and quantity. Additional consideration must be given to factors such as income, tastes and preferences for various goods, and, finally, the prices of other goods. In the traditional demand relationship we also examine prices given various specific units of the good in question. While these are the primary questions of economics, they may not apply to something as broad as health care because health care is not a single product but a variety of products. However, among the most important specific elements in health care are physicians' services and hospital services.

Demand for Physicians' Services

As one would expect, the demand for physicians' services depends upon the amount of money that people are willing to spend relative to the number of doctors available. The price for the service of a physician could then be estimated at given levels of service. Unfortunately, the situation is not nearly so simple; complications in pricing arise. One such complication is the price discrimination practiced by physicians. The discrimination occurs in the sliding scale of fees which the medical profession employs. People are charged according to their income for the service rendered. While we recognize that this is a form of price discrimination, it is a means, though perhaps modest, of redistribution of income downward. Another aspect of this price discrimination is that it has made medical services available to large numbers of people within the community. Even today the tradition of free care for the poor is nurtured in medical education.[2] Whether one accepts this kind of income redistribution practice in the medical industry is a value judgment, but we can see that such practices demonstrate that the market for physicians' services is not a competitive market.

While it is true that a tradition of free care and sliding fee scales has existed in the medical profession for many years, it is likely less significant today than it was.[3] One reason for the discontinuance of sliding scales has been the rise of health insurance. Logically, health insurance tends to equalize charges for medical care. While the traditions of charging have been altered with the introduction of health insurance, probably the principal idea in the pricing of physicians' services lies with the physician himself. Charges by the physician are directly related to the amount of medical care which he prescribes for his patients, sometimes taking into account their ability to pay. It is the service itself rather than the price of an individual form or unit of that service which is significant.

Another pricing custom pervasive in medical care is the standardization of the base of medical fees. The range of established fees for particular types of medical services are agreed upon by medical societies, and these fee schedules are used to charge for those services. In spite of this monopolistic practice there is still wide variation in charges made in any large community for physicians' services. For example, doctors may charge for telephone consultation; on the other hand, many do not. In addition, office calls may vary in price and frequency depending upon the physician's choice. In some cases a doctor may charge for an initial visit for a particular ailment and yet not see the patient again during the entire time of treatment and make no additional charge for this treatment.

Yet another example of pricing distortion which leads to variations in physicians' prices is the emergency call. In an emergency, consumers are inclined to act as if price were no object.[4]

There are other aspects to demand. A very unfortunate aspect is the acute shortage of doctors. For some this shortage makes a traditional pricing discussion somewhat irrelevant. People in many small towns could not, for any price, have the services of a physician. Even in cities it is not always possible to receive the particular form of medical care required or wanted by the ill person. In many cases the customer (patient) is pretty much at the mercy of the individual doctor in terms of the price which will be extracted from him. Medical care is also curious in that the demand for the physician's services is defined by the physician. Once the patient goes to the physician, the demand function is no longer exclusively that of the patient.

[2] Klarman, *The Economics of Health*, p. 21.

[3] Klarman, *The Economics of Health*, p. 22.

[4] Klarman, *The Economics of Health*, p. 23.

When we consider the patient himself, the demand function is dependent upon his income, his tastes and preferences, and the time and locational availability of the physician. Some people seek medical care when none is necessary. Others refuse medical care when it is essential to their well-being. Socially, we cannot assume that consumer rationality exists in medical care sufficiently so that individuals will seek proper amounts, since "proper amounts" are defined differently at various times by individuals, physicians, and society at large.

Demand for Hospital Services

Rates charged by hospitals are mainly for three distinct types of accommodations: private, semiprivate, and ward. Their respective prices reflect the degree of privacy but can also reflect differences in service. As Klarman points out, it is intended that the price of the semiprivate room reflects the cost of care, and that the charge for the private room should yield a net gain for the hospital while the ward patient will pay as much as he can afford.[5] Health insurance tends to equalize and raise the price of, and the amount of, hospital care and eliminate or diminish the relative number of patients in the wards as compared to private and semiprivate rooms.

The discussion of physicians' and hospitals' pricing suggests that the demand for services is reasonably inelastic. Consequently, changes in the price of either are not due to any particular responsiveness to the demand for the service. It would appear that the price and quantity relationships of both hospital care and physicians' services are more subject to tradition and the social environment in which these services are offered than to precise economic considerations.

Other Elements of Demand for Medical Care

Reder, in discussing the demand for hospital facilities, suggests that an individual's demand for a hospital bed appears to be based on his financial situation, alternative care (outside of hospitals), attitudes of doctors towards length of stay, economic status of hospitals (whether they are military, public, voluntary, etc.), the diagnosis, and the attitudes of the hospital administrators.[6]

In addition to the foregoing determinants of medical care demand, we must consider the traditional factors, namely income, relative prices, and consumer tastes and preferences. With regard to income, it appears that while the level of expenditures for medical care increases with income, the proportion to total income declines. Among all income recipients, medical care expenditures have been rising (table 24). From 1950 to 1968, medical care expenditures rose from 4.6% to 7.2% of total personal consumption expenditures. At the same time, as

[5] Klarman, *The Economics of Health*, p. 23.

[6] Melvin J. Reder, "Economic Theory and Nonprofit Enterprise: Some Problems in the Economics of Hospitals," *Papers and Proceedings of the American Economic Association, American Economic Review* 55 (1965): 472–80.

TABLE 24

U.S. MEDICAL CARE EXPENSES IN DOLLARS
AND AS A PERCENTAGE OF PERSONAL CONSUMPTION EXPENDITURES
FOR SELECTED YEARS

Year	Medical Care Expenditures (In Billions)	Percentage of Personal Consumption Expenditures
1950	$ 8.8	4.6
1955	12.8	5.0
1960	19.1	5.9
1965	28.1	6.5
1966	31.1	6.7
1967	34.6	7.0
1968	38.6	7.2

Source: U.S. Bureau of the Census, Department of Commerce, *Statistical Abstract of the United States, 1971* (Washington, D.C.: U.S. Government Printing Office, 1971), table 476, p. 314.

a part of the consumer price index, medical costs have been rising faster than other prices.

Consumer preferences or tastes are not (as one would expect) directly similar to the preference functions for normal goods. Medical care in a city is positively associated with education. Particularly is this true in the case of prevention. As well, the "tastes" for medical care are directly related to whether or not you have sunk such costs as medical care insurance. A person with such insurance is more apt to use medical care facilities and services than one who does not belong to an insurance plan.

In some sense age and family structure vary the taste for medical care. There appears to be greater demand for medical care among families than among unmarried individuals. There appears to be greater demand among the old than among the young. It should also be noted that few people really have (even if they can afford it) a substantial health care program of regular checkups, preventive activities, and extensive physical examinations.

Many other factors not considered in this discussion affect health care. Included among these are the possible irrationality of patients, the impossibility of revealed preferences, uncertainty about quality and cost, the unavailability of fair and equitable insurance, and the fact of relative poverty among residents.[7]

II. Supply of Medical Services

Just as in the case of demand, attempts to deal with the supply of medical services in the city lead to confusion. While the principal markets are the hos-

[7] For a discussion of these and other variables see A. J. Culyer, "The Nature of the Commodity 'Health Care' and Its Efficient Allocation," *Oxford Economic Papers* 23 (1971): 189–211.

pitals and physicians' services, the related industries include insurance, drug, physical equipment, and the many support systems of the two basic services. In some instances, we can eliminate an analysis of some facets of health care such as drugs, because drugs are not price responsive and are produced in oligopolistic markets. A supply schedule of drugs would be an exercise in futility.

Supply of Physicians

Traditional supply schedules applied to the physician in general are inappropriate, but in a given urban space the promise of larger incomes does draw forth an additional number of doctors. Thus supply in the single urban community is conceptually logical when we consider such items as physicians' services. Further, since it is the physician and his work that calls forth the related services of nurses and technicians, the supply of these labor segments is largely dependent upon the supply of physicians.[8]

First we should note that the supply curve for physicians in the short run is highly inelastic. However, the supply in the short run can appear to be quite elastic when incomes in a community are rising rapidly. This form of elasticity of supply occurs primarily among beginning physicians, however, and cannot be applied to physicians generally. Unless we segment the supply into particular groups by experience, speciality, etc., we must conclude that supply of physicians is relatively inelastic.

Secondly, there are significant restrictions to entry among physicians. Within most states, only residents of that state may enter state medical schools. The total number of students admitted to medical schools is limited by the high cost of medical education. A further barrier and one related to the mobility of physicians is whether a physician may be appointed to the staff of a hospital. In a few cases, physicians are barred from a hospital and appointment to a particular hospital is seldom certain.

The supply of physicians is difficult to comprehend because of three additional factors. Klarman notes that the length of work week, productivity as measured by the number of patients seen, and the performance of functions other than patient care are significant if one is to understand supply.[9]

Finally, a significant factor in the supply of physicians in a given community is the impact of specialization on the medical profession. The decline of the general practitioner makes the assessment of community medical care difficult since total physicians' services are fragmented. Specialization also differentiates the market and generates price increases for the services, whether or not the quality of the services are better. Specialization also calls forth an increased house staff for a given hospital and increases costs of hospitalization.

[8] Klarman, *The Economics of Health*, p. 78.
[9] Klarman, *The Economics of Health*, pp. 80–81.

Specialization is not limited to physicians. All industries and professions involved in medical care are undergoing increasing specialization. There is some degree of specializing among nurses, even though the principal gradation appears to depend more upon the administrative responsibilities of the nurse than her specialty. On the other hand, among hospitals there appears to be some evidence that specialty hospitals are on the decline relative to the general hospital.[10]

Before turning to the supply of hospitals we should discuss briefly one important source of efficiency in the supply of physicians — group practice. While only a small percentage of the doctors in the United States are in group practice, lower costs can be obtained by the collectivization of equipment and the business management aspects of medical practice. Further efficiencies come from the potential for improved quality of medical care in that doctors in group practice have readily available consultants. The question of whether any of these cost saving possibilities are passed onto consumers is not, however, well documented.

Supply of Hospital Services

Our principal concern with the supply of hospital services lies with the general hospital which is designed to offer the community treatment for short-term but acute illnesses. The general hospital is only one kind of hospital, but it represents the most significant service in most communities.

In the short run, the cost curves of individual hospitals (where we assume the number of beds to be fixed, with some factors variable) may well be linear; that is, marginal costs may be constant over a relevant range of production.[11] If marginal costs are constant, an explanation might be the necessity of having a flexible output. This flexibility, as Stigler points out, is not free; efficiencies under such a constraint tend to be found in minimizing costs.[12]

Likewise, we can assume that the marginal costs of an additional patient day in a hospital is slight relative to average cost.[13] As long as there is idle capacity in plant and equipment and as long as the staff is not overworked, then the costs of an additional patient day are slight. In the short run, marginal costs appear to be less than average costs indicating that average costs are declining.[14]

The long-run cost curves for hospitals appear to be somewhat U shaped.[15] As one might expect, idle capacity tends to generate relatively high costs at a low capacity. As a hospital grows, increases to the kinds of services and increased managerial costs could cause the long-run curve to turn upward again when output is high.

[10] Klarman, *The Economics of Health*, p. 84.
[11] Klarman, *The Economics of Health*, p. 105.
[12] George J. Stigler, *The Theory of Price*, rev. ed. (New York: Macmillan, 1952), p. 118.
[13] Klarman, *The Economics of Health*, p. 106.
[14] Klarman, *The Economics of Health*, pp. 106–7.
[15] Klarman, *The Economics of Health*, p. 107.

In recent years, costs for hospital services have been increasing, thus the supply curve has been shifting upward and to the right. The rise in these costs appears to be principally due to increasing costs of labor in hospitals; hospital jobs have been generally low paying until recent years, except for doctors and administrators. Similarly, many medical advances increase costs as new techniques and services are introduced. Finally, costs appear to rise in the long run because hospitals, by their nature, are not capable of efficiency comparable to other "plants" in the economy.

The quantity and quality of medical care service the hospital provides varies according to its ownership. The three basic forms of hospital ownership include proprietary hospitals, government hospitals, and voluntary or general hospitals. The proprietary hospital is thought to be socially undesirable because it is essentially a profit-making activity which may skimp on services. Many proprietary hospitals do not qualify for accreditation because of a failure to meet minimum standards of safety in health care. Likewise, many such hospitals are small and do not offer a full range of hospital services. It is sometimes charged that the proprietary hospital serves only those with financial ability to pay and only those who must be hospitalized for extended periods of time. On the other hand, proprietary hospitals can sometimes move quickly to meet changing community needs. Also, they can provide hospital services for physicians who are discriminated against by the larger hospitals.[16]

The voluntary hospital, or nonprofit hospital, operates on a larger scale than private proprietary hospitals. When we say nonprofit, recognize that many such hospitals are "well-off" and, further, recognize that many persons such as physicians make considerable income from hospital practice. The voluntary hospital usually provides services for all income levels in a community and can adjust its budgets to better respond to changes in local incomes. The voluntary hospital normally offers some outpatient care and operates an emergency facility. One problem with the voluntary hospital (though not unique to it) is that there is little incentive to keep costs down compared to the incentives of a competitive business firm. The hospital administrator is interested in enlarging his operation. The staff is interested in performing its tasks but not in keeping costs down. The patient certainly does not worry too much about costs since the doctor is prescribing the care and the patient may have medical insurance. Physicians have no particular interest in lowering costs in hospitals, and insurance companies, who have some incentive to keep costs low, either limit coverage or raise premiums to deal with increasing costs. All hospitals can suffer from the failure to be concerned about costs relative to other goals, but the voluntary hospital is particularly heir to such difficulties.

The government hospital serves a limited population as in the example of veterans' hospitals. Military hospitals only reluctantly accept the care of mili-

16 Klarman, *The Economics of Health*, pp. 111, 112, 113.

tary dependents. Characteristic of the government hospital is the fact that few services are purchased by the hospital. Its financing and production are almost wholly an inside or "in-house" operation. Thus, V.A. hospitals do not contract for services from other hospitals; what services the government hospital needs, it will most likely provide for itself.[17]

An additional factor affecting the quality and quantity of medical services in hospitals is utilization of hospital capacity. If there is high occupancy, there may be a tendency for admissions which are diagnosed as postponable or discretionary to generate longer stays in hospitals than would be the case if the occupancy rate were lower.[18] It is not difficult to imagine that overcrowded hospitals generate inefficiencies in the services rendered.

III. Economies of Scale in the Medical Firm

When we consider productivity in the medical care industry, we begin by raising questions about the presence of economies of scale. It has been said that the medical care industry is largely a declining cost industry. It is easy to imagine the advantages of specialization and group practice as being efficient in reducing costs, thus individual practice is generally thought to be less efficient.

Questioning the concept of declining costs, Richard Bailey suggests that the efficiency of such assumptions depends upon the degree to which we can (1) define the output as a given product, (2) use dollar measures as proxies for the real production, (3) identify the substitution among factor inputs in the production process, and (4) assert that physicians would avail themselves of opportunities to lower costs.[19] Until answers to the above definitional requirements are made, it is argued that the assumption of declining costs is only a guess. Bailey argues that one must separate the outputs of the medical industry in order to analyze economies of scale and suggests that we separate physicians' services from other services such as administration, laboratory analysis, record keeping, etc. Bailey notes that while economies of scale may obtain in group practice under the latter services, most of the economizing possibilities in the supportive or complementary services can be contracted and can thus be made available to an individual doctor.

Reder, in criticizing Bailey's position, notes that the production function of the medical firm may not be separated into physician-generated and laboratory-generated outputs. Rather, according to Reder, the laboratory-generated outputs are really inputs in the process of rendering patient care by physicians.

[17] Klarman, *The Economics of Health*, pp. 114, 116.

[18] J. A. Rafferty, "Patterns of Hospital Use: An Analysis of Short-Run Variations," *Journal of Political Economy* 79 (1971): 154–65.

[19] Richard M. Bailey, "Economies of Scale in Medical Practice," in *Empirical Studies in Health Economics: Proceedings of the Second Conference on the Economics of Health*, ed. Herbert E. Klarman (Baltimore: Johns Hopkins Press, 1970), p. 256.

Reder further comments that the number of patient visits as the output measure limits any consideration of the quality of medical care.[20]

Martin S. Feldstein has argued that the appropriate measure of output of hospitals is an index which combines case cost and the patient week. Thus:

$$C_i^* = \frac{\Sigma_j n_{ij} c_{ij}}{\Sigma_j n_{ij} c_{.j}}$$

where: C_i^* = costliness of hospital i

   n_{ij} = number of cases of type j treated per year in hospital i

   c_{ij} = average ward cost per case of type j in hospital i

   c_j = national average cost per case of type j[21]

In assessing economies of scale in medical firms, though the output can be thought of as patient care or units of patient care, methods to measure this output are not completely agreed upon. The question of whether medical firms operate under constant, increasing, or decreasing costs is uncertain.

IV. Problems in Urban Health Care

Health care in cities in the United States is becoming a problem of increasing urgency. With rising costs of medical care and increasing demands, the urban dweller of the 1970s is presented with a complex of choices concerning the medical care of his family. While the United States devotes a larger share of resources to health care than do most other countries in the world, it lags behind many developed countries in indices of health. In general, as more information is available on the nature of health care and health services in the United States, the word crisis takes on increased meaning.

While it is still not possible to determine what an ideal medical care system would be for any urban society, it is nevertheless possible to point out certain deficiencies in thinking, facilities, and services which are attendant to the existing medical care industry. One severe problem in improving medical care in the United States is the historic attitude of Americans that they are the healthiest people in the world.

The Healthiest Nation Myth

Senator Abraham Ribicoff describes the wife of a 43-year-old house painter in Alabama who was hospitalized for cancer of the cervix and colon while pregnant with the couple's fifth child. Over an 18-month period she had several

---

[20] Bailey, "Economies of Scale," in *Empirical Studies in Health Economics*, ed. Klarman, pp. 274, 276. Comments by Melvin J. Reder.

[21] Martin S. Feldstein, *Economic Analysis for Health Service Efficiency. Econometric Studies of the British National Health Service* (Chicago: Markham Publishing Co., 1968), pp. 24–26.

major operations, intensive care, and many expensive drugs; in the end, however, she died. Her husband was left with a $30,000 medical bill of which only $9,000 was covered by medical insurance. While some of the best medical care in the world is available in the United States, it is not available on a widespread basis because of the high costs. As Senator Ribicoff points out, medical bills like the instance cited are only one example of what is wrong with American health care. If in 1969 the house painter had lived in Sweden where there is a national health insurance plan, his wife's hospital bill would have been $1.40 a day, doctor visits would have cost $1.35 each, and drugs, if not free, would have been provided at a very low cost. The seriousness of the problem is reflected in the fact that the house painter's wife was one among 100,000 Americans to die of cancer in 1968 who might have been saved.[22]

Historically, the American has imagined that he is a healthy person. Perhaps it is part of the economic traditions of private initiative in the society which suggests to us that we are the best judges of our own particular conditions. There would seem, therefore, to be some resistance to seeking medical care. It is probably just as well, however, because, as noted earlier, in any community citizens may have great difficulty in finding medical care. Many Americans, even when they can pay for it, cannot find a doctor. Doctors are unevenly distributed around the United States, just as are specialized hospital facilities. For example, the Presidential Commission on Heart Disease, Cancer, and Stroke surveyed 777 United States hospitals equipped to perform open heart surgery. One-third of the hospitals surveyed had no open heart cases that year, more than 60% had fewer than one a week, and 30% had fewer than one a month.[23]

Other evidence which tends to discredit the healthiest nation myth is the fact that hospital standards are generally not what they should be. Ribicoff cites stories of heart attack patients placed in halls when cardiac units are full, of hospitals failing to separate infectious patients from obstetric areas, emergency units without any blood supplies, and where x-ray service is available only during daytime hours and not at all on weekends.[24]

An argument for the healthiest nation myth has been our high expenditures on medical care. Spending 6.7% of our 1969 gross national product generated a health expenditure of 63 billion dollars a year or $294 per person per year. While no other country spends this much money, the United States is fourteenth in the world in infant mortality with a rate of 22.1 infant mortalities per 1,000 infant births.[25] The countries which are ahead of us, Sweden, the Netherlands, Finland, and Japan, have fewer resources to devote to medical care than we do

[22] Abraham Ribicoff, "The 'Healthiest Nation' Myth," *Saturday Review of Literature*, Aug. 22, 1970, p. 18.

[23] Ribicoff, "The 'Healthiest Nation' Myth," p. 19.

[24] Ribicoff, "The 'Healthiest Nation' Myth," p. 19.

[19] Ribicoff, "The 'Healthiest Nation' Myth," p. 19.

in the United States. Further, twelve nations also have a lower maternal mortality rate. In seventeen countries men live longer than in the United States; in ten other countries women live longer. As Ribicoff suggests:

> Obviously we are not the healthiest nation in the world. We are not even close. Personal habits, life-styles, education, income, genetics, and physical and social environment have combined, along with medical care deficiencies, to produce the data that destroys this myth.[26]

The Doctor Shortage

What has been called the professional birth control of the American Medical Association has resulted in a severe shortage of doctors. This control of a labor force by a professional association is one of the most severe problems of American medicine today. The difficulty in finding a doctor in many communities even when they exist has already been noted, but there are many communities where there are no qualified doctors.

Physicians tend to cluster in cities where a large clientele exists and specialization is profitable. When regressions were run on the number of physicians per 100,000 population among SMSAs with 250,000 population or more, some interesting correlations resulted (table 25). For example, population size was influential as a locational factor. Whether consciously or not, physicians tended to cluster where incomes were higher. High correlation coefficients were obtained for physicians per 100,000 population, and birth rates, death rates, and marriage

TABLE 25

SIMPLE LINEAR CORRELATION OF PHYSICIANS PER 100,000 PERSONS
IN 110 SMSAs OF 250,000 OR MORE PERSONS
FOR 1969, BY SELECTED VARIABLES

Variables Regressed with Physicians per 100,000	Coefficient of Correlation
Total population of SMSA	.674
Birth rate	.755
Death rate	.737
Marriage rate	.669
Per capita income	.632
Per capita income as a percent of national per capita income	.632
Total Social Security payments monthly	.609
Hospital beds per 100,000	.711

Source: Compiled from U.S. Bureau of the Census, Department of Commerce, *Statistical Abstract of the United States, 1971* (Washington, D.C.: U.S. Government Printing Office, 1971), table 1, pp. 842–71.

[26] Ribicoff, "The 'Healthiest Nation' Myth," p. 19.

rates all associated positively with the physician rate. There were strong associations between the number of hospital beds per 100,000 and the physicians' rates. Physicians seem to cluster in cities where social security payments are high. With wide variations in medical services among cities, it is not surprising that there tends to be a reinforcing of a particular city's medical care problems. It may well be a situation in which the rich get richer and the poor communities get poorer.

Wide variations exist in urban medical services among cities, even large cities. For example, among SMSAS of population size of 250,000 or more residents, the range of hospital beds per 100,000 persons is quite wide (table 26) — Honolulu has less than 250 beds per 100,000, while Omaha, Duluth, and Superior have in excess of 600 beds per 100,000 population. While this is only one evidence of medical services, a range of this extent is considerable. Most cities fall into the 301 to 500 hospital bed rate.

Not only can we speak of a shortage of doctors generally and a poor geographic distribution of them, but we can also speak of the uneven training of particular kinds of doctors. Currently we are faced with a situation where there are an increasing number of neurosurgeons, thoracic surgeons, and general surgeons, while the number of general practitioners has declined greatly. In surveying medical schools, one may not find a general practitioner among the graduating class.[27]

Other problems account for the doctor shortage. Medical schools in 1970 turned down 15,000 qualified students who wanted places in freshman classes

TABLE 26

HOSPITAL BEDS PER 100,000 PERSONS
AMONG SMSAS OF 250,000 POPULATION OR MORE FOR 1969

Hospital Beds per 100,000 Population	Number of Cities
201–250	1
251–300	8
301–350	13
351–400	24
401–450	20
451–500	19
501–550	4
551–600	1
601–650	1

Source: Compiled from U.S. Bureau of the Census, Department of Commerce, *Statistical Abstract of the United States, 1971* (Washington, D.C.: U.S. Government Printing Office, 1971), table 1, pp. 842–71.

[27] Ribicoff, "The 'Healthiest Nation' Myth," p. 19.

which had only enough space for 10,000. Medical schools are not numerous and many are faced with serious financial problems. Forty-three of the 107 medical schools in the United States received special financial distress grants from the federal government to continue operations. At the same time, severe restrictions in federal funds appear to have limited construction money. It is estimated that the federal government, given current efforts, will generate only 1,600 new doctors by 1975 or a .5% increase in the current physician population.[28]

Self-Diagnosis and Proximity to Markets: A Problem in Consumer Economics

While we are used to the desirable aspects of the urban community as a diverse marketplace where goods are located readily available to the consumer, we seldom think in terms of the community as a source of waste and inefficiency because of this same proximity. Does inaccessibility to formal health care generate undesirable spin-offs in the form of self-medication?

It is easy to acquire highly advertised but inefficacious drugs and nostrums, yet sometimes difficult or expensive to receive formal medical care. While one may argue that physicians' services may be overpriced, self-medication for many complaints is dangerous and wasteful from a medical care standpoint. Such waste as the economy generates includes such items as vitamins in wide variety, mouthwashes, miracle cures for arthritis, eyewashes, and cough medicines.

Other possible spin-offs which are undesirable are the health problems which urban congestion generates generally. Respiratory diseases, heart disease, and many other ailments have much higher incidence in cities than in rural areas or small communities.

Still another proximity problem in urban areas relates to the economy of scale of illicit enterprise. Markets such as illicit drugs demand congestion or density of consumers to be effective. Likewise, quack medicine demands a market which is densely populated.

From a strictly economic point of view, there is no doubt that bad health contributes to the waste of vital human and capital resources in the city. Some examples include losses due to absenteeism, therapy costs in otherwise preventable diseases, inefficient production among the labor force when afflicted by minor illnesses, loss of life, and loss of the production values which the diseased no longer generate. Magnitudes of these forms of waste are capable of development and should be generated for the evaluation of health programs in cities.

From a social and psychological point of view there is great waste in illness; not all can be eliminated, but preventable illnesses and consequent losses are significant contributors to mental breakdowns and family problems. While

---

[28] Ribicoff, "The 'Healthiest Nation' Myth," p. 18. The extent of the doctor shortage in dispassionate terms is best seen in Rashi Fein's work, *The Doctor Shortage: An Economic Diagnosis* (Washington, D.C.: Brookings Institution, 1967).

studies are not numerous, it is possible to suggest that family illness of either parent can aid in the creation of juvenile delinquency and numerous other social pathologies.

One additional significant problem is that of medical service to persons at various places as opposed to a central place. Many urbanites have limited access to regular care because of lack of transportation. Transportation services, such as a publicly sponsored dial-a-bus system, could improve accessibility to medical services. Likewise, a mobile unit can offer quite a variety of health services.

There are numerous other aspects of health care which are problematical. We have seen only a few examples. The extent to which some of these problems can be acted upon at the local level is limited, but urban policy in health care planning and implementation can bear fruit.

V. Policies for Urban Health

There are distinct limits to what local governments may at this time do to improve medical care for citizens. Several avenues, however, appear to be open.

Local Government as an Insuror

One possible policy for the improvement of local health care comes in the form of local government either becoming an insuror of health or, at a minimum, providing a group health plan for residents through existing private health plans. For residents in the city who are not otherwise covered, group rates for hospitalization insurance (and even more sophisticated coverage) could be made available. The possibility of the government as insuror would demand more competence than local governments can now muster, but offering group plans to residents is well within local government capability. It would be feasible to introduce a plan of variable cost insurance where costs are varied in order to overcome the inefficiencies in demand for uniformly high-quality hospitals in the face of a lack of variance in cost to the consumer.[29]

The Community Health Plan[30]

Few cities in America have community sponsored health plans, the only major exceptions being the health care provided by Kaiser programs, in planned cities, or at military bases. One example is Columbia, Maryland, the community developed by the James Rouse Company between Baltimore and Washington, D.C. In this planned community a health program has been devised which is essentially comprehensive, and, through the Columbia Hospital and Clinics Foundation, any resident of Columbia may enroll at prices which are comparable to those of private hospitalization insurance firms.

[29] For a discussion of Variable Cost Insurance see J. P. Newhouse and V. Taylor, "The Subsidy Problem in Hospital Insurance," *Journal of Business* 43 (October 1970): 452–56.

[30] From descriptive literature of the Columbia Hospital and Clinics Foundation, Columbia, Maryland.

An important feature of this health plan, developed in association with the Johns Hopkins Medical School, is its heavy emphasis upon prevention. While developed with private insurance companies, the preventative services are thought to aid in the reduction of cost to the general plan. Currently, flat fees are levied for visits to a Columbia clinic for participants in the amount of $2 per visit. Any prescription obtained bears a cost of $2. The following excerpt from the *Columbia Medical Plan* notes the major provision of the plan, as currently offered to residents in or near Columbia.

The Columbia Hospital and Clinics Foundation, a new institution affiliated with The Johns Hopkins Hospital and The Johns Hopkins University, is establishing the Columbia Medical Plan, a voluntary, comprehensive, prepaid health care plan for residents of the new city of Columbia, Maryland, and the surrounding area. The Plan provides a wide range of medical and hospital services and emphasizes prevention of illness, early detection of disease, and comprehensive ambulatory medical care. Objectives are to improve and maintain the overall physical and mental health of Plan members and to deliver quality medical care at reasonable cost.

Individuals enrolled in the Plan receive medical care at Columbia from a group of physicians representing a wide range of medical specialties. These physicians are members of the medical faculty and staff of The Johns Hopkins University School of Medicine and The Johns Hopkins Hospital, and they are augmented by the full medical staff at Johns Hopkins.

Members of the Plan receive care and treatment in the new Columbia Hospital and Clinics Foundation medical office building located on Banneker Road in Columbia. In late 1971, an expanded outpatient facility and a hospital was opened in Columbia. Until the hospital was constructed, hospital services were provided at The Johns Hopkins Hospital in Baltimore. Plan members have access, when necessary, to the extensive resources of The Johns Hopkins Medical Institutions in Baltimore for services that cannot be provided economically or efficiently in Columbia.

Members are enrolled in the Prepaid Plan by health insurers. Participating carriers offer the Plan to groups, primarily at places of employment. Residents of Columbia and its immediate area have the option to join the Plan in this way, and in addition, special group plans are arranged for Columbia residents through village associations, Medicare and Medicaid beneficiaries, and others.

How the Plan Works

Members obtain care in the Plan's facilities. Physicians will be available on a 24-hour, 7-day-a-week basis in the facility or on-call after hours. Out-of-area coverage assures members that they have full protection in other hospitals and clinics when medical emergencies preclude coming to the Columbia facility. Members receive physician services from a newly formed group practice of salaried physicians. The physician group consists of specialists in internal medicine, pediatrics, gynecology-obstetrics, surgery, psychiatry, opthalmology, and radiology, and will be augmented by other specialists at Johns Hopkins in Baltimore. The group, while initially small, is expected to grow to about seventy physicians. Members of the Plan and their families will be free to select a physician from among the group working in Columbia. In addition to the physicians, paramedical health workers, such as physicians' assistants, will be employed to assist the physicians.

Premium Cost

Monthly premium charges are determined by the insurance carriers participating in the Plan. Premiums are comparable to presently available comprehensive health insurance. Minimum co-payments and deductible charges are made for certain services.

Comprehensive Care

Comprehensive care includes prevention, diagnosis, and treatment of disease. It is a continuous process provided in the doctor's office, in the hospital, and, when necessary, in the patient's home. It uses modern techniques and specially trained personnel for medical screening, diagnosis, and treatment. It encourages individuals to seek medical care on a regular basis, not just when illness occurs, by making available in an organized system a broad range of medical services which include:

Ambulatory Care

Visits for certain emergencies, preventive, diagnostic, therapeutic, or follow-up care, eye examinations, immunizations, injections, a periodic health review, and laboratory and x-ray examinations are included in this care. Drugs prescribed by a Plan physician and obtained through the Columbia Medical Plan will be covered by the Plan with a low co-payment per prescription by the Plan member.

Hospital Care

The full range of care normally provided by a general hospital and the services of a Plan physician are offered. This benefit includes payment of hospital charges in full for confinement in a semiprivate (or private if prescribed by a Plan physician) room. Intensive care and private duty nurses are also covered in full if medically necessary. There is no duration limit as long as confinement is considered medically necessary by the physician.

Home Care

House calls if ordered by a Plan physician are covered with a co-payment for the first visit per each episode of illness. Subsequent house calls for the same episode are covered with a smaller co-payment per visit.

Special Provisions

1. Maternity care — All appropriate maternity care (including pre and postnatal and well baby care) is covered in full after $100 co-payment. If pregnancy begins before the effective date of coverage (or after coverage has terminated) care is provided on a fee-for-service basis.

2. Mental illness — Hospitalization for acute mental illness is covered up to 30 days per calendar year. Also available is partial hospitalization for

day care. The ambulatory psychiatric care by (or controlled by) the Plan staff is covered with a small co-payment per visit for fifteen visits per calendar year, with a larger co-payment per visit thereafter.

3. Ambulance service — This is covered when ordered by a Plan physician. At a future date, dental services, nursing home care, and other benefits will be considered for addition to this comprehensive package.

While the above plan has the advantage of prepaid and comprehensive (or nearly so) medical care, like most private plans it fails to provide health care for a "comprehensive population"; that is, the plan is open to those who can afford it and no one else. As a model for a given community, its principal failing is this very point. Some members of the Columbia community are involved in attempts to devise a plan for subsidizing those who cannot afford the rates at this time. Currently monthly rates vary from $30 to $50 for a family and will be increased as subsidization by the principal insuror is discontinued.

Such plans as exist in Columbia, Maryland, are close to what is referred to as the Health Maintenance Organization, an organization developed within a community with private initiative and voluntary membership to begin to deal with the question of comprehensive medical care. Federal funding of Health Maintenance Organizations has increased to sixty-six programs that have been supported in recent years by HEW. Such programs are, as has been pointed out, not available to all since, unlike a National Health Insurance program, fees are required.[31]

Health Care vs. Medical Care

To this point, all we have talked about is medical care; the economist has not been heavily involved with health care.

Health care in the United States should not be confused with medical care. Health should be thought of as the state of a human being's physical and mental well-being. Medicine is the process of curing, by diagnosis and therapy, a human physical or mental illness. Health care is not widely viewed in our society as a desired goal; the society up to this point has concentrated its efforts on medical care. The distinction between the two is important and often confused. The medical profession, for example, when it thinks of health care, tends to think in terms of the physical state of the person and only secondarily of the mental state. Even then mental health is usually limited to the narrow confines of what is currently accepted in medical practice. The sad fact of the matter is that in this complex society, few are thinking in terms of an entire urban health care system with its many spatial, economic, political, and social dimensions.

[31] For a discussion of health maintenance organizations see Gerald F. Pyle and Gary F. Stein, "Some Spatial Implications of Health Maintenance Organizations at the National Scale," paper presented to the Annual Meeting of the Association of American Geographers, Atlanta, Georgia, April 1973.

While not totally comprehensive, the efforts of members of the health field are shown in figure 8. Seen as a process, health care consists of prevention, diagnosis, and therapy leading to the outputs of health care. Unfortunately, only the medical industry and the public health organizations now recognize themselves as health organizations. The necessary support agencies, such as public schools, welfare organizations, employers in the private sector, and public recreation agencies, fail for the most part to consider the health of people they serve. Of equal importance is that in the medical care industry and the public health sector, no organizations exist which recognize or act to generate comprehensive health care. Functions are divided and operate separately or, if together, they are more apt to be on the basis of collusion rather than cooperation. Another point is that individuals for the most part do not have access to anything like comprehensive health care. Even in the case of well-organized community health plans such as Columbia's, there is little or no cooperation between the community health plan and other social agencies in the city.

Even if comprehensive health care is conceptually possible, cities do not have the institutions today to provide such health care. What care is provided is provided by powerful economic groups such as associations of doctors, powerful federal agencies, and monopolistic local hospitals. Other powerful elements within the community such as school authorities, local government officials, and private insurors work hard to protect their particular domains. One could not expect to either finance or administer effective health care in the city except through the expansion of such collectives as the Kaiser plan in Seattle into more comprehensive activities and with national health insurance — to wit, socialized medicine. Tendencies toward socialization of medicine continue as medical care packages are developed by Congress, and the most likely form of such care will be variants of medicare. Until nationally provided medical care and basic medical insurance are made available to all residents, it is unlikely that the local role can be very effective. The provision of hospitals, clinics, insurance plans, interface programs between medical care and other urban institutions, and local controls are all local roles of the future, but probably cannot be effectively implemented until national health insurance is available for all.

VI. Evaluating the Costs and Benefits of Medical Care Expenditures

The question of whether "good health" is desirable is in general not arguable, but what is meant by "good health" and to what extent and in what amount and by what means is it to be provided? As is customary in a "private" society, some goods and services cannot be provided effectively except on some collective basis. For example, a man cannot afford to build a hospital emergency room in order to have a blood transfusion. On the other hand, we cannot argue that since this (hospitalization) is a desired or "demanded" service it will be provided by the

FIGURE 8
A COMPREHENSIVE HEALTH CARE SYSTEM

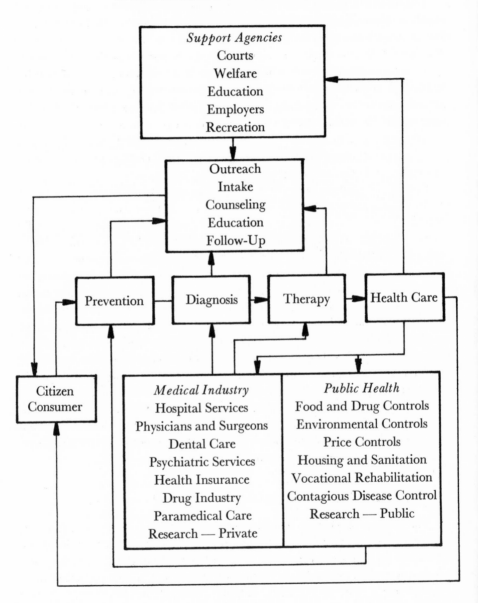

private sector at an economic level. As Weisbrod argues, "whenever production or consumption of a commodity involves significant external effects, we may expect its volume in the free market to be nonoptimal." [32] Such is the case with medical care and general health activities.

Improvement in the health of one person has a desirable impact upon the health of others. For example, if a group of persons is innoculated for smallpox, then it reduces the risk (probability) of catching that disease for the rest of the population. Weisbrod uses the illustration of the problem of indivisibilities in such things as mosquito control programs. The benefits of such programs can be realized by individuals in many cases without paying for them. In short, paraphrasing Weisbrod, it is argued that there are three ways in which a person can benefit from the health expenditures of others:

1. Through reduction of risk in communicable disease which is a function of the externalities of health expenditures by "being" more healthy;
2. Through the "actions" taken (that is, the physical programs and facilities developed) to improve health which is a function of the "indivisibilities" of health resources; and
3. Through reductions in health cost as a service expands (assuming the service is produced at a less than optimal level).

Thus persons reap benefits from the combined health expenditures of others and without the necessity of making contributions themselves. Because of the lack of success of voluntary attempts to provide better health care (the three reasons above), private individual expenditures for improvement to health are likely to be suboptimal. Following the argument that the welfare of one may not coincide with the welfare of society, we can conclude that the public, in attempting to provide such goods, will have difficulty in determining the demand for such goods since individuals will tend to hide their wishes in the knowledge that the good will be provided anyway. A similar problem could be exemplified in the revenues to a church where voluntary contributions do not provide an even estimate of the value which its members place on the institution. [33]

Weisbrod lists a number of monetary losses due to poor health:

1. Premature death and the consequent loss of production,
2. Sickness and the loss of production,
3. Reduced productivity as a result of aftereffects of disease,
4. Restructuring of the production process in which the absented member functions may reduce total productivity,
5. Change in the size and composition of the labor force,

[32] Burton A. Weisbrod, *Economics of Public Health: Measuring the Economic Impact of Diseases* (Philadelphia: University of Pennsylvania Press, 1961), p. 16. Note: This section on evaluation depends heavily upon Weisbrod.

[33] Weisbrod, *Economics of Public Health*, pp. 18, 20, 21.

6. The costs of treatment, detection, and rehabilitation,

7. The existence of disease may cause persons to make costly attempts to avoid disease.

The means at our disposal for placing a monetary value on the items above vary. In the case of death and loss of production, we use the estimate of the future income a person would have generated then multiply that number by 95% which is an adjustment for "full employment." Still another adjustment must be made to weight the probability of the person gaining the full productive life. Thus we multiply adjusted average earnings for each age by the survival probability of that age group. This figure must, in turn, be discounted back to the present and summed to provide the value of the person lost as a net producer. Thus, the cost of the disease under item 1 is the value item for various age groups multiplied by the various age groups who die from a particular disease.[34]

Temporary disability from disease leads to a loss in production. Weisbrod's method for calculating this loss is as follows: For a given disease we need to know the average duration of disability it causes, the age-sex incidence of its cases, and the average earnings of its victims. Thus, if a male age 32 falls victim to a disease which results in a mean period of disability of four weeks, the loss of his production is 4/52 of the average annual earnings of males of age 32. Data problems in this case will be difficult to overcome but they can be assessed simply by gaining the reportable items and measures of average duration.[35]

In the case of permanent disabilities which impair productivity, we first look to the diseases which cause this impairment. Weisbrod suggests polio, TB, heart disease, and we could probably include others. To estimate the loss suffered, we would determine the percent of disability within age-sex groupings and multiply this times annual earnings (with appropriate discounted values previously described). The percent disabled is a weak figure and at this point is probably not possible to ascertain; likely, we will leave it as a real but unidentifiable cost.

The same is true of the impact of absenteeism upon the total production process; data for these costs are simply not available.

In the case of the population effects of disease which affects the structure of the economy as well as the distribution of income, no sound device has been developed for such measurements.

Treatment costs are to some degree obtainable from hospital records, doctors, and insurance companies. Avoidance costs (not sufficiently valid to use insurance records) and rehabilitation costs are not easy to develop, and the latter is not significant in the case of most diseases.

[34] Weisbrod, *Economics of Public Health*, pp. 30–31, 34.

[35] Weisbrod, *Economics of Public Health*, pp. 38, 39.

In conclusion, when we talk about the costs to society of poor health we are speaking of a number of items of which the following can be quantified:

1. Premature death
2. Sickness
3. Treatment

The costs or losses so included should be compared to the costs of given programs for public health and medical care so that the program costs become the monetary costs of the program, and the benefits become the losses no longer incurred by society.[36]

The foregoing description of health care evaluation is not a completely detailed model which one employs; its use has been to present the major economic concepts relevant to the evaluation of health care expenditure.[37]

Summary: Medical Care

In this chapter we have discussed some of the economic aspects of urban health care. In speaking of health we concentrated on the medical care industry which includes the services of the physicians, dentists, and other medical labor. Additional medical services include hospital services, outpatient services, and the support systems of medical care such as health insurance, the drug industry, public health agencies, and producers of medical equipment.

When demand for medical care is discussed, it is usually convenient to consider the demand for physicians' services and the demand for hospital services separately. The demand for physicians' services is clouded by the fact that the market for physicians is far from competitive. One facet of this lack of competitiveness is found in the still existing but declining price discrimination practiced by physicians. Standardization of fees is another instance of lack of competition. The shortage of doctors accounts for the possibilities for such pricing patterns, but the situation is further confused when one considers that it is the doctor, once contacted, who determines the amount of services the consumer needs. Traditional factors of demand which are present in this market include income, tastes and preferences, and the prices of other goods and services.

The demand for hospital services likewise is not directly determined by the consumer. The physician determines the need for hospitalization. Health insurance tends to raise and equalize the rates charged indicating the likelihood of an inelastic demand. Demand for hospital services is also accounted for by income, alternative care, economic status of hospitals, and attitudes of administrators and

---

[36] Weisbrod, *Economics of Public Health*, p. 47.

[37] For detailed discussions of the economics of health in addition to Weisbrod and Klarman, see Feldstein, *Economic Analysis for Health Service Efficiency*.

doctors. Tending toward the operation of Say's Law, the supply of hospital beds appears to create its own demand.

In addition to the demand factors for hospitals and physicians, there are general elements which appear to affect the level of demand for medical care — education, family status, and the availability of preventive medicine. Education and medical care seem to be positively associated. Families are more likely to seek medical care than individuals. Preventive medicine appears also to be positively associated with health care expenditures, perhaps in affecting the taste for medical care.

The supply of physicians is highly inelastic in the short run, but, in the long run, accumulations of doctors may be found in cities where incomes are rising rapidly. There are interstate barriers to entry into medical practice. Supply of physicians is difficult to comprehend because of complicating factors including the failure of productivity measures as applied to medical care, the length of the work week, and the specialization that exists among doctors. Group practice by physicians appears to generate efficiencies in supply.

The supply of hospitals is equally confusing. Short-run cost curves may appear to indicate a constancy of marginal cost over the relevant range of production. Consequently, these short-run cost curves for hospitals may show average costs declining. The quantity and quality of hospital care varies with the ownership. Proprietary hospitals appear to provide the poorest quality of health care, while the voluntary hospital offers a generally higher level of service. The government hospital offers the greatest degree of services; however, neither the voluntary nor the government hospital has any real incentive to keep costs down.

Turning to problems of urban health, we noted the myth to which Americans subscribe in which we imagine ourselves the healthiest nation. A critical problem does exist in the shortage of doctors, absolutely and spatially. The limited number of medical schools, the high cost of education, and the monopolization by the American Medical Association appear to be factors which create this numerical shortage. Likewise, specialization generates the need for more doctors; however, when specialists are produced rather than general practitioners, the shortage is even more acute. Shortages of hospitals and the unevenness of their distribution were also noted as medical care problems.

The concentration of health care facilities and supportive markets tends to bias medical care markets in favor of the urbanite and generate a tendency on his part to overspend in nostrums and in some formal health care services.

The local government should aspire to the role of local health insuror or, at a minimum, should provide group health insurance to local residents at reduced costs. An example of a community health plan was cited as an illustration of how one community is attempting to deal with comprehensive medical care. Health care was distinguished from simple medical care, and a lack of coordination and cooperation as well as medical specialization were seen as principal reasons for our failure to concentrate on health care as opposed to the more limited concept of medical care.

In evaluating the costs and benefits of medical care, it would appear that the principal benefit measures include the economic productivity "saved" for the community by a reduction in illness and a lowering of death rates. Externalities appear to be very much in evidence when one considers the benefits of preventive medicine or the therapy and cure of contagious disease.

In conclusion, let us consider the question of health care and the premise of this work — that planning can assist and should assist the individual. Conflicts arise when we consider health care. The individual consumer needs the support of good health institutions, and planners can aid both through formal health planning and accessibility supports. Yet we are struck by the reliance that health care of the individual has upon the individual physician. Narrow specialization of the medical profession renders the medical practitioner a "fender man" or a "tune-up specialist" rather than a professional interested in the general health of the patient. The one to one relationship between doctor and patient becomes at best a partial relationship, and the needs of the patient must in some sense suffer. Thus it is as a final thrust that we argue for an increase to the number of general practitioners in order to return health care to a supportive role of the individual through a one to one relationship with a professional who is competent in general and concerned with the total person rather than the partial health of the individual.

Selected Bibliography

Health

ARNION, J. "Costs and Efficiency of Health and Social Welfare Institutions." In *Cost-Benefit Analysis of Social Projects*, United Nations, Research Institute for Social Development. Report no. 7. Geneva, Switz.: United Nations, 1966.

ARROW, KENNETH J. "Uncertainty and the Welfare Economics of Medical Care." *American Economic Review* 53 (1963): 941–73.

BARLOW, ROBIN. "The Economic Effects of Malaria Eradication." In "Economics of Health," *American Economic Review* 57 (1967): 130–48.

BURNS, EVELINE M. "Health Insurance: Not If, or When, But What Kind?" *American Journal of Public Health* 61 (1971): 2164–75.

CORREA, HECTOR. "Health Planning." *Kyklos* 20 (1967): 909–21.

CULYER, A. J. "The Nature of the Commodity 'Health Care' and Its Efficient Allocation." *Oxford Economic Papers* 23 (1971): 189–211.

EHRENREICH, JOHN, AND EHRENREICH, BARBARA. *The American Health Empire: Power, Profits, and Politics.* New York: Vintage Books, 1971.

FELDSTEIN, MARTIN S. "Economic Analysis, Operational Research, and the National Health Service." *Oxford Economic Papers* 15 (1963): 19–31.

———. *Economic Analysis for Health Service Efficiency. Econometric Studies of the British National Health Service.* Chicago: Markham Publishing Co., 1968.

————. *The Rising Cost of Hospital Care.* Washington, D.C.: Information Resources Press for National Center for Health Services Research and Development, 1971.

FRANKEL, M. "Federal Health Expenditures in a Program Budget." Research Memorandum, RM-4612-RC. Santa Monica, Cal.: Rand Corporation, June 1965. Also in David Novick, ed., *Program Budgeting, Program Analysis and the Federal Budget.* Washington, D.C.: U.S. Government Printing Office, 1965.

HAUGHTON, J. G. "Can the Poor Use the Present Health Care System?" *Inquiry*, Mar. 1968, pp. 43–48.

HERMAN, MARY W. "The Poor: Their Medical Needs and the Health Services Available to Them." *Annals of the American Academy of Political and Social Science* 399 (Jan. 1972): 12–21.

KLARMAN, HERBERT E. *The Economics of Health.* New York: Columbia University Press, 1965.

————, ED. *Empirical Studies in Health Economics: Proceedings of the Second Conference on the Economics of Health.* Baltimore: Johns Hopkins Press, 1970.

————. "Syphilis Control Program." In *Measuring Benefits of Government Investments: Papers Presented at a Conference of Experts Held November 7–9, 1963,* ed. Robert Dorfman, pp. 367–414. Washington, D.C.: Brookings Institution, 1965.

LAVE, JUDITH R. "A Review of the Methods Used to Study Hospital Cost." *Inquiry*, May 1966, pp. 57–81.

————, AND LAVE, LESTER B. "Economic Analysis for Health Service Efficiency: A Review Article." *Applied Economics* 1 (1970): 293–305.

LINNENBERG, CLEM C. "How Shall We Measure Economic Benefits from Public Health Services?" In *Economic Benefits from Public Health Services,* publication no. 1178. Washington, D.C.: U.S. Public Health Service, 1964.

LONG, MILLARD F., AND FELDSTEIN, PAUL J. "Economics of Hospital Systems: Peak Loads and Regional Coordination." In "Economics of Health," *American Economic Review* 57 (1967): 119–29.

MARSHALL, A. W. "Cost-Benefit Analysis in Health." Paper P-3274. Santa Monica, Cal.: Rand Corporation, 1965.

MUSHKIN, SELMA J. "Health as an Investment." *Supplement: Oct. 1962. Journal of Political Economy* 70 (1962): 129–57.

PACKER, A. H. "Cost-Effectiveness Concepts to the Community Health System." *Operations Research* 16 (1968): 227–53.

PAULY, MARK V. *Medical Care at Public Expense: A Study in Applied Welfare Economics.* Praeger Special Studies in U.S. Economic and Social Development. New York: Praeger, 1971.

REDER, MELVIN J. "Economic Theory and Nonprofit Enterprise: Some Problems in the Economics of Hospitals." *Papers and Proceedings of the American Economic Association. American Economic Review* 55 (1965): 472–80.

ROTTENBERG, SIMON. "The Allocation of Biomedical Research." In "Economics of Health," *American Economic Review* 57 (1967): 109–18.

SCITOVSKY, A. "Changes in the Costs of Treatment of Selected Illness." *American Economic Review* 57 (1967): 1182–95.

U.S. DEPARTMENT OF HEALTH, EDUCATION AND WELFARE, PUBLIC HEALTH SERVICE. *Disability Days: United States — July 1965 — June 1966.* Vital and Health Statistics, Data from the National Health Survey. National Center for Health Statistics, series 10, no. 27. Washington, D.C.: U.S. Government Printing Office, 1968.

————. *Economic Benefits from Public Health Services: Objectives, Benefits and Examples of Measurement.* Publication no. 1178. Washington, D.C.: U.S. Government Printing Office, 1964.

———. *The Plan for Implementing a Planning-Programming-Budgeting System in the Public Health Service.* Washington, D.C.: U.S. Government Printing Office, 1965.

WAGNER, L. C. "The Role of Private Insurance in Meeting Personal Health Care Costs." *University of Washington Business Review,* Winter 1970, pp. 45–56.

WEISBROD, BURTON A. "Costs and Benefits of Medical Research: A Case Study of Poliomyelitis." *Journal of Political Economy* 79 (1971): 527–44.

———. *Economics of Public Health: Measuring the Economic Impact of Diseases.* Philadelphia: University of Pennsylvania Press, 1961.

———. "Some Problems of Pricing and Resource Allocation in a Non-Profit Industry — The Hospitals." *Journal of Business* 38 (1965): 18–28.

8

Technology
and the City

I. Introduction

Technology is a form of human knowledge but it is necessary to distinguish between science and technology if we wish to understand technology.

Technology and Science

Skolimowski argues that it is an error to consider technology as an applied science, that technology is not a science, and that the difference between science and technology can be understood only by comprehending the ideas of scientific progress and technological progress.[1]

Technology is not merely derived from science; it cannot be dissected into other particular sciences because such a view overlooks technological progress. Scientific progress comes from improvements and enlargements to the scientific store of knowledge; it arises from more simple, more universal, more detailed, and more accurate (in prediction) theories.[2]

Does technology seek truth? Does it aim at an enlargement of knowledge? No — "in science we investigate the reality that is given; in technology we create a reality according to our own designs."[3]

Science is concerned with what is, while technology is concerned with what is to be.[4] Technology is concerned with producing new objects and improving existing objects. Improvement means to make them: (a) more durable, (b) more

---

[1] Henry K. Skolimowski, "The Structure of Thinking in Technology," *Technology and Culture* 7 (1966): 372.

[2] Skolimowski, "The Structure of Thinking," pp. 373, 374.

[3] Skolimowski, "The Sturcture of Thinking," p. 374.

[4] Skolimowski, "The Structure of Thinking," p. 375.

reliable, (c) more sensitive, (d) faster, or (e) any combination of the above. Technological progress is characterized then by its ability "to produce more and more diversified objects with more and more interesting features, in a more and more efficient way." Science aims at creating better theories while technology aims at creating new artifacts through means of increasing effectiveness. Science can aid technology and technology can aid science, but they are essentially different.[5]

Societies and urban communities within society have technological problems. In broad aspects, technological problems include the basic questions of food, clothing, shelter, and transportation. As we narrow the focus, questions come in the form of how to effect small changes in current ways of doing things is cities. It should be pointed out that these fundamental questions are not exclusively technological, but they are essentially technological.

This chapter argues that technological forces operating upon cities are largely uncontrolled except in the context of the market economy. Because of this lack of effective social consideration and subsequent control, technology is seen as partially disruptive to the development of high quality urban life. Technology is seen as an externality on the human life of the city with significant social costs and benefits. The pollution literature of economics is extensive, but in the view of the author, pollution is a relatively minor externality compared to some other effects of technology.

This chapter examines some of the effects of technology but in a largely speculative way. No claim is made that each idea is in itself sufficient to point out total technological effects; rather, the discussion should be viewed as attempting to generate a recognition of certain aspects of life in the technological city which are not commonly treated.

Some Characteristic Effects of Technology

Nowhere is the evidence of change in the community more obvious than in the impact of machine technology. The dying neighborhood is a function of obsolescence in the face of new means of accomplishing housing and housing amenities. The decrepit downtown to some degree dies in the anger of the unparked automobile. The empty bus rattles on the street, a needless relic. Pawnshop and Goodwill stores become histories of dying arts. Vast walls of deceased toasters line their shelves, dead from lack of mechanics to service them. The service manager at the auto dealership fumes over the shoddy work of his senior mechanic. The implication of technology from the above examples is the evidence of lost skills. New technology makes existing tools and existing knowledge obsolete. Thus we lose the ability to operate a form of machine technology and at the same time lose a certain body of knowledge and labor skills.

---

[5] Skolimowski, "The Structure of Thinking," pp. 375, 376.

A second characteristic of importance is the fact that new technology typically builds on top of old technology. New cities are erected on the sites of old cities. Evidence abounds of this transitional dependence of technological advance on older technology. Old streetlights give a candle glow in the shadow of their mercury vapor progeny. Old houses with gingerbread mock the new houses with gingerbread. The iron fence falls and gives way to the electronic beam. Men gather on street corners to watch one building technology replace another building technology. Everywhere we are propping up, tearing down, rebuilding, razing, creating and making cities rise and fall on the horizon.

A third and very important characteristic of technology is that it may make the working man obsolete. Technology has the power to bring him high, but often it brings him low; it can make him an obsolete piece of "economic machinery" in a very short time. Skills, like current fashions, are rapidly replaced. The modern working urbanite may find himself in a wave of change which sets him loose, a transient seeking secure ports of employment over his working life. He must learn to navigate the seas over and over again to prevent his own obsolescence, and, in such a sea, while few are lost, many live in fear of being so. If urban man lives in a constantly changing environment of technology, then in a sense technology makes urban man homeless. The city is no longer a walled refuge; while rural areas have a sense of permanence, the city, as the home of man, is ever subject to change. This change is in part due to "advanced technology." An advanced technology is one which can economically destroy another technology. Schumpeter saw this clearly in *The Theory of Economic Development* in what he called the process of "creative destruction." [6] If in the market one set of ideas deposes another set of ideas which are less efficient than what replaces them, this is "creative destruction." The innovation of ideas and means of organizing economic production are processes whereby creative destruction takes place. Innovations in the normal process of capitalistic economic development cause changes in the economic institutions, and, consequently, the labor markets which surround these institutions. The urban labor force can be seen as a constantly changing body of requirements, a mix of old and new skills. While one can be sentimental about the destruction of old machine technology, the idea of the "creative destruction" of human beings, i.e., their skills and their means of living, is quite another thing.

The fact of obsolescence suggests another unsettling consequence for the urban labor market, namely that technology affects different people in different ways. To the employer who buys a machine to increase production efficiency, the value is positive, but the person replaced by the machine is without a job. Thus, a fourth characteristic of technology is that the one who pays for and the one who gains from technology may not be the same person.

[6] Joseph A. Schumpeter, *The Theory of Economic Development* (Cambridge, Mass.: Harvard University Press, 1934), pp. 57–94.

While the above discussion serves to introduce some of the effects of technology, it does not by any means exhaust the list. To understand the technological developments which have had impact upon cities is to trace the long road of change through a myriad number of mechanical, epistemological, and scientific ideas. To understand the impact of technology upon men working in cities is to trace and describe all of man's relations to materials and ideas about materials. Thus a fifth point of importance is the extensiveness of the relation of man and his material objects. Our identities are much bound in our possessions and skills.

Because of the close interrelationship of man to his work and to his tools a different view of technology is suggested. That view is that man's objects are man; that is to say that man in a cultural sense is his toaster. Our neckties, our freezers, our autos define us; they are our deeds and our identities. Following this one step further, you are the ghetto and the country club all rolled into one rather curious set of reactions. Our common identity within cities lies in the objects and organizations which define us. If we have unrest in the city, perhaps riots are self-hate, a common statement of futility and impotence which we in our cities may communicate. While this view of cities leads to a certain cynicism, to say that technological developments will save us or destroy us is somewhat like saying that my right hand will save me from my recalcitrant left hand.

As we approach some more specific ideas about technology and life in the city, let us summarize the initial ideas we have discussed: (1) technology causes a loss of knowledge as well as a creation of new ideas or skills; (2) technology builds on old technology; (3) we recognize that technology can make man obsolete, thus cities are flows of rapid change which can be threatening; (4) those who pay for technological advance may not be the ones who gain from technological advance; (5) technology is enormously complex because of its extensive interrelationships with all of man's activities, and this suggests that less is known about its impact than might be the case in less complex phenomena; and (6) the above interrelations put us in prospect of identifying ourselves by our machines and suggest that there is an essential conflict in looking to technology to solve problems precipitated by technology.

The six effects mentioned above may have social costs and benefits attached to them. Such externalities are not easily discussed nor are they always measurable. Finally, external effects may or may not be significant in loss or gain.

II. Man, His Machines, and His City

As has been suggested, the machine is very much with us. If the idea of the machine is expanded to include all devices, both mechanical and electronic, which extend human powers, we recognize that without the machine the entire fabric of society would collapse. This present central fact of dependence has a logical historical development.

The word "machine" is derived from the Greek "machane" and its Latin cognate "machina." The Greeks noted five particular types of devices which represented most machines. These included the lever, the wheel and axle, the pulley, the wedge, and the screw. All tools can be seen as extensions of these five types. A chisel is simply a sharpened wedge, a shovel is a form of lever, and an auger is a form of screw. Men discovered that by the application of these primitive machines there was considerable mechanical advantage. Machines differ from tools principally in that tools lend themselves to manipulation by skills whereas machines are more nearly automatic in function.

In the history of the development of machines we learn about the forging of metal so that man could cease to be so dependent upon stone for tool making. A second major era of advance was the development of the wheel and axle about 3000 B.C. and probably came from the extension of the potter's wheel into other uses. It is notable that the wheel allowed man to be on the treadmill for the first time, probably in the course of using the water wheel for irrigation purposes; by adding the second vertical wheel he could hook up his oxen and get off the treadmill. The history of machines is the story of man undertaking tasks to fulfill his needs and, upon discovering proper methods, relieving himself of the physical burden of accomplishing that task .

The machine has been associated historically with our diversion, work, and our war making. Battering rams, towers, and Archimedes' claw are examples of war use. Wind machines and organs are examples of machines for diversion. Vertical water wheels are an example of the machine for work purposes. We see today a proliferation of machines in modern cities. In the complex mechanics of entertainment, in sophisticated machines for mass production, and in our security and weapons systems we extend the three basic uses of machines.

The City as a Machine

In many respects the city is the product of man's use of machines. While it is possible to view the city as more, at one level at least, the city is a complex machine in which people live. Its principal shape or structure ought then to reflect it as a tool for man's purpose.

War is no longer significant to cities, but work and pleasure are. When one views the urban landscape he sees technology applied for the narrow purpose of the local economy, the production and distribution of goods and services. Skyscraper densities in central business districts are centers of congestion because they were created out of the old need for close proximity of business affairs. Communications technology has made that congestion largely unnecessary, but the monuments in the central city in the United States are office buildings — monuments to an economic tradition creating the congestion of a medieval marketplace.

Yet were not these mammoths of the central business district built to more efficiently provide for the production of goods and services in the city? If this city machine in its organization today is largely economic, its method for achieving organizational goals is technological efficiency. While business firms may be efficiently located, planned, and staffed, this does not necessarily mean that the city will also be efficiently located, planned, and staffed. The needs of economic efficiency do not necessarily coincide with the needs of an efficient city. Indeed, a city which is efficient in the social sense may be inefficient in the economic sense. Yet cities develop more for the convenience of economic production than for any other human requirements.

But what of diversion? In the modern city diversion is also machine dependent, thus the production of recreational goods tends to overwhelm the fact of diversion. The fact of the television is more significant than the content of television programs.

Some further examples of the city as an economic machine may be cited. Every transportation system in the country is organized around the necessity to move people to work and to move goods. With the exception of winding lanes in large parks and curves in residential areas (done ostensibly for aesthetic purposes), city streets are grid-like conveyor belts moving goods and people much like Henry Ford's assembly lines. Rapid transit systems, expressways, and bus systems, reduced to their essentials, are all forms of economic conveyors.

If technological function is the point, why then do we, for example, have such relatively inefficient autos? Machine efficiency and function may conflict with economic organization. Auto makers build a fashion into autos, "gilding the lily" to protect their markets. If something as essential as the auto were truly functional, like a water pump, then men would opt for keeping it as efficiently inexpensive as possible. But then auto makers would have to compete. Why? Because if they built the efficient machine they could quickly saturate the market and be forced to move to other forms of goods production. What an odd result! While the basic force for improvement of transportation is technological efficiency, we find ourselves in the curious position of maintaining the system by inefficient means. The light bulbs in Thomas Edison's home are the original ones and still working, even after twelve hours of use each day for many years. In modern society the better mousetrap is apt to be hidden away.

The examples of the auto and the light bulb are not unique. Large-scale enterprise is fundamentally interested in efficiency but only within the constraints of protecting itself. One may imagine that the major forms of technological advance come from large corporations because these firms have the financial capacity to undertake innovation. However sparse, evidence suggests that it is the middle-sized firm which, relative to capacity, generates the most innovative activity. What is suggested is that size and stage of development alters the innovative pattern. Once the large-scale firm gains a large share of the market, then it seeks to protect its capital investments and to protect its markets — output becomes frivolous, as in the case of the auto, or shoddy, as in the case of the light bulb.

This result is what can be called a "vested interest" in a particular capital technology. Both the public and private sector of the local economy are subject to it.

The fact of vested interest in a particular technological form leads to a strong resistance to change. If cities develop this same resistance, then we must recognize that it is not simply scarce resources which limits technological improvement of the city machine, but it is sunk costs in the form of vested interests in particular technological ways and means or forms of undertaking city functions. A bureaucratization of technology is very evident; while planners or engineers may talk of technological solutions to city problems, they do so in the context of an accepted vested form. What then results? The result is that the city, an economic machine initially formed by tradition and historical condition, operates as an imperfect artifact of the present for which one may only buy improved parts. We can scarcely start over; it is very difficult to totally rebuild this outdated entity to make it more effective. Thus it is that our large cities, particularly our older ones, can be considered as partially worn out and patched machines for man.

Vested interest in technology is evident in both the public sector and the private sector. The private sector makes use of outdated physical facilities long past the time of their best efficiency. The public sector likewise maintains its old school buildings, its old forms of parks, its outdated street systems, and its antiquated courthouses. Yet it is not the use of old physical facilities that is most important in the "make-do" attitudes of public and private officials. Rather, it is the habits of mind that accompany any old technology which represent the most significant resistance to change among officials, both in the public and private sectors of local authority. Why do we do this today? Answer: Because we did it that way yesterday. Somehow old or traditional patterns are assumed proven by use over time when, in fact, they may never have been appropriate to the tasks at hand.

An illustration of what happens when the grip of vested technology is broken can be seen in the so-called new towns. In England there was great resistance to move into the new towns around London, yet once people moved they became mobile and the problem was to keep them from moving out. They did not become mobile to move back to London or whatever city was "home." No, the residents generally moved to other communities. The new town increased mobility; it broke up traditional ways of thinking about things.

New towns may be worth investigating to see if they can be agents of social and economic change. Public new towns could be somewhat venturesome, but it is likely that the privately built new towns as are planned and developed in North America may be too bound to tradition to serve as social and economic experiments and may be too bound to the profit motive to be able to move far enough ahead of the existing suburb. On the other hand, perhaps it is logical to assume that any set of physical structures built with current technology will of necessity be limited in its capacity to change. Exceptions are perhaps only a matter of degree, but while some may suggest that Paolo Soleri's planned cities are "visionary," it is more likely that the work of Wright in Broadacre City and Soleri in 3-D New Jersey is really the most practical direction in which to move. At least, in such cases, a great leap in technology is a force for change rather than a base upon which immediate resistance to change is built.

The Discipline of the Machine

If the city is a machine, then urban life is a machine life. For the urban resident, the discipline of this life comes in a number of ways. Work is measured by machines, evaluated by machines, overseen by machines, and man working in the city is disciplined by the machine. To Marx this domination by machine technology would have suggested the problem of alienation from specie-life; that is, man working to perform a specialized task in which the product and the work are separated is alienated both from nature and from his labor. Specialization creates "cogs" in the machine making unclear the distinctions between man and production man or between man and machine.

In addition to its impact on work, the machine separates man from his leisure. He becomes a leisure specialist just as he is a labor specialist. Catching (producing) a fish becomes more important than the pleasure of pursuing leisure skills. The reliance upon technology and the consequent alienation of man from his leisure and recreation is evidenced by sonar for fishing, complex power boats, automated tuning television, autos heavily laden with power assists, "convenience" foods for camping, recreation vehicles with all the comforts of home, motels in national parks, artificially created environments such as Disneyland, and many other aspects of leisure time pursuits. Mountain climbing with aids, hiking with lots of equipment, and all recreational activities served by industrial technology tend to supplant human ingenuity and effort with machine effort.

Even in medical care, technology supplants human activity with machine activity. No one would deny that medical care technology can be efficient, accurate, and inexpensive, yet, as we saw in the chapter on medical care, the specialization of doctors diminishes the quality of health care. The lack of the personal care responsibility traditional to the general practitioner is largely lost today in the clinic of specialists. The loss of the generalist doctor is precisely the same thing as the loss of the generalist citizen — an ideal long fostered by democratic theory. Just as the citizen is removed from the responsibility for his state, the doctor is removed from responsibility for his medical care.

Not only has medical technology isolated personalized medical care from the citizen by depending on specializing doctors, but the responsibility for medicine has to a considerable degree been taken away from both the patient and the doctor. The drug industry develops and markets drugs and to some degree prescribes them. For every human ailment there is a drug or nostrum, and, as Nickolas Johnson of the FCC suggested, television is the pusher supplying a junkie society with all manner of drugs and other stimulants.

In education the discipline of the machine is revealed in the heavy reliance upon the physical facilities of the school building. Learning is acceptable as long as it is confined to the classroom building. Likewise, audio-visual equipment is purchased and widely used as a time filler for the teacher. Interestingly enough, in modern public school libraries, the audio-visual equipment such as tape players synched to slide shows is often held on display like the autos at the auto show. Too expensive for the children to use, the equipment is a proud but idle monument to educational technology.

Another essentially machine oriented process is evidenced in the packaged programs for courses in public schools. There are packages on the environment, packages on mathematics, etc., all of which aid the teacher to such an extent that no additional preparation is really necessary. Machine teaching through the computerized programmed text is, of course, widely touted as desirable "individualized" education.

The foregoing points suggest that man is widely disciplined by technology. This need not be negative; indeed, the majority of city dwellers find such discipline comforting and generally supportive. Negative aspects, however, do exist; for example, when we educate by machine we appear to educate exclusively on content, not on humanitarian principles, and by educating exclusively on course content, an educational system is created which produces a good worker but little else. Is a good worker a good citizen? Does he have a satisfactory urban life?

III. Technology and Urban Space

Another essentially spatial impact on the city results from technology — a centralizing force which has brought us together.

Centralization

Most obvious of the centralizing forces of technology has been the industrial revolution and its drawing together of productive facilities into large factories. Economies of scale have enlarged this process over many years. When we include the specialization of labor called for by the rise of the factory system, a second pervasive reason is suggested for the growth of large cities. Specialization of labor demands the clustering of the population. Third, agricultural technology in recent history has left large numbers of our current crop of urban-bound rural dwellers unemployed. Developments in management, communications, transportation, city services, building technology, and educational technology all blend with other systems to force the growth of cities.

In the face of this growth, man made only personal rather than social plans as to what he intended in coming together. As Tawney mentions, perhaps we are more interested in the condition of the roads than in where they are going. We have awakened to find ourselves a very centralized and congested urban population.

Decentralization

As centralization continued we discovered another recurring phenomena, a tendency toward a relative decentralization within an area larger than the central city, namely the metropolitan region. The early wave of crowding into the central city and the related retreat to its margins can be partially accounted for by technological change. The economies of large-scale enterprise brought people to the city, but people cannot live in factories, thus a congested habitat becomes expensive and unacceptable.

Unfortunately the economic forces which centralized people in the first place have followed them to the suburbs. Job opportunities continue to rise in the suburbs relative to the central city. Dorothy K. Newman used building permits issued in the central city and other than central city areas within metropolitan areas as evidence of increasing economic activity in the suburbs.[7] The trend toward new buildings in the suburbs is especially marked in the northern part of the United States where central cities are old and the exodus of the population has been going on for many years. Even in office construction and recreation construction there is an increasing tendency to locate out of the central city area (table 27).

In a study of twelve SMSAs between 1959 and 1965 there was a large increase to the percentage of total payrolls in employment which existed within the SMSA but outside the central city county (table 28). Of all working age people in SMSAs who were poor, half the whites and 80% of the nonwhites lived in the central cities; blacks continue to bear the greatest rate of unemployment and poverty within the central city. It is also true that holding a suburban job is considerably more difficult for central city residents than for the suburban commuter working in the city. Central city residents using public transportation probably spend more money and time to reach their suburban jobs than the suburbanites do in commuting to the city. Dependence upon public transportation is particularly acute for nonwhite families living in central cities because fewer of them have automobiles.

Suburban employment is growing more rapidly than central city employment. In looking at changes in employment between 1959 and 1965 between

[7] Dorothy K. Newman, "The Decentralization of Jobs," *Monthly Labor Review* 90 (May 1967): 7–13.

TABLE 27

PERCENTAGE OF NEW, PRIVATE, NONRESIDENTIAL BUILDING OUTSIDE THE CENTRAL CITIES
OF SMSAS, BY REGION, 1960–65 AND 1954–65*

Type of New, Nonresidential Building	Percentage of Valuation of Permits Authorized For New, Nonresidential Building				
	United States	North-east	North Central	South†	West†
			1960–65		
All types‡	47	53	49	34	53
Business	47	54	47	33	52
Industrial	62	71	59	46	69
Stores and other mercantile buildings	52	68	57	34	56
Office buildings	27	26	30	22	32
Gasoline and service stations	51	61	52	39	57
Community	45	47	47	33	53
Educational	45	47	46	34	50
Hospital and institutional	35	35	36	20	48
Religious	55	66	57	42	60
Amusement	47	41	60	46	45
			1964–65§		
All types‡	49	55	51	34	55
Business	46	56	50	33	50
Industrial	63	73	59	47	72
Stores and other mercantile buildings	53	69	55	33	58
Office buildings	27	25	31	20	32
Gasoline and service stations	53	66	54	40	59
Community	45	52	50	33	57
Educational	50	53	54	36	58
Hospital and institutional	36	38	36	21	50
Religious	54	67	55	39	62
Amusement	48	48	51	41	50

* Data for groups of years are used to avoid erroneous impressions from erratic year-to-year movements in building construction.

† Data for southern and western SMSAs reflect a more significant degree of annexation and area redefinition and are therefore less reliable than figures for other regions.

‡ Includes types not shown separately and excludes major additions and alterations for which type of building is not known.

§ Excludes data for 1959, for which comparable information is not available.

Source: Unpublished data of the Bureau of the Census, Department of Commerce, Washington, D.C.

TABLE 28

PERCENTAGE OF PAYROLL EMPLOYMENT OUTSIDE THE CENTRAL CITY–COUNTY

Standard Metropolitan Statistical Area	1959	1965
Total of 12 SMSAs	23	27
Atlanta	11	13
Boston	59	61
Chicago	10	12
Cleveland	6	7
Dayton	14	14
Detroit	20	26
Indianapolis	9	10
New Orleans	18	22
New York	15	19
Philadelphia	40	45
San Francisco	53	57
Washington	38	46

Source: Dorothy K. Newman, "The Decentralization of Jobs," *Monthly Labor Review* 90 (May 1967): 9.

SMSAs and the noncentral cities segment of the SMSAs examined by Miss Newman, the growth of suburban employment is pervasive (table 29). Whether in manufacturing, retailing, wholesaling, construction, transportation, public utilities, finance, insurance, real estate, or in services the story is the same. There are an increasing number of jobs available in the rings around the central city.

IV. Technological Effects on Employment

We have discussed some of the implications of technology on man and his city. What evidences of employment change aside from spatial change can we suggest?

Labor Force Trends

Total employment in the goods producing sector of urban economies has not changed much over the past thirty-five years, and there has been a pronounced shift from blue-collar to white-collar work. The machine has reduced employment relative to output in most sectors of the urban economy except the service sector. Further, we spend in excess of $20 billion annually in product research and development, but little in human resource development; as a result, we can contend that fewer and fewer people are playing a role of any importance in the economy.[8]

[8] Eli Ginzberg, *Manpower Agenda for America* (New York: McGraw-Hill, 1968), p. 27.

TABLE 29

PERCENTAGE CHANGE IN PAYROLL EMPLOYMENT IN SELECTED SMSAs AND IN THEIR RING, BY INDUSTRY GROUP, 1959–65

Industry Group	Total of 12 SMSAs	Atlanta	Boston	Chicago	Cleveland	Dayton	Detroit	Indianapolis	New Orleans	New York	Philadelphia	San Francisco	Washington
All industries													
Total SMSA	12%	32%	9%	10%	10%	17%	16%	11%	24%	9%	9%	19%	34%
Ring	30	51	14	34	36	20	48	25	54	37	22	27	61
Manufacturing													
Total SMSA	4	21	−24	6	3	10	11	10	26	1	1	6	34
Ring	15	39	−2	27	34	20	36	20	12	15	12	13	75
Trade, retail													
Total SMSA	15	26	14	16	14	12	16	−1	14	11	11	25	28
Ring	39	58	24	47	35	8	57	29	77	40	37	37	58
Trade, wholesale													
Total SMSA	8	38	7	9	5	33	11	14	−1	4	3	10	24
Ring	46	138	37	60	9	……	76	10	17	66	44	29	57
Construction													
Total SMSA	18	67	27	5	18	36	14	8	53	4	8	19	43
Ring	31	80	31	6	10	27	80	8	151	24	14	19	59
Transportation and public utilities													
Total SMSA	14	35	−1	……	16	23	7	14	20	20	23	12	10
Ring	19	130	18	11	33	20	67	13	48	19	4	21	13
Finance, insurance, and real estate													
Total SMSA	14	44	12	10	20	10	19	14	18	7	17	31	47
Ring	55	88	23	30	29	11	276	20	125	51	41	35	106
Services													
Total SMSA	30	37	32	24	27	42	34	24	34	26	28	36	47
Ring	55	81	42	60	71	48	82	52	73	58	49	50	78

Source: Compiled from U.S. Bureau of the Census, Department of Commerce, *County Business Patterns, 1959 and 1965* (Washington, D.C.: U.S. Government Printing Office, 1959, 1965).

An additional aspect of technological change has been that work in our cities and the entire society has shifted from brawn to brain. As Ginzberg points out, advanced technology has created larger and more complex bureaucratic corporations and power tends to flow to the top. Just a few up front will be putting out special effort to maintain themselves in the increasing professionalization of the work force. As the complex economy is increasingly dependent upon education, we will be more concerned with quality distinctions than simple quantity distinctions. For example, the classification of "college man" is less significant today because it is a simple quantity distinction. Students who now come from our best high schools probably know more of the course materials in areas such as English and mathematics than the people who graduate from our less developed colleges. Further, increased specialization results in increases to the quantity of education required. The American Psychoanalytic Association conducted a study in which it determined that the average age at which its members completed their education was 40.5 years.[9]

As a further result of technology, increased specialization creates a lessening job security since the special talents developed by a high degree of professionalization may not translate to another position.[10] Such insecurity may lead to an increase in white-collar unions and to an increasing pressure for early retirement.

Ginzberg also suggested that the 1970s will probably not be as favorable for women seeking employment as the last decade. Although women currently account for only one-third of the labor force, more women than men have of late gotten jobs. In the present decade many more young men will be competing for jobs. As more married women choose to work, employers seeking to hire or to move a man may also have to consider what they can do for his wife. This possible expanding surplus of labor is unusual. Historically we have been a nation short of labor supply and rich in resources. With the shortage of labor, wages in the United States have always been high, even during the Colonial period. Today, however, a surplus of labor may be developing.[11]

During the prosperity of the 1920s and since the end of World War II, in spite of rapid economic growth, employment opportunities did not expand at a rate sufficiently rapid to provide jobs for all that were dislocated by technological and other changes. Further, there has been more than a 50% increase in the total American labor force since 1929, but almost all of the gain in employment occurred in the service sector. Unfortunately there are several difficulties in shifting employment from manufacturing to services: (1) in many parts of the service sector people are needed with substantial education; (2) there are wage differentials in the shift from manufacturing to services — typically manufactur-

---

9 Ginzberg, *Manpower Agenda for America*, pp. 27, 31.

10 Ginzberg, *Manpower Agenda for America*, p. 32.

11 Ginzberg, *Manpower Agenda for America*, pp. 34, 39.

ing wages have been higher; (3) the flight of middle-class people from the cities has meant the need for many services in urban centers has declined. If we consider shifting persons from manufacturing to services, we need to be very careful about the bias in the American economy for governmental spending on defense expenditures. If we eliminate the impact of the military budget, government and nonprofit institutions (particularly educational and medical) have accounted for almost all of the net growth in employment since 1929.[12]

It is known that while the private sector continues to expand its output it is able to do so with fewer people. The logical outcome of this is likely to be increased unemployment in the future. For example, we will have an increasing number of young men seeking employment and we have few plans to accommodate them. On the one hand we can anticipate that unions will become increasingly interested in reduction of the work week as a means of sopping up excess unemployment. A shorter workday, work week, and larger number of three- and four-day weekends should help to stimulate the growth of the local economy and employment by encouraging the expansion of the educational and recreational industries among others. From a dynamic viewpoint, the urban economy requires shorter work hours for sustained growth.[13] But these measures are stopgap. We do not plan for long-run contingencies because we have not determined which segments of the population will be most affected.

Automation

We have mentioned some effects of technology on the city. A most significant form of that technology is automation. According to Charles Killingsworth, automation is the mechanization of sensory control and thought processes. Killingsworth argues that applications of automation techniques need not involve both elements.[14] To distinguish between technological change, economic change, mechanization, and automation refer to Killingsworth's chart in figure 9 which he calls a nest of change. Economic change, as the broadest concept, refers to the alteration of economic institutions. Moving closer to the center, technological change is a form of economic change but does not require the alteration of economic institutions. Examples include changes in technique which are not merely changes in mechanics, but are scientific changes which alter an economic process. Going further, mechanization is one kind of technological change. Mechanization refers to the physical activity of the use of tools. According to Killingsworth's chart, there may be no sharp dividing line between mechanization and automation. The use of tools does not imply automatic operation, but that element might be present in mechanization. Any system of economic, technological, or

[12] Ginzberg, *Manpower Agenda for America*, pp. 46–47, 48.

[13] Ginzberg, *Manpower Agenda for America*, p. 49.

[14] Charles C. Killingsworth, "Automation, Jobs and Manpower," in U.S. Congress, Senate Committee on Labor and Public Welfare, Subcommittee on Employment, Manpower, and Poverty, *The Manpower Revolution: Its Policy Consequences*, ed. Garth L. Mangum (Garden City, N.Y.: Doubleday, 1965), p. 98.

FIGURE 9
NEST OF CHANGE

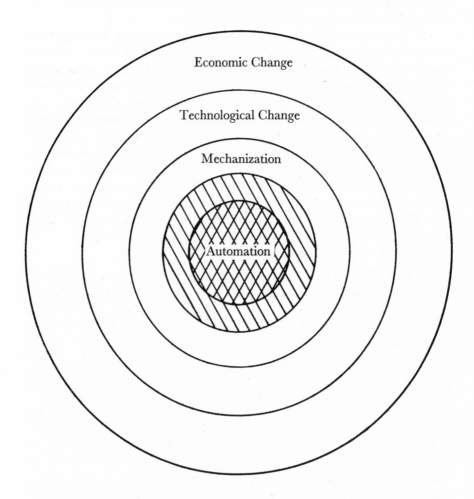

Economic Change

Technological Change

Mechanization

Automation

Source: Charles C. Killingsworth, "Automation, Jobs and Manpower: The Case for Structural Unemployment," in *The Manpower Revolution*, ed. Garth L. Mangum, p. 100. Copyright © 1965 by Doubleday & Co., Inc. Reprinted by permission.

mechanized change is automated only to the degree that it generates a completely self-regulating complex system.

One of the most startling examples of automation is the use of computers in an ever increasing number of applications. For example, in the area of traffic control many communities have computer controlled traffic systems in which sensors monitor the streets and measure the number of cars; this is fed into a computer and traffic lights are regulated.

Computers can aid psychiatrists in rearranging patients' random experiences and concepts into a more meaningful order so that the patient can understand himself better. Eyeglasses with photocells can measure light reflected from the wearers' eyes and feed this information into a computer that can diagnose brain disorders. In disease diagnosis, high-speed computers are being programmed to culture and analyze bacteria in order to immediately identify infectious diseases.

Other examples abound. Computers enable manufacturing firms to link their plants to sales offices in such a manner that instant transmission of production statistics and information as well as product inventory is readily possible. Obviously one of the widest applications lies in automated manufacturing where the computer can control the assembly of electronic gear such as radios easily and quite rapidly. The FBI's crime data retrieval system can enable a policeman thousands of miles away to know within ninety seconds whether a man is wanted by the police anywhere or an item of property has been stolen. A computer controlled training unit now enables airline pilots on the ground to learn the conditions of flight. The Bar Association has a computer which enables lawyers to place the facts of a given case into the computer and in a matter of minutes come up with appropriate data for the writing of a brief. Even Mother Bell is computerized to a highly significant degree as witnessed by the fact that 170,000 long-distance operators with the aid of computerized techniques handle calls equal in volume to that which only a few years ago would have demanded 750,000 operators. Likewise, when one makes an airline reservation it is instantly possible to have the availability of a seat for the entire trip confirmed. The field of simulation has made it possible to avoid the costly aspects of trial and error by allowing testable situations to be structured whether it be in research, business policy, or space flight.

It would not be possible to list even a partial grouping of applications of the computer and computer technology to the various activities of mankind. To do so with such an enormous volume would best be done by a computer.

While there may be many positive things that one may say about automated machinery and computers in particular, we should consider the advantages and the disadvantages. For example, Hailstones, Martin, and Wing note some of the advantages to the business firm. First, automatic machines in many cases do their work faster, better, and more safely than people. Second, they have the capacity to do things which are beyond human capacity. Third, machines do not become tired or sick, although we may say this advisedly. Fourth, automation improves managerial control particularly in office operations. Fifth, automation can make management better informed and, therefore, more efficient. Sixth, because people can be eliminated, the automated process makes it possible to run a continuous round-the-clock operation. Seventh, production ceases to be constrained by the limitations of human beings, their faculties, and skills.[15]

Automation has some disadvantages even to the business firm. Again, calling upon Hailstones, Martin, and Wing, we note: (1) the automated process tends to downgrade the status of the workers; (2) capital expenditures as we substitute automated machinery for men become quite high; (3) strikes by even a small number of workers can close up an automated factory; (4) automated equipment is very subject to rapid obsolescence; and (5) there are transitional difficulties upon the introduction of automation into the plant.[16]

There are many positive effects of automation but there are negative effects as well. It is possible to conclude that any automated process which generates benefits also creates costs to the user. It is, therefore, unlikely that it is possible to imagine an optimal amount of technology when all its effects are considered.

Technological Unemployment and Its Effects on Urban Development

We know that in the urban area the ability of the local government to undertake any meaningful manpower policy is subject to the ability of the city to sustain growth. One important factor for unemployment within the growth context is that of the impact of technology. A knowledge in the community of frictional job displacement due to technological change as well as job creation due to technological change is required. While this is essential data, it is not sufficient to describe the impacts of technology. In fact, if the rate of displacement is the same as the rate of employment, the data suggests that unemployment has not changed. If the time it takes to generate this reconversion is too long, unemployment problems have increased. As Thompson suggests, this possible characteristic can be simply demonstrated as follows:

$U = dl$ when $d = r$

Where:

$U =$ number of workers unemployed at any point in time
$d =$ number of workers displaced per month
$l =$ time lag from displacement to reemployment
$r =$ the number of workers reemployed each month[17]

[15] Thomas J. Hailstones, Bernard L. Martin, and George A. Wing, *Contemporary Economic Problems and Issues* (Cincinnati: Southwestern Publishing Co., 1966), p. 125.

[16] Hailstones, Martin, and Wing, *Contemporary Economic Problems and Issues*, p. 128.

[17] Wilbur R. Thompson, *A Preface to Urban Economics* (Baltimore: Published for Resources for the Future by Johns Hopkins Press, 1965), p. 4.

The rate of displacement described by Thompson refers to the impact of technology. The frictional component of the above would largely be technological and separated from the structural component of the technological impact by an investigation of who was reemployed and who was not.

Unemployment, when displacement and reemployment of the same person occurs, would be deemed frictional, but only if some judgment is made about the length of time of transition. If technological impact displaces 400 workers and 300 of them are reemployed within some "reasonable" amount of time at comparable wage rates, we can say that the 300 suffered frictional unemployment. On the other hand, if the 100 are unemployed for longer than a "reasonable" period of time, we can say that they are structurally unemployed. In frictional and structural unemployment we have not accounted for the person who is displaced by technology and is forced into a lower wage job.

A further caveat is the definition of "reasonable." By this we must imagine a "reasonable" period of time in some sense as an average for all displaced workers, something like mean time. The problem in such a suggestion is that the mean time would be much increased by those who are chronically unemployed due to technological change.

There are other problems implicit in the nature of technological unemployment and its apprehension. While we talk about the decline of industrialism in goods making in general, Perlman deals with an additional feature of industrial decline: "mal-allocation" due to industrial decline. He discusses the relative decline of several major manufacturing cities as places in which people can work. Technological reasons for industrial decline fall into two categories: (1) technological change causes industries to expand and contract, and (2) technological change within given industries requires new kinds of labor forces.[18]

Technological unemployment according to Perlman calls for three solutions; first, bringing in new industry to absorb surplus labor, second, helping the surplus labor to adapt to the situation by acquiring new skills, and, third, encouraging the unemployed to migrate to areas which have industrial growth rather than decline.[19] There are no specific ways in which we can systematically describe the means whereby new industries could be encouraged to come to a particular market. The second solution, that of reeducating technologically unemployed labor, has some advantages, but only if we have a delivery system into which these people can be fitted. This is determined by the degree to which there are distinct labor shortages which can be ascertained in sectors of the existing urban economy. The third solution suggests encouraging people to migrate. Migration becomes somewhat of a disadvantage to the economic development of the com-

---

[18] Mark Perlman, "The Economics of Human Resources in the American Urban Setting: Some Concepts and Problems," in *Human Resources in the Urban Economy*, ed. Mark Perlman (Washington, D.C.: Resources for the Future, 1963; distr. by Johns Hopkins Press, Baltimore), p. 4.

[19] Perlman, "Economics of Human Resources," in *Human Resources*, ed. Perlman, p. 5.

munity because the most mobile persons within it would likely be younger people of potential. Thus this final suggested solution may be self-defeating.

In order to present viable solutions around the first and second alternatives Perlman suggests, appropriate data are needed which will allow a match of human resources to industrial resources. For Perlman this information would consist of: "(1) age and sex distribution of the population, (2) participation by persons 14 years and older in a labor force, (3) years of formal schooling completed by persons 25 years and older, (4) class of worker in major occupation groups of employed persons, and (5) industry groups of employed workers." These data are available by smsa, but Perlman further suggests we need additional components like:

1. Size, participation, and rates in the labor force,
2. Age structure of the labor force,
3. Formal educational structure of the labor force,
4. Definition of and knowledge of quantities of types of skills available in the areas,
5. The principal secondary skill in classification which workers might have.[20]

Taking the above indicators and comparing them with the Department of Labor's *Dictionary of Occupational Specifications* introduces a degree of sophistication into the determination of possibilities of industrial location or expansion relevant to individual cities.

Another major area of employment problems in the urban context is what Perlman refers to as mal-allocation because of industrial specialization. This form of urban economic structure arises in the steel town or the rubber town — cities which have developed principally because of a single major industry. In the provision of public services, which are typically low in such communities, economies of scale make it possible for large individual firms to provide many of their own external economic services such as trucking, restaurant services, accounting services, etc. To the extent that this happens, secondary industries may not develop to the degree that would otherwise be possible. When large industrial firms do not contract services out "there are fewer external economies of scale for firms engaged in the particular service industries." [21] For the stunted industries, the economy of operation keeps their costs high and consequently their prices significantly higher than would otherwise be. This may well have the effect of discouraging other industries from locating in this particular community. In sum, in those instances where there is a dominant firm or a dominant industry in the community, the economic conditions surrounding its operation may stunt growth and diversification of development of the community.

[20] Perlman, "Economics of Human Resources," in *Human Resources*, ed. Perlman, pp. 6, 7.
[21] Perlman, "Economics of Human Resources," in *Human Resources*, ed. Perlman, pp. 7–8.

V. Technology and Social Policy

In previous sections we discussed technology, its physical form, the machine, and the automated machine from a number of viewpoints. In these earlier discussions, technology was occasionally lauded and often damned for its impact upon cities. A thread running through the discussion generates a paradox, namely, that technology is progressive and regressive. How can it be both? First, as a narrow progressive force, technology has been the major form of economic progress in cities. The machine as man's servant (or man as the machine's servant) is capable of creating a more efficient material world. At the same time, however, we noted that technology in current cities was vested in the sunk costs of old methods and the physical decay and old habits of mind. Vested technology and the consequent resistance to change are essentially regressive and may result in significant social costs.

Technology and Planning

Technology, as a problem in cities, may be a result of its nearly exclusive use for private economic gain. Following Heilbroner, under a system which abdicates planning to the profit motive, technology becomes a disruptive force.[22] If private enterprise cannot contain technology, then the controlling forces must come from other social institutions. Heilbroner suggests that the increasing rise of technological phenomena will end capitalism as we have known it as an increasing amount of planned control becomes a reality. Technology will force a larger and larger controlling role on the local government.

Veblen believed that the basic capital of the society is the accumulation of knowledge through which technology itself is derived. He said that all scientific knowledge, the real basis of all wealth, is public property.[23] Technology, therefore, may represent a private expropriation of property in the public domain. Were we to accept Veblen's notion, the organization of the American city would be quite different. Technological improvement would in the main become publically owned for anyone's use.

Without public ownership, control of technology, if possible, is required. The external effects of technology suggest that technology is not in today's cities exclusively problem solving but also problem creating. As a result, planners of cities are faced with an overwhelming job — that of responsibility to the public for technology and its control, and a systematic attempt to reduce technology as a negative externality while at the same time not eliminating its desirable aspects.

The Technologically Balanced City

To reduce the impact of the technology upon cities is to dismantle some of what has been done in cities. We do not move backward toward a primitive city

[22] Robert L. Heilbroner, *The Limits of American Capitalism* (New York: Harper & Row, 1966): pp. 97–98.

[23] Thorstein Veblen, "Ownership and the Industrial Arts," in *The Portable Veblen*, ed. Max Lerner (New York: Viking Press, 1948), pp. 324–34.

but forward toward a full city, one which is not narrowly dominated by the machine. The components of this city are numerous. First, the city is reduced in size; fortunately central cities have a real advantage in this direction. To the extent that the central city may be cleared of people, the diminished size of the city population makes planning possible on a more human scale. Real property in the emptying city is taken into the public domain and useless structures demolished. The area can be turned into open space and parklands. The relation between nature and man has real potential for recreating the human scale of cities. Sadly, as the city empties, incomes decline, tax revenues decline, and the community is less capable of taking advantage of the opportunities for redesign. Here is an opportunity for federal assistance. Urban Renewal, even in town centers, could have been a desirable force had the renewal been towards creating open space as opposed to new commercial buildings and activities. The doughnut of the central business district turned into a large park has much to commend it. Recognize that the current decline in revenues is only a short-run effect. Cities can readjust to a smaller scale in the long run.

Second, if transportation facilities in the city are inadequate, we may not build more freeways. Rather, tax the automobile more heavily and ration the use of streets. In particular, tax the second automobile very heavily. Reducing some dependence upon technology may have a salutary effect upon the quality of urban life. As a further means of improving the transportation system in cities, reduce taxes on small autos relative to large ones. Enormous expenditures on public transit may not be necessary for considerable improvement to the city transportation system. By following a careful tax policy on autos and trucks and by instituting a dial-a-bus system, most residents could be accommodated at a considerably reduced cost from current individual and public transportation expenditures.

Third, redevelop building codes to accommodate to more simple housing requirements from an electrical, mechanical, and plumbing context, but enforce the less demanding code vigorously. At the same time, tax the user of electricity more heavily. Place a graduated tax on use of power sources to discourage the "electric home." In short, place a luxury tax on the luxurious uses of resources and provide relief to those who are not large users of resources.

Fourth, and perhaps most importantly, do not build for permanence in the city unless it is absolutely required. Temporary housing, which is safe, warm, dry, and comfortable could be provided for everyone in the city. The urban house could be an investment which the owner and the city see as a temporary and relatively inexpensive habitat. The logical consequence of such impermanence would be to create a great deal of flexibility in the city for planning purposes and flexibility for people living in the city. Also, the provision of temporary housing on public land would do much to immediately improve the lot of those in substandard housing. As a basic unit, the temporary abode is less complex and, therefore, less dependent upon technology. In addition, public authorities may wish to encourage the citizenry to be self-reliant in housing. Subsidize those who wish to create their own housing units.

Fifth, attempt to reduce the workday, the workweek, and the work year. Urban policy should create more leisure time while providing uses and facilities of substance for the additional leisure time.

Reduce the dimension of city services which are essentially physical as opposed to those which are essentially human. Generally the city should not attempt to develop sewer systems which accommodate to tomorrow's needs. More appropriately, the city may simply limit what it wishes to accomplish in such directions instead of assuming a continual expansion of physical services. A limitation to such services suggests a form of planned capacity for the city beyond which it will not grow. A control and limitation to maximum growth size should be a formal part of planning.

Other questions could be raised; the modest proposals above, though outrageous to some, are not a complete list. The point is that the city needs to learn to plan for and control technology and economic growth in order to have any basis for further high quality development. A complete acceptance of the elaborated technological house, cafe, business, and public institution is not progressive — it is probably imbecilic if we accept the premise that technology creates problems for the city.

But then one may argue that the residents of the city do not wish to give up their full-wall televisions, their autos with baroque interiors, their houses with many convenience circuits and intercoms. That, after all, is the good life . . . or is it?

We do not propose the abandonment of technology. We do not propose throwing out the technological baby with the environmental bath water. We merely propose that the impact of machine technology has been dominant in cities and needs rather to be dominated by the citizens. Technological effects on life styles and the quality of city life should be treated as externalities, some positive and some negative. Whether these are social costs or social benefits, we need to understand how the city machine has narrowed our perceptions of urban life. To define these effects is necessary, and while we cannot at this time do so except in the limited area of pollution, study of externalities has generated sufficient thinking to conceptualize possible modes of solution.

Avenues of Policy

If the urban community has any opportunities to regulate the impact of technology upon the urban environment and the citizens who live in this environment there are a number of ways to do so. Davis and Kamien mention ways in which the problems of externalities can be solved. Their ideas seem appropriate to the most massive externality of all — technology. Solutions can come in the form of prohibition, directive, voluntary action, taxes and subsidies, regulation, payments, and by governmental action. In discussing solution by prohibition, the point is made that the use of prohibition in almost every case prevents optimal economic behavior.[24] There is little point in not using resources, but what constitutes a desirable level of use? In the case of solution by directive, there is the problem of ascertaining the level of appropriate use plus the problem of not knowing all of the possible effects of the directive. Voluntary action appears to be of little aid; a desired change in behavior from some urban malfactor would require some change in the conditions under which he operates, whether he be corporation or individual.

Turning to solution by means of taxes and subsidies, Davis and Kamien suggest that there are real possibilities, but caution: "In essence, what has to be balanced in this situation is the cost of acquiring the needed information against the losses to society if nothing is done or another imperfect policy is followed." [25] To deal with technology as an externality, public authorities must have considerably more skill and information than most presently have. Further, tax and subsidy payments require wider legislative powers than many communities possess.

Solutions derived from regulation are numerous in government. The major commissions of the federal government are regulatory commissions and their experience is relevant. Regulation in many instances becomes a situation in which the regulatory body becomes a supporter and promoter of the regulated activity rather than its regulator. Further, as Davis and Kamien suggest: "The administrative costs of enforcing the regulation are relevant and cannot be overlooked." [26] Costs of regulating certain types of activities may be more than the costs which the public bears in having the undesired activity.

Incentive payments are another solution, yet in many instances they are crude devices and not altogether socially acceptable. We would not, for example, pay the burglar to stop breaking into houses because of the fear his action creates in the city. Another limitation to incentive payments is that they are likely to work well only when capital costs are the only significant block to elimination of the undesirable conditions.[27] For example, we may provide subsidy for the improvement of redoing a sewer system (subsidize the capital costs), but we have no means of knowing if incentive payments will work in a situation where the action

[24] Otto A. Davis and Morton I. Kamien, "Externalities, Information, and Alternative Collective Action," in *Public Expenditures and Policy Analysis*, ed. Robert H. Haveman and Julius Margolis (Chicago: Markham Publishing Co., 1970), pp. 74–95.

[25] Davis and Kamien, "Externalities," in *Public Expenditures and Policy Analysis*, ed. Haveman and Margolis, p. 92.

[26] Davis and Kamien, "Externalities," in *Public Expenditures and Policy Analysis*, ed. Haveman and Margolis, p. 93.

[27] Davis and Kamien, "Externalities," in *Public Expenditures and Policy Analysis*, ed. Haveman and Margolis, p. 94.

is a continuous one such as reducing the tax on an auto on the proviso that it will not be used at certain hours of the day.

A final solution idea lies in the area of direct action. When, for example, a lake is overfished and stock is low, the subsequent fishermen may not catch fish (as a direct result of previous fishermen's catches). Davis and Kamien suggest that the simple direct action of stocking the lake overcomes this externality.[28]

The point of solution to the external effects of technology in the city lies finally in the evaluation of the social costs of the external effects and their regulation and a careful consideration of which if any of the solution modes is relevant. Unfortunately, aside from the rather large body of literature on externalities related to pollution of various kinds, the economic literature in this crucial area is limited. To consider technology as an externality on the life styles of the city presents many conceptual problems which demand further work before one could begin to consider which if any solution modes were applicable.

Technology: A Warning

Samuel Butler observed in *Erewhon* that

> we cannot calculate any corresponding advances in man's intellectual or physical powers which shall be set off against the far greater development that seems in store for the machine. Some people may say that man's moral influence will suffice to rule them; but I cannot think that it will ever be safe to repose much trust in the moral sense of a machine.[29]

Butler's warning seems particularly timely when we have had a number of decades to see a rapid development of machine technology and automation.

As Mumford says, automation is paradoxically similar to the Sorcerer's Apprentice.

> Our civilization has found a magic formula for setting both industrial and the academic brooms and pails of water to work by themselves in ever increasing quantities at an ever increasing speed. But we have lost the master magician's spell for altering the tempo of the process, or halting it when it ceases to serve human functions and purposes. . . .[30]

Without systems of feedback and evaluation, we have rapid development of technology which can certainly be destructive or it can accidentally be a great boon. The point is that we need the "magic spell" of evaluation of technology to prevent its "sweeping" us away.

By failing to acquire the "magic spell" of which Mumford speaks we leave ourselves open to uncontrolled expansion of technology. Our interest in Butler's

---

[28] Davis and Kamien, "Externalities," in *Public Expenditures and Policy Analysis*, ed. Haveman and Margolis, p. 94.

[29] Samuel Butler, *Erewhon* (New York: E. P. Dutton & Co., 1917), p. 240.

[30] Lewis Mumford, *The Pentagon of Power* (New York: Harcourt, Brace and Jovanovich, 1964), p. 180.

notion of the morals of machines lies in the fact that machines are used to make decisions, and all decisions are value laden and have moral implications. The machine, as it greatly regiments human life, is theoretically capable of doing all of man's work for him, but in so doing the machine is given greater and greater responsibility for valuing man. Mumford's picture of the astronaut in the capsule as "encapsulated man" in the fetal position is no fantasy. Man in accepting his machines conforms to them and to their "needs."

The optimistic prospect for man, however, lies in such examples as the blackout in New York in 1965 in which people were forced to live without their machines and in many cases were enlivened cooperatively to help, assist, and seek each other. Tragedy can serve as an illustration of just how easily man could break the dependence upon technology where he may decide it is an unwarranted dependence. Perhaps it is safe to suggest that each person can evaluate his own position by imagining which technologies he can live without. This may be more important to us than we imagine, for it may be that satisfaction in our possessions is only possible when we can safely walk away and, thereby, reject them. Rejection in some cases may be the only answer, because one must recognize that if he wishes petroleum products for his car, he may also gain petroleum products for his beaches.

Summary: Technology

Following a distinction between scientific progress and technological progress, discussion in this chapter turned to six characteristic effects of technology. Defined as possible externalities are:

1. Technology causing a loss of knowledge as well as the creation of new skills,
2. New technology building on old technology,
3. Technology possibly making man obsolete and transient,
4. Those paying for technological advance may not be the ones who gain from technology,
5. The enormous complexity of technology because of its interrelations with all of man's activities. This suggests that we know less of its impacts than we do of less complex phenomena.
6. Man's tendency to define himself by his machines.

Social costs and benefits may be associated with the six externalities.

Historically, man developed his basic tools of lever, wheel and axle, pulley, wedge, and screw for the principal purposes of war making, recreating, and working. The city when viewed as a machine is seen as a device for man living and pursuing his major goals with considerable attention given to efficiency.

Transportation systems, therefore, may be viewed as technologies designed to move people and goods, the conveyors of the city.

In the pursuit of developing the efficient city we have limited the scope of our technological innovation as a result of our vested interest in existing technology. This reliance on existing technology results in worn-out cities and a failure to fully utilize long-run potentials of technology. Unemployment is created by this resistance to radical change in technology, a resistance brought about by both capitalists and laborers.

Another significant impact of technology on the city includes some centralizing factors and some decentralizing factors. Centralizing factors include the rise of the factory system in which large numbers of laborers are drawn together. Specialization of labor logically draws laborers together in central places in the face of increasingly complex economic units. Agricultural technology has created surplus labor which sought employment in cities.

Decentralizing factors include the dispersal of an urban population as the city grows and transportation technologies that make the suburbanite possible. Job opportunities appear to be following the worker to the suburbs emptying the central city.

We then turned our attention to technological effects on the labor force. For example, total employment in the goods producing sector has not changed in the past thirty-five years. Employment has shifted from "brawn" to "brain" and increased specialization of labor. Increasing specialization generates insecurity in employment, and with increasing numbers of women entering the labor force, we may be generating a labor surplus.

Increases to the labor force have come in the service sectors. Government and (nonprofit) institutions have accounted for the greatest increases to the labor force. Relative declines can be seen in employment throughout much of the private sector of the economy. Attempts to maintain employment levels may be aided by shorter work weeks and extended vacations.

In the segment on automation, this term was defined as automatic operation in which a self-regulating tool is developed. Computers were cited as the most prominent examples, but the astonishing variety of their uses leaves some doubt as to our ability to really comprehend their effect upon us.

In considering the advantages and disadvantages of automation to business firms it was noted that a concern for labor was largely absent. This void of economic concern calls forth governmental concern for the external effects of technology and automation. It was suggested that where planning is abdicated in favor of the profit motive, technology can be disruptive and eventually end capitalism as we know it. Veblen saw scientific knowledge as public property, thus technological development may be a private expropriation of public property.

The major idea discussed relating technology to planning emphasized that local authorities must learn to control technology's impact upon the city. Suggestions were posed to break the hold of technology upon the quality of life in the city. Solution modes to control technology were discussed.

Technology need not create problems. In many situations technological development has been job creating. Perhaps it is the largely unplanned and uncontrolled aspects of technological growth that are cause for greatest concern. As long as we are heavily dependent upon material possessions, we are unlikely to be willing to control technology.

Selected Bibliography

Technology

ADELSTEIN, MICHAEL E., AND PIVAL, JEAN, EDS. *Ecocide and Population.* New York: St. Martin's Press, 1972.

ALCOTT, JAMES. *Technology and Urban Needs.* A Statement from the Engineering Foundation Research Conference on the Social Consequences of Technology. Kansas City, Mo.: Midwest Research Institute, 1966.

AYERS, CLARENCE E. *Toward a Reasonable Society: The Values of Industrial Civilization.* Austin, Tex.: University of Texas Press, 1961.

BUNGE, MARIO. "Technology as Applied Science." *Technology and Culture* 7 (1966): 329–47.

CAPRON, WILLIAM M., ED. *Technological Change in Regulated Industries.* Studies in the Regulation of Economic Activity. Washington, D.C.: Brookings Institution, 1971.

CARTER, ANNE P. *Structural Change in the American Economy.* Harvard Studies in Technology and Society. Cambridge, Mass.: Harvard University Press, 1970.

CROCKER, THOMAS D., AND ROGERS, A. J., III. *Environmental Economics.* Hinsdale, Ill.: Dryden Press, 1971.

DAVIS, OTTO A., AND KAMIEN, MORTON I. "Externalities, Information, and Alternative Collective Action." In *Public Expenditures and Policy Analysis*, ed. Robert H. Haveman and Julius Margolis, pp. 74–95. Chicago: Markham Publishing Co., 1970.

DOLAN, EDWIN G. *Tanstaafl: The Economic Strategy for Environmental Crisis.* New York: Holt, Rinehart and Winston, 1971.

GALBRAITH, JOHN KENNETH. *The New Industrial State.* Boston: Houghton Mifflin, 1972.

GARVEY, GERALD. *Energy, Ecology, and the Economy.* New York: W. W. Norton, 1972.

GINZBERG, ELI. *Manpower Agenda for America.* New York: McGraw-Hill, 1968.

GOLDSMITH, MAURICE, ED. *Technological Innovation and the Economy.* Chichester, Engl.: Wiley-Interscience, 1970.

HARRIS, BRITTON. "The New Technology and Urban Planning." In *Urban Research and Policy Planning*, ed. Leo F. Schnore and Henry Fagin, pp. 363–88. Urban Affairs Annual Reviews, vol. 1. Beverly Hills: Sage Publications, 1967.

HEILBRONER, ROBERT L. *The Limits of American Capitalism.* New York: Harper & Row, 1966.

JACOBY, NEIL H. "What is a Social Problem?" *Center Magazine* 4 (July/Aug. 1971): 35–40.

JARRETT, HENRY, ED. *Environmental Quality in a Growing Economy.* New York: Holt, Rinehart and Winston, 1971.

KNEESE, ALLEN V.; AYRES, ROBERT U.; AND D'ARGE, RALPH C. *Economics and the Environment: A Materials Balance Approach.* Washington, D.C.: Resources for the Future, 1970; distr. by Johns Hopkins Press, Baltimore.

MUMFORD, LEWIS. "Technics and the Nature of Man." *Technology and Culture* 7 (1966): 303–17.

———. *The Pentagon of Power.* New York: Harcourt, Brace and Jovanovich, 1964.

NEWMAN, DOROTHY K. "The Decentralization of Jobs." *Monthly Labor Review* 90 (May 1967): 7–13.

PERLMAN, MARK, ED. *Human Resources in the Urban Economy.* Washington, D.C.: Resources for the Future, 1963; distr. by Johns Hopkins Press, Baltimore.

PLATT, JOHN. "Science for Survival." *Center Magazine* 4 (Mar./Apr. 1971): 63–66.

SCHUMPETER, JOSEPH A. *The Theory of Economic Development.* Cambridge, Mass.: Harvard University Press, 1934.

SCOTT, ELLIS L., AND BOLZ, ROGER W., EDS. *Automation and Society.* Athens, Ga.: Center for the Study of Automation and Society, 1969.

SHEPARD, JON M. *Automation and Alienation: A Study of Office and Factory Workers.* Cambridge, Mass.: M.I.T. Press, 1971.

SILBER, JOHN R. "The Pollution of Time." *Center Magazine* 4 (Sept./Oct. 1971): 2–9.

SKOLIMOWSKI, HENRY K. "The Structure of Thinking in Technology." *Technology and Culture* 7 (1966): 371–83.

TAVISS, IRENE; BURBANK, JUDITH; AND ROTHSCHILD, JOAN. *Technology and the City.* Harvard University Program on Technology and Society. Research Review no. 5. Cambridge, Mass.: Harvard University Press, 1970.

U.S. CONGRESS, SENATE COMMITTEE ON LABOR AND PUBLIC WELFARE, SUBCOMMITTEE ON EMPLOYMENT, MANPOWER, AND POVERTY. *The Manpower Revolution: Its Policy Consequences*, ed. Garth L. Mangum. Garden City, N.Y.: Doubleday, 1965.

WERTHEIMER, RICHARD F., II. *The Monetary Rewards of Migration Within the U.S.* Washington, D.C.: The Urban Institute, 1970.

9

A Concluding Note

No one can say with precision what the future shape of the city will be or that cities will exist in forms we currently know. Complexity of the city makes it far from predictable. Nonetheless, we know that certain kinds of trends are likely to continue, and we recognize that cities will continue to exist in the United States in the forseeable future and the number of large cities will increase. Our largest cities may decline slightly and some of our middle-sized cities will grow larger, but none of our cities will disappear.

Growth in cities will likely continue in patterns of sprawl, but some may rejuvenate and increase density. For most, densities will likely decline as sprawl continues, and some few new towns will grow up as satellites. New cities will tend to be too expensive when they are isolated from existing major cities, but satellite new cities will be common as the building industry becomes the urban development industry.

Inner cities will continue to be problematical for people who live in them and to some small extent for the rest of the community because inner city problems are not amenable to desirable market solutions. At least some market solutions to inner city problems (such as illicit drug markets, contract theft markets, and other inner city programs for a private redistribution of income) do not appear to be completely acceptable to us.

On the other hand, city problems can diminish if effective policy is devised and sufficiently funded to attack problems of chronic unemployment, inadequate medical care, poor educational opportunity, and weak recreational programs. Combined with income programs at the federal level and combined with improved state and federal programs of welfare, efficient local policy can have a significant beneficial impact upon life in the cities, yet at the same time such programs will not completely solve urban problems.

Racism will continue to limit solutions to urban problems. The social, economic, and psychological advantages of racism are too ingrained in our mores to allow a ready dissemination of the racist features of urban life. As Anthony Downs has pointed out, there are numerous advantages to racism, advantages which Downs classifies into economic, political, and psychological.[1] The economic benefits of racism include the reduction in competition for jobs, the exploitation of minorities by low wages and higher prices, and the avoidance by the white population of dead-end jobs.

The political benefits to whites of discrimination against minorities include the manipulation of voters and boundaries, political job discrimination, and the advantage that whites do not support nonwhite candidates.

The psychological benefits to whites of racism include feelings of superiority, projection to another of one's problems, the promotion of white solidarity, and the avoidance of dealing with social problems by blaming such problems on the characteristics of minorities.

When we turn to specific areas of urban policy at various levels of government several things obtain. First, the federal government will support income guarantees to individuals living in America. Second, federally sponsored basic medical care will be provided in the near future. This is not to say that everyone will have sufficient health care, merely that the medical care services which are available will be available to most people. A third factor is guaranteed education which will probably be a mix of federal, state, and local policy. While in the future we may limit the educational choices of individuals, we will likely develop programs which provide for the education of citizens as far as their talents will take them. A fourth development important at all levels of government will be the provision of recreational opportunity. Recreation, a significant possibility for social intervention, leads toward socialization of the populace. Through the permissive potential of recreational interaction, citizens may be increasingly educated toward citizenship as well as meaningful use of leisure time. Largely unexploited now, public recreation may in the future take on an importance which places it on a par with formal schooling. Fifth, manpower policy will undoubtedly expand and will blend in with the social policies related to health, welfare, and recreation. Specialized programs of urban policy will increasingly be coordinated and gaps will be filled as urban planning and policy originating at local, state, or federal levels will cease to be considered in isolation from other policies which affect cities.

One cannot help but imagine that technology policy is a vastly undeveloped area. Safety regulations, pollution abatement programs, and local beautification ordinances are all activities which attempt to control technology directly, but they are all programs which attack single aspects of technology or particular forms of technology. The extent to which citizens must in the future give up some of their present consumption patterns and levels is vague and difficult to pre-

[1] Anthony Downs, *Urban Problems and Prospects* (Chicago: Markham Publishing Co., 1970), pp. 90–96.

dict, but we can be certain that significant changes are in store for technological application in the future. Social values toward the environment and toward the control of corporate behavior suggest that the purveyors of technology in the future, both public and private, will operate under some distinctly different game rules.

In *The Unheavenly City*, Banfield argues that most federal programs are designed for comforts and amenities for upper- and middle-class citizens rather than to end the critical problems of the poor in cities.[2] Where Banfield is correct is that such programs generate problems for some in the city. Where Banfield may be in error is in failing to recognize that public programs may not have gone far enough, may not have been sufficiently comprehensive, and have not resulted in strong local institutions. What is needed is policy to employ those with low incomes who are employable, and income policy to support those who are poor and are not employable, as well as first-class health, recreation, and education programs. Cities cannot develop as long as the poor of cities are not included in that development.

But will the development of human potentials socially and economically improve the quality of life in cities? Can improved policies generate more successful human lives? Hopefully. Cities are satisfying and desirable places for most people to live. There is little reason to doubt that cities can be better in the future, but there are a considerable number of questions as to whether significant improvements will be sufficient.

For years cities in America have been concerned with their economic development. Local development groups have arisen in most cities of some size and have bent their efforts toward creating jobs with the relocation of industry to that city as the primary device for job creation. While the activities of these groups and the activities of others such as the Urban League and local government are necessary, they operate under a premise which, if examined thoroughly, may not hold. The premise under which all such groups operate is that jobs are the principal responsibility of the private sector of the local economy. Manpower policy as defined in Washington has constantly been developed to train, educate, and reactivate the worker for jobs in the private sector, or it has moved to subsidize business activity toward the creation of jobs in the city. Nowhere and at no time has local government been able to, or in most cases even wished to, become the prime employer in manpower programs, yet it has been a major premise of this work that local government has the capacity and will obtain the resources necessary to become the principal manpower agent and the employer of last resort.

One may challenge the efficacy of such a possibility, but in so doing one should note where the private sector as principal employer has taken us. It has

[2] Edward D. Banfield, *The Unheavenly City: The Nature and Future of Our Urban Crisis* (Boston: Little, Brown & Co., 1970).

taken us to high levels of employment and high incomes for most people, but it has left out large groups of persons who live in cities. Second, the private sector has taken us to jobs and high incomes in cities with considerable external costs. Pollution, sprawl, transportation congestion, inferior housing, inadequate schools, and, indeed, inadequate local governments are all results of our heavy dependence upon the private sector and the values it creates. The private sector has created numerous goods, but in so doing it has convinced us that we must react as individuals and reject collective efforts to spend our incomes. The principal externality of private production and consumption for urban development has been not less than the domination of our entire thinking about how cities should be and how we as residents in cities should think. As Galbraith wisely pointed out, the polluted stream and the fancy car are the results of our overstimulation toward private means of production and consumption.[3]

If society is to move from a private goods bias, local governments must assume new and positive roles. We cannot have "safe" cities and desirable urban environments without individual income sacrifices, the funds from which will be spent in collective ways at local levels.

Making the city better depends as well upon other policy themes. For example, as noted earlier, significant increases to local government planning for human development must occur. The expanded planning should consider the individual, not the "typical individual," but programs in education, manpower, recreation, and health designed around service to each person. This requirement for flexibility and concern is based on the easily conceived but difficult to implement democratic rationale of the educated individual as the best arbiter of his needs.

The quality of life for the resident of the city depends upon the extent of his or her associations with the "new entrepreneurs," institutions of collective action for the exercise of political, social, and economic power. Equity demands a regrouping of urban institutions since we do not perceive sufficient checks and balances within the community to create effective bargaining units. Some presently powerful institutions may be reduced while other weak institutions may have to gain strength through both completely acceptable legal means and, in some instances, by legal but antisocial means. Explicitly, it is then suggested that new, strong collective institutions arise in cities.

Yet strong public institutions are capable of great mischief if they are not effectively countered by strong consumer's and citizen's groups. The check and balance of urban interaction is rigged today in favor of a few strong economic interests in the local economy, a strong educational bureaucracy, which need not either lead or respond to citizens' educational needs, and a strong medical care industry which limits health care responses. Likewise, the local public recreation

[3] John Kenneth Galbraith, *The Affluent Society* (New York: New American Library, 1958), pp. 198–200.

programs are made flabby by their own bureaucracy and by strong commercial domination of citizens' leisure tastes. Mischief results because countervailing power is not operative.

The need for strong collectives challenging local bureaucracies and private economic power requires the coordination of the basic human services of the city. Coordination comes from strong local government planning, programming, and organizing the interactions and interdependencies of local institutions. A school system must recognize its health, recreation, and manpower roles. Each of the sets of institutions involved in these four service areas we have discussed has some responsibility in the primary activities of the others. Philosophies of goals, operation, and coordination are required — not mere competition among the local institutions. The school system becoming a heavy competitor in recreation does much to damage the already limited public recreation institution. That each institution has its primary role and that each has its secondary role creates an overlap in service that has two results: it may cause neither institution to fulfill the required service, or it may cause duplication of services. Either result is undesirable, and both are the result of lack of effective coordination. Coordination, not competition, is required.

Finally, then, the city is a set of individuals and a set of collectives. It is only by acting collectively that we may set priorities, determine problems, plan and implement programs, and evaluate them in the light of democratically agreed upon goals and objects. The point of it all is that individual citizens "getting it together" in cities means individual fulfillment through collective action. Effective bargaining does not demand that we all love one another; it simply provides mechanisms for successfully living together in cities.

Subject Index

A

Accounting costs, 74
Administered price, 180
Administered taste, 180
Adult Basic Education Program, 130, 132
Adult Education Act, 130
Advocacy planning, 25. *See also* Planning
AFL-CIO, 130. *See also* Labor unions
Aged, employment for, 153–55
Aggregation, distortions of, 188, 191
American Medical Association, 254
Apprentice Outreach Program, 130
Area Redevelopment Act (ARA), 124, 132
Assets. *See* Resources
Automation, 285–88
Average costs, 60

B

Bargaining. *See* Decision costs
Behavioral Research Laboratory, 194
Benefits: of municipal services, 65–66; specification of, 67; maximization of, 71–74, 85; primary and secondary, 72; tangible and intangible, 73; measures for, 73; and discounting, 80–83; from economic progress, 123; from manpower programs, 160–62; from education, 173–74; 179–89. *See also* Costs; Cost-benefit analysis; Planning, programming, and budgeting systems
Blue-collar worker. *See* Labor; Labor force; Workers
Brown decision, 194
Buddy system, 130
Budgeting: of programs, 39–40; functions of, 66; as a systematic process, 68
Building codes, 292
Bureaucracy, 32, 284
Bureau of Outdoor Recreation, 205

C

Capital costs, 75
Capitalization, 227
Centralization, 279–80
Cities: development of, 1–2, 3–5, 8–9, 29–30; life in, 1–2; as economic units, 2; and human development, 3; labor force in, 114; as machines, 275–78; limitation of size of, 293; future forms of, 301. *See also* City planning; Urban development; Urban economic development
Citizens' participation, 5, 33–34, 41
City Demonstration Agency, 25
City planners: role of, 16; two schools of, 17; changes in thinking of, 17–18; comprehensive, 17–25; and transportation, 18–19; and industry, 20; and businesses, 20–21; and residential planning, 21–22; and recreation, 22–23; and the urban space, 23–24; vs. citizens' goals, 41–43; tools of, 45. *See also* City planning; Planning; Social planning; Urban development
City planning: definition of, 15–16; coordination of, 15–16; principal aspects of, 16; role of local government in, 16–17; principal schools of, 17; comprehensive, 17–25; social vs. physical, 17, 24–25, 28; physical bias in, 17, 24–25, 28; and transportation, 18–19; and industry, 20; and businesses, 20–21; and residential planning, 21–22; and recreation, 22–23; and the urban space, 23–24; problems of, 28–30; as a control mechanism, 29, 45; vs. private planning, 29; and the individual, 28–35; and freedom of choice, 30–32; and the planning unit of one, 32–35; costs of, 35; goals of, 39–45; complexity of, 42; as national policy, 43–45. *See also* City planners; Planning; Social planning; Urban development
Civilian Conservation Centers, 129, 132
Civil Rights Act, 153
Coleman Report, 192

307

M

Machine technology: man's dependence on, 210, 275–77; discipline of, 210, 278; city and, 275–78; efficiency of, 276; advantages of, 287–88

Mack and Myers model, 227–31

Mal-allocation, 289–90

Manpower: definition of, 104; dangers of, 104–5; development of, 148, 149, 150, 151, 154, 187; for the aged, 154–55. *See also* Manpower planning; Manpower policy; Manpower programs

Manpower data system, 157–60

Manpower Development Training Act (MDTA), 125–26, 132, 138

Manpower planning: definition of, 104; problems for, 104–5, 135–36, 144, 146; resources devoted to, 138; and information collection, 157–60; and education, 183, 187. *See also* Manpower; Manpower policy; Manpower programs

Manpower policy: reasons for, 120–22; active, 122–24; purpose of, 122; and federal government, 124–30, 132, 138, 146, 303; problems of, 135–36; and local government, 139, 154, 303; development of, 148, 149, 150, 151; and discrimination, 149, 153, 154. *See also* Manpower; Manpower planning; Manpower programs

Manpower process, 147–48

Manpower programs: for minorities, 130, 148–49, 151–54; role of local government in, 139–45, 303; role of federal government in, 139, 146, 303; funding of, 136, 142, 145, 146; role of education in, 142–43, 146; and training, 143, 160; role of private firms in, 143, 145, 303–4; role of health care in, 143, 146; scope of, 146–48; data research for, 157–60; evaluation of, 160–64; benefits of, 160–62; costs of, 162; discounting and, 162–64. *See also* Manpower; Manpower planning; Manpower policy

Manpower training, 143, 160

Manpower Training Skill Centers, 125

Marginal cost pricing, 60

Market mechanism, 59–60

Measures: of economic development, 10; for cost-benefit analysis, 86; of human resource development, 185–86

Mechanization, 285–87. *See also* Automation; Machine technology

Medical care: demand for, 244–47; supply of, 247–51; vs. health care, 260–61; and technology, 278. *See also* Health care

Medical care industry: definition of, 243; demand for, 244–47; supply of, 247–51; economies of scale for, 251; and self-medication, 256–57; socialization of, 261. *See also* Health care; Health services industry

Medical firms, 251

Merit-weighted user day, 230

Migration. *See* Mobility

Minorities: manpower programs for, 130, 153–54; discrimination against, 148–50, 153–54, 234–35, 284, 301–2; and transportation, 280

Mobility, 120, 121, 143, 182, 189, 289–90

Model Cities, 25–28, 33, 39, 43, 45

Motivator hygiene theory, 107

N

National Alliance of Businessmen (NAB), 130, 141

National Defense Education Act, 125

National Health Insurance, 260

National labor force, 112–13. *See also* Labor force

National urban policy, 43–46

Neighborhoods, 21–23, 193–94

Neighborhood Youth Corps (NYC), 128, 130, 132

New entrepreneurs. *See* Entrepreneurs

New towns, 277–78

O

Objective function, 71–74

Obsolescence, 272–73

Occupations. *See* Labor force; Work

Office of Economic Opportunity (OEO), 44

On-the-Job Training (OJT), 125, 126

Operation Mainstream, 130

Opportunity cost rate. *See* Social opportunity cost rate

Opportunity costs, 15. *See also* Social opportunity cost; Social opportunity cost rate

Optimality, 61–62, 67, 72

Outdoor Recreation Resources Review Commission, 227

Overhead costs, 74

P

Pareto optimality, 61, 62, 72

Park administrators, 216, 233–34

Parks: and planning, 22–23; spatial aspects of, 22; and recreation, 23; users of, 23; goals of, 64; evaluation of, 73, 218–31; for children, 213; definition of, 214; long-run aspects of, 215; placement of, 215–16; costs of, 226–27; benefits from, 231–33; administration of, 233–34; demand for, 233; land for, 234; and discrimination, 234–35; and private firms, 235. *See also* Recreation; Recreation sites

Peak loading, 60, 216–17, 236

Pecuniary spillovers, 78

Pecuniary transfer, 78

Per capita income, 10, 187

Peripheral worker, 150

Physicians, 244–46, 248–49, 254–56

Planners. *See* City planners

Planning: economic, 11; role of local government in, 12; coordination of, 12, 15–16;

Name Index

A

Ackoff, Russell L., 179
Alinsky, Saul D., 34–35
Anderson, C. Arnold, 182
Anderson, Nels, 207–10
Arrow, Kenneth, 61

B

Bailey, Richard M., 251
Banfield, Edward D., 303
Baumol, William J., 82
Becker, Gary, 177–78
Berg, Ivar E., 157
Bergson, Abram [pseud. Burk], 61
Boulding, Kenneth E., 104
Bowen, William G., 109–11, 158, 173
Branch, Melville C., 18–24
Brazer, Harvey, 182
Brown, Carol A., 144
Buchanan, James M., 35
Bugbee, George, 182
Burk, Abram. *See* Bergson, Abram
Burton, T. L., 218
Butler, Samuel, 295

C

Carol, Arthur, 177
Chamberlain, Neil W., 16, 87, 105
Clawson, Marion, 214–15, 221

D

David, Henry, 104
David, Martin, 177, 182
Davis, Otto A., 293–95
Doell, Charles, 216
Downs, Anthony, 302

E

Eckstein, Otto, 75, 81

F

Faulkner, William, 8
Feldstein, Martin S., 252
Finegan, T. Aldrich, 109–11, 158
Freeman, Roger, 178
Friedman, Milton, 175
Fulcher, Margaret N., 218

G

Galbraith, John Kenneth, 304
Ginzberg, Eli, 118–20, 128, 284
Glick, Paul C., 176–77
Goodman, Paul, 182

H

Hailstones, Thomas J., 287–88
Harbison, Frederick, 183, 185, 186
Hatry, Harry P., 68–69
Heilbroner, Robert L., 291
Hinrichs, Harley H., 71, 82
Hirsch, Werner Z., 178, 190
Hirshleifer, Jack, 84
Holland, Susan, 111
Holloman, J. Herbert, 184–85
Houthakker, H. S., 176

J

Jacob, Philip E., 181
Johnson, Pres. Lyndon B., 128

K

Kaldor, Nicholas, 61
Kamien, Morton I., 293–95
Karp, H. B., 107

Typography for Economics for Urban Social Planning *by Donald M. Henriksen. The text type is Intertype Baskerville with handset Lydian foundry display type. The text paper is Wausau Exact Matte, the endsheets are Strathmore Americana, and the cover material is Columbia Riverside Linen. This book was printed by the University of Utah Printing Service and bound at Mountain States Bindery.*

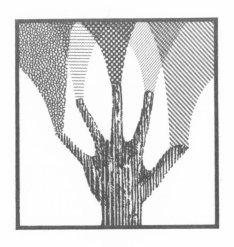